Schizotypy

Schizotypy

Implications for Illness and Health

Edited by

GORDON CLARIDGE

Department of Experimental Psychology
Oxford University

Oxford   New York   Tokyo
OXFORD UNIVERSITY PRESS
1997

Oxford University Press, Great Clarendon Street, Oxford OX2 6DP

Oxford   New York
Athens   Auckland   Bangkok   Bombay
Calcutta   Cape Town   Dar es Salaam   Delhi
Florence   Hong Kong   Istanbul   Karachi
Kuala Lumpur   Madras   Madrid   Melbourne
Mexico City   Nairobi   Paris   Singapore
Taipei   Tokyo   Toronto
and associated companies in
Berlin   Ibadan

Oxford is a trade mark of Oxford University Press

Published in the United States
by Oxford University Press Inc., New York

A catalogue record for this book is available from the British Library

Library of Congress Cataloging in Publication Data
Schizotypy: implications for illness and health/edited by Gordon Claridge.
Includes bibliographical references and index.
1. Schizotypal personality disorder.   2. Psychoses.   I. Claridge, Gordon.
[DNLM: 1. Schizotypal Personality Disorder.   2. Cognition
Disorders–psychology.   3. Creativeness.   4. Spiritualism.   WM 203
S33989 1997]   RC569.5.S36S35 1997   616.89'82–dc21   96–45523
ISBN 0 19 852353 X

Typeset by Palimpsest Book Production Limited,
Polmont, Stirlingshire

Printed in Great Britain by
Bookcraft (Bath) Ltd,
Midsomer Norton, Avon

Preface

There always seems to have been a dispute about whether madness is brain disease or something else—religious possession, moral degeneracy, or, in the modern period, more or less understandable psychological deviation. For the 1960s generation the dilemma was articulated in criticisms of a psychiatry that was relatively ineffectual therapeutically, as well as weak in its ability to explain very scientifically the disorders on which it was supposed to be expert. The two populist challenges came from the so-called antipsychiatry and radical psychiatry movements, associated with, respectively, Thomas Szasz and R. D. Laing. Although politically and philosophically distinct, these two departures from the psychiatric orthodoxy have since been generally bundled together. This is partly because of the belief they shared in an exclusively social/environmental, as distinct from a biological/genetic, explanation of mental disorder; and partly because together they captured and fired the sense of protest against the Establishment (of which psychiatry is both the mirror and the agent) that swept Western European and North American society at that time. The order of the day was self-discovery and the psychological understanding of—to use Szasz's terminology—our 'problems in living', rather than their labelling and treatment as medical conditions.

The criticism of orthodox psychiatry was largely justified. It indeed *had* failed to fit mental disorder into a medical model; *was*, consequently, unable to devise physical treatments rationally based upon that view of the disordered mind; and still *did* lack the factual knowledge that justified its continuing belief that this was, nevertheless, the way forward. It is therefore not surprising that an alternative psychiatry—or, as perceived by some, an alternative to psychiatry —flourished, especially given the romantic appeal of the language in which the ideas were couched and the guru status of its proponents. Indeed, such was the excitement generated, that any other kind of questioning of the received wisdom about mental illness was almost bound to go unnoticed. The public debate was very much a two-sided affair: a dialectic between traditional medical psychiatry and an assortment of social constructionist rebels from within and outwith the profession.

Yet, other challenges did exist. They stemmed, in the immediately preceding past at least, from a non-medical, science-based abnormal psychology—or experimental psychopathology—which also saw itself as having a legitimate say in discussions about the nature of psychiatric disorder. It was there that treatments like behaviour therapy originated, and extensive laboratory research programmes developed, applying to the study of mental illness experimental paradigms derived from several branches of academic psychology, including perception, cognition, learning theory, and the biology of behaviour. At minimum, this work succeeded in bridging an empirical gap between normal and abnormal, not much attempted by psychiatrists themselves. More forcefully interpreted, it led some academic psychologists to voice their own versions of 'antipsychiatry'. Notable here was Hans Eysenck, who contemporaneously with Laing and Szasz, also questioned the wisdom of a narrow neurological model of the psychological disorders, preferring to construe them simply as extremes of normal personality. Of course, Eysenck's reasoning was quite different from that of the existentialist and social theorists, his being a superficial trait approach to personality and his view of human variation thoroughly biological—aligning him very much with conventional psychiatry about the need to look towards the brain for an explanation of mental illness. But he and Laing were oddly in agreement about two things: the essential connection between normalcy and deviance and the conviction that the study of one can advance (indeed is essential to) our understanding of the other. If there is a common theme running through the chapters of the present book, it is to be found in that shared observation by two otherwise very disparate thinkers. Which is appropriate, since the contributions to the book vary considerably in content and theoretical style: while most are in the strict scientific tradition of experimental psychopathology, this is by no means true of all—illustrating the healthy mix of ideas that still pervades the field we attempt to cover.

The book focuses on madness (psychotic disorder), especially schizophrenia, and its normal counterpart—for which we have used the term 'schizotypy'. The latter will be strange to many readers and, for this and other reasons, requires brief comment. As I elaborate in my own first chapter, and as will be evident in chapters by several of my co-authors, there is a subplot to be aware of in historical and theoretical discussions of madness. 'Schizophrenia' has emerged as the most commonly used label; so, inevitably, when a linguistic variant has been needed it has tended to be fashioned in a form such as 'schizotypy'. However, it has been suggested that all of this is arbitrary classifying of what is actually a very heterogeneously expressed condition—madness—for which other, more appropriate, descriptors could, and should, be found. I personally tend to agree. In which case the title of the book is a bit of a misnomer (and unfamiliar to boot!). But unavoidably so, since the choice was between reflecting the reality of usage within the research literature we draw upon or introducing a friendlier, but even more idiosyncratic or misleading, term.

I am pleased to record that all of the contributors to the book were, or are, colleagues of mine, either as graduate students or in some other capacity. I am also amused to recall that, such was the perceived extent of this local involvement, one unfavourable reviewer of the manuscript projected the opinion that I was really just trying to organize my own *Festschrift*! What strikes me more is how gratifying it has been over the years to discover such diverse expertise in one place on what is still a relatively specialized topic. For it is worth noting that this is only the second book ever to appear with 'schizotypy' in the title. The other, recently published and edited by American colleagues, covers the area with a slightly different view of schizotypy. I like to think that the two volumes will happily complement each other and that, if there is an incestuous element in our own, it reflects (with due respect, of course, to my Antipodean friends and contributors to the book!) a European, rather than narrowly Oxonian, perspective on the topic.

There is, however, one particular local connection I would like to mention, since it helps to trace out part of the origins of the book and allows me to place on record a debt of gratitude. More than twenty years ago—at a point where I was, I recall, at a particularly low ebb of inspiration about my research—a young undergraduate from St Anne's College, Sharon Reichenstein, came to me and asked if I would supervise her research project. She explained that she wanted to devise a questionnaire for assessing schizophrenic features in healthy subjects —at that time a fairly novel idea, with few such instruments available and the whole field of schizotypy research only just beginning to open up. I agreed and largely through her own efforts she produced a very workable scale; this formed the prototype for other questionnaires we later developed and really marked the beginning of our programme of 'schizotypy research.' And the undergraduate? She took her BA and slipped out of sight . . .

Among more recent acknowledgements, I thank all of the contributors for making this volume possible; the staff of Oxford University Press for steering the manuscript painlessly through to publication; and my daughter, Emma, for putting up with my tantrums while she was helping me index the book.

Oxford   G.C.
January 1997

Contents

Part IV   Schizotypy in healthy subjects

Part V   Conclusions

Appendices

Contributors

Note: Any e-mail enquiries can be addressed in the first instance to
Gordon.Claridge@psy.ox.ac.uk.

Anthony Beech Department of Forensic Psychology, Fair Mile Hospital,
Wallingford, Oxon OX10 9HH

J. H. Brod Department of Experimental Psychology, University of Oxford,
South Parks Road, Oxford OX1 3UD

Paul Broks School of Psychology, University of Birmingham, Edgbaston,
Birmingham B15 2TT

Helen J. Cassaday Department of Psychology, University of Nottingham,
University Park, Nottingham NG7 2RD

Gordon Claridge Department of Experimental Psychology, University of
Oxford, South Parks Road, Oxford OX1 3UD

Simon Enright Department of Clinical Psychology, Fair Mile Hospital,
Wallingford, Oxon OX10 9HH

Julie L. Evans Department of Psychology, London Guildhall University,
Calcutta House, Old Castle Street, London E1 7NT

Justin L. Freeman School of Behavioural Science, Department of Psychology,
University of Melbourne, Parkville, Victoria 3052, Australia

Michael Jackson School of Psychology, University of Wales, Bangor, Gwynedd
LLS7 2DG

Charles McCreery Institute of Psychophysical Research, 118 Banbury Road,
Oxford OX2 6JU

Oliver Mason School of Psychology, University of Wales, Bangor, Gwynedd
LLS7 2DG

David Rawlings   School of Behavioural Science, Department of Psychology, University of Melbourne, Parkville, Victoria 3052, Australia

A. J. Richardson   Academic Department of Psychiatry, Charing Cross Hospital and Westminster Medial School, St Dunstan's Road, London W6 8RP

Leanne Williams   Department of Psychology, University of New England, NSW 2351, Australia

Abbreviations

CSTQ	Combined Schizotypal Traits Questionnaire
DSM	*Diagnostic and statistical manual of mental disorders* (American Psychiatric Association)
E	Extraversion Scale (Eysenck's)
EPQ	Eysenck Personality Questionnaire
HOP	Hypomania Scale (Chapman's)
L	Lie Scale (Eysenck's)
LH	left hemisphere
LVF	left visual field
MMPI	Minnesota Multiphasic Personality Inventory
MgI	Magical Ideation Scale
N	Neuroticism Scale (Eysenck's)
O–LIFE	Oxford–Liverpool Inventory of Feelings and Experiences
P	Psychoticism Scale (Eysenck's)
PAb	Perceptual Aberration Scale
RH	right hemisphere
RISC	Rust Inventory of Schizoid Cognitions
RT	reaction time
RVF	right visual field
SAWCI	semantic activation without conscious identification
SPQ	Schizotypal Personality Questionnaire
STA	Schizotypal Personality Scale (Claridge and Rawlings')
STB	Borderline Personality Scale (Claridge and Rawlings')
STQ	Combined STA and STB Scales
WAIS-R	Wechsler Adult Intelligence Scale (Revised)

Part I Schizotypy: concept and measurement

1

Theoretical background and issues

GORDON CLARIDGE

It is worth reminding those who have read the Preface to this volume—and explaining to those who have not—that there is something of a mismatch between the title of the book and its subject matter. 'Schizotypy' is a narrow term unambiguously connected to schizophrenia: historically, conceptually, clinically, and of course etymologically. No one even half familiar with the field could therefore be blamed for believing that, in so far as the book refers to mental illness, it will do so mostly with regard to schizophrenia. Yet there are other forms of madness, and even those who set out to study 'schizophrenia' soon find themselves straying beyond its boundaries, however defined. Furthermore, they do so—and this is the point—unavoidably. So, although in starting this chapter as I have, I might appear to be prejudging one of its conclusions and so biasing the reader, this is not the case. It is merely a matter of fact—and part of the background we need to discuss here—that the ideas presented in the book have originated from a number of different sources; and that, where these origins have been psychiatric, they are not always strictly to be found in the schizophrenia literature *per se*. It is simply that schizophrenia has become the dominant idea, the shorthand term, the everyday metaphor for madness—whichever way one wishes to look at it—in the field of study that we are concerned with.

Attempts to extrapolate from the abnormal to the normal—the other, in some of its forms more controversial, theme of the book—have naturally been shaped by the clinical *Zeitgeist*. Consequently, 'schizotypy', as the less deviant bedfellow of 'schizophrenia', has come into common usage among professionals as a way of expressing, for those who believe in it, the apparent dimensionality of psychosis. As we shall see, there are other labels but, for one reason or another, none is an ideal substitute: either a label is as restricted in meaning as 'schizotypy', but less well-known; or it sounds clumsy and is awkward to use grammatically; or it is already in use with a different meaning. To anticipate, I am referring here to, respectively, 'schizoidness', 'psychosis-proneness', and 'psychoticism'. For the moment, for want of a neat alternative, we are stuck with 'schizotypy' as the best generic descriptor we can find. I will certainly mostly use it here, though, like the authors of later chapters, sometimes in a rather loose or extended sense, and occasionally, where the context demands it, I shall resort to other terminology.

The above preamble serves to introduce the two main strands of the discussion in this chapter. One concerns the question of continuity in serious mental illness: whether it exists and, if so, how far it can be generalized—into other, lesser forms of psychological disorder or even the healthy personality; and, if the latter, how that can be reconciled with the notion of a pathology for the abnormal state. The other strand is contained in the point we started from, viz. the overall scope of the subject matter with which we are dealing. This can be translated into the question taken up first, concerning the heterogeneity of psychosis.

VARIETIES OF PSYCHOSIS

Although not a formal psychiatric criterion for the distinction between 'mad' and 'not mad' (or 'psychotic' and 'not psychotic'), there is a good working agreement about what roughly distinguishes these two classes of mental illness. The 'not mad' (or 'not psychotic') refers to forms of distress or departure from the norm—for example neurotic anxiety, mild depression, antisocial attitudes, excessive narcissistic preoccupation—for which the average person can summon up some sympathy; he or she may already have been there or have become aware of the possibility, or they might have enough insight into their own personalities to know that they are not too far removed from the deviant characters they read about in novels, newspaper reports, or psychiatric glossaries.

The 'mad' (or 'psychotic'), on the other hand, evoke puzzlement, fear, a feeling of alienation, and a sense that the sufferer's behaviour and experience are strange and beyond the reach of empathy and ordinary rationality. As it happens, and as all of the subsequent chapters of this book, in one way or another, will show, this is a false comparison. On closer inspection and with more careful thought, the sense of 'there but fortune' attends, for many people at least, *both* the more serious, mad, psychotic aberrations *and* those of a lesser quality. Nevertheless, there *is* some distinction—the degree of insight into the state of the self when most disturbed is probably as good a rule of thumb as any for drawing it— and the notion survives of madness (psychosis) as somehow being recognizably different from other forms of psychopathology.

From the earliest times it has been observed that these serious disorders of mind can manifest themselves in various forms. Indeed, despite differences in terminology and explanation, there is a surprising continuity over the ages in the described phenomenology (see Cutting (1985) for a useful chronological listing). Distinctions encountered frequently refer to groupings according to such features as: deranged emotions or 'affections' (from melancholia to manic excitement); disturbed volition, deteriorating into apathy or 'dementia'; and disordered thinking, sometimes amounting to 'possession' by delusional beliefs that fly in the face of reality. The credit for first moving to shape these observations into the beginnings of a modern psychiatric nosology is commonly ascribed, jointly, to Emil Kraepelin (1919) and Eugen Bleuler (1911). As Berrios (1995) has recently pointed out, the account is an oversimplification of the historical progression which, not unusually, proceeded more unevenly than is usually portrayed. Nevertheless, as influential figures, Kraepelin and Bleuler certainly represent landmarks in the attempt, throughout the nineteenth and early twentieth centuries, to provide a classification of serious mental illness that acknowledged both its unity and its variety. Kraepelin's contribution was the distinguishing of an affective, manic-depressive form from *dementia praecox*. The latter term gathered together several conditions—hebephrenic, catatonic, and some forms of paranoid illness—into what were perceived to be deteriorating mental diseases. It was the third group that Bleuler subsequently wrote about as 'the schizophrenias', a term that soon became singularized; misleadingly so, and for reasons which seem only to do with the awkwardness of linguistic usage. For even in the modern psychiatric glossaries, ICD-10 (World Health Organization 1992) and DSM-IV (American Psychiatric Association 1994), the criteria for an overall diagnosis of 'schizophrenia' can be made on the basis of widely differing sorts of criteria: the classic ones of delusions and hallucinations, certainly, but also disorganized or derailed speech, or flattened emotional expression.

Several issues that we now need to consider lie in the background to these attempts to describe and classify the psychotic disorders. The first is the stance, taken currently and in the past, on the question of there being a discoverable neuropathology for such conditions. Although later appearing to have some doubts, Kraepelin certainly considered initially that the composite illness, *dementia praecox*, was an organic disease. Bleuler, however, was less sure from the beginning and his explanation of schizophrenia was more of a compromise between the biological and the psychological. This reflected his view that among the primary features of schizophrenia—and perhaps constituting its biological substrate—is a loosening of associative thought. According to Bleuler, this then led—through a 'splitting' of psychological functions—to hallucinatory and delusional experiences. Yet it is the very presence of the latter, more bizarre features—the so-called 'first-rank symptoms' of Schneider (1959)—that has persuaded others to have a more straightforward medical view: that these are the direct signs of an underlying neurological disease process.

The failure, as yet, to find a unique pathology for schizophrenia—or most of its forms—means that the debate about its nature rumbles on, with organic, psychological, and psychobiological accounts still in play (see *Journal of Mental Health* 1993). For the moment, the most we can probably conclude is that, given the very strange nature of psychotic experiences, it is intuitively unlikely that there will be *no* associated aberrant brain function. On the other hand, it is equally unlikely that any pathology that is discovered will be as unsubtle as it is in most genuine neurological diseases, such as Alzheimer's disease, which is often used as a paradigm by some schizophrenia researchers. Of the three options considered above, a psychobiological perspective on schizophrenia seems the most promising, leaving open for consideration the full range of theoretical and empirical approaches. This means, as far as the ideas presented in this book are concerned, that although of interest—and certainly referred to—such biological evidence as presently exists is not crucial one way or the other to the central thesis about schizotypy, or any broader equivalent, as they relate to psychosis.

There are, incidentally, other reasons for drawing attention here to Alzheimer's and other neurological diseases as poor models for understanding schizophrenia. Despite the early use of the term 'dementia' in connection with it, there is no evidence that schizophrenia leads to any cognitive impairment (in the dementing sense), or indeed to any impairment that cannot be explained as a secondary consequence of other factors. On the contrary, as any perceptive clinician can vouch, individuals with the diagnosis can retain remarkable powers of intellect and creativity despite years of illness, social neglect, hospitalization, and damaging drug regimes. This is unlike neurological diseases proper which—to paraphrase Jaspers (1913), who drew a similar comparison—merely 'smash' the brain and generally, in the end, kill the person.

Turning to a second point at issue that runs through the classification of the psychoses, a persisting question has been whether Kraepelin was right to separate off manic-depressive insanity (bipolar affective disorder) from *dementia praecox* (schizophrenia). The attraction of doing so was that it helped to sustain a sound medical model that relied on being able to identify distinct diseases, definable according to their clinical course, treatment response, prognosis, and hopefully, eventually, a knowledge of their aetiology. The argument has been a persuasive one for psychiatrists right up until the present day, and schizophrenia and bipolar disorder remain officially listed as different illnesses in both ICD-10 and DSM-IV. However, this tradition has not gone unchallenged. Indeed the notion of there being only a *single* form of insanity goes back well into the early history of psychiatry, long antedating Kraepelin, and expressed as several versions of an *Eintheitpsychose* (or unitary psychosis) theory (see Berrios 1995).

In recent years there has been something of a revival of the unitary psychosis theory, centering partly on observations that bipolar affective psychosis and schizophrenia do not appear to be as distinguishable as was once thought, and partly on the failure to establish what McGuffin *et al.* (1987), writing from a genetics viewpoint, call 'lines of cleavage' among the schizophrenias as a group.

The overlap between bipolar and schizophrenic psychoses is evident in a number of ways (Taylor 1992). Most obviously, at the symptom level statistical analyses trying to find a clear point of rarity between these two forms of psychosis have generally failed to do so (Brockington *et al.* 1979; Kendell and Brockington 1980). Writing about the evidence elsewhere, Kendell (1991) comments that ... it is time we questioned Kraepelin's paradigm of distinct disease entities and of two discrete types of functional psychosis'. To an extent, of course, this is already acknowledged in the inclusion in the psychiatric glossaries—both ICD and DSM—of a 'schizoaffective' form of psychosis; though, interestingly, the condition is listed as a variant of schizophrenia, rather than being recognized as genuinely intermediate.

Other evidence for the *Eintheitpsychose* theory comes from the effective interchangeability of treatments between the two forms of psychosis (Klein and Fink 1963; Overall *et al.* 1964; Delva and Letemendia 1982; Abraham and Kulhara 1987). Then, on a more scientific front, there are observations that many experimentally established differences claimed for schizophrenia can often be found in affective disorder. Kendell (1991) comments, too, on this phenomenon, as follows:

Time after time research workers have compared groups of schizophrenics and normal controls and found some difference between the two which they assumed to be a clue to the aetiology of schizophrenia, only for someone else, years later, to find the same abnormality in patients with affective disorders. Of all the dozens of biological abnormalities reported in schizophrenics in the last 50 years, none has yet proved to be specific to that syndrome. All have been found, although often less frequently, in patients with affective psychoses, and none has been demonstrated in more than a minority of schizophrenics. (pp. 14–15)

Examples of this overlap in experimental data range from pursuit eye movement aberrations (Iacono *et al.* 1982) and enlarged ventricles (Dolan *et al.* 1985) to the demonstration that 'overinclusive thinking'—a classically described feature of *schizophrenic* cognition (Cameron 1938; Payne *et al.* 1959)—also occurs in mania (Andreasen and Powers 1974).

Genetic findings (for example, Baron and Gruen 1991) on the intermingling of familial liabilities to schizophrenia and affective disorders can also be used to support the *Eintheitpsychose* model. The most explicitly stated psychiatric interpretation of such evidence is that offered by Crow (1986, 1991). He has argued forcefully for a continuum of psychosis, running from normal, through affective disorder, to schizophrenia, and biologically mediated by genetic influences on the neurodevelopment of brain asymmetry (Crow 1990). It remains to be seen whether such a sweeping generalization about aetiology proves fruitful; the theory has difficulties, for example, explaining the differences in clinical presentation between the schizophrenias or between the latter and affective psychosis. Nevertheless, together with Kendell's opinions, it puts down a strong marker that even psychiatry is having new (or at least renewed) thoughts about the viability of its earlier, more discrete disease modelling of psychosis to which it has been wedded for most of this century.

The blurring of the edges between the major forms of functional psychosis is not, however, the only point at issue in defining their status as psychiatric illnesses. An additional question about continuity concerns the extent to which they themselves merge into other, less serious, disorders. This is taken up in the next section.

BORDERLANDS OF PSYCHOSIS

For reasons similar to those already outlined, post-Kraepelinian, organic psychiatry has also been slow to acknowledge that the outer boundaries of psychotic disorder are not as clearly demarcated as it would like. As discussed elsewhere (Claridge 1987), this 'fuzziness' does not in any way threaten the idea of psychological disorders as diseases, though it does open up further issues about psychiatric classification and its relation to the medical model. With a long-standing awareness of such questions, and despite its inherent conservatism, psychiatry has actually generated a considerable amount of interest in the topic of 'the borderline'. (I should mention that for the moment I am using this term in a very general sense, simply to refer to any psychological disorder that could represent a mild variety of, or be phenomenologically continuous with, one of the major forms of psychosis. As becomes clear later, 'borderline', also has a more technical meaning.)

The history this century of the general notion of 'the borderline' can be traced to several quite different clinical and theoretical perspectives. In an early guise it emerged as the notion of 'schizoidness', which from the very beginning formed an intrinsic part of the concept of schizophrenia. Manfred Bleuler (1978), who inherited his father's psychiatric mantle, makes this very clear. The term 'schizoid personality', he points out, took 'shape in conversations among the doctors of Burghölzi [the Zurich hospital where he and his father worked] in connection with the expression of "schizophrenia" around 1910'. The description was partly intended to capture the mental state of individuals who were strange or eccentric, but not showing the full-blown symptoms of schizophrenia. Since then it has established itself as part of the psychiatric nomenclature, finding its way into the psychiatric glossaries as 'schizoid personality disorder'. The defining features (as an Axis II disorder in DSM-IV (American Psychiatric Association 1994) include such signs as indifference to social relationships, constricted affect (cold, aloof), and a preference for solitary activities.

'Schizotypy' emerged much later. It was first used by Rado (1953), an American psychoanalyst, who coined it—in the form 'schizotype'—as an abbreviation for 'schizophrenic genotype.' As the derivation of the term indicates, it was meant to signify the hereditary disposition to schizophrenia, being roughly equivalent to 'schizoid personality' and to another descriptor used by E. Bleuler (1911), viz. 'latent schizophrenia'. Rado considered that schizotypy stemmed from psychodynamic personality traits concerned with the self-regulation of hedonic tone and expressed as 'an integrative pleasure deficiency' (anhedonia). According to him, adaptations that cope more or less effectively with this deficiency—preventing breakdown into open schizophrenia—nevertheless leave the individual with a personality structure identical to what would now be called 'schizoid personality disorder'.

The most vigorous immediate proponent of Rado's ideas was Paul Meehl (1962). He sharpened up the genetic formulation of schizotypy by coining the term 'schizotaxia' to denote what, in the genotype, is supposedly inherited in schizophrenia. For Meehl 'schizotypy' defined the phenotype, according to four behavioural traits: cognitive slippage (a mild form of thought disorder), interpersonal aversiveness, anhedonia, and ambivalence. At that stage, like Rado, he regarded anhedonia as the primary expression of schizotaxia, but in a later revision (Meehl 1990) he placed greater emphasis on the cognitive slippage component of schizotypy.

Meehl's change of opinion on this last point might partly reflect the general widening that has occurred in the definition of 'schizotypy' since Rado first introduced it. For two meanings have emerged, brought out by Kendler (1985) in a review of some ideas in the area. Kendler notes two different ways in which observers have attempted to characterize the 'schizophrenia spectrum'. One—signified by 'schizoid' (though Kendler does not note this) and closer to the original usage of 'schizotypy—stresses *personality* features. The other includes the latter, but also places emphasis on expression of the schizophrenia spectrum as attenuated forms of psychotic *symptoms*. It is a bias towards the latter that has crept into some recent usage. This is revealed by the kinds of psychometric instrument developed to measure schizotypy (see Chapter 2). It is also evident in the clinical indicators chosen to define Schizotypal Personality Disorder (SPD), another of the Axis II disorders related to schizophrenia, included in the DSM. As well as personality traits, such as social anxiety and eccentricity, the criteria also cover manifestly symptom-like features, for example transient illusory experiences and odd speech.

Most of the current research on the dimensionality of schizophrenia (the schizophrenia spectrum) is done under the umbrella of this broadened schizotypy concept (see Raine *et al.* (1995) for recent 'collected works'). This, in turn, is underpinned by the theory—for which there is reasonably good evidence (Ingraham 1995)—that schizotypy describes some aspect of the genetic basis for the predisposition to the schizophrenias. Twin questions that remain uncertain concern the precise definition of the schizophrenia spectrum itself (Levinson and Mowry 1991) and the exact components of schizotypy that relate to it. Regarding the latter point it has been argued (Torgersen 1994) that, from a genetics perspective at least, it is just a few of the specifically personality-based (schizoid) elements that are critical. On the other hand, there is evidence that narrowly schizoid and broader schizotypal subtypings overlap considerably (Coid 1992), as do the so-called Cluster A personality disorders in DSM-IV (viz. schizotypal, schizoid, and paranoid) in their relation to schizophrenia (Varma and Sharma 1993). For the moment there would seem to be an advantage in continuing to work within a wide, rather than a narrow, construction of schizotypy/schizoidness. (For an excellent recent discussion of this issue from a developmental perspective see Wolff (1995).)

It could be argued that the remit for schizotypy research should be—indeed already is—even broader, given the discussion in the previous section about the arbitrary division between schizophrenic and affective psychosis. Attempts to pursue 'the borderline' in the case of the latter have been less successful than for schizophrenia—strangely perhaps, though it might simply reflect comparatively less, or a different kind of, research effort. Nevertheless, there is a large, albeit somewhat chaotic, background literature on aspects of 'the borderline' that lie outside that referred to so far with respect to schizotypy (see Stone (1980) and, for a summary account, Claridge (1995)).

The work in question started from a similar point as that now subsumed under schizotypy research; also influenced by attempts—mostly by psychoanalysts—to define the outer boundaries of schizophrenia. Coining the term 'schizoaffective' formed part of this, as did the appearance of labels such as 'borderline schizo-phrenia' and 'pseudoneurotic schizophrenia'. Eventually the focus of attention shifted towards examining some of these intermediate conditions more from a view of their being personality disorders and the descriptor, 'borderline', in its more technical sense, was born. The main landmark here occurred through the revision that produced the DSM-III (American Psychiatric Association 1980)—

specifically the recognition of two forms of 'borderline' disorder: one schizotypal (SPD), already referred to, and the other BPD. Unlike SPD, BPD is defined much more explicitly in terms of personality-based features of an aberrant kind, such as impulsivity, affective instability, and self-damaging patterns of behaviour.

Given the strong mood element in its definition, it would be a neat solution if BPD bore a relation to affective psychosis which mirrored that connecting schizotypy to schizophrenia. The evidence being equivocal, opinions on the issue are strongly polarized. Some (For example Paris 1994) dismiss the idea of a primary association to any Axis I psychosis; others (Stone 1977; Marziali *et al.* 1994) have argued that there is evidence connecting some forms of BPD to major mood disorder. A third view is that BPD is so ill-defined that, given nevertheless that it describes some fairly disturbed psychological functioning, it is bound almost by default to show a degree of relationship to psychosis (Tyrer 1994). If this were true then presumably it would be expected that the association would be to the affective (or schizoaffective), rather than to the narrowly schizophrenic, form of psychotic disorder.

Two other points are relevant here. One is evidence, some dating back to the DSM revision (Spitzer *et al* 1979), that there is a considerable overlap between the schizotypal and borderline forms of personality disorder (see also George and Soloff 1986). This in itself, together with the co-morbidity of both BPD and SPD with several other types of Axis II personality disorder, would argue for a broad interpretation of continuity in this clinical domain, in the form of a *'psychosis spectrum'*. The second point, however, is that the existing psychiatric nosology already contains a clinical entity—in DSM-IV 'cyclothymic mood disorder'— which could provide an alternative or additional way of pursuing the 'borderline' variant in affective psychosis. Interestingly, with one small exception to be noted in the next chapter, this possibility has been entirely ignored by schizotypy researchers.

Although by no means a fully delineated framework for research or clinical practice, it is beyond reasonable doubt that in the illness domain there is strong dimensionality, connecting the psychoses to lesser variants of abnormal behaviour, particularly the personality disorders. A further, more radical question is how far this continuity can be extended back into the normal, healthy population.

DIMENSIONS OF PSYCHOSIS

Except for an oversimplistic, all-or-none, theory of disease, the ideas presented in the previous section are perfectly compatible with a medical model of psychiatric disorder. Dimensionality within the clinical sphere is easily explicable in terms of a *forme fruste* concept of disease, viz. that the symptoms of illnesses can manifest themselves with varying severity, dependent upon the degree of expression of the relevant underlying cause. This, in turn, will be influenced by the presence or absence, or strength or weakness, of other modifying factors in the aetiology.

In personality psychology the concept of dimensionality is somewhat different, if only because it refers to continua that describe smoothly varying individual differences in healthy functioning that have no necessary reference point in abnormality (except in a purely statistical sense). Yet the two constructions of continuity do often come close together—and can do so unproblematically. Anxiety is a case in point. The notion of anxiety as a healthy personality trait (or transient adaptive state) is perfectly reconcilable with its expression as anxiety *disorder*. One is seen as merely flowing from the other, only a slight twist being needed to transform healthy into less-healthy functioning. Even the measured signs give us little clue as to where the transition occurs: scales of anxiety traits do not look all that different from scales of anxiety symptoms.

Viewing psychosis—especially schizophrenia—in a similar way has, predictably, proved more difficult. But not impossible. Here I am *not* referring to the ideas of the existentialist radical psychiatry of the 1960s. Long before that, 'dimensionality' formed part of a more received psychiatric (and psychological) wisdom about psychosis. The coining of 'schizoid', in connection with schizophrenia, is an example. As mentioned earlier, Eugen Bleuler was always somewhat uncertain about the status of schizophrenia as organic disease: there was a hint from the outset that the idea of disordered personality within schizophrenia could not be fully separated from the concept of schizophrenia itself and that something in the condition, while puzzling, was understandable, perhaps even continuous with normality. Jung (1960), a colleague of E. Bleuler's at the Burghölzi, with a deep interest in schizophrenia at that time, contributed to the debate.

Taking up this historical theme, Manfred Bleuler (1978) comments on why the 'discovery' of schizoid personality seemed so important to the appreciation of the quality of psychosis. He writes:

To anyone who had accepted the concept, much of what constitutes the essence of schizophrenia was bound to appear to him as not quite so 'crazy' psychologically. The magic touch of the concept lay in the fact that it brought the mental patient closer to the heart and to the understanding of his doctor. It helped to establish a clear pathway to a 'psychodynamic' schizophrenia theory and to a sympathetic meeting with the mentally ill patient that was unencumbered by the hard, cold dogmas depicting the mental patient as something different, inaccessible, and beyond the reach of human empathy. (p. 434)

As M. Bleuler further notes, all of this resulted in schizoidness (or 'schizoidia') being seen sometimes as personality deviation and sometimes as an incipient sign, or mild form, of disease.

One person who combined both usages of 'schizoid' was Kretschmer (1925). He considered schizoid qualities as both clinical manifestations and traits of normal temperament, and established the first important dimensional model of psychosis in the modern period. His theory is also significant because it brought schizophrenia and affective psychosis (as manic depression) into the same domain: these two disorders defined the end-points of a dimension of normal personality, 'schizothymia – cyclothymia', which had 'schizoid' and 'cycloid' temperaments as intermediate aberrant forms. Kretschmer considered that variations along this dimension were constitutional, related to somatotype. His biological perspective accorded well with an emerging organic (genetic) view of psychosis that prevailed in the 1930s. But in other respects Kretschmer's theory was out of line and before its time. For example, it failed to identify a mechanism whereby temperamentally normal or mildly aberrant personality disorder could be seen to translate into manifest psychotic illness. Dimensional theories of psychosis remained, and to an extent still remain, only half-formed, the inherent ambiguities in them not fully articulated.

Figure 1.1 summarizes some of the above discussion by highlighting one source of confusion—the way in which dimensionality in psychosis has been variously construed. It draws a distinction between what, on the right of the diagram, I have labelled 'quasi-dimensional' and 'fully dimensional' interpretations, respectively. Quasi-dimensional corresponds to the *forme fruste* view of illness referred to earlier: continuity in psychosis certainly exists, but only in so far as it represents a variation in an underlying disease process. The aetiological questions for this type of theory concern the nature and cause of the neurological 'lesion' or functional incapacity. Regarding diagnosis and nosology, typical issues for debate

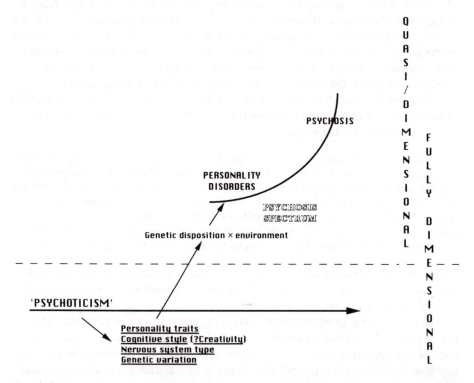

Fig. 1.1. Comparison of quasi-dimensional (disease-based) and fully dimensional (personality-based) continuity modes of psychosis. Note that, in the fully dimensional part of the model, the term 'psychoticism' has a more comprehensive meaning than Eysenck's usage (see footnote in, and later part of, main text for further elaboration).

include those discussed in the previous section about the relationship between full-blown psychosis and personality disorders, such as SPD, and the nature of the schizophrenia spectrum.[1]

The fully dimensional version is very different: it *encloses* the quasi-dimensional component but is otherwise more personality-based. Crucially, it adds another level of continuity, in the form of psychotic traits that constitute part of normal individual differences. These traits describe *both* sources of healthy variation *and* predisposition to disorder (psychosis-proneness). In other words, the fully dimensional model pursues the similarity to trait anxiety and anxiety disorder discussed above. The only difference from that example would seem to lie in the sharper discontinuity that might accompany the shift from the healthy state to disorder (represented in the figure as crossing the dotted line into the zone of functioning to which quasi-dimensional theorists confine themselves). It will be recalled that it was this bigger leap—and perhaps only that—which seemed to make the difference between extrapolating the fully dimensional view from the lesser (neurotic) illnesses to psychosis.

A radical feature of the fully dimensional construction of psychosis—distinguishing it from the quasi-dimensional alternative—concerns its approach to the study of 'aetiology'. Instead of taking the pathological as its only possible reference point, it also pays attention to a full range of data about normal individual differences: cognitive, personality, social, genetic, and so on. As predisposing influences, all of these are intrinsically part of the antecedent causes of psychotic illness, as well as of the intermediate disorders of personality associated with it. By the same token, a variable expression of these same predispositions also allows for the possibility of other, more healthy or adaptive outcomes, in favourable circumstances or enriching environments.

The two versions of dimensionality shown in Fig. 1.1 roughly align to the psychiatric and the psychological; not surprisingly, the quasi-dimensional view finds more favour among medical observers. However, there is not a perfect correspondence in that respect. Among psychologists, at least, there is a marked Transatlantic difference in usage. Most North American workers on schizotypy, for example, are very committed to a quasi-dimensional explanation of the schizophrenia spectrum. Their theoretical position on this is largely due to the influence of Meehl, for whom schizotypy, as noted earlier, lies firmly in the domain of disease—as partially expressed 'schizotaxia'. Furthermore, the latter is considered by Meehl to be mediated by a single major gene. If true, this is certainly compatible with a continuum theory of the *quasi*-dimensional type (Roberts and Claridge 1991); but it probably rules out a *fully* dimensional interpretation, of the kind presented in Fig. 1.1.

---

[1] In Fig. 1.1 I have borrowed the term 'psychoticism' from Eysenck. However, it is important to note that I have used it in a much broader, and in several other respects different, sense from that in which he uses it (Eysenck 1992; and see later in this text). For the purposes of the figure I have preferred this to 'schizotypy' because it illustrates the general case better. In practice it would be expected that different expressions of 'psychoticism' might generate their own versions of the model, e.g. 'SPD' would substitute for 'personality disorders' along a 'schizophrenia spectrum' (Claridge 1994).

The notion of psychotic traits having healthy qualities seems quite foreign, then, to North American schizotypy researchers. Here, by way of illustration, I might mention one strong adherent of Meehl's theory who recently looked at me in complete incomprehension when I tried to explain to him the notion of the 'happy schizotype', a term which Charles McCreery, the author of Chapter 12 in this book, has coined to designate individuals who seem perfectly content in their 'psychotic' personalities.

A diametrically opposite point of view to Meehl's—on the continuity question— and illustrating the Transatlantic divide is Eysenck's. He proposes a fully dimensional model close to that shown in Fig. 1.1—indeed his theory partly inspired it. If there is a difference, it lies in the fact that Eysenck's version is even more 'fully' dimensional than that suggested here. This is because Eysenck appears to take little or no account of the discontinuities between traits and symptoms implied in the transition from adaptive personality to illness. For him all psychiatric disorders, including the psychoses, do seem merely to represent the end-points of continuously variable dimensions (Eysenck 1960).

This last feature of Eysenck's theory is, in my view, a weakness. As the late Graham Foulds (1965) pointed out many years ago, there is a logical distinction to be made between personality traits and the symptoms of illness, as two different universes of discourse. Admittedly, in some instances—for example anxiety, referred to previously—the differentiation can in practice be difficult to make, but it is nevertheless necessary to preserve it, in order to accommodate the fact that functional shifts do occur on entry into ill (or other unusual) states to which the relevant traits predispose the person. It is particularly important to recognize this in the case of psychosis, where such discontinuities may be very marked. However persuasive the personality-based dimensional view is in accounting for certain features, it is not an *alternative* to a medical paradigm for psychological disorders, as Eysenck has sometimes argued. It can, in fact, provide only a partial explanation, needing also to incorporate—as the fully dimensional model proposed here does—the element of discontinuity contained in disease theory.

Eysenck's theoretical position is also notable in two other respects. One is for his having formulated his views of psychosis largely outside the mainstream of schizotypy research; he has been driven more by attempts to develop his own ideas on personality structure, extending them into the sphere of 'psychoticism' and psychosis. The other is for his embracing *Eintheitpsychose* theory. He did so very early on (Eysenck 1952b), in the face, it has to be said, of considerable derision from some members of the psychiatric Establishment and long before some of them rediscovered the concept for themselves!

Taken together, the above two qualities of Eysenck's theory have caused it to emerge as a distinct alternative to all other contemporary views on the dimensionality of psychosis. His individual-differences approach is historically more in line with the personality, than with the now more prevalent clinical, constructions of psychosis-proneness, Eysenck being particularly influenced by Kretschmer's early schizothymia—cyclothymia theory of temperament (Eysenck 1952a). But Eysenck even departs drastically from that, with his proposal of 'psychoticism' (P) as a general personality factor common to *all* psychosis and introversion–extraversion (I–E) as the dimension differentiating the schizophrenic and manic-depressive forms (Eysenck and Eysenck 1976). This suggested arrangement certainly deals, in principle at least, with the questions raised earlier, arising from the apparent overlap between the two types of psychosis and the probable need to try to bring them within the same domain.

Yet Eysenck's further development of his ideas about psychoticism over the years has had other consequences that have caused his theory to appear to stand even more alone. The most significant is the adoption of what many would regard as an idiosyncratic approach to the questionnaire measurement of 'psychoticism'. This theme will be taken up in the following chapter, but it is worth making some brief observations, in order to put Eysenck's theory in context, in relation to the other ideas about schizotypy that have been discussed here.

In evaluating Eysenck's approach to the subject matter of this book, I believe it is necessary to bear in mind an important distinction. I am referring to the different contributions Eysenck has made to the topic, as reflected in (1) his original very general theoretical statements about the dimensional structure of personality; and (2) his later, more current, interpretations of 'psychoticism' within that structure. The former, *qua* pure theory, could be claimed to be a quite viable, if unusual, alternative to more conventional approaches currently in vogue in schizotypy research: locating individuals in a dimensional framework of E, P (and N) might well be as informative a guide to their 'psychoticism', 'schizotypy', or 'psychosis-proneness' as more symptom-based evaluations, or accounts in terms of traditional personality descriptors, like 'schizoid' or 'cycloid'. However, Eysenck has gone further than that and, in doing so, has somewhat foreclosed the debate on the meaning of 'psychoticism' as an individual-differences construct. He has chosen to interpret psychoticism as a general dimension of antisocial behaviour and to formulate a theory of clinical psychosis based on the notion of a continuum of what is, effectively, aggressiveness; this runs from altruism at one end, through normal hostility, psychopathic personality disorder, and affective psychosis, to schizophrenia at the other (Eysenck 1992). The scheme Eysenck proposes certainly offers a partial solution to some of the questions raised here about the nature of the 'psychosis spectrum' and its relation to psychosis itself; for example the possible merging of some forms of personality and psychotic disorder. But, as brought out in later chapters here, his theory seems to fall short of what a *comprehensive* account of 'psychoticism'—in the broader sense in which we would like to use it here—should look like.

CONCLUSIONS

Several issues have been brought out in this chapter: the breadth of the concept of madness; the relationship to less serious, but apparently associated, personality disorders; the defining role of biological or organic factors; and the terminology that can best capture the continuity within psychosis. But the main issue was the comparison drawn between the two models of dimensionality that have implicitly shaped research on the subject matter with which this book is concerned. Indeed, as the title indicates, that theme lies at the centre of the book. For, among other implications that later chapters deal with, probably one of the most important questions that currently needs to be answered is about schizophrenia: whether it is a neurological disease or a personality deviation.

To anticipate an obvious retort to that statement, 'it' is probably neither, in two senses. First, some individuals who can be labelled 'schizophrenic' undoubtedly do have a diagnosable organic brain disease. But for the majority of cases—those that fall within the purview of this book—the evidence suggests that is not the case, and a more subtle explanation has to prevail. Even so—and this is the second reply to the expected objections to my earlier remark—neither simple biological aberrations nor understandable psychological reactions are likely to suffice as an explanation. Both Bleulers, and many other authors, have taught us that. Subsequent chapters do not answer the questions that still persist, but perhaps they will give pause for thought to those readers who feel that they already 'know' what schizophrenia is.

REFERENCES

Abraham, K. R. and Kulhara, P. (1987). The efficacy of electroconvulsive therapy in the treatment of schizophrenia: a comparative study. *British Journal of Psychiatry*, **151**, 152–5.

American Psychiatric Association. (1980). *Diagnostic and statistical manual* (3rd edn). APA, Washington, DC.

American Psychiatric Association. (1994). *Diagnostic and statistical manual* (4th edn). APA, Washington, DC.

Andreasen, N. J. C. and Powers, P. S. (1974). Overinclusive thinking in mania and schizophrenia. *British Journal of Psychiatry*, **125**, 452–6.

Baron, M. and Gruen, R. S. (1991). Schizophrenia and affective disorder: Are they genetically linked? *British Journal of Psychiatry*, **159**, 267–70.

Berrios, G. E. (1995). Conceptual problems in diagnosing schizophrenic disorders. In *Advances in the neurobiology of schizophrenia* (ed. J. A. Den Boer, H. G. M. Westenberg, and H. M. van Praag), pp. 7–25. Wiley, Chichester.

Bleuler, E. (1911). *Dementia praecox or the group of schizophrenias* (trans. J. Zinkin, 1950). International Universities Press, New York.

Bleuler, M. (1978). *The schizophrenic disorders* (trans. S. M. Clemens). Yale University Press, New Haven.

Brockington, I. F., Kendell, R. E., Wainwright, S., Hillier, V. F., and Walker, J. (1979). The distinction between the affective psychoses and schizophrenia. *British Journal of Psychiatry*, **135**, 243–8.

Cameron, N. (1938). Reasoning, regression and communication in schizophrenics. *Psychological Monographs*, **50**, 1–34.

Claridge, G. (1987). 'The schizophrenias as nervous types' revisited. *British Journal of Psychiatry*, **151**, 735–43.

Claridge, G. (1994). Single indicator of risk for schizophrenia: Probable fact or likely myth? *Schizophrenia Bulletin* **20**, 151–68.

Claridge, G. (1995). *Origins of mental illness* (new impression). Malor Books, Cambridge, Mass.

Coid, J. W. (1992). DSM-III diagnoses in criminal psychopaths: a way forward. *Criminal Behaviour and Mental Health* 2, 78–94.

Crow, T. J. (1986). The continuum of psychosis and its implication for the structure of the gene. *British Journal of Psychiatry*, 149, 419–29.

Crow, T. J. (1990). Temporal lobe asymmetries as the key to the etiology of schizophrenia. *Schizophrenia Bulletin*, 16, 434–43.

Crow, T. J. (1991). The failure of the Kraepelinian binary concept and the search for the psychosis gene. In *Concepts of mental disorder. A continuing debate* (ed. A. Kerr and H. McClelland), pp. 31–47. Gaskell, London.

Cutting, J. (1985). *The psychology of schizophrenia*. Churchill Livingstone, Edinburgh.

Delva, N. J. and Letemendia, F. J. J. (1982). Lithium treatment in schizophrenia and schizoaffective disorders. *British Journal of Psychiatry*, 141, 387–400.

Dolan, R. J., Calloway, S. P., and Mann, A. H. (1985). Cerebral ventricular size in depressed subjects. *Psychological Medicine*, 15, 873–8.

Eysenck, H. J. (1952a). Schizothymia—cyclothymia as a dimension of personality. II. Experimental. *Journal of Personality*, 20, 345–84.

Eysenck, H. J. (1952b). *The scientific study of personality*. Routledge and Kegan Paul, London.

Eysenck, H. J. (1960). Classification and the problems of diagnosis. In *Handbook of abnormal psychology* (ed. H. J. Eysenck), pp. 1–31. Pitman, London

Eysenck, H. J. (1992). The definition and measurement of psychoticism. *Personality and Individual Differences*, 13, 757–85.

Eysenck, H. J. and Eysenck, S. B. G. (1976). *Psychoticism as a dimension of personality*. Hodder and Stoughton, London.

Foulds, G. A. (1965). *Personality and personal illness*. Tavistock, London.

George, A. and Soloff, P. H. (1986). Schizotypal symptoms in patients with borderline personality disorders. *American Journal of Psychiatry*, 143, 212–15.

Iacono, W. G., Peloquin, L. J., Lumry, A., Valentine, B. H., and Tuason, V. B. (1982). *Journal of Abnormal Psychology*, 91, 35–44.

Ingraham, L. J. (1995). Family-genetic research and schizotypal personality. In *Schizotypal personality* (ed. A. Raine, T. Lencz, and S. A. Mednick), pp. 19–42. Cambridge University Press.

Jaspers, K. (1913). *General psychopathology* (trans. J. Hoenig and M. W. Hamilton, 1963). Manchester University Press.

Journal of Mental Health (1993). Perspectives on schizophrenia. What is schizophrenia? (Special section featuring articles by E. C. Johnstone, A. Farmer *et al.*, R. P. Bentall, and P. K. Chadwick; and commentaries by G. Claridge), 2, 193–253.

Jung, C. G. (1960). *The psychogenesis of mental disease*, Vol. 3 of *The collected works of C. G. Jung* (trans. R. F. C. Hull). Routledge and Kegan Paul, London.

Kendell, R. E. (1991). The major functional psychoses: are they independent entities or part of a continuum? Philosophical and conceptual issues underlying the debate. In *Concepts of mental disorder. A continuing debate* (ed. A. Kerr and H. McClelland), pp. 1–16. Gaskell, London.

Kendell, R. E. and Brockington, I. F. (1980). The identification of disease entities and the relationship between schizophrenic and affective psychoses. *British Journal of Psychiatry*, 137, 324–31.

Kendler, K. S. (1985). Diagnostic approaches to schizotypal personality disorder: A historical perspective. *Schizophrenia Bulletin*, 11, 538–53.

Klein, D. F. and Fink, M. (1963). Multiple item factors as change measures in psychopharmacology. *Psychopharmacologia*, 4, 43–52.

Kraepelin, E. (1919). *Dementia praecox and paraphrenia* (trans. R. M. Barclay). Churchill Livingstone, Edinburgh.

Levinson, D. F. and Mowry, B. J. (1991). Defining the schizophrenia spectrum. *Schizophrenia Bulletin*, 17, 491–514.

Kretschmer, E. (1925). *Physique and character* (trans. W. J. H. Sprott). Kegan, Trench, and Trubner, London.

McGuffin, P, Farmer, A., and Gottesman, I. I. (1987). Is there really a split in schizophrenia? The genetic evidence. *British Journal of Psychiatry*, 150, 581–92.

Marziali, E., Munroe-Blum, H., and Links, P. (1994). Severity as a diagnostic dimension of borderline personality disorder. *Canadian Journal of Psychiatry*, 39, 540–4.

Meehl, P. E. (1962). Schizotaxia, schizotypy, schizophrenia. *American Psychologist*, 17, 827–38.

Meehl, P. E. (1990). Toward an integrated theory of schizotaxia, schizotypy, and schizophrenia. *Journal of Personality Disorders*, 4, 1–99.

Overall, J. E., Hollister, L. E., and Meyer, F. (1964). Imipramine and thioridazine in depressed and schizophrenic patients. *Journal of the American Medical Association*, 189, 605–8.

Paris, J. (1994). *Borderline personality disorder. A multidimensional approach*. American Psychiatric Press, Washington, DC.

Payne, R. W., Mattusek, P., and George, E. I. (1959). An experimental study of schizophrenia thought disorder. *Journal of Mental Science*, 105, 627–52.

Rado, S. (1953). Dynamics and classification of disordered behavior. *American Journal of Psychiatry*, 110, 406–16.

Raine, A., Lencz, T., and Mednick, S. A. (eds) (1995) *Schizotypal personality*. Cambridge University Press.

Roberts, D. and Claridge, G. (1991). A genetic model compatible with a dimensional model of schizophrenia. *British Journal of Psychiatry*, 158, 451–6.

Schneider, K. (1959). *Clinical psychopathology* (trans. M. W. Hamilton). Grune and Stratton, New York.

Spitzer, R. L., Endicott, J., and Gibbon, M. (1979). Crossing the border into borderline personality and borderline schizophrenia: the development of criteria. *Archives of General Psychiatry*, 36, 17–24.

Stone, M. H. (1977). The borderline syndrome: evaluation of the term, genetic aspects, and prognosis. *American Journal of Psychotherapy*, 31, 345–65.

Stone, M. H. (1980). *The borderline syndromes*. McGraw Hill, New York.

Taylor, M. A. (1992). Are schizophrenia and affective disorder related? A selective literature review. *American Journal of Psychiatry*, 149, 22–32.

Torgersen, S. (1994). Personality deviations within the schizophrenia spectrum. *Acta Psychiatrica Scandinavica*, 90 (suppl. 384), 40–4.

Tyrer, P. (1994). What are the borders of borderline personality disorder? *Acta Psychiatrica Scandinavica*, 89, 38–44.

Varma, S. L. and Sharma, I. (1993). Psychiatric morbidity in the first degree relatives of schizophrenic patients. *British Journal of Psychiatry*, 162, 672–8.

Wolff, S. (1995). *Loners. The life path of unusual children*. Routledge, London.

World Health Organization (1992). *ICD: The ICD–10 classification of mental and behavioural disorders—clinical descriptions and diagnostic guidelines*. WHO, Geneva.

2

Questionnaire measurement

OLIVER MASON, GORDON CLARIDGE, AND LEANNE WILLIAMS

INTRODUCTION

Over the past thirty years the theoretical ideas introduced in the previous chapter have been operationalized as self-report questionnaires in a variety of ways. Picking up on the discussion there, it is possible to discern, in the aim and content of such questionnaires, two major respects in which they vary, reflecting the two lines of cleavage that have divided the way the notion of psychotic traits has been conceptualized, in Europe and the United States, and by psychologists and psychiatrists. One concerns the extent to which investigators have been inspired by a 'fully dimensional' view, constructing scales of a general individual-differences kind, or, alternatively, by a 'quasi-dimensional' perspective, seeking a more clinical, dichotomous content for their questionnaires. The second source of difference has been the relative emphasis placed on narrowly schizophrenic, as distinct from more general, and/or additional, psychotic characteristics. Then, in a more minor vein, questionnaires also vary in whether they have been designed according to a wide brief—for example 'schizotypal personality'—or focus on more specific features, such as 'perceptual aberration' or 'predisposition to hallucinate'. These themes can be illustrated by referring to the scales themselves, listed in Table 2.1.

Most obviously, on the one hand are the many scales produced by the Chapmans in Wisconsin, who have taken single schizotypal or psychotic features and produced long item-lists that are perhaps similar to the regular symptom checklists of psychiatry, adjusted for use in the non-psychiatric population. One of the concerns of users of these clinically based scales has been the attempt to derive indices that detect the so-called schizoid taxon. On the other hand, and in complete opposition to the clinical approach, Eysenck has adopted a more personality-based, fully continuous view, as well as arguing for the existence of a general dimension of psychoticism, measured by his P-scale. Other researchers, including ourselves, have combined elements of both approaches, working within a personality model but attempting to bridge the gap—more than Eysenck does—to the clinical pheneomena. In some cases this has entailed leaving open for the moment the *Einheitpsychose* question; hence the ambiguity deliberately retained here in the use of the term 'schizotypy'.

The above issues have been raised—and are slowly being resolved—by a new trend that has emerged over the past decade in schizotypy questionnaire research, namely the comparison of scales using a variety of multivariate techniques,

Table 2.1 Psychosis-proneness scales

Scale	References	Comments
Schizoidia	Golden and Meehl (1979)	seven-item scale derived from MMPI
Chapman *et al.* scales		
Perceptual Aberration	Chapman *et al.* (1978)	tendency to perceptual distortion
Physical and Social Anhedonia Scales	Chapman *et al.* (1976)	loss of pleasure from sensory and social sources
Revised Social Anhedonia Scale	Eckblad *et al.* (1982)	schizoid indifference
Magical Ideation	Eckblad and Chapman (1983)	superstitions and other magical beliefs
Social Fear	Raulin and Wee (1984)	
Intense Ambivalence	Raulin (1984)	
Cognitive Slippage	Miers and Raulin (1985)	
Hypomanic Personality	Eckblad and Chapman (1986)	impulsive and manic behaviour
Schizotypal Personality Scale (STA) and Borderline Personality Scale (STB)	Claridge and Broks (1984)	modeled on DSM-III criteria for schizotypal and borderline disorders
Launay-Slade Hallucination Scale	Launay and Slade (1981)	measure of predisposition to hallucinate
Schizophrenism Scale	Nielsen and Petersen (1976)	attentional difficulties and social anxiety
Rust Inventory of Schizoid Cognitions (RISC)	Rust (1987, 1988)	taps positive aspects of schizotypy
Psychoticism Scale	Eysenck and Eysenck (1975) Eysenck *et al.* (1985)	part of four-scale Eysenck Personality Questionnaire
Schizophrenism and Anhedonia scales	Venables *et al.* (1990)	measures of both positive and negative aspects of schizotypy
Schizotypal Personality Questionnaire (SPQ and SPQ-B)	Raine (1991) Raine and Benishay (1995)	modelled on DSM-III-R criteria for schizotypal personality disorder

including principal components analysis, factor analysis, and cluster analysis. Such work lies behind the new scales we shall refer to towards the end of this chapter. First, however, we shall examine in more detail some of the individual scales shown in Table 2.1, roughly divided according to their theoretical origins.

APPROACHES TO MEASUREMENT

Clinical

Paul Meehl believed that the Minnesota Multiphasic Personality Inventory (MMPI) could identify the combination of traits present in the schizotype. This clinical questionnaire works by producing a profile of scores across a number of scales. The schizotypal profile is one of high scores on 'Depression' (no. 2), 'Psychasthenia' (no. 7), and 'Schizophrenia' (no. 8): this has been called the 2–7–8 profile. The full MMPI is extremely unwieldy, with over 500 items; a shorter scale has benefits for the researcher and respondents alike. Golden and Meehl (1979) therefore used a process known as criterion referencing to arrive at a seven-item scale of 'Schizoidia'. Criterion referencing involves choosing items one after another that best separate the respondents according to a defined criterion, such as membership of a particular group, in this case schizophrenia. Items are chosen for their ability to select this group in a different way from other items, so that between them an adequate separation is achieved. While the method is ambitious and economical in using few items, it is difficult to see how the scale can achieve reliability and validity. One form of reliability assesses the internal consistency of a scale and this is poor for MMPI-based scales. In terms of validity, one study (Miller *et al.* 1982) found that the Schizoidia scale identified a greater proportion of depressives (71%) than schizophrenics (53%). It seems that with so few items the scale cannot discriminate between different clinical groups.

The Chapmans and their associates have taken up Meehl's theoretical approach, but operationalized his ideas quite differently. The Chapman scales are based on the notion that non-patients experience attenuated forms of psychotic experience. One of the most widely used of their scales (Perceptual Aberration) taps experiences of distortions in body image. Another, Magical Ideation, asks about experiences of precognition, thought transmission, spirits, and the transfer of psychic energies between people. Notably, items focus on personal *experiences* of, rather than simply *belief in*, these phenomena, for it is the former that characterize schizotypy as an attenuatated version of the similar schizophrenic symptomatology. In this same tradition, anhedonia is regarded as an important psychological deficit, marked by the lifelong inability to experience pleasure. The Social and Physical Anhedonia scales access sources of pleasure from, respectively, a variety of social situations and physical stimuli such as sport, sex, and other leisure pursuits.

Typically all of the Chapman scales use many items for each trait, this being seen as one solution to the problem of unreliability, referred to earlier. Because the Chapmans' items are often essentially weak versions of symptom-identifying ones, many are very rarely endorsed in normal populations. This is not a problem in itself: it may indeed indicate that 'the schizotype' is statistically rare and so support the quasi-dimensional view. On the other hand, for certain experimental purposes the distribution of responses is not ideal, since the majority of respondents score similarly and so are not discriminated; consequently the distribution of scores is not well suited to parametric statistics.

Users of the Chapmans' scales have rarely been concerned by these limitations, however, since a major enterprise has been to identify a discrete taxon of people at risk (Lenzenweger and Korfine 1995). The fact that the questionnaire scores of people in the taxon are in practice continuous with the rest of the population is regarded as being due to the flawed psychometric properties of the scales. Given this absence of 'points of rarity', sophisticated statistical techniques have been needed to separate the taxons. One of these, admixture analysis, attempts to model the 'latent structure' underlying the continuous distributions that questionnaires inevitably produce. Lenzenweger and co-workers have arrived at a figure of 15% (Lenzenweger and Moldin 1990) for the proportion of schizoid taxon members in the general population, as identified by the Perceptual Aberration scale.

Aside from these measurement issues, the Chapman scales do have an impressive range of content and depth of validation, rare among rivals (see Edell (1995) for an extensive review of their use in a variety of relevant research settings). Deserving special mention here—because it is crucial to the psychosis-proneness concept—is a recent report on the predictive validity of the scales, after a 10-year follow-up of a large subject cohort (L.J. Chapman *et al.* 1994). Although not predictive of schizophrenia itself, Perceptual Aberration, Magical Ideation, and Social Anhedonia were, in various combinations, good prognosticators of other major psychoses, as well as schizotypal symptoms and psychotic-like experiences.

Turning to other questionnaires, some have made use of the shared ground, referred to in Chapter 1, between psychosis and the personality disorders, especially Schizotypal Personality Disorder (SPD). This was true in the design of the Oxford STQ (discussed in the next section); while Adrian Raine has similarly used the DSM-IIIR diagnostic criteria for SPD to construct a nine-scale questionnaire, appropriately called the Schizotypal Personality Questionnaire. Notably, anhedonia, a central feature in some constructions of schizotypy, is largely absent from Raine's scale, because the DSM definition of Schizotypal Personality Disorder does not include it as a feature. Raine and Benishay (1995) have subsequently developed a brief scale for identifying SPD in clinical or research screening.

Modelling measures of psychosis-proneness on the personality disorders does carry some hazards. Although the relevance to SPD is undeniable, the personality disorders as a whole form a somewhat open-ended list of overlapping conditions. Co-morbidity is very high (Widiger *et al.* 1987), with many diagnostic features being shared among the different disorders in DSM. Particularly confusing is the clustering together of schizotypal and schizoid personality disorders (Tyrer and Ferguson 1988); the relation of both of these, together with paranoid personality, to schizophrenia (Varma and Sharma 1993); and the strong correlation between schizotypal and borderline forms of personality disorder (Spitzer *et al.* 1979). Another way of looking at such data, however, is to consider that they might reflect genuine connections between different conditions within a broad psychosis spectrum, a fact which clinicians, theorists, and constructors of questionnaires in the area would then simply need to live with.

Other sources of inspiration for questionnaire constuction have been the research programmes into high risk for schizophrenia (Watt *et al.* 1984). One British investigator influenced by this is Peter Venables, whose concern has been to identify early predictors of risk for subsequent psychosis, using a combination of both questionnaire and laboratory measures. Here, Venables (1993) found that psychophysiological markers used to choose probands at age four could predict later scoring on a Schizophrenism scale that he constructed (Venables 1990). In subsequent analyses of large sets of data from this questionnaire, Venables and Bailes (1994) have identified several factors among the items, as referred to later.

Personality

Undoubtedly the prime move of more personality-based measures has been Hans Eysenck, whose dimensional model of individual differences, including psychotic traits, has dominated the scene for nearly half a century. Eysenck's radical approach to theory is mirrored in his P-scale measure of general psychoticism, an instrument that has developed over several versions (Eysenck and Eysenck 1975; Eysenck *et al.* 1985). The early form (part of the PEN questionnaire, measuring psychoticism, extraversion, and neuroticism) had several items with a manifestly psychotic content but suffered from poor internal consistency (reliability) and produced very low endorsement rates. Subsequent revision of the scale to correct these weaknesses was successful but shifted the content more towards coverage of antisocial, impulsive, and socially nonconformist traits, causing at least one author (Zuckerman 1993) to label it more a measure of psychopathy. As it happens, this is not a particularly devastating criticism, given the evident multidimensional nature of psychotic traits and the possible connections, already noted, between psychosis and personality disorder. However, the published P-scales have been criticized on a number of other grounds, including their specificity and criterion validity (Claridge 1981, 1983) and their relatively weak predictive validity (J. P. Chapman *et al.* 1994).

Other researchers have been highly influenced by Eysenck, usually in the course of trying to construct improvements to the P-scale. Nielsen and Petersen (1976) made an early attempt to measure some of the characteristics of premorbid schizophrenia, their scale being intended to work much as Eysenck had intended for Psychoticism, but due to the exclusion of the affective psychoses from their remit the authors substituted 'Schizophrenism' as the title of the scale. Its content can be conveyed by such items as 'I often have difficulties in controlling my thoughts' and 'Sometimes I am so nervous that I am blocked'; these stress the cognitive difficulties and resultant social anxiety of many schizotypes and schizophrenics and cause the scale to be very highly correlated with Neuroticism.

Along not dissimilar lines is the RISC, a questionnaire of 'schizotypal cognitions' produced by Rust (1987, 1988). This was conceived as a deliberate substitute for the Eysenck P-scale, likewise being constucted, with relatively mild items, for use in normal populations; as contrasted, for example, with the Chapman scales, referred to earlier. The RISC was deliberately designed not to, and indeed does not, correlate with the P-scale and is considered by the author to tap a quite different aspect of 'psychoticism' (Rust 1988). Apart from the Eysenck scale, it is the only instrument of those reviewed here that is commercially published; a fact which Chapman *et al.* (1995) have commented on somewhat critically, referring to the lack of good standardization data that would normally be expected of a questionaire that might be advertised for clinical or other applied use.

The origins of schizotypy measurement in Oxford also lie in the Eysenckian school of individual-differences psychology; or, more strictly, in an attempt to blend together the personality and clinical approaches to the measurement of psychotic traits. The first effort is attributable to Sharon Reichenstein (1976), an undergraduate under G. C.'s supervision, who took J. Chapman's (1966) classic paper on the symptoms of early schizophrenia as a starting point for constructing a questionnaire for use with normal subjects. This early questionnaire was then revised in collaboration with several later graduate students, notably David Rawlings, with whom the STQ scales took their final form (see Appendix I). It is here that the influence from clinical research on the personality disorders becomes apparent, since the STA and STB were based on, respectively, the Schizotypal and Borderline Personality Disorders criteria as described in DSM III (American Psychatric Association 1980).

MULTIVARIATE ANALYSES

Principal components and factor analysis

With measures differing so much in name and item content, it has been of interest to compare the aspects of schizotypy, or psychosis pronenesss, they purport to represent. Both factor analysis (FA) and principal components analysis (PCA) have been used to compare items within some of the questionnaires individually, and to compare across scales. Here the interested reader is directed to several recent reviews of the flurry of analyses carried out to date (Claridge 1994; Venables 1994; Vollema and van den Bosch 1995). For present purposes we shall summarise the main findings and then present some further work carried out on those data collected in our own laboratory.

The factors

Table 2.2 contains a fairly comprehensive list of these studies, arranged so as to draw out the similarities between the factors identified. It should be noted that these are grouped in the table under four headings, even though not every analysis has produced all four factors, nor are the factors contained in the same column necessarily well matched. Indeed, there are some obvious disparities between the

Table 2.2 Summary of factor analytic studies of schizotypal traits

	Factors			
Study	Positive schizotypy Perceptual/cognitive	Negative schizotypy Introvertive Anhedonia	Social Anxiety and Cognitive Disorganization	Impulsive Nonconformity
Muntaner et al. (1988)	STA, STB, MgI, PAb, N	SoA, PhA, E (–ve)		P, STB, L (–ve)
Raine and Allbutt (1989)	STA, STB, PAb, LSHS, NP			P, SoA
Kendler and Hewitt (1992)	PAb, MgI, LSHS, STA (MI and PA)	SoA, STA (PI), E (–ve)	STA, N, ImpNon,	ImpNon, P, PhA, SoA
Kelley and Coursey (1992)	STA, MgI, PAb, 278, ImpNon, MMPI Schiz., NP	PhA, PAb (–ve), MgI (–ve)		
Obiols et al. (1992)	PAb, STA, N	PhA, E (–ve)		P
Claridge et al. (1996) after Bentall et al. (1989)	PAb, MgI, HoP, LSHS, STA, STB, P	SoA, PhA, E (–ve)	N, NP, STA, MMPI schiz.	P, L (–ve), HoP, STB
Gruzelier et al. (1995) Raine et al. (1994) Analysis of SPQ subscales	Ideas of reference, magical thinking, unusual perceptual experiences		Social anxiety, paranoid ideation, no close friends, constricted affect	Odd behaviour, odd speech
Venables and Bailes (1994) Analysis of items	'Unusual Perceptual Experiences, paranoid and magical ideation'	'Social Anhedonia'	'Social Anxiety/Cognitive Disorganization'	('Physical Anhedonia'?)

Key:
Chapmans' Scales: PAb, Perceptual Aberration; MgI, Magical Ideation; ImpNon, Impulsive Nonconformity; SoA, Social Anhedonia; PhA, Physical Ahedonia; HoP, Hypomania. Claridge's Scales: STA, (schizotypal personality) and STB, (borderline personality). NP, Nielsen Petersen's Schizophrenism Scale. Eysencks' Scales: E, Extraversion; N, Neuroticism; P, Psychoticism; L, Lie. MMPI schiz., Golden and Meehl's MMPI schizoidia scale. 278, MMPI scales 2, 7 and 8.

studies. For one thing, different investigators have used different scales, or items from scales, and without sufficient variables a factor cannot emerge: in other words a clear marker for a trait needs to be present. The studies have also differed in the respondents they have used. Furthermore, some have employed small numbers of subjects that come close to minimum acceptable limits—this also tends to lead to underestimation of the number of factors.

The most consistent component to emerge from all of the studies has loadings from scales pertaining to unusual perceptual experiences, thinking styles, and beliefs. Particularly characterizing this factor are features described earlier as represented in the Chapmans' Magical Ideation and Perceptual Aberration scales. Such magical or religious beliefs may have their origin in the seemingly altered perceptions and sensations that some individuals have of their own bodies and the aspects of the world around them. Hypersensitivity to sounds and smells, a heightened or altered awareness of their visual world, and a sense of *déjà vu* and *présque vu* (its opposite) are some of the phenomena surrounding this predisposition. Rather more unusual phenomena that still occur in the normal population include 'hearing voices'. These may be 'true' auditory hallucinations, so-called 'pseudo-hallucinations' (where the hearer is aware that the voice is self-generated), or may simply be thoughts taking on a 'heard' quality. It is interesting that these experiences co-exist with beliefs in the supernatural, ESP, and other phenomena of a quasi-magical or religious content. Because of the likeness to hallucinatory and delusionary experiences this factor might be clinically labelled 'positive symptoms'; however it is important to clarify that this component is not pathological in and of itself. Many individuals appear at ease with these experiences and successfully assimilate their contents (see Chapters 11 and 12).

Very reliably distinguished from the 'positive symptom/unusual experiences' factor is a social withdrawal component, defined particularly by anhedonia. It occurs frequently in analyses and is strongly associated with introversion. Social anhedonia seems to be the most reliable marker for this component, as physical anhedonia is sometimes also associated with other factors. Part of the reason for the latter's 'floating behaviour' in some analyses may be the presence of the P-scale, which has some physically anhedonic items. It it important to appreciate that this factor is not simply extreme introversion but rather what Bleuler would have called schizoid: solitary, withdrawn, and lacking the everyday feelings that motivate social action.

Several of the factor analyses (Bentall *et al.* 1989; Kendler and Hewitt 1992; Venables and Bailes 1994; Claridge *et al.* 1996) have found that when a wide variety of scales are used with sufficient subjects, another cognitive component consistently emerges. Some items from the STA, the MMPI, and the Nielsen-Petersen Schizophrenism Scales appear to be the best descriptions of this factor, which Venables and Bailes (1995) called 'Cognitive Disorganization/ Social Anxiety'. When Eysenck's scales are included in the analyses, Neuroticism has a high loading on this factor. One of the studies (Hewitt and Claridge 1989) divided the STA scale into three subscales on the basis of FA of the scale itself.

These were 'Magical Ideation', 'Perceptual Aberration', and 'Paranoid Ideation'. Just as one would have predicted, the first two subscales loaded on the 'unusual experience/positive symptom' factor whilst 'paranoid ideation' was associated with neuroticism. Given the other analyses describing a 'cognitive disorganization' factor, it may be that paranoia is also part of this constellation of attributes. David Rawlings has investigated this concept, which has received little attention to date (see Chapter 3).

A fourth component to emerge from PCA and FA studies was present in perhaps four of the six studies in the table. It relies heavily on the presence of psychoticism and in some studies appears to be confused with anhedonia. Called variously 'impulsive nonconformity', 'odd behaviour', or 'asocial schizotypy', it seems to be clearly distinguished from anhedonia in several studies. A rarely used scale, 'Impulsive Nonconformity' (Chapman *et al.* 1984) might be said to capture the component best; its items describe thoughts of harming others and oneself and uncontrollable urges to abuse a variety of substances. Both Bentall *et al.* (1989) and Claridge *et al.* (1996) found that the tendency towards subclinical hypomania was associated with this factor.

Claridge *et al.*'s 1996 analysis—the largest to date with respect to sample size and included variables—was a replication of an early, smaller study (Bentall *et al.* 1989). The data for both analyses came from the Combined Schizotypal Traits Questionnaire (CSTQ), which in addition to a large set of regular psychosis-proneness scales (and other parts of the Eysenck Personality Questionnaire (EPQ)) also contained four delusional scales (Foulds and Bedford 1975). The latter measures are very clinical in content and, in normal samples, their score distributions quite skewed; the scales were therefore technically ill-suited for use in the kinds of analysis performed. However, they were included in the Bentall *et al.* analysis as possible 'markers' for the factors extracted. In fact their inclusion caused four, rather than three, recognizable components to emerge, leaving the exact factor structure of schizotypy unclear at that stage.

Subsequent data collection, due in large part to Charles McCreery, enabled the sample size for the CSTQ to pass a thousand. The resulting four-factor solution (see Table 2.2) was unambiguous, even without the delusional scales. A further refinement of the Claridge *et al.* study was to repeat the analysis without the three 'non-psychotic' scales from the EPQ—Extraversion, Neuroticism, and Lie (or Social Conformity). This was done in order to test the possibility that the factor structure might simply have reflected the three major Eysenckian dimensions. (This is a general argument about the structure of schizotypy, used by Eysenck and Barrett (1993), following a reanalysis of Kendler and Hewitt's (1989) data.) In fact, our reanalysis of the CSTQ data without the three EPQ scales revealed the same four components as before; this suggested a factor structure over and above—rather than being explained by—Eysenck's dimensions.

There are other arguments for concluding that the factors identified in studies of psychosis-proneness are not merely redescriptions of E, N, and P. First, the strongest and most consistent factor to appear in all of the analyses reported—'unusual cognitions'—does not have high loadings on any of Eysenck's scales and is substantially different in content from his contender, the P-scale. Secondly, while other factors do align with Extraversion and Neuroticism, they have substantially different contents; viz. items that do not simply redescribe E and N but have particular 'flavours' relevant to psychopathology. Neuroticism is the undiscriminating predictor *par excellence* of all psychopathology and it remains to be seen how well a more specific 'psychosis-prone' trait can be isolated from it. Thirdly, the theoretical links between Eysenck's Psychoticism and schizophrenia are weak. Other schizotypy scales and the empirical work with them seem to offer better possibilities for theory building, encompassing evidence from both the personality and clinical domains.

Confirmatory factor analysis (CFA)

An extension of the factor-analytic method is to include an element of formal model testing by importing other statistical methods. This requires one to have a much better understanding of the relationships that are likely to emerge from what is already known and develop models on *a priori* grounds. By specifying the number and type of factors, the algorithm is able to calculate the plausibility of such a set of interrelationships given the actual data. Obviously there is always some discrepancy, but the indices for 'goodness-of-fit' (essentially chi-square statistics) indicate the degree to which the predicted and actual results diverge. As well as providing a test of the structure obtained by exploratory FA, it is possible to compare models based on different theories. Raine *et al.* (1994) used the nine subscales of the SPQ to compare several models of schizotypal traits. Using theories of the relationships between positive and negative symptoms, several two-and three-factor models were compared. Of these, a three-factor solution provided the best fit, confirming analyses that Gruzelier *et al.* (1995) had made of the subscales. As noted earlier, the Schizotypal Personality Questionnaire contains little of an anhedonic nature, so this factor was largely absent. The authors interpreted a factor containing the subscales Paranoia, Anxiety, No Friends, and Blunt Affect as an 'Interpersonal' or withdrawn trait. In the light of the other analyses this seems to combine something of the 'Cognitive Disorganization/Social Anxiety' component with that of Anhedonia/Withdrawal.

Recent confirmatory factor analysis in our own laboratory (Mason 1995) has followed the direction of research on the CSTQ referred to above (Bentall *et al.* 1989; Claridge *et al.* 1996). This compared several plausible models of one, two, three, and four factors (see Table 2.3). The two-factor solution was constructed to mirror a distinction between 'positive and 'negative' schizotypy, terms that have arisen from a common distinction made about schizophrenic symptoms (see later). In contrast, the three-factor solution suggested a factor of 'cognitive disorganization/social anxiety' in addition to the other factors. As several of the studies discussed earlier (including that by Bentall *et al.* 1989) had found three factors, this was a plausible model. The final model

Table 2.3 Goodness-of-fit indicators for CFA models

Model	χ^2	d.f.	$\Delta\chi^2$/ d.f.	NFI	ΔNFI
2 Factors					
orthogonal	1304	57	0.841		
oblique	1266	56	38/1[a]	0.846	0.005
3 Factors					
orthogonal	1665	54	0.797		
oblique	1297	51	368/3[a]	0.842	0.045
4 Factors					
orthogonal	1286	54		0.844	
partial obl.	681	50	605/4[a]	0.917	0.073
full obl.	678	48	2.8/2ns	0.918	0.001

χ^2 = chi-square statistic; d.f. = degrees of freedom; $\Delta\chi^2$/ d.f. = change in chi-square with d.f.; NFI= normed fit index (>0.9 indicates good fit); ΔNFI = change in NFI (significant improvements indicated at >0.01) [a] P<0.01. [b] Model illustrated in Figure 2.1.

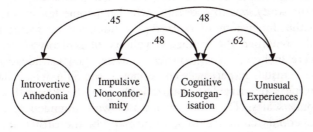

Fig. 2.1. Correlations between schizotypy factors.

(see Fig. 2.1) used the same (four-factor) structure found by Claridge *et al.* (1996).

The models are compared using several indices of fit including the normed-fit index (NFI), which can vary between a complete absence of fit at zero to a perfect fit of one. Only the four-factor models have respectable-fit indices and the best fitted is shown in Fig. 2.1 as a diagramatic representation. Notice that some of the factors have been allowed to correlate (so-called oblique factors) but that not all are correlated, since freeing extra constraints did not improve the model further.

It is important to note that the correlations are not 'real' but 'virtual' figures, estimated as the relationships between *latent*, rather than measured, variables. What can these statistical abstractions tell us? Although unusual experiences and cognitive disorganization are separate factors, they are likely to correlate in the general population. Impulsive nonconformity is also likely to correlate to a lesser extent with both components. The trait of introvertive anhedonia is rather separate, although it does correlate with cognitive disorganization.

Cluster analysis

Evidence from the factor-analytic studies described so far indicates that schizotypy is clearly a multidimensional construct, made up of at least three components. However, factor analysis provides information based on the the interrelationships between *measures* of, in this case, schizotypal traits. It does not tell us how *individuals* might be grouped according to their responses on these measures. That is, factor analysis does not indicate whether *people* form distinct groups, defined by different combinations of schizotypal traits. One of us (LW) has addressed this question by applying cluster analysis to schizotypy data.

Cluster analysis identifies groups of individuals, commonly referred to as 'types' (Hair *et al.* 1992). The value of this technique is that it identifies such types on the basis of 'natural' groupings in the data themselves. In this way cluster analysis produces a 'numerical taxonomy' of people with regard to their schizotypal traits. Although several studies have used the technique to develop a typology of schizophrenic symptoms (Farmer *et al.* 1983; Gur *et al.* 1991; Morrison *et al.* 1990; Van der Does *et al.* 1993), only one study—that referred to here—has attempted the same for schizotypy (Williams 1994).

The aim of the study was to determine whether people fall into clusters that correspond to the dimensions of schizotypy established by factor analysis. If so, this would strengthen the ecological validity of schizotypy measurement. Four scales were included in the cluster analysis: Magical Ideation (a good marker for the Unusual Experiences component), the STA which has a varied content (including Cognitive Disorganization), and the Physical and revised Social Anhedonia scales. These last two scales were intended to capture the introvertive anhedonia component found in many of the earlier analyses. One issue of particular interest was whether different aspects of anhedonia consorted with different profiles of schizotypy in different individuals; it was thought that this might shed some light on the different locations that had been found for the anhedonia scales in different factor analyses.

Scores from 70 undergraduates on these four schizotypy scales were analysed using Ward's method of cluster analysis which relies on an agglomerative hierarchical procedure and was chosen because it forms groups of people in such a way that the variance within groups is minimized. The standardized scores produced four clusters after one outlying individual was omitted. Fig. 2.2 shows the profile of mean scores (and associated standard error) on the four schizotypy scales for each of the clusters.

The numbers of people in each cluster, while not equal, none the less suggested that no single cluster could be considered more prevalent than any other. As indicated in Fig. 2.2., Cluster 1 is made up of 22 people with a generally low level of schizotypal traits. For fairly obvious reasons this cluster was called the 'Low Schizotypy' group.

The relatively high magical ideation for the 14 people in Cluster 2, along with a low level of both physical and social anhedonia, suggests that these people experience primarily 'positive' aspects of schizotypy—in particular, ideational

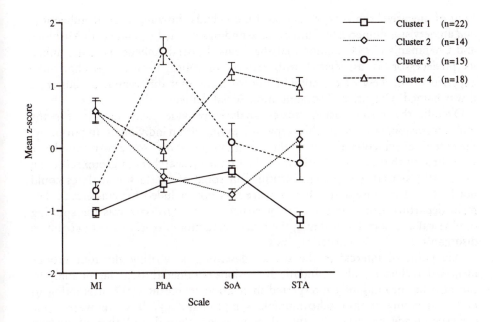

Fig. 2.2. Clusters of responders to four schizotypy scales.
Key: MI, Magical Ideation; PhA, Physica Anhedonia; SoA, revised Social Anhedonia;
STA, Schizotypal Personality.

disturbances. The average STA scores for this cluster may also reflect the presence of disturbances of ideation; Hewitt and Claridge (1989) found that one component of the STA taps distortions in ideation as well as perception. Cluster 2 was referred to as the 'Ideational/Perceptual Disturbance' group.

The 18 people in Cluster 3 are differentiated most clearly from other individuals by a very high level of physical anhedonia. They also show a generally average level of social anhedonia, slightly below average STA scores, and a low level of magical ideation. In contrast to Cluster 2, these individuals seem to experience mostly 'negative' aspects of schizotypy; but reflected in physical (rather than social) anhedonia. The cluster was called the 'Physical Anhedonia' group.

Cluster 4 was made up of 18 people characterized by very high scores on all of the scales, except Physical Anhedonia. The presence of very high STA scores could be taken to suggest that these individuals had endorsed all components of the scale: unusual ideation and perceptual experience, as well as aspects of cognitive disorganization and social anxiety, were previously found to load with paranoid ideation (Hewitt and Claridge 1989). The coexistence of these features, and magical ideation, with social anhedonia suggests two possibilities about the people in Cluster 4. First, social anhedonia might share some common elements with social anxiety and hence contribute to the latter's association with cognitive disorganization Secondly, social anhedonia might be construed specifically as a 'trait of 'negative' schizotypy, Cluster 4 individuals showing separate anhedonia *and* anxiety simultaneously. Both of these findings would be in line with Mishlove and Chapman's (1985) finding that the Revised Social Anhedonia scale, unlike its predecessor, is associated with reports of more 'positive' psychotic-like experiences. In view of the combination of traits that differentiated Cluster 4, it was named 'Cognitive Disorganisation/Social Anhedonia'.

Overall, the results using cluster analysis provide clear support for the multidimensional nature of schizotypy, as it exists within individuals. Importantly, the pattern of schizotypal traits in these four clusters shows some correspondence with three of the clusters identified by the Oxford researchers (a group reflecting the fourth, asocial 'component identified in some of the factor analyses could not be found because a suitable measure was not included for clustering). The main departure from the three-factor structure of schizotypy was the splitting of physical and social anhedonia, the latter being more associated with cognitive disorganization in the cluster analysis.

One point of interest in the studies described is whether the four groups identified in cluster analysis, and the dimensions obtained through factor analysis, can also be meaningfully interpreted in relation to recent work attempting to find a structure within schizophrenic symptomatology. If there were some correspondence between the two domains—the clinical and that of normal individual differences—it would add one more plank of support for the validity of the schizoptypy concept. This question is considered in the next section.

A comparison with schizophrenic symptomatology

We have already in a sense anticipated the conclusions from this section, in repeated reference to the distinction between 'positive' and 'negative' schizotypy. In neuropsychiatry the terminology is an old one (Jackson 1831), but enjoyed some revival a few years ago as a proposed division of schizophrenic symptoms into two types: 'positive' ones, such as hallucinations and delusions, and negative ones, including alogia, avolition, and flattened affect. The dichotomy was recast by Crow (1980) in a suggestion of a dual-process model, separating Type I (positive symptoms having a functional basis) from Type II (negative symptoms having a structural basis).

More recent work has thrown doubt on the validity of these models, suggesting that at least three factors are present (Liddle and Barnes 1990; Arndt *et al.* 1991; Gur *et al.* 1991, Peralta and Cuesta 1992). Arndt *et al.*, for example, performed factor analyses of three published studies of 93, 62, and 52 schizophrenic patients and a large pooled sample to demonstrate that more than two distinct dimensions are required to categorize symptoms in schizophrenia All of the analyses found some kind of 'cognitively impaired/disorganized' factor, in addition to the traditional positive and negative factors. In a study of chronic schizophrenics, Liddle (1987) named this factor 'cognitive disorganization', represented in tangentiality and derailment of thought, pressure of speech, distractibility, and poverty of speech content (poverty of speech loaded on the negative 'psychomotor poverty' factor). Thought disorder, attentional impairment, bizarre behaviour, and inappropriate affect are the symptoms most commonly loading on this factor in other analyses. Liddle's system also has the benefit of external validation in the form of cerebral regional blood flow results. The different syndromes appear to have different neuroanatomical foci. Nevertheless he stresses that the syndromes are overlapping and not mutually exclusive in any way.

Liddle's 'Reality Distortion' syndrome has the features of hallucinations and delusions and bears a close resemblance to the hallucinatory tendencies, odd beliefs, and distorted perceptions of reality of the Unusual Experiences component found in schizotypy research. We have already noted the comparison of Introvertive Anhedonia to negative symptoms, and experimental work in normals and patients has offered some evidence that these are related (Simons 1981; Bernstein and Riedel 1987). (It is important to note that some symptoms such as alogia and the loss of facial and verbal expression cannot be easily tapped as normal traits.)

The third schizophrenic and schizotypal factors have often been given the same name: 'cognitive disorganization', although 'social impairment' and 'disorders of relating' are sometimes used. Both make reference to distractibility, difficulties with speech, and attentional difficulties. The only obvious analogue in schizophrenic symptomatology to the antisocial 'impulsive nonconformity' schizotypal factor is the manifest antisocial behaviour of some psychotics. However, aspects of bipolar affective disorder and borderline personality disorder are related to this factor. These include mood swings, irritability, callousness, self-harm, and disinhibition, sometimes leading to aggression.

In summary, several of the dimensions of schizotypy appear to have parallels in the clinical dimensions of schizophrenia. However, it is not clear whether a distinct pattern of schizotypic characteristics gives rise to parallel patterns of symptoms or whether traits play differentially important roles in the breakdown process and maintenance of schizophrenic disorders.

A new measuring instrument

The discussion so far provides many reasons for continuing to develop measures that combine elements of the several approaches to (and questionnaires in) this now broad domain. The results of the multivariate analyses suggested the components needed for a comprehensive view and we wanted to develop rigorous psychometric scales, firmly based on the now well-replicated structure which our own and others' analyses have provided. The development of these new measures will only be described briefly (the interested reader is directed to the original report (Mason et al. 1995). Essentially, we aimed to develop scales for use in the *normal* population that avoided the pathological feel and content of some other scales and which also provided good coverage of each of the four components described earlier. To do this we chose between 20 and 30 items that correlated highly with each one of the factors. This produced four new scales that we named after the factors. After some initial pilot work we were able to settle on items that gave a good coverage of each factor's content and produced reasonable rates of endorsement, together with high reliability (as assessed by Cronbach's alpha); see Appendix 2 for item lists. Of course, this hardly justifies the new measures— further evidence is needed of their validity and usefulness in experimental and laboratory contexts.

The completed questionnaire was named, with an eye for an acronym, the Oxford—Liverpool Inventory of Feelings and Experiences (O-LIFE). We retained the tried and trusted STA scale (see Appendix 1) for comparison and also inserted the Eysenck E and L scales for filler items. How do the new scales perform in a group drawn from the general population? Over 500 subjects of all ages completed the questionnaire as part of different studies in different research centres. The scales were reasonably internally consistent and the distribution of respondents' scores very suitable for the scales' use in normal samples. Sex differences were in the expected direction for each of the scales: females score more highly on Unusual Experiences and Cognitive Disorganization, but lower on Introvertive Anhedonia. Age was significantly correlated with all of the scales, indicating that schizotypal trait scores tend to decrease with age. Introvertive Anhedonia is the exception and increases with age. The age and sex results mirror findings in schizophrenics: positive symptoms are more prevalent in females who tend to have a more schizoaffective presentation. In contrast, the 'classic' schizophrenic male progresses to a greater preponderance of negative symptoms. There is a steady decline in onset of all psychoses as age increases from the risk periods of late adolescence and early adulthood. The drop in schizotypy scores with age may mirror this or it may be that some individuals are actually removed from the available sample by frank or subclinical psychopathology.

REFERENCES

Arndt, S., Alliger, R. J., and Andreasen, N. C. (1991). The distinction of positive and negative symptoms. The failure of a two-dimensional model. *British Journal of Psychiatry* 158, 317–22.

American Psychiatric Association (1980). *DSM-III: Diagnostic and Statistical Manual of Mental Disorders*, (3rd edn). APA, Washington.

Bentall, R. P., Claridge, G. S., and Slade, P. D. (1989). The multidimensional nature of schizotypal traits: A factor analytic study with normal subjects. *British Journal of Clinical Psychology*, 28, 363–75.

Bernstein, A. S. and Riedel, J. A. (1987). Psychophysiological response patterns in college students with high physical anhedonia: Scores appear to reflect schizotypy rather than depression. *Biological Psychiatry*, 22, 829–47.

Chapman, J. (1966). The early symptoms of schizophrenia. *British Journal of Psychiatry*, 121, 225–63.

Chapman, J. P., Chapman, L. J., and Kwapil, T. R. (1994). Does the Eysenck Psychoticism Scale predict psychosis? A ten year longitudinal study. *Personality and Individual Differences*, 17, 369–75.

Chapman, L. J., Chapman, J. P., and Raulin, M. L. (1976). Scales for physical and social anhedonia. *Journal of Abnormal Psychology*, 87, 374–82.

Chapman, L. J., Chapman, J. P., and Raulin, M. L. (1978). Body image aberration in schizophrenia. *Journal of Abnormal Psychology*, 87, 399–407.

Chapman, L. J., Chapman, J. P., Eckblad, M., and Kwapil, T. R. (1984). Impulsive nonconformity as a trait contributing to the prediction of psychotic-like and schizotypal symptoms. *Journal of Nervous and Mental Disease*, 172, 681–91.

Chapman, L. J., Chapman, J. P., Kwapil, T. R., Ecblad, M., and Zinser, M. C. (1994). Putatively psychosis-prone subjects 10 years later. *Journal of Abnormal Psychology*, 103, 171–83.

Claridge, G. S. (1981). Psychoticism. In *Dimensions of Personality. Papers in Honour of H. J. Eysenck*, (ed. R. Lynn). Pergamon, Oxford.

Claridge, G. S. (1983). The Eysenck Psychoticism Scale. In *Advances in Personality Assessment*. (ed. J. M. Butcher and C. D. Spielberger) Erlbaum, Hillsdale, New Jersey.

Claridge, G. S. (1994). Single indicator of risk for schizophrenia: probable fact or likely myth? *Schizophrenia Bulletin*, 20, 151–68.

Claridge, G. and Broks, P. (1984). Schizotypy and hemisphere function: I. Theoretical considerations and the measurement of schizotypy. *Personality and Individual Differences*, 5, 633–48.

Claridge, G., McCreery, C., Mason, O., Bentell, R., Boyle, G., Slade, P., and Popplewell, D. (1996) The factor structure of 'schizobypal' traits: A large replication study. *British Journal of Clinical Psychology*, 35, 103–15.

Crow, T. (1980). Molecular pathology of schizophrenia: more than one disease process? *British Medical Journal*, 280, 1–9.

Eckblad, M. and Chapman, L. J. (1983). Magical ideation as an indicator of schizotypy. *Journal of Consulting and Clinical Psychology*, 51, 215–25.

Eckblad, M. and Chapman, L. J. (1986). Development and validation of a scale for hypomanic personality. *Journal of Abnormal Psychology*, 95, 214–22.

Eckblad, M. L., Chapman, L. J., Chapman, J. P. and Mishlove, M. (1982). The Revised Social Anhedonia Scale. Unpublished test. University of Wisconsin-Madison.

Edell, W. S. (1995). The psychometric measurement of schizotypy using the Wisconsin scales of psychosis proneness. In *The behavioral high-risk paradigms in psychopathology*, (ed. G. A. Miller), pp. 3–46. Springer, New York.

Eysenck, H. J. and Barrett, P. (1993). The nature of schizotypy. *Psychological Reports*, 73, 59–63.

Eysenck, H. J. and Eysenck, S. B. G. (1975). *Manual of the Eysenck Personality Questionnaire*. Hodder and Stoughton London.

Eysenck, S. B., Eysenck, H. J. and Barrett, P. (1985). A revised version of the Psychoticism scale. *Personality and Individual Differences*, 6, 21–9.

Farmer, A. E., McGuffin, P., and Spitznagel, E. L. (1983). Heterogeneity in schizophrenia. A cluster-analytic approach. *Psychiatry Research*, 8, 1–2.

Foulds, G. A. and Bedford, A. (1975). Hierarchy of classes of personal illness. *Psychological Medicine*, 5, 181–92.

Golden, R. R. and Meehl, P. E. (1979). Detection of the schizoid taxon with MMPI indicators. *Journal of Abnormal Psychology*, 88, 217–33.

Gruzelier, J., Burgess, A., Stygell, J., Irving, G., and Raine, A. (1995). Patterns of cerebral asymmetry and syndromes of schizotypal personality. *Psychiatry Research*, 56, 71–9.

Gur, R., Mozley, D., Resnick, S., Levick, S., Erwin, R., Saykin, A. J., and Gur, R. (1991). Relations among clinical scales in schizophrenia. *American Journal of Psychiatry*, 148, 472–8.

Hair, J. F., Anderson, R. E., Tatham, R. L., and Black, W. C. (1992). *Multivariate data analysis with readings*, (3rd edn). MacMillan; New York.

Hewitt, J. K. and Claridge, G. (1989). The factor structure of schizotypy in a normal population. *Personality and Individual Differences*, **10**, 323–9.

Jackson, J. H. (1931). *Selected writings*. Hodder and Stoughton, London.

Kendler, K. S. and Hewitt, J. (1992). The structure of self-report schizotypy in twins. *Journal of Personality Disorders*, **6**, 1–17.

Launay, G. and Slade, P. (1981). The measurement of hallucinatory predisposition in male and female prisoners. *Personality and Individual Differences*, **2**, 221–34.

Lenzenweger, M. F. and Korfine, L. (1995). Tracking the taxon: on the latent structure and base rate of schizotypy. In *Schizotypal personality*, (ed. A. Raine, T. Lencz., and S. A. Mednick), pp. 135–67. Cambridge University Press, Cambridge.

Lenzenweger, M. F. and Moldin, S. O. (1990). Discerning the latent structure of hypothetical psychosis proneness through admixture analysis. *Psychiatry Research*, **33**, 243–57.

Liddle, P. F. (1987). The symptoms of chronic schizophrenia: A reexamination of the positive-negative dichotomy. *British Journal of Psychiatry*, **151**, 211–34.

Liddle, P. F. and Barnes, T. R. (1990). Syndromes of chronic schizophrenia. *British Journal of Psychiatry*, **157**, 67–79.

Mason, O. (1995). A confirmatory factor analysis of the structure of schizotypy. *European Journal of Personality*, **9**, 271–83.

Mason, O., Claridge, G., and Jackson, M. (1995). New scales for the assessment of schizotypy. *Personality and Individual Differences*, **1**, 7–13.

Miers, T. C. and Raulin, M. L. (1985). The development of a scale to measure Cognitive Slippage. Presented at the Fortieth Eastern Psychological Association Convention. Boston, MA.

Miller, H. R., Streiner, D. L., and Kahgee, S. L. (1982). Use of the Golden-Meehl indicators in the detection of schizoid-taxon membership. *Journal of Abnormal Psychology*, **91**, 55–60.

Mishlove, M. & Chapman, L. J. (1985). Social anhedonia in the prediction of psychosis-proneness. *Journal of Abnormal Psychology*, **94**, 384–96.

Morrison, R. L., Bellack, A. S., Wixted, J. T., and Mueser, K. T. (1990). Positive and negative symptoms in schizophrenia. A cluster-analytic approach. *Journal of Nervous and Mental Disease*, **178**, 377–384.

Muntaner, C., Garcia, S. L., Fernandez, A., and Torrubia, R. (1988). Personality dimensions, schizotypal and borderline personality traits and psychosis proneness. *Personality and Individual Differences*, **9**, 257–68.

Nielsen, T. C. and Petersen, N. E. (1976). Electrodermal Correlates of extraversion, trait anxiety, and schizophrenism. *Scandinavian Journal of Psychology*, **17**, 73–80.

Obiols, J. E., Domenech, E., Garcia, D. M., and de Trincheria, I. (1992). Anhedonia fisica y estructura de la personalidad en varones jovenes. (Physical anhedonia and personality structure in young men). *Pisquis Revista de Psiquiatria, Psicologia y Psicosomatica*, **13**, 25–8.

Peralta. V. and Cuesta, M. J. (1992). Are there more than two syndromes in schizophrenia? A critique of the positive-negative dichotomy. *British Journal of Psychiatry*, **161**, 353–72.

Raine, A. (1991). The SPQ: A scale for the assessment of schizotypal personality based on DSM-III-R criteria. *Schizophrenia Bulletin*, **17**, 555–64.

Raine, A. ad Allbut, J. (1989). Factors of schizoid personality. *British Journal of Clinical Psychology*, **28**, 31–40.

Raine, A. and Benishay, D. (1995). The SPQ-B: A brief screening instrument for schizotypal personality disorder. *Journal of Personality Disorders*, **9**, 346–55.

Raine, A., Reynolds, C., Lencz, T., Scerbo, A., Triphon, N., and Kim, D. (1994).

Cognitive-perceptual, interpersonal and disorganised features of schizotypal personality. *Schizophrenia Bulletin*, 20, 191–201.

Raulin, M. L. (1984). Development of a scale to measure intense ambivalence. *Journal of Consulting and Clinical Psychology*, 52, 63–72.

Raulin, M. L. and Wee, J. L. (1984). The development and initial validation of a scale of social fear. *Journal of Clinical Psychology*, 40, 780–84.

Reichenstein, S. (1976). A pilot study into the incidence of schizophrenic symptoms in a normal population. Undergraduate dissertation, Department of Experimental Psychology, University of Oxford.

Rust, J. (1987). The Rust Inventory of Schizotypal Cognitions (RISC): a psychometric measure of psychoticism in the normal population. *British Journal of Clinical Psychology*, 26, 151–2.

Rust, J. (1988). The Rust Inventory of Schizotypal Cognitions (RISC). *Schizophrenia Bulletin*, 14, 317–22.

Simons, R. F. (1981). Electrodermal and cardiac orienting in psychometrically defined high-risk subjects. *Psychiatry Research*, 4, 347–56.

Spitzer, R. L., Endicott, J., and Gibbon, M. (1979). Crossing the border into borderline personality and borderline schizophrenia: the development of criteria. *Archives of General Psychiatry*, 36, 17–24.

Tyrer, P. and Ferguson, B. (1988). Development of the concept of abnormal personality. In *Personality disorders: diagnosis, management and course*, (ed. P. Tyrer), pp. 1–11. Wright, London.

Van der Does, A. J. W., Linszen, D. H., Dingemans, P. M., Nugter, M. A., and Scholte, W. F. (1993). A dimensional and categorical approach to the symptomatology of recent-onset schizophrenia. *Journal of Nervous and Mental Disease*, 181, 744–9.

Varma, S. L. and Sharma, I. (1993). Psychiatric morbidity in the first degree relatives of schizophrenic patients. *British Journal of Psychiatry*, 162, 672–8.

Venables, P. H. (1990). The measurement of schizotypy in Mauritius. *Personality and Individual Differences*, 11, 965–71.

Venables, P. H. (1993). Electrodermal indices as markers for the development of schizophrenia. In *Progress in electrodermal research* (ed. J. C. Roy, W. Boucsein, D. C. Fowles, and J. H. Gruzelier), pp. 187–206. Plenum Press, New York.

Venables, P. H. and Bailes, K. (1994). The structure of schizotypy, its relation to subdiagnoses of schizophrenia and to sex and age. *British Journal of Clinical Psychology*, 33, 277–94.

Venables, P. H., Wilkins, S., Mitchell, D. A., and Raine, A. (1990). A scale for the measurement of schizotypy. *Personality and Individual Differences*, 11, 481–95.

Vollema, R. and van den Bosch, E. (1995). The multidimensionality of schizotypy. *Schizophrenia Bulletin*, 21, 1–18.

Watt, N. F., Anthony, E. J., Wynne, L. C. and Rolf, J. E. (1984). *Children at risk for schizophrenia. A longitudinal perspective.* Cambridge University Press, Cambridge.

Widiger, T., Francis, A., and Trull, T. (1987). A psychometric analysis of the social-interpersonal and cognitive-perceptual items for schizotypal personality disorder. *Archives of General Psychiatry*, 44, 741–5.

Williams, L. M. (1994). The multidimensional nature of schizotypal traits: A cluster analytic study. *Personality and Individual Differences*, 16, 103–12.

Zuckerman, M. (1993). P-impulsive sensation seeking and its behavioral, psychophysiological biochemical correlates. International Symposium: Psychobiology: Psychophysiological and psychohumoral processes combined (1992, Giessen, Germany). *Neuropsychobiology*, 28, 30–6.

3

Measuring paranoia/suspiciousness

DAVID RAWLINGS AND JUSTIN L. FREEMAN

INTRODUCTION

The senior author's first involvement with the area of 'schizotypy' was at Oxford during the early 1980s. The STQ scale, and its immediate predecessor, the ST1, were employed in a doctoral research programme concerned with a general examination of the concept of Psychoticism. The scale proved particularly useful in the examination of individual differences, especially in the study of differential hemisphere functioning, both at Oxford (Rawlings and Claridge 1984) and later at Melbourne (Rawlings and Borge 1987).

More recently, following the various studies showing the multidimensional nature of schizotypy, our interest has centred on an aspect of the construct which we perceived to be both important and relatively neglected. As we shall argue later, no substantial scale has been developed within the schizotypy framework to measure paranoid and suspicious behaviour. For example, the recently developed four-factor O-LIFE schizotypy scales do not include a 'paranoia' factor. In fact, while the unidimensional STA scale had at least five questions which were unambiguous measures of paranoia/suspiciousness, not one of these original five 'paranoia' items was retained when the longer questionnaire was produced.

The present chapter describes a paranoia/suspiciousness scale which we believe forms a useful complement to the O-LIFE. Before describing the stages in the development of this scale, we shall first provide evidence for the importance of the concept of paranoia in psychiatric classification, consider several possible markers of paranoid mental disorder, and discuss some earlier questionnaire measures of paranoia, suspiciousness and related concepts. Stages in the development of the Paranoia/Suspiciousness Questionnaire (PSQ) will be briefly described, and the scale and its subscales will be related to the O-LIFE schizotypy measure as well as to several other measures of personality. Finally, some suggestions will be made for further research into paranoia within the schizotypy framework.

THE CONCEPT OF PARANOIA IN PSYCHIATRY

Used by Hippocrates, and in pre-Hippocratic times, to refer to a general form of insanity, it was Emil Kraepelin who gave 'paranoia' its modern meaning as a mental state characterized by extreme suspiciousness. As early as 1896, Kraepelin viewed paranoia as a third major category of functional psychosis which was qualitatively different and more limited than either *dementia praecox* or manic-depressive insanity (Kendler 1988). Whereas the latter disorders produced striking disturbances in a vast range of psychological functions, paranoia resulted from impairment in a single psychological capacity which Kraepelin called 'judgment'. Paranoia was later included in Kraepelin's (1919) classification of *dementia praecox*, being one of the three forms (with catatonia and hebephrenia) of that disorder. It was Bleuler who subsequently noted that these three syndromes share several features in common and could be considered variants of a single clinical entity, which he termed 'schizophrenia' (Bleuler 1950).

The continued importance of paranoia within psychiatric classification is illustrated by the fact that the DSM-IV (APA 1994) includes at least five mental disorders that contain 'paranoia' constructs:

1. Paranoid Personality Disorder is included as a 'cluster A' personality disorder, defined as '. . . a pattern of pervasive distrust and suspiciousness of others such that their motives are interpreted as malevolent' (p. 264).

2. Also in cluster A is Schizotypal Personality Disorder, which is diagnosed on finding five (or more) of its nine symptoms, one of which is labelled 'suspiciousness or paranoid ideation'.

3. Borderline Personality Disorder is included as a 'cluster B' personality disorder, and is diagnosed on finding at least five of its nine symptoms, one of which is transient, stress-related, paranoid ideation.

4. The Paranoid Type of Schizophrenia is maintained as one of the main schizophrenia subtypes.

5. The Persecutory Type of Delusional Disorder is included as a form of psychosis separate, though not always clearly distinguishable, from the Paranoid Type of Schizophrenia.

As with the other disorders in DSM-IV, an attempt is made to distinguish essential from various associated features. Of particular interest here is the distinction made between the essential feature of the 'Paranoid Type of Schizophrenia', as the presence of 'prominent delusions or auditory hallucinations'. These (frequently bizarre) delusions are typically persecutory, grandiose, or both, and the hallucinations are typically related to the content of the delusional theme. Associated features include 'anxiety, anger, aloofness, and argumentativeness'.

The continued relevance of the concept of paranoia to the classification of schizophrenia has been specifically noted by several recent writers. McGlashan and Fenton (1991) reviewed published studies and unpublished presentations, as well as relevant data from their own ongoing study on schizophrenic subtypes; they concluded that there was particular support for the paranoid subtype. Nicholson and Neufeld (1993) reviewed the various methods of subtyping schizophrenia and concluded that the paranoid—non-paranoid distinction is the method most consistently supported both clinically and in experimental research. For example, they discuss Morrison's (1974) findings based on an examination of records of admissions to a state psychiatric hospital over 46 years Morrison found that, although the frequency of schizophrenia remained constant, there was considerable variability from year to year in the frequency of the diagnosis of most subtypes, with the exception of the paranoid subtype. The study supported the division of schizophrenia into paranoid and non-paranoid subtypes, but suggested that further subdivision of the non-paranoid type is likely to be susceptible to environmental influences or diagnostic fads.

There is some support for the view, which underlies much of the schizotypy research, that the concept of paranoia may be understood within the framework of a dimensional rather than a categorical approach. Thus, several writers have noted a continuum of severity linking the various types of paranoid disorder. Altrocchi (1980) writes:

Differentiating the various kinds of paranoid behaviours from one another is often difficult. There is a continuum of severity from transitory paranoid behaviour (paranoid personality, non-delusional) through paranoid behaviour patterns and paranoid states (delusional) to paranoid schizophrenic behaviour. (p. 355)

In fact, the view of a continuum linking the paranoid mental disorders is not a recent conceptualization. Bernstein *et al.* (1993) point out that paranoid personality disorder has historically been thought of by several authors as a possible precursor to more severe conditions, such as paranoid psychoses (Kraepelin 1921) and paranoid delusional disorder (Herbert and Jacobson 1967).

A more genuinely dimensional view is proposed by Nicholson and Neufeld (1993), who posit a continuum of disorder with paranoid and non-paranoid schizophrenia located towards the milder and more severe poles, respectively. Orthogonal to this continuum is a separate 'severity of symptom' dimension. The writers discuss the advantages and disadvantages of the dimensional approach compared with a categorical approach and argue for a genetic vulnerability—environmental stress model of schizophrenia, which has considerable similarity to the 'fully-dimensional' view of schizotypy suggested by Claridge (1994; also Chapter 1)

In this section, it has been argued that 'paranoia' is an important nosological concept in psychiatry. Its importance in the classification of schizophrenia has been specifically emphasized. Further, it is appropriate to understand the concept of paranoia within the framework of dimensional assumptions of the type which underlie the approach to schizotypy taken by many researchers in this area, including the authors of the O-LIFE scales.

POSSIBLE MARKERS OF PARANOID DISORDERS

A number of empirical studies have been conducted to investigate the aetiology of paranoia. This section will briefly look at some epidemiological data, and then at research attempting to establish specific genotypic and endophenotypic markers.

Paranoia does not appear to vary much with culture. However, there is evidence that it is more common in groups undergoing severe, rapid cultural changes involving relocation of many people (Eitinger 1959; Mezey 1960; Swanson *et al.* 1970). Altrocchi (1980) argues that the association between paranoia and relocation may result from such factors as social estrangement, language difficulties, and difficulties in competing for jobs, security, and status in a new culture. It was suggested that these factors lead to lowered self-esteem and ultimately to paranoid behaviour. Paranoid forms of behaviour may also be more common in people with sensory handicaps and in people subjected to sensory overload or sensory deprivation due to the effects of drugs or extreme environments (Kay and Roth 1961; Sarvis 1962; Busse and Pfeiffer 1977). Paranoia might be associated with sensory handicap because people who cannot fully see what others are doing or hear what they are saying are forced to makes inferences on the basis of their own thoughts and fears, and may fail to check these with other people (Altrocchi 1980). In summary, the limited epidemiological research in this area suggests no clear risk factor for paranoid mental disorder (Bernstein *et al.* 1993).

The possibility of a genetic basis for paranoid mental disorder has been suggested by Onstad *et al.* (1991), who showed that the occurrence of paranoia is higher amongst those having a biological relative with psychiatric paranoia. Indeed, a number of authors have suggested possible genotypic markers for paranoid mental disturbances. Cowen *et al.* (1993) suggest that, for some individuals, paranoid psychosis may be in part due to genetic and epigenetic defects in the expression and interaction of dopamine and oestrogen, which are essential for the normal functioning of tanycyte brain cells. They also suggest that other major tanycyte regulators may be central to other psychoses. Holland and Gosden (1990) studied three generations of a family in which some of the members had paranoid psychotic disorder. They propose that one factor facilitating a susceptibility to develop paranoid psychosis may be a balanced 6;11 chromosomal translocation abnormality, and that one of the genes at the breakpoints may be aetiologically important in this form of psychosis. Holland and Gosden hasten to add that the genetic factor appears to be neither a necessary nor a sufficient condition for the development of paranoid psychosis—the aetiology of paranoid mental disorder appears to be heterogeneous. These writers point to several psychiatrically normal family members who inherited the genetic abnormality but appear to be protected either for environmental reasons or because of variable penetrance. It might be argued that the genetic research on paranoia is not inconsistent with the model of continuous vulnerability which has been proposed for the various forms of schizotypy (cf. Roberts and Claridge 1991).

Several biological endophenotypic markers of paranoid disorders have been proposed. In one study, Gupta (1993) investigated differential cerebral hemisphere processing of information in paranoid and non-paranoid schizophrenics and controls. Schizophrenics showed superior performance for material presented to the left than to the right hemisphere; in controls the pattern was reversed. However, Gupta found no evidence to support the hypothesized difference in performance between paranoid and non-paranoid subjects.

Several other biologically oriented studies have been more successful. In support of the view that paranoia may be associated with specific biochemical abnormalities, Galinowski *et al.* (1992) found a significant increase of various autoantibody levels in their group of paranoid schizophrenics, compared with a healthy control group. Monteleone *et al.* (1992) established 24-hour profiles of plasma melatonin and cortisol in a group of paranoid schizophrenics. Compared with normals, the paranoid subjects showed an absence of circadian rhythms for plasma melatonin, whereas their 24-hour profile of plasma cortisol was preserved at a higher level and their melatonin/cortisol ratio was significantly lower than for normals. In a study by Macciardi *et al.* (1990), the blood concentration of the amino acid glycine was found to be abnormally elevated in subjects with paranoid schizophrenia.

Abnormalities in particular brain areas are sometimes proposed, with at least two studies implicating the basal ganglia (Miller 1986; Lauterbach 1991). On the other hand, Krieckhaus *et al.* (1992) suggest that the hyperactivity of particular neuron synapses in the hippocampus may serve as a possible endophenotypic marker of paranoid schizophrenia. They posit that explicit consolidation of memory, or fixation of declarative belief, appears to be physically represented in changes of the synaptic conductance of neurons in the parietal-temporal-occipital association cortex (PTO). They then argue that the concentrations of dopamine relate to the ability of hippocampal pyramidal cells from the so-called CA1 area of Ammon's horn (*cornu Ammonis*) to update the neural net weights in the PTO. The delusions of paranoid schizophrenics are held to be caused by a hyperactivity of the same dopamine-sensitive CA1 neurons that are responsible for the fixation of normal beliefs.

While the wide-ranging results outlined above are of considerable interest in suggesting that certain biological mechanisms may underlie paranoid conditions, it is important to note that most await replication, many are based on small samples, and few are set within a substantial theoretical framework. These deficiencies are generally well recognised by the researchers, who sometimes note that the biological correlates with paranoid behaviour which do occur are neither necessary nor sufficient for the development of the behaviour (Miller 1986; Macciardi *et al.* 1990). A typical viewpoint is that of Krieckhaus *et al.* (1992), who propose that physiological structure, as represented in their case by the level of CA1 activity, predisposes an individual to respond in a particular way to the surrounding environment, while the triggering event (for example stress), as well as the form of the delusions, are most likely determined by specific environmental factors.

Non-biological accounts of paranoid ideation continue to be given within the framework of traditional approaches such as psychoanalysis and social-learning theory. Thus, many current psychoanalysts have modified Freud's view of paranoia as homosexual projection; paranoids use projection as a defence not just for unacceptable homosexual impulses, but for unacceptable feelings in general (Heilbrun *et al.* 1985). The social-cognitive view of Meyer and Salmon (1988) contends that paranoid individuals have not properly learned to share responsibility or to be open to constructive feedback from others. When normal stressors occur, these individuals isolate themselves, which negates the ability to share their vulnerability and dissipate their anxiety, and instead they alter their perception of society.

Several authors have departed from traditional approaches in attempting to establish non-biological endophenotypic markers of paranoid mental disturbance. Frequently, these approaches attempt to elucidate paranoid delusional phenomena by using models of normal psychological functioning. Thus, Hemsley and Garety (1986) suggested that research on normal-belief formation, from the perspective of Bayesian theory, could help our understanding of the cognitive processes underlying deviant (delusional) beliefs.

The work of Oxman *et al.* (1988) also exemplifies the 'psychological' approach. These researchers conducted a computerized content analysis of the free speech of paranoia patients in order to identify and compare dimensions of self-concept related to lexical choices. In comparison to other groups, the categories used by the paranoia patients portrayed an artificially positive, grandiose self-image, suggesting that this group utilized a particular style when dealing with psychological distress. Specifically, the lexical profile suggests an avoidance of personal exposure and any reflection of distress or negative self-image; reality is distorted in an attempt to bolster impaired self-esteem.

A promising line of recent research is based on the view of Zigler and Glick (1988) that paranoia might be a defence against low self-esteem and that certain forms of paranoid schizophrenia result from an attempt to defend against depression. This area of research is particularly associated with the work of Bentall and his colleagues. It is put forward as a valid psychological alternative to biomedical approaches, which are seen to be deficient on empirical, pragmatic, and ethical grounds (Bentall *et al.* 1988). The framework of attribution theory is employed and paranoid defensiveness is seen as an exaggeration of the ordinary tendency to abnegate responsibility for negative events (Bentall *et al.* 1994). It is proposed that the attributional style varies across distinct levels of information processing within the paranoid individual. At the *underlying* level, the paranoid individual has a self-blaming attributional bias which leads to emotional depression of mood; the self is blamed for negative events and attributes positive events to external causes. At the *conscious* level, the paranoid individual simultaneously has a self-serving attributional style which functions to decrease depressed mood. That is, paranoid individuals engage in self-deceit to prevent themselves from becoming aware of their own negatively self-referent attitudes. This view has received some support from studies using both clinical patients (Kaney and Bentall 1989; Candido and Romney 1990; Bentall *et al.* 1991; Kinderman *et al.* 1992) and normal subjects differing on a measure of 'schizotypy' (Jackson, unpublished thesis, 1994). Trower and Chadwick (1995) have recently argued that this approach can account for what they call the 'poor-me' type of paranoia, but not the 'bad-me' type; they propose an interpersonal theory of the self in an attempt to explain both of these paranoid types.

In summary, the wide range of findings briefly discussed above point to a number of areas for further research as investigators attempt to establish conceptual frameworks which will be useful for theory and practice.

QUESTIONNAIRE MEASURES OF PARANOIA

A variety of questionnaire measures of paranoia and related concepts have already been developed, reflecting a number of theoretical perspectives. The most well-known of these is the Pa scale of the MMPI. Various writers have derived subscales from this scale. For example, Wiener and Harmon (1946) divided the items of the scale into 'obvious' and 'subtle' components. Harris and Lingoes (1955) identified three content areas in their subscales: persecutory ideas, poignancy, and naivety. Most of the MMPI scales were derived by contrasting a group of nonclinical subjects with a relevant clinical group. Specifically, the Pa scale was derived

by contrasting normal persons with a group of clinic patients who were characterized by suspiciousness, oversensitivity and delusions of persecution, with or without expansive egotism. The diagnoses were usually paranoia, paranoid state or paranoid schizophrenia (Hathaway and McKinley 1951, p. 50).

In the area of paranoia, as in other areas, the MMPI has remained a rich source of items in the development of other scales. A recent example is the 20-item scale of Fenigstein and Vanable (1992) which was designed for use with normal individuals, but was made up entirely of MMPI items.

An early 'Psychoticism' scale of H. J. Eysenck, contained in his unpublished Psychoticism-Extraversion-Neuroticism (PEN) inventory; this included many items adapted from the MMPI. In later refinements of the scale many of the original items were excluded, in a attempt to make the scale conform to psychometric criteria, including normality and orthogonality (with respect to the Neuroticism dimension). Claridge (1981) argued that the early psychoticism scale was higher in face validity than the more recent, published versions, including as it did many 'weird', distinctly psychotic items. In this context, an early study by McPherson *et al.* (1974) is of interest. These writers administered what is presumed to be the early P-scale to a number of clinical groups: high scores were obtained by subjects with the diagnoses of paranoia and mania, whereas relatively low scores were obtained by subjects with schizophrenia and depression. Certainly, the early P-scale contains several items which seem at face value to measure aspects of suspiciousness and paranoia.

As well as MMPI-derived scales, several other measures of paranoia and related concepts have been devised. Kreiner *et al.* (1990) developed a paranoia scale for use with clinical subjects, with items derived from the Millon Clinical Multiaxial Inventory (Millon 1983). Factor L of the 16PF (Cattell *et al.* 1970) has been labelled alexia—protension or trust—suspiciousness, and was identified as a factor of normal personality in the various studies of Cattell and his colleagues. In several factor analytic studies aimed at describing the factor structure of aggressiveness, Buss and Perry (1992) identified four different factors, labelled physical aggression, verbal aggression, anger, and hostility. The short (eight-item) hostility scale includes several items that are unambiguous measures of paranoid and suspicious behaviour. Indeed, the early Buss and Durkee (1957) scale—on which the present revision is based—included among its seven scales two correlated scales labelled Suspiciousness and Resentment.

The area of paranoia has not been completely neglected in recent schizotypy research. Raine (1991) produced a battery of nine short (seven- to nine-item) schizotypy scales; items relevant to the areas of paranoia and suspiciousness appear in his Suspiciousness, Ideas of Reference, and Excessive Social Anxiety scales. In their factor analysis of the original STA schizotypal personality scale, Hewitt and Claridge (1989) identified five factors labelled magical thinking, unusual perceptual experience, and paranoid ideation. This last (eight-item) scale actually included only four items which were unambiguous measures of paranoia and, as noted earlier, none of these was included in the most recent revision of the scale; in fact, only two items from this subscale were included in the O-LIFE, both in the 'Cognitive Disorganization' subscale. Furthermore, although the Raine and the Hewitt and Claridge scales provide useful starting points to the development of more substantial scales, it might be argued that they do not fully reflect the importance of the paranoia construct within the psychiatric literature.

In summary, while numerous scales have already been produced to measure paranoia and related concepts, none was entirely adequate for measuring the broad concept of paranoia/suspiciousness in normal individuals.

DEVELOPING THE PSQ

Rawlings and Freeman (1996) describe the stages in the development of the PSQ. We shall outline these briefly.

1. Five criterion scales were selected as a source of 'paranoia' items, each of which is referred to in the previous section. These were the Psychoticism scale from the unpublished PEN Inventory of H. J. Eysenck; the STA Paranoia Ideation subscale; the 16PF Suspiciousness scales (forms A to D); the Hostility scale from the Buss and Perry Aggression Questionnaire; and the Paranoia scale from the MMPI. In fact, a shortened version of the MMPI scale was used—items were excluded if they appeared on other scales or had been shown in the MMPI Manual to have very low endorsement rates.

2. Several other scales were included as a source of 'filler' items, including the Impulsiveness and Empathy scales of the I-7 questionnaire (S. B. G. Eysenck *et al.* 1985*a*); the Narcissistic Personality Inventory (Raskin and Hall 1979); the Machiavellianism scale (Allsopp *et al.* 1991); and the Physical Aggression, Verbal Aggression, and Anger subscales of the Buss and Perry (1992) Aggression Questionnaire. There was a total of 213 items in the final questionnaire.

3. Where necessary, items were rewritten to fit a two-choice question (YES/NO) format.

4. A rotated, generalized, least-squares factor analysis of the scale scores of

264 first-year psychology students (202 females and 62 males) produced a general factor of paranoia/suspiciousness which had a high loading on all five criterion measures mentioned above and also the Anger scale from the Buss Aggression Inventory. This last scale was subsequently added as a criterion measure.

5. All items from the full 213-item scale were correlated with the factor score of the above general factor *and* with the total score on the six criterion scales. The 47-item PSQ was thus produced. On the basis of this study, and a later factor analysis in a similar group, the reliability of the scale was found to be 0.89. In a subsequent small study (N = 74), the test-retest reliability after about 3 months was 0.82.

6. Using a sample of 561 first-year psychology students (136 males and 425 females), which included the original 264 subjects, the 47-item scale was factor-analyzed using the generalized least-squares method followed by orthogonal (oblimin) rotation. This produced a scale with five subscales (as well as six items which did not belong in any subscale). The five subscales were named Interpersonal Suspiciousness/Hostility (IS); Negative Mood/Withdrawal (NM); Anger/Impulsiveness (AI); Mistrust/Wariness (MW); Perceived Hardship/Resentment (PH). The subscales were moderately intercorrelated (between 0.33 and 0.50), had reasonable internal consistency (alphas between 0.65 and 0.77), and in the subsequent small study were found to have reasonable test-retest reliabilities (between 0.59 and 0.82).

Appendix III shows the PSQ divided into its subscales. Original item numbers are given; note, however, that the items should normally be included among other items—such as those of the O-LIFE.

The PSQ and its subscales were related in a number of obvious ways to some of the earlier questionnaires on which our questionnaire was based. This is particularly true of the Buss and Perry (1992) Aggression Questionnaire. Six of the nine items with loadings above 0.45 on our 'general' factor were from the Buss and Perry Hostility scale. Five of the nine items in our AI subscale, including the four highest loading items, were from the Buss and Perry Anger scale.

A few less obvious comparisons with earlier scales will be mentioned briefly.

1. All six items from the original STA that were included in the PSQ were in the IS or NM subscales.

2. Of the five items from H. J. Eysenck's unpublished PEN P-scale that were included in the PSQ, three were in the PH subscale and the other two were among the six miscellaneous items not in any subscale.

3. The Manual of the MMPI-2 (Hathaway and McKinley 1989) cites two attempts to group the items of the Pa scale. Our factor structure bore no relation at all to Wiener and Harmon's division of the scale into subtle and obvious components. However, two of the groupings identified (on an intuitive basis) by Harris and Lingoes show some overlap with our subscales. Their Persecutory Ideas component shows some relation to our PH, and, to a lesser extent IS, and their

Poignancy component bears some relation to our NM. However, their Novety component is not clearly related to any of our subscales.

4. Several of the original 'filler' scales were represented in the PSQ, including the I–7 (Impulsivity (3 items) and Empathy (1 item)), the Narcissistic Personality Inventory (3 items), and the Machiavellianism scale (3 items). While the loadings obtained by these items were generally lower than those attained by items from the original criterion scales, two of the items from the Narcissistic Personality Inventory did attain loadings on the general factor of 0.44 and 0.40, respectively.

Examination of the items of the NNM/OM and AI subscales suggested that these may be usefully considered to measure what DSM-IV describes as the associated features of Paranoid Schizophrenia. Specifically, our NM subscale may measure the associated features of 'anxiety' and 'aloofness', and the AI scale the associated features of 'anger' and 'argumentativeness'. The other three scales would seem to index different aspects of the more central features of the paranoid personality structure, including both the ideational and affective aspects of such traits as suspiciousness, hostility, mistrust, and resentment.

FACTOR ANALYSIS OF THE O-LIFE ITEMS

As outlined above, the PSQ was developed largely in response to the perceived neglect of the paranoia/suspiciousness concept in current schizotypy research. The recently developed O-LIFE scales were used as a reference point when developing the scales; for example, questions were produced in the same two-choice question format as contained in that scale. All subjects who were involved in the development of the PSQ also completed the O-LIFE.

While a major purpose of the present chapter was to report the results of a factor analysis of the combined O-LIFE and PSQ items, a factor analysis of the O-LIFE items was first carried out. This was done in order to provide further confirmation of the O-LIFE factor structure reported by Mason *et al.* (1995) in their original publication of the O-LIFE (see also Chapter 2). It also served to show that the sample and procedures employed in our study were appropriate for the further examination of the O-LIFE with the PSQ items.

A generalized least-squares factor analysis was carried out on the items of the four schizotypy scales of the O-LIFE. This method of factor analysis was employed here and in later analyses because it has been shown to produce more robust solutions than the more commonly used principal components method (McDonald 1985). Four factors were selected for rotation, based substantially on the use of two criteria—the scree test and the parallel analysis method (Horn 1965). When rotated using oblimin, the four-factor solution explained a cumulative variance of 19.9 per cent. The factor structure provided strong confirmation of a the original O-LIFE structure. The factors clearly represented (in order) Unusual Experiences, Introvertive Anhedonia, Cognitive Disorganization, and Impulsive Nonconformity. All Unusual Experience items loaded on factor 1, with the exception of item 96 on the original scale which loaded (0.25) on factor 4 with a (0.17) cross-loading on factor 1. All of the items in the Introvertive Anhedonia scale loaded on factor 2. The items in the Cognitive Disorganization scale loaded on factor 3, with the exception of item 2 whose loading was marginally higher on factor 2 (−0.249) than on factor 3 (−0.248). The items in the Impulsive Nonconformity scale loaded on factor 4, with the exceptions of items 81 and 106, which were the two lowest-loading items on factor 3 and had cross-loadings on factor 4 of 0.10 and 0.21, respectively. In all, there were 15 items of the 104 O-LIFE items which failed to load positively (>0.25) and unambiguously on the relevant factor, compared with ten items in the Mason *et al.* study.

The internal consistency of the four original scales was calculated. The alpha coefficients obtained in our sample of 561 Australian subjects were 0.88 for Unusual Experiences, 0.84 for Cognitive Disorganization, 0.80 for Introvertive Anhedonia, and 0.70 for Impulsive Nonconformity. With the exception of Impulsive Nonconformity, our coefficients were close to those obtained by Mason *et al.* in their original publication of the O-LIFE. Using a sample of 508 English subjects, these writers obtained alpha coefficients of, in the same order as above, 0.89, 0.87, 0.82, and 0.77. The small sample ($N = 74$) mentioned in the previous section was required to complete the tests twice, about three months apart. Test-retest reliabilities in the small sample were, in the same order as above, 0.77, 0.81, 0.85, and 0.72. Again using the large sample, we obtained, as did Mason *et al.*, almost identical means for males and females on the Unusual Experiences scale. Females were significantly higher than males on Cognitive Disorganization and significantly lower on Introvertive Anhedonia. Males scored higher than females on Impulsive Nonconformity but, unlike Mason and his colleagues, we did not find this difference significant.

Given the different nationality and narrower composition of our sample, and the different factor-analytic methods employed, our results may be interpreted as providing strong confirmation of the English results as well as suggesting that our sample and procedures were suitable ones for comparing the O-LIFE with the PSQ.

FACTOR ANALYSIS OF PSQ AND O-LIFE ITEMS

The items of the PSQ and the four schizotypy scales of the O-LIFE were included together in a generalized least-squares factor analysis. Using the same criteria as in the previous analysis, a five-factor solution was suggested, explaining 21.1 per cent of the variance. The first four factors clearly represented, respectively, Cognitive Disorganization, Introvertive Anhedonia, Unusual Experiences, and Impulsive Nonconformity. The structure of these factors was very similar to the analysis of the O-LIFE items reported above, though appearing in a different order. Our fifth factor consisted largely of items from the PSQ; in fact, there were four items in this factor from the O-LIFE, but only one had a loading > 0.25. The similarity with the earlier analysis is illustrated by the fact that, even with the fifth factor included, only 19 of the original 104 items of the O-LIFE did not load unambiguously on its appropriate factor.

A noteworthy feature of the analysis of the combined scales was the tendency for three of the five PSQ subscales to be respectively associated with one O-LIFE subscale. This is summarized in the points below, where the various item numbers refer to the version of the PSQ in Appendix III.

1. Nine of the twelve items in the IS subscale loaded on factor 1 (cognitive disorganization), eight of these loadings being above 0.25 (items 47, 33, 11, 14, 43, 27, 2, and 3). Only two other items from the PSQ loaded > 0.25 on this factor—item 4 (from the PH subscale) whose loading of 0.38 was the same (to two decimal places) as it obtained on factor 5; and item 18 (from the NM subscale) which had a loading of 0.28 on the factor.

2. Four of the seven items in the NM subscale loaded on factor 2 (introvertive anhedonia)—these were the four items which originally attained the highest loadings on the NM subscale. No other PSQ item attained a loading > 0.25 on factor 2.

3. No PSQ item loaded > 0.25 on factor 3 (Unusual Experiences).

4. Eight of the nine items in the AI subscale loaded on factor 4 (Impulsive Nonconformity), seven of these attaining loadings above 0.25 (items 23, 40, 35, 37, 29, 36, and 9), while item 17 had a loading of 0.24. In fact, the first four of these items attained higher loadings than any of the original Impulsive Nonconformity Items on factor 4. Item 41 (a PSQ item without a subscale) attained a loading of 0.30 on this factor.

Our factor 5 was made up substantially of items from two subscales of the PSQ. All MW items and all but one PH item obtained loadings > 0.25 on this factor. As noted above, the only item from these two subscales whose primary loading was not with factor 5 was PH item number 4, which obtained an almost identical loading on factor 1 as on factor 5. Loadings > 0.25 were also obtained by a PSQ item without a subscale (item 21), one AI item (item 31), two IS items (items 15 and 42), and one item from the original O-LIFE. Three items from the O-LIFE also loaded on this factor, but with very low loadings.

RELATING THE PSQ TO THE O-LIFE

The above analysis suggests that there are aspects of paranoia which are associated with the various forms of schizotypy. In that analysis, PSQ items load on all O-LIFE scales except Unusual Experiences, sometimes quite strongly. This point is further strengthened by the consistently positive correlations between PSQ subscales and O-LIFE scales shown in Table 3.1.

The factor analysis also reveals that there are aspects of paranoia that are not

Table 3.1   Pearson correlations of the full PSQ and its subscales with the four O-LIFE scales

		PSQ subscales				
	Full PSQ	IS	NM	AI	MW	PH
O-LIFE scales						
Unusual Experiences	0.47	0.38	0.32	0.37	0.26	0.25
Cognitive Disorganization	0.66	0.65	0.48	0.45	0.31	0.42
Introvertive Anhedonia	0.32	0.17	0.49	0.13	0.23	0.15
Impulsive Nonconformity	0.52	0.39	0.30	0.58	0.24	0.26

Note: All correlations were significant $P< 0.01$, using a two-tailed test

measured strongly by the current O-LIFE scales. These aspects are most clearly identified with our MW and PH scales.

The PSQ does seem to provide a useful complement to the O-LIFE. Three suggestions for how the PSQ and the O-LIFE may be meaningfully used together will be briefly advanced and their advantages and disadvantages considered.

1. It could be argued that, as three of the five PSQ subscales are already measured in some way by three O-LIFE scales, it is only necessary to measure the two other aspects of paranoia—as represented by the MW and PH subscales. In fact, if these two subscales are put together, a 13-item 'scale' with a respectable alpha value of 0.76 is produced.

This alternative, while attractive in terms of economy of administration, ignores the fact that there are paranoia 'components' of several other aspects of schizotypy, which it would seem useful to measure.

2. A second possible approach involves administering the whole PSQ scale and, as well as having a combined MW/PH scale (as discussed in point 1), combining the subscales with the O-LIFE scales in the manner suggested by the factor analysis. A combined IS/Cognitive Disorganization scale would, in our sample, obtain an alpha value of 0.88. A composite of NM and Introvertive Anhedonia would have an alpha of 0.84. A combined AI/Impulsive Nonconformity scale would have an alpha of 0.80. This approach seemed particularly attractive with respect to the production of an AI/Impulsive Nonconformity composite because of the fact that these two scales are correlated at 0.58, because the first four items on our 'factor 4' were AI items, and because of the boost to the alpha coefficient (from 0.70 to 0.80) provided by this process. The argument for the other 'composites' are considerably weaker, however, particularly for NM/Introvertive Anhedonia. The main point against this approach is that it places considerable weight on our single factor analytic study. A major revision of the O-LIFE would seem to require further replication of our model.

3. The third alternative, and the one which is recommended by the authors, is

that the PSQ and O-LIFE should be used together, but maintained for the time being as separate questionnaires. Hints about how they might be meaningfully combined, if at all, will no doubt appear as they are employed together with different samples and in different experimental contexts.

PARANOIA AND OTHER PERSONALITY FEATURES

The dimensional approach to schizotypy lends itself naturally to description within the framework of models of 'normal' personality.

Several of the studies that have investigated the relationship of normal personality to schizotypy employed the popular framework of Eysenck and Eysenck (1976) which measures individual differences in personality on the three independent dimensions of extraversion (E), neuroticism (N), and psychoticism (P), as well as a lie scale (L). More recently, a five factor ('Big-5') model of personality has emerged as a useful paradigm for personality research, associated particularly with writers such as Goldberg (1993) and Costa and McCrae (1992a). The five-factor theorists concur with the Eysencks on the first two dimensions (E and N), but differ about the nature of the other dimensions. Although there is some debate among five-factor theorists about the most suitable label for the 'fifth' factor, the other three factors in the five-factor model are typically referred to as agreeableness (A), conscientiousness (C), and either openness (O) or intellect (I). Five-factor theorists, such as Goldberg, who use lexical (mostly adjective) studies are inclined to call the fifth factor 'intellect', whereas questionnaire theorists like Costa and McCrae obtain a broader factor more readily interpreted as 'openness'.

We shall report the correlations of the PSQ and its subscales with the four factors from the Eysenck Personality Questionnaire-Revised (EPQ-R) (S. B. G. Eysenck *et al.* 1985b) and a lexical measure of the five factors, the Melbourne Adjective Checklist (MADJ; Rawlings 1994). The MADJ is an unpublished checklist providing reliable measures of the five factors of the five-factor model of personality which closely parallel the American scales published by Goldberg (1990). It was developed on a sample of approximately 650 Australian students similar to the sample used in the development of the PSQ.

Factor analysis was employed in analysing the relationship between the PSQ and the NEO-PI-R (Costa and McCrae 1992b). The five factors or 'domains' of the NEO-PI-R are each divided into six 'facets'. Factor analysis seemed to be the most appropriate way of summarizing the large number of intercorrelations between these facets and the various PSQ subscales. The scales of the O-LIFE were also included in the factor analysis in an attempt to provide an overall 'picture' of how the PSQ and O-LIFE scales relate to the five factors of the Big-5 model.

Certain specific relationships between the PSQ and personality were expected. For example, we anticipated that there would be some correlation between scores on the PSQ and the EPQ-R P-scale. It may be recalled that, in developing our original scale, an early unpublished P-scale was used as a source of items because of the obvious 'paranoid' content of the items. While few of these items remain in the P-scale of the EPQ-R, we might anticipate a certain amount of overlap in variance between the two versions of the scale. In fact, when the first published version of the P-scale appeared in 1975, writers such as Block (1977) argued that it was more likely to measure 'aggressive, impulsive, conscienceless' behaviour rather than predisposition to psychosis (Zuckerman 1989). Accordingly, the item content of our Anger/Impulsiveness subscale suggests that it might obtain the highest loadings with P.

Trull (1992) computed correlations between raw scores on the NEO-PI and the presence of the symptoms of DSM-III-R personality disorders. The symptoms of personality disorder were measured using a semi-structured interview and two self-report inventories. Trull found that paranoid personality disorder was particularly associated with high scores on the N-scale (correlations from 0.24 to 0.46) and low scores on A (−0.35 to −0.48). Correlations with the other three NEO domains were weak. On the basis of studies such as Trull's, Widiger (1993) and Widiger and Costa (1994) have argued that the dimensions and facets of the NEO questionnaire may be used to characterize the various DSM-III-R personality disorders. Specifically, Widiger has suggested that paranoid personality disorder is likely to be related to high loadings on the C-facet of 'Competence' and the N-facets of 'Anxiety' and 'Hostility'; and low loadings on the E-facets of 'Warmth', 'Gregariousness', and 'Positive Emotions', the O-facets of 'Aesthetics', Feelings', and 'Actions', and the A-facets of 'Trust', 'Straightforwardness', 'Compliance', 'Modesty', and 'Tender-Mindedness'.

Table 3.2 shows the correlations of the PSQ and its subscales with the four scales of the EPQ-R and the five scales of the MADJ, using a sample of 297 student subjects (223 females and 74 males).

Table 3.2 Pearson correlations of the full PSQ and its subscales with the four EPQ-R scales and the five MADJ scales

		PSQ subscales				
	Full PSQ	IS	NM	AI	MW	PH
EPQ-R scales						
Psychoticism	0.31**	0.15**	0.29**	0.34**	0.17**	0.12*
Extraversion	0.03	0.01	−0.18**	0.18**	−0.16**	0.01
Neuroticism	0.66**	0.64**	0.47**	0.43**	0.33**	0.38**
Lie	−0.22**	−0.25**	−0.06**	−0.32**	−0.10	0.01
MADJ scales						
Neuroticism	0.58**	0.51**	0.52**	0.38**	0.31**	0.33**
Extraversion	−0.12*	−0.06**	−0.27**	0.08**	−0.17**	−0.06
Openness	0.07	−0.07	0.23**	0.06	0.02	0.01
Agreeableness	−0.36**	−0.19**	−0.28**	−0.30**	−0.27**	−0.21**
Conscientiousness	−0.09	−0.09	−0.01	−0.23**	0.04	0.04

* significant $P<0.05$, using a two-tailed test
** significant $P<0.01$, using a two-tailed test

From Table 3.2 it can be seen that several of the expected relationships were obtained. The full PSQ scale had a high correlation with N, and its five subscales correlated more highly with this scale than any of the others. The full scale obtained a moderate correlation with P, as well as a small but significant negative correlation with L. As expected the AI subscale obtained a higher correlation with P than with other subscales, and the correlation of this subscale with L was almost as strong.

As might be expected from the fact that the EPQ-R and MADJ Neuroticism scales were highly correlated ($r = 0.67$), the correlations between the PSQ and the MADJ N-scale closely paralleled the correlations of the PSQ with the EPQ-R N-scale, though they were slightly weaker. The correlations between the PSQ and MADJ A-scale were quite similar (although negative) to those between the PSQ and the EPQ-R P-scale, with a tendency to be slightly stronger.

The five subscale scores of the PSQ, the four O-LIFE scale scores, and the 30 NEO domain scores were included in a factor analysis of 350 student subjects ($F = 248$, $M = 102$), all different to those in the earlier large-scale study. A scree-test suggested a clear five-factor solution, with the eigenvalue on factor 5 more than twice that on factor 6. The five-factor solution was supported by the parallel-analysis method mentioned earlier. The table shows an oblique (oblimin) rotation of the five factors, following a generalized least-squares extraction. The five factors accounted for 57.8 per cent of the variance in the correlation matrix. Table 3.3 gives the results of this analysis, showing loadings above 0.25.

The five factors in the rotated factor analysis closely parallel the five factors of the Big-5 model, corresponding respectively to neuroticism, extraversion, agreeableness, conscientiousness and openness. As anticipated, paranoia is closely associated with the N-factor and to a lesser degree with the A-factor. Anger/Impulsiveness is the only PSQ subscale which has its highest loading on a factor other than N; though there are also substantial loadings of NM on the E-factor and of MW on the A-factor.

The O-LIFE scales are related in a predictable way to the five O-LIFE factors. Given the large number of neuroticism items in the Cognitive Disorganization scale, and of extraversion items in the Introvertive Anhedonia scale, it is not surprising that these two scales have their highest loadings on the first two factors. The tendency for the Impulsive Nonconformity scale to load on A, and to a lesser extent on C, is consistent with the high number of P items in this O-LIFE scale. H. J. Eysenck (1992*a,b*) and Costa and McCrae (1992*c*) agree that P is (negatively) correlated with both A and C, and factor analytic studies (for example Zuckerman *et al.* 1993) have shown that P cuts across these two factors. The loading of Unusual Experiences on the O-factor argues against the view put forward by writers such as H. J. Eysenck and Barrett (1993) that the three personality scales in the Eysenckian system can adequately account for the variance associated with schizotypy.

More generally, the analysis provides some support for the construct validity of the NEO as a measure of the 'Big-5' factors. Only two of the thirty facet

Table 3.3   Oblique rotation of generalized least-squares factor analysis comprising the five PSQ subscales, four O-LIFE scales, and 30 NEO-PI-R facets. Items are grouped according to factor (only loadings >0.25 reported).

	Factor				
	1 (N)	2 (E)	3 (A)	4 (C)	5 (O)
NEO-PI-R N1: Anxiety	0.86				
NEO-PI-R N3: Depression	0.76				
O–LIFE Cognitive Disorganization	0.71				
PSQ IS	0.69				
NEO-PI-R N6: Vulnerability	0.67			-0.30	
NEO-PI-R N2: Angry Hostility	0.65		0.47		
NEO-PI-R N4: Self-Consciousness	0.61		-0.29		
PSQ PH	0.57				
PSQ NM	0.51	-0.41			
PSQ MW	0.39		0.35		
NEO-PI-R N5: Impulsiveness	0.38	0.31		-0.33	
NEO-PI-R E2: Gregariousness		0.85			
NEO-PI-R E1: Warmth		0.81			
NEO-PI-R E6: Positive Emotions		0.69			
O–LIFE Introvertive Anhedonia		-0.65			
NEO-PI-R E5: Excitement-Seeking		0.50	0.32		
NEO-PI-R A1: Trust	-0.27	0.47	-0.37		
NEO-PI-R E4: Activity		0.38	0.35	0.36	
NEO-PI-R A4: Compliance			-0.72		
NEO-PI-R A2: Straightforwardness			-0.68		
NEO-PI-R A3: Altruism		0.51	-0.56		
NEO-PI-R A5: Modesty			-0.51		
O–LIFE Impulsive Nonconformity			0.49	-0.33	0.25
PSQ AI	0.44		0.48		
NEO-PI-R A6: Tender-Mindedness			-0.44		
NEO-PI-R E3: Assertiveness	-0.26	0.39	0.42	0.30	
NEO-PI-R C4: Achievement Striving				0.85	
NEO-PI-R C5: Self-Discipline				0.76	
NEO-PI-R C3: Dutifulness				0.74	
NEO-PI-R C1: Competence				0.73	
NEO-PI-R C2: Order				0.68	-0.25
NEO-PI-R C6: Deliberation			-0.38	0.55	
NEO-PI-R O2: Aesthetics					0.78
NEO-PI-R O5: Ideas					0.72
NEO-PI-R O3: Feelings	0.28				0.64
NEO-PI-R O1: Fantasy					0.60
NEO-PI-R O6: Values					0.54
NEO-PI-R O4: Actions					0.51
O–LIFE Unusual Experiences	0.27				0.45

scores loaded on a factor other than their original factor, and both of these facets have substantial cross-loadings on their original factor.

The above interpretation is based on a generalized least-squares analysis, followed by oblique rotation. To allow direct comparison with many earlier studies in this area, a principal components analysis followed by orthogonal (varimax) rotation was carried out. The results obtained were very similar to those in the above analysis.

FUTURE DIRECTIONS

A number of steps must still be taken to consolidate the PSQ as a valid measure which can be used alongside established indices of vulnerability to specific forms of psychosis or personality disorder. Although it has already been employed in correlational and factor analytic situations with two large samples, it would seem useful to validate the factor structure of the scale using more sophisticated statistical procedures such as confirmatory factor analysis.

It would also be interesting to see how the scale performs in clinical situations. However, as with similar measures of psychosis proneness and schizotypy, it would not be surprising if subjects who are clinically diagnosed as 'paranoid' did not obtain scores considerably higher than the norm. A more useful approach might be to employ the scale with normal individuals scoring high and low on the PSQ and its subscales, using tasks previously shown to differentiate paranoid from non-paranoid individuals. There is already considerable evidence, some of it detailed in this book, that individuals scoring high on these measures show similarities with psychotic patients at the levels of phenomenology, cognitive performance, neuropsychological functioning, and psychophysiological respond- ing. Chapman *et al.* (1994) have reported longitudinal research suggesting that certain measures of psychosis proneness contribute to the prediction of psychiatric breakdown. Paranoia has received little attention in this type of research. Our early section on 'markers' of paranoid disorder suggests a number of possible starting-points for the exploration of paranoia in normal individuals. The attribution research recently reported by Bentall and his colleagues may be particularly worthy of note in this respect.

Research on paranoia will need to consider developments in other fields, such as the more general area of 'schizotypy'. We would suggest two useful, though somewhat different, approaches to the measurement of schizotypy. On the one hand, it will continue to be productive in certain circumstances to employ schizotypy measures with a narrow focus, particularly those which aim to measure 'symptoms' rather than 'syndromes'. The Launay and Slade Hallucination Scale (Launay and Slade 1981) is an example of such a scale. These types of measure will assist in the understanding of specific psychotic phenomena as they manifest themselves in attenuated form in non-clinical populations.

At the other extreme, the O-LIFE questionnaire defines schizotypy very broadly. In the present writers' view, this is a useful development, in showing how previous tests of schizotypy can be summarized in terms of four main factors, and in demonstrating how these factors can be incorporated into the framework of normal personality. However, it might be argued that the O-LIFE has been so successful in achieving these aims that it would now seem inappropriate to call it a schizotypy measure. Three of the O-LIFE scales closely reflect the three factors of the Eysenckian system of normal personality. The O-LIFE enriches this tripartite system by the inclusion of many items from published schizotypy measures, and extends it by the inclusion of a fourth scale (Unusual Experiences) which is substantially independent of E, P, and N. Thus, the O-LIFE may be seen as a general personality questionnaire with a schizotypic slant. If the logic of this approach were to be applied more fully, the study of schizotypy would become even more intertwined with general personality study. Research on 'schizotypy' would then be directed towards the examination of how the various dimensions and subcomponents of personality might contribute to our understanding of psychotic phenomena.

Conceptual and empirical developments using both of the above general approaches will influence the direction of future research on paranoia and suspiciousness.

REFERENCES

Allsopp, J., Eysenck, H. J., and Eysenck, S. B. (1991). Machiavellianism as a component in psychoticism and extraversion. *Personality and Individual Differences*, 12, 29–41.

Altrocchi, J. (1980). *Abnormal Behaviour*. Harcourt Brace Jovanovich, New York.

APA (American Psychiatric Association) (1994). *Diagnostic and statistical manual of mental disorders*. APA, Washington, DC.

Bentall, R. P., Jackson, H.F., and Pilgrim, D. (1988). Abandoning the concept of 'schizophrenia': Some implications of validity arguments for psychological research into psychotic phenomena. *British Journal of Clinical Psychology*, 27, 303–24.

Bentall, R. P., Kaney, S., and Dewey, M. E. (1991). Paranoia and social reasoning: An attribution theory analysis. *British Journal of Clinical Psychology*, 30, 13–23.

Bentall, R. P., Kinderman, P., and Kaney, S. (1994). Cognitive processes and delusional beliefs: Attributions and the self. *Behaviour Research and Therapy*, 32, 331–41.

Bernstein, D. P., Useda, D., and Siever, L. J. (1993). Paranoid personality disorder: Review of the literature and recommendations for DSM-IV. Special Feature: DSM-IV reviews of the personality disorders: III, *Journal of Personality Disorders*, 7, 53–62.

Bleuler, E. (1950). *Dementia praecox or the group of schizophrenias*. International Universities Press, Madison.

Block, J. (1977). P scale and psychosis: Continued concerns. *Journal of Abnormal Psychology*, 86, 431–4.

Buss, A. H. and Durkee, A. (1957). An inventory for assessing different kinds of hostility. *Journal of Consulting Psychology*, 21, 343–9.

Buss, A. and Perry, M. (1992). The aggression questionnaire. *Journal of Personality and Social Psychology*, 63, 452–9.

Busse, E. W. and Pfeiffer, E. (ed.) (1977). *Behaviour and adaptation in late life* (2nd edn). Little, Brown, Boston.

Candido, C. L. and Romney, D. M. (1990). Attributional style in paranoid vs. depressed patients. *British Journal of Medical Psychology*, 63, 355–63.

Cattell, R. B., Eber, H. W., and Tatsuoka, M. M. (1970). *Handbook for the Sixteen Personality Factor Questionnaire*. Institute for Personality and Ability Testing, Champaign, IL.

Chapman, J. P, Chapman, L. J., and Kwapil, T. R. (1994). Does the Eysenck psychoticism scale predict psychosis? A ten year longitudinal study. *Personality and Individual Differences*, 17, 369–75.

Claridge, G. S. (1981). Psychoticism. In *Dimensions of personality. Papers in honour of H. J. Eysenck* (ed. R. Lynn), pp. 79–109. Pergamon, Oxford.

Claridge, G. (1994). Single indicator of risk for schizophrenia: Probable fact or likely myth? *Schizophrenia Bulletin*, 20, 151–68.

Costa, P. T. and McCrae, R. R. (1992a). Four ways five factors are basic. *Personality and Individual Differences*, 13, 653–65.

Costa, P. T. and McCrae, R. R. (1992b). *Revised NEO Personality Inventory (NEO-PI-R) and NEO Five-Factor Inventory (NEO-FFI) [Professional manual].* Psychological Assessment Resources, Odessa, FL.

Costa, P. T. and McCrae, R. R. (1992c). Reply to Eysenck. *Personality and Individual Differences*, 13, 861–5.

Cowen, M. A., Green, M. R., and Bertollo, D. N. (1993). A proposed neuroendocrine model of the schizophrenias. *Psychoneuroendocrinology*, 18, V–X (Editorial).

Eitinger, L. (1959). The incidence of mental disease among refugees in Norway. *Journal of Mental Science*, 105, 326–38.

Eysenck, H. J. (1992a). Four ways five factors are *not* basic. *Personality and Individual Differences*, 13, 667–73.

Eysenck, H. J. (1992b). A reply to Costa and McCrae. P or A and C—The role of theory. *Personality and Individual Differences*, 13, 867–8.

Eysenck, H. J. and Barrett, P. (1993). The nature of schizotypy. *Psychological Reports*, 73, 59–63.

Eysenck, H. J. and Eysenck, S. B. G. (1976). *Psychoticism as a dimension of personality.* Hodder and Stoughton, London.

Eysenck, S. B. G., Pearson, P. R., Easting, G., and Allsopp, J. F. (1985a). Age norms for impulsiveness, venturesomeness and empathy in adults. *Personality and Individual Differences*, 6, 613–19.

Eysenck, S. B. G., Eysenck, H. J., and Barrett. (1985b). A revised version of the psychoticism scale. *Personality and Individual Differences*, 6, 21–9.

Fenigstein, A. and Vanable, P. A. (1992). Paranoia and self-consciousness. *Journal of Personality and Social Psychology*, 62, 129–38.

Galinowski, A., Barbouche, R., Truffinet, P., Louzir, H., Poirier, M. F., Bouvet, O. *et al.* (1992). Natural autoantibodies in schizophrenia, *Acta Psychiatrica Scandinavica*, 85, 240–2.

Goldberg, L. R. (1990). An alternative 'description of personality': The big-five factor structure. *Journal of Personality and Social Psychology*, 59, 1216–29.

Goldberg, L. R. (1993). The structure of phenotypic personality traits. *American Psychologist*, 48, 26–34.

Gupta, A. (1993). Differential hemisphere processing of information in schizophrenia. *Journal of Psychiatric Research*, 27, 79–88.

Harris, R. E. and Lingoes, J. C. (1955). *Subscales for the MMPI: An aid to profile interpretation.* Mimeographed materials, Department of Psychiatry, University of California at San Francisco.

Hathaway, S. R. and McKinley, J. C. (1951). *Manual of the Minnesota Multiphasic Personality Inventory.* The Psychological Corporation, New York.

Hathaway, S. R. and McKinley, J. C. (1989). *Manual for administration and scoring of the Minnesota Multiphasic Personality Inventory-2.* University of Minnesota Press.

Heilbrun, A., Blum, N., and Goldreyer, N. (1985). Defensive projection: An investigation of its role in paranoid conditions. *Journal of Nervous and Mental Disease,* 173, 17–25.

Hemsley, D. R. and Garety, P. A. (1986). The formation of maintenance of delusions: A Bayesian analysis. *British Journal of Psychiatry,* 149, 51–56.

Herbert, M. E. and Jacobson, S. (1967). Late paraphrenia. *Journal of Psychiatry,* 113, 461–9.

Hewitt, J. K. and Claridge, G. (1989). The factor structure of schizotypy in a normal population. *Personality and Individual Differences,* 10, 323–9.

Holland, T. and Gosden, C. (1990). A balanced chromosomal translocation partially co-segregating with psychotic illness in a family. *Psychiatry Research,* 32, 1–8.

Horn, J. L. (1965). A rationale and test for the number of factors in factor analysis. *Psychometrika,* 30, 179–85.

Jackson, M. C. (1994). 'Delusional' attributional biases in relation to schizotypy and depression in a normal sample. Unpublished D. Phil. thesis. University of Oxford.

Kaney, S. and Bentall, R. P. (1989). Persecutory delusions and attributional style. *British Journal of Medical Psychology,* 62, 191–8.

Kay, D. W. K. and Roth, M. (1961). Environmental and hereditary factors in the schizophrenias of old age ('late paraphrenia') and their bearing on the general problem of causation in schizophrenia. *Journal of Mental Science,* 107, 649–86.

Kendler, K. S. (1988). Kraepelin and the diagnostic concept of paranoia. *Comprehensive Psychiatry,* 29, 4–11.

Kinderman, P., Kaney, S., Morley, S., and Bentall, R. P. (1992). Paranoia and the defensive attributional style: Deluded and depressed patients' attributions about their own attributions. *British Journal of Medical Psychology,* 65, 371–383.

Kraepelin, E. (1896). *Psychiatrie: Ein Lehrbuch fur studirende und aerzte* (5th edn). Barth, Leipzig.

Kraepelin, E. (1919). *Dementia praecox and paraphrenia* (trans. R. M. Barclay). Livingstone, Edinburgh.

Kraepelin, E. (1921). *Manic-depressive insanity and paranoia.* Livingstone, Edinburgh.

Kreiner, S., Simonsen, E., and Mogensen, J. (1990). Validation of a personality inventory scale: The MCMI P-scale (paranoia). *Journal of Personality Disorders,* 4, 303–11.

Krieckhaus, E. E., Donahoe, J. W., and Morgan, M. A. (1992). Paranoid schizophrenia may be caused by dopamine hyperactivity of CA1 hippocampus. *Biological Psychiatry,* 31, 560–70.

Launay, G. and Slade, P. D. (1981). The measurement of hallucinatory predisposition in male and female prisoners. *Personality and Individual Differences,* 2, 221–34.

Lauterbach, E. C. (1991). Serotonin reuptake inhibitors, paranoia, and the ventral basal ganglia. *Clinical Neuropharmacology,* 14, 547–55.

Macciardi, F., Lucca, A., Catalano, M., Marino, C., Zanardi, R., and Smeraldi, E. (1990). Amino acid patterns in schizophrenia: Some new findings. *Psychiatry Research,* 32, 63–70.

McDonald, R. P. (1985). *Factor analysis and related methods.* Lawrence Erlbaum Associates, London.

McGlashan, T. H. and Fenton, W. S. (1991). Classical subtypes for schizophrenia: Literature review for *DSM-IV. Schizophrenia Bulletin,* 17, 609–22.

McPherson, F. M., Presly, A. S., Armstrong, J., and Curtis, R. H. (1974). 'Psychoticism' and psychotic illness. *British Journal of Psychiatry,* 125, 152–60.

Mason, O., Claridge, G., and Jackson, M. (1995). New scales for the assessment of schizotypy. *Personality and Individual Differences,* 18, 7–13.

Meyer, R. G. and Salmon, P. (1988). *Abnormal Psychology* (2nd edn). Allyn and Bacon, Mass.

Mezey, A. (1960). Personal background, emigration and mental disorder in Hungarian refugees. *Journal of Mental Science*, 106, 618–27.

Miller, L. (1986). Conversion, paranoia and brain dysfunction. *British Journal of Psychiatry*, 148, 481.

Millon, T. (1983). *Millon clinical multiaxial inventory (MCMI) manual* (3rd edn). Interpretive Scoring Systems (division of National Computer Systems), Minneapolis.

Monteleone, P., Maj, M., Fusco, M., Kemali, D., and Reiter, R. J. (1992). Depressed nocturnal plasma melatonin levels in drug-free paranoid schizophrenics. *Schizophrenia Research*, 7, 77–84.

Morrison, J. R. (1974). Changes in subtype diagnosis of schizophrenia: 1920–1966. *American Journal of Psychiatry*, 131, 674–7.

Nicholson, I. R. and Neufeld, W. J. (1993). Classification of the schizophrenias according to symptomatology: A two-factor model. *Journal of Abnormal Psychology*, 102, 259–70.

Onstad, S., Skre, I., Torgensen, S., and Kringlen, E. (1991). Subtypes of schizophrenia-Evidence from a twin-family study. *Acta Psychiatrica Scandinavica*, 84, 203–6.

Oxman, T. E., Rosenberg, S. D., Schnurr, P. P., and Tucker, G. J. (1988). Somatization, paranoia and language. *Journal of Communication Disorders*, 21, 33–50.

Raine, A. (1991). The SPQ: A scale for the assessment of schizotypal personality based on DSM-III-R criteria. *Schizophrenia Bulletin*, 17, 555–64.

Raskin, R. N. and Hall, C. S. (1979). A narcissistic personality inventory. *Psychological Reports*, 45, 590.

Rawlings, D. (1994). A five-factor model of personality. Unpublished study. The University of Melbourne.

Rawlings, D. and Borge, A. (1987). Personality and hemisphere function: Two experiments using the dichotic shadowing technique. *Personality and Individual Differences*, 8, 483–8.

Rawlings, D. and Claridge, G. S. (1984). Schizotypy and hemisphere function. III. Performance asymmetries on tasks of letter recognition and local-global processing. *Personality and Individual Differences*, 5, 663–7.

Rawlings, D. and Freeman, J. L. (1996). A questionnaire for the measurement of paranoia/suspiciousness. *British Journal of Clinical Psychology*, 35, 451–61.

Roberts, D. and Claridge, G. (1991). A genetic model compatible with a dimensional view of schizophremia. *British Journal of Psychiatry*, 158, 451–6.

Sarvis, M. A. (1962). Paranoid reactions. *Archives of General Psychiatry*, 6, 157–62.

Swanson, D. W., Bohnert, P. J., and Smith, J. A. (1970). *The paranoid*. Little, Brown, Boston.

Trower, P. and Chadwick, P. (1995). Pathways to defense of the self: A theory of two types of paranoia. *Clinical Psychology: Science and Practice*, 2, 263–78.

Trull, T. T. (1992). DSM-III-R personality disorders and the five-factor model of personality: An empirical comparison. *Journal of Abnormal Psychology*, 101, 553–60.

Widiger, T. A. (1993). The *DSM-III-R* categorical personality disorder diagnoses: A critique and an alternative. *Psychological Inquiry*, 4, 75–90.

Widiger, T. A. and Costa, P. T. Jr (1994). Personality and personality disorders. *Journal of Abnormal Psychology*, 103, 78–91.

Wiener, D. N. and Harmon, L. R. (1946). Subtle and obvious keys for the MMPI: Their development. *Advertisement Bulletin*, 16. Regional Veterans Administration Office, Minneapolis.

Zigler, E. and Glick, M. (1988). Is paranoid schizophrenia really camouflaged depression? *American Psychologist*, 43, 284–90.

Zuckerman, M. (1989). Personality in third dimension: a psychobiological approach. *Personality and Individual Differences*, 10, 391–418.

Zuckerman, M. D., Kuhlman, M., Joireman, J., Teta, P., and Kraft, M. (1993). A comparison of three structural models for personality: The Big Three, the Big Five, and the Alternative Five. *Journal of Personality and Social Psychology*, 65, 757–68.

Part II Neurocognitive investigations

4

Investigations of cognitive inhibitory processes in schizotypy and schizophrenia

LEANNE WILLIAMS AND ANTHONY BEECH

INTRODUCTION

Researchers reporting in the attention literature have put substantial effort into understanding the mechanisms that allow the brain to attend to certain features of the environment and, at the same time, to screen out information that seems to be irrelevant. An ongoing controversy concerns where this screening takes place: whether it is at an early, preconscious stage of processing in which the environment is comprehended only in terms of elementary physical and sensory features (Broadbent 1958, 1971) or at a much later stage, where objects in the environment have reached a level of representation that allows us to become consciously aware of them (Allport 1980; van der Heijden 1981). These contrasting views are most commonly referred to as the 'early selection' and 'late selection' theories. To date, the weight of evidence is in favour of the late selection theory (for example Mackay 1973; Corteen and Wood 1974; Underwood 1976; Marcel 1983).

In the last ten years interest has shifted towards the fate of ignored information in selective attention. Specifically, when selecting information to pay conscious attention to what are the associated mechanisms involved in effectively ignoring distracting information? For example, how does a predator pick a particular prey animal and manage to ignore competing stimuli in its environment? Some have suggested that unselected information decays passively. Proponents of this view include both early and late selection theorists (for example, Broadbent 1958; van der Heijden 1981). Others have argued that the way selection works is by active suppression of information that has not been specifically attended to (Neill 1977; Lowe 1979; Tipper 1985). These latter researchers have reported that if information has been presented in such a way as to invite an experimental subject to ignore it, and if this information is quickly re-presented, the time taken to attend to re-presented stimuli is longer than if it had not been ignored in the first place.

A typical example of an experiment showing this 'suppression' effect uses Stroop words. These are colour words written in another colour, for example the colour word RED written in *blue* ink. If a subject is asked to report the ink colour of the word, the argument is that the selection process involves active inhibition of the word itself, i.e. by attending to the ink colour *blue* there is an active inhibition of the concept RED. If *red* is the ink colour of the next Stroop word it takes longer to report this than if the last colour word had been, say, GREEN. Tipper (1984) termed this effect 'negative priming', in contrast to 'positive priming' where, if a subject had responded to the ink colour *red* and then *red* has to be named again, the reaction time to the second presentation is speeded up.

REDUCED INHIBITION AND SCHIZOPHRENIA

The mechanism that produces active suppression of irrelevant information has interested us because it may provide a clue to some of the problems involved in schizophrenia. Such an idea has a long history; for example Dixon (1981) has suggested that intrusions of irrelevant information into consciousness seen in schizophrenics' performance on selective attention tasks, such as dichotic listening (reported by, among others, Marchbanks and Williams (1971) and Wishner and Wahl (1974)) could be explained in terms of a defect in the mechanism that controls the flow of information into conscious awareness. Frith (1979) proposed that this defect is due to a breakdown in the inhibitory processes that 'control and limit the contents of consciousness' and that the 'positive' symptoms of schizophrenia— hallucinations, delusions and thought disorder (Schneider 1959)—are due to a sufferer's inability to screen out distracting information.

From such a formulation several aspects of schizophrenics' symptoms could be accounted for (although it should be noted that Frith himself does not adhere to this theory any longer). Auditory hallucinations, for example, could have their basis in real sounds which activate various representations in the brain. Some initial processing might then result in various interpretations which, in most people, do not reach a conscious level of experience. However, because of a weakened filtering of information between preconsciousness and consciousness these incorrect interpretations could become consciously experienced as auditory hallucinations.

As for delusions, the thoughts that an individual is currently aware of would obviously seem to be the most pertinent to that person (Posner and Boies 1971); so, if there are strange ideas arriving in consciousness, they need to be explained. Frith argues that delusions are an attempt to put these strange thoughts and experiences into some form of context. He notes that some evidence for this proposition can be found in the observation that those suffering from paranoid delusions tend to be more intelligent than non-paranoid sufferers; paranoid schizophrenics are therefore more able to fit irrelevant percepts into their cognitive schemata.

Thought disorder can only be inferred from problems in speech and language. Frith (1981) suggested that the processing of thought may not actually be the problem, but rather that it is a failure at the output stage of *language* processing, a failure to suppress the alternative meanings of words, producing abnormal speech output. Say, for example, a sentence is about the level of traffic in London and the phrase 'traffic jam' is used. In most individuals alternative meanings of the word 'jam' are suppressed (Marcel 1980), but if this does not happen then the rest of the sentence could well turn into one about strawberry jam.

Research by Bullen (Bullen and Hemsley 1984, 1987) tested this proposition in several experiments using a semantic priming task where subjects had to identify target words (for example WRIST) that were preceded by two semantically related primes (for example HAND—PALM or TREE—PALM). The latter were presented at above-threshold levels of detection, the target words just below threshold. The primes were either *concordant* with the target word (for example HAND preceded PALM which semantically primes WRIST) or *discordant* with the target word (for example TREE precedes PALM so that the meaning of the polysemous word PALM is semantically unrelated to WRIST). In such an experimental procedure the target word has been shown to be facilitated in the *concordant* condition, but inhibited in the *discordant* condition in normal subjects (Schvaneveldt *et al.* 1976). Bullen found that there was less inhibition in the *discordant* condition in schizophrenic patients compared with non-psychotic controls, suggesting that there the clinical subjects were relatively less able to inhibit the alternative meaning of PALM. However, a failure to find the expected facilitation effects in the *concordant* primes in both schizophrenic and non-schizophrenic subjects weakens Bullen's argument concerning the ability of the priming stimuli to have any effect upon the target words.

As Bullen's results were not clear-cut, the present authors, influenced by the work of Tipper and his co-workers, have employed more robust experimental designs to investigate Frith's notion of weakened inhibition as being the cause of positive schizophrenic symptoms, investigating both schizophrenic and schizotypal performance on various negative priming tasks.

HIGH SCHIZOTYPES AS ANALOGUES OF SCHIZOPHRENICS

There are a number of problems when conducting experiments with schizophrenic patients. By the very nature of their illness they are extremely easily distracted, so it is very difficult to get them to concentrate on the task at hand. In addition, since most are probably on medication to stabilize their illness, this may well have an impact upon the inhibition effect that we were interested in measuring. Therefore, the initial approach taken to the investigation of inhibitory processes and schizophrenia was to compare non-clinical individuals who had high or low schizotypy scores.

Inhibitory processes in high and low schizotypes

The first published study (Beech and Claridge 1987) investigating inhibitory processes using ideas from Tipper employed a priming procedure where subjects had to name a colour bar presented in the centre of a screen and ignore flanking stimuli that were either a series of crosses or colour words. In the second part of the procedure subjects had to name the ink colour of a Stroop word presented for

100 ms. This procedure was based on an experimental design also reported by Tipper (1984). He had found that normal subjects showed a measurable inhibition effect, i.e. increased reaction time (in the region of 40 ms) to name the ink colour of the Stroop word when the *to-be-named* colour in the second part of the procedure was the same as the *to-be-ignored* colour word (distractor) in the priming condition. This was when compared with a control condition where the ignored distractor in the priming part of the experiment, rather than being a colour word, was a series of crosses.

In the Beech and Claridge study it was found that, when subjects were divided into high and low schizotypy scorers on the basis of a median split of scores on the STA scale of the STQ (Claridge and Broks 1984; see Chapter 2 for a description of this scale), low scorers showed an inhibitory effect (again of about 40 ms), whereas high scorers did not. With regard to the high schizotypy group's performance, if anything they showed a facilitation effect of about 15 ms rather than an inhibition effect. It was also found that there was a significant *negative* correlation between schizotypy score on the STA scale and the amount of inhibition shown, indicating that the measured inhibition effect decreases with the degree of schizotypy.

This particular experimental design was considered unsatisfactory because of the different natures of the stimuli in the priming and control trials. In a subsequent study, therefore, (Beech *et al.* 1989) lists of Stroop words were presented under a number of conditions, the two main ones of interest here being control and negative priming conditions. Subjects had to name the ink colour of Stroop words presented at one of three presentation times: 100, 250, and 500 ms. In the negative priming condition the *to-be-ignored* Stroop colour word was the same as the *to-be-named* ink colour of the subsequent Stroop word. In the control condition the *to-be-ignored* Stroop colour word was unrelated to the subsequent *to-be-named* ink colour of the next Stroop word. A measure of inhibition was obtained by comparing the difference in performance, in terms of reaction time, between the control and negative priming trials.

Participants were again divided into low and high schizotypal groups on the basis of a median split of STA scores. At the 100 ms presentation time, low schizotypal subjects showed a substantial inhibition effect (about 30 ms), whereas again, as in the earlier Beech and Claridge study, there was a suggestion of a facilitation effect in high schizotypal subjects (24 ms). For very high schizotypes (i.e. those scoring higher than one standard deviation above the mean on the STA scale) there was a significant facilitation effect (49 ms). This result suggests that, rather than distracting information merely being less available for subsequent processing in this group, such information can actively enhance later processing.

Also, it should be noted that at the 250 ms presentation time both groups showed a measurable inhibition effect, while at the 500 ms presentation no inhibitory or facilitatory effect was measured in either group. These observations may have happened because at longer presentation times conscious biases begin to affect performance, possibly masking the effect of inhibition or facilitation associated with preconscious selection.

It was suggested above that distracting information, rather than being less available for subsequent processing in high schizotypes at the 100 ms presentation time, is actually more available. However, an alternative explanation needs to be considered. High schizotypes might have shown reduced or reversed negative priming because they may have been able to analyse only a fragment of the irrelevant distractor information when it was presented so briefly. In other words, high schizotypes might not be able to complete their perceptual analysis of distractor information in this pre-attentive time frame. This explanation would be consistent with evidence from other studies that schizotypal subjects and schizophrenics use local rather than global pre-attentive grouping strategies (Schwartz-Place and Gilmore 1980; Rawlings and Claridge 1984). A second possibility is that the masking stimulus, routinely used in such experiments to prevent further processing at the end of the stimulus presentation time, had a greater effect upon the processing of information in high schizotypes than in low schizotypes. This proposal would appear to fit with the findings from backward masking studies, that there is slower information transfer in both schizotypal and schizophrenic subjects (for example Saccuzzo *et al.* 1974; Merritt *et al.* 1986). However, an argument against this idea is that it would seem likely that the significant facilitation effect found for those having very high schizotypy scores could only have been produced if they were able to analyse distractors to a semantic level of representation.

Nevertheless, to discount these possibilities completely, and to provide a more definitive test of the reduced inhibition hypothesis, a further negative priming study was carried out (Beech *et al.* 1991). In this study there were a number of conditions, using either repeated words or semantically related words (for example CAT-DOG). The task was to verbally name the semantic category of each word (for example say 'animal' when the word DOG was presented). The experimental procedure was as follows. Two overlapping words were presented in a prime condition, followed by a probe condition; the ink colour of one of these words would be red, the other green. The subject's task in half of the trials was to categorize the red word and ignore the green word; in the the other half of the trials the opposite procedure applied. Two negative priming conditions were used. In the *repetition negative priming* condition, words that had been ignored in the prime condition were presented to be categorized in the probe condition (for example red DOG to green DOG). In the *semantic negative priming* condition, words in the probe condition were presented for naming that were semantically related to words that had previously been ignored (for example red CAT-green DOG). The use of this latter condition meant that if facilitation occurred in high schizotypal subjects, it could not be attributed to their failure to fully analyse the distracting information.

Subjects were again split on the basis of high and low schizotypy, their results revealing a double dissociation in the data. High schizotypes showed significant facilitation in the *semantic negative priming* condition compared with a control condition, but no effect when the distractor was identical to the target. Low schizotypes, on the other hand, exhibited significant inhibition in the *repetition negative priming* condition, but no effect in the *semantic negative priming* condition.

The observation, that irrelevant material which should have been actively suppressed in the prime condition actually facilitates the recognition of subsequently presented semantically related material in high schizotypes, suggests a possible way of understanding what is happening in the positive symptoms of schizophrenia. What may be regarded as an apparently irrelevant stimulus in the environment may set off a chain of associations in the sufferer that could be experienced as an unwanted intrusion into consciousness, as hallucinations or a tangential stream of thought.

Inhibitory processes in schizotypal subgroups

The work outlined above has recently been extended (Williams 1995). Rather than relying on a single measure of schizotypy to identify high and low groups, cluster analysis of various questionnaires has produced clearer definitions of schizotypy. In Chapter 2 evidence is provided for the existence of four different subgroups of schizotypal traits: Low; Ideational/ Perceptual Disturbance; Cognitive Disorganization/Social Anhedonia; and Physical Anhedonia. Comparisons of the information processing styles of these groups, identified by distinct patterns of positive and negative schizotypal traits, provide a better test of the hypotheses under investigation than the study of groups defined by a single broad measure of schizotypy. At least, that was our assumption at the outset.

The Ideational/Perceptual Disturbance and Cognitive Disorganization/ Social Anhedonia subgroups of schizotypy were both predicted to show *reduced* negative priming. This was based on the argument than they might reflect a predisposition to two of Liddle's (1987) three syndromes of schizophrenic symptoms, i.e. Reality Distortion and Disorganization, both of which are considered to be positive symptom syndromes. However, it should be noted that the social anhedonia component of the Cognitive Disorganization/Social Anhedonia schizotypal subgroup has usually been regarded as a negative schizotypal feature, whereas the alogia and attentional deficit aspects of the Disorganization clinical subgroup have been commonly defined as non-deficit negative symptoms in schizophrenia (for example Andreasen and Olsen 1982). Thus, evidence for a lack of negative priming in the Cognitive Disorganization/Social Anhedonia group could also indicate that reduced cognitive inhibition might underlie some aspects of negative symptomatology. The availability of a purely negative schizotypal trait group (viz. the Physical Anhedonia subgroup) meant that it was possible to test out the prediction that reduced inhibition is primarily a correlate of the vulnerability to positive symptomatology.

The study again included both *repetition negative* and *semantic negative* priming conditions, but employed a different priming task: the verbal identification of word stimuli. Such a procedure was designed to encourage an orthographical focus (requiring only a lexical level of analysis for response), as opposed to the Beech *et al.* (1991) study, which used semantic categorization that obviously biased subjects to focus on semantic processing. Previous studies have indicated that an orthographic method of processing is promoted by the inclusion of both concrete and abstract words and the use of low and medium frequency words (Balota and Chumbley 1984; Seidenberg and McClelland 1989). For this reason, the stimuli included words that met such criteria. Also, a larger number of prime and target words were used, compared with previous studies, to decrease the potential response benefit that could accrue from familiarity with the experimental words (Seidenberg and McClelland 1989; May *et al.* 1995).

The results for the four schizotypal subgroups revealed some interesting differences in negative priming. Both the Low and the Physical Anhedonia subgroups showed inhibition effects in both the *repetition negative priming* and *semantic negative priming* conditions. The performance of the Low subgroup was consistent with the low schizotypy group in the Beech *et al.* study, confirming the earlier proposal that efficient inhibitory processes are associated with a low level of schizotypal features as a whole. The findings for the Physical Anhedonia group indicate that efficient inhibitory mechanisms are also found in the presence of purely negative schizotypal features.

Results in the Ideational/Perceptual Disturbance and Cognitive Disorganization/Social Anhedonia subgroups indicated either reduced inhibition or facilitation in both the *repetition negative priming* and *semantic negative priming* conditions. The pattern for these subgroups thus corresponds to the performance of Beech *et al*s. high schizotypy group in the *semantic negative priming* condition.

As the Cognitive Disorganization/Social Anhedonia subgroup also showed reduced inhibition, and this group has coexistent positive and negative schizotypal features, it might appear that the reduced cognitive inhibition hypothesis is not restricted to an explanation of positive symptoms. However, the failure to find inhibitory effects in this group could instead reflect a very high level of *positive* schizotypal traits (as evidenced by very high STA scores) in the Cognitive Disorganization subgroup. Therefore, the conclusion can be drawn that presence of negative schizotypal traits is not associated with reduced inhibition unless there are also high levels of coexistent positive features.

SCHIZOPHRENIA STUDIES

Inhibitory processes in schizophrenics

Beech *et al.* (1989) investigated schizophrenic patients' performance in an experimental procedure based on that used in normal schizotypes by Beech *et al.* (1989) (described earlier on p. 66). The study compared schizophrenics (with predominantly positive symptoms) and a neurotic control group. The latter group showed a level of cognitive inhibition that was equivalent to results found in non-psychiatric patients in previous studies (roughly 30 ms) Schizophrenics showed reduced negative priming (approximately 9 ms). However, they did not show the facilitation effects observed in highly schizotypal subjects seen by

Beech *et al.* (1989). This result could be due to testing the schizophrenic sample when in comparative remission. In an unpublished study, one of us (A.B.) tested five sufferers over a period of weeks (on the same task as reported above). It was observed that when sufferers appeared to be more floridly ill they showed less cognitive inhibition than when they seemed comparatively well. However, these observations did not concur with the sufferers' self-reports, or psychiatric ratings by ward staff, of their current mental state. A second explanation of the failure to find facilitation effects in the schizophrenic group may be linked to the fact that all of the schizophrenic sample were on some form of neuroleptic medication and this may have had the effect of 'normalizing' inhibitory processes. This idea is discussed later.

Inhibitory processes in schizophrenic subgroups

Recently, the first author has reported a study investigating inhibitory processes in schizophrenic subgroups (Williams 1996). Cluster analysis was used to produce subgroups of schizophrenic symptoms. The analysis was performed on ratings from the Scale for the Assessment of Positive Symptoms (SAPS; Andreasen 1984) and the Scale for the Assessment of Negative Symptoms (SANS; Andreasen 1981). From these scales are derived four positive symptom subscales: hallucinations, delusions, positive formal thought disorder, and bizarre behaviour; and five negative symptom subscales: affective flattening, alogia, avolition, anhedonia, and attentional impairment. As found in the analysis of the schizotypy data (referred to above and in Chapter 2), four distinct clusters emerged. Three of these show a broad correspondence with Liddle's (1987) schizophrenic subtypes, i.e. Reality Distortion syndrome, Disorganization syndrome, and Psychomotor Poverty syndrome. The fourth cluster was characterized by a general absence of symptoms. As participants in this last cluster reported intermittent episodes of primarily positive symptoms, they were termed the Episodic group.

The priming task completed by schizophrenic subjects was identical to that used in the schizotypy subgroup study reported earlier. Results showed that both Reality Distortion and Disorganization were associated with reduced inhibition, and indeed facilitation in some subjects in the *repetition negative priming* and *semantic negative priming* conditions. The Episodic subgroup also showed a lack of inhibition in these two conditions, perhaps indicating a latent presence of positive symptoms. In contrast, the Psychomotor Poverty subgroup displayed negative priming for both *repetition negative priming* and *semantic negative priming* conditions.

The observation that there were facilitation effects in the Reality Distortion and Disorganization schizophrenic subgroups mirrors the pattern of results seen in the Ideational/Perceptual Disturbance and Cognitive Disorganisation/Social Anhedonia *schizotypal* groups. Similarly, the finding that the Psychomotor Poverty subgroup showed a normal negative priming effect parallels the results found in the Physical Anhedonia schizotypal group. This latter result suggests that purely negative symptoms *cannot* be explained in terms of reduced inhibition.

Overall, the results indicate that there are analogues of schizophrenic-like performance in non-psychotic schizotypal subjects and tend to confirm the construct validity of these clusters as they relate to schizophrenia. Given the parallel in both phenomenology and priming performance between the schizotypal and schizophrenic subgroups, it is apparent that the three high schizotypy groups might indeed represent the personality and cognitive dispositions to Liddle's (1987) three schizophrenic syndromes.

Analysis of the errors made by schizophrenic groups also produced some interesting results. Errors were scored in the following way. Full-word errors were taken to be those responses in which the match with the actual experimental word represented no more than one letter in the correct position for one syllable words (for example 'fat' instead of 'fork') and no more than one letter in each syllable in the correct position for two syllable words (for example 'ignore' instead of 'eyebrow'). Full-word errors also included semantic substitutions (for example 'funny' instead of 'laugh'). Part-word errors were defined as responses in which the match with the stimulus word represented at least two letters in the correct position for one syllable words (for example 'spoon' instead of 'stool'), and at least one syllable in the correct position for two syllable words (for example 'forehand' instead of 'forehead'). Part-word errors also covered responses that represented an extension of the stimulus word (for example 'bowling' instead of 'bowl').

It was found that the Disorganization subgroup made a particularly high number of full-word errors in their responses to target words. Inspection of these responses revealed a surprising number of incorrect answers that comprised words semantically associated with the correct target word. For example, the response 'police' was given instead of 'rules', and the response 'working' instead of 'student'. Such errors suggest that individuals in the Disorganization subgroup, i.e. those with the highest overall level of thought disorder and other positive symptoms, experienced intrusions into their consciousness of irrelevant, yet semantically associated, information. These findings are in line with those of Kwapil *et al.* (1990) where schizophrenics characterized by the presence of thought disorder showed heightened activation of semantic information.

THE IMPACT OF NEUROLEPTICS ON INHIBITORY PROCESSES

The observation that there was reduced inhibition, but a failure to find facilitation effects, in schizophrenic subjects in the first patient study described here was explained by the fact that all of the schizophrenics were on some form of neuroleptic medication which may have had a 'normalizing' influence upon their performance in the experimental task. This proposal was tested in a study reported by Beech *et al.* (1990). Here the effects of medication on negative priming in a non-schizophrenic sample were examined using a double-blind placebo procedure. Participants completed the Stroop task twice, with a one-week interval between sessions. Half the participants were administered 25 mg of chlorpromazine before the first testing session, the other half a syrup placebo. This procedure was reversed at the second testing session. In line with expectation, medication was found to increase the amount of measured inhibition compared with the placebo condition. These results appear to support the proposal that neuroleptic medication has a 'normalizing' effect on negative priming in schizophrenia. However, the chlorpromazine dosage of 25 mg used in this study is substantially lower than that prescribed for most schizophrenics, and the effect of this medication on psychiatrically healthy normals may differ from that for schizophrenics.

In the second patient study reported here, 80 per cent of the participants were taking some form of anti-psychotic medication, with dosages ranging from 100 to 1750 mg (chlorpromazine equivalent). As there were insufficient numbers of unmedicated schizophrenics to conduct a between-groups comparison (medicated versus unmedicated) in relation to inhibitory performance, the level of medication was co-varied with priming performance for each subgroup. Medication was not found to co-vary significantly with subgroups and priming conditions, a result which fails to provide support for the idea that medication normalizes performance in schizophrenics. This result, taken together with the observation that the Episodic schizophrenic subgroup failed to show inhibitory effects, suggests that reduced inhibition is a stable phenomenon for sufferers experiencing manifest as well as latent positive symptoms. Therefore the results from the Beech *et al.* study could well reflect the the temporary use of neuroleptics in a healthy non-schizophrenic sample. Neither strategy for investigating the effect of medication on the patient samples was ideal and this is a topic that deserves further investigation, preferably by comparing medicated and non-medicated clinical samples on therapeutic doses of the drugs concerned.

THE MECHANISMS UNDERLYING POSITIVE SYMPTOMS

A model of inhibitory and facilitatory mechanisms

A theoretical model was subsequently constructed to attempt to explain the findings reported here, based on two observations from the Beech *et al.* (1990) study: (a) that high schizotypes showed significant facilitation in a *semantic negative priming* condition, but no effect when the distractor was identical to the target; and (b) that low schizotypes exhibited significant inhibition in the *repetition negative priming* condition, but no effect in the *semantic negative priming condition*.

From the observation that ignored information had significant effects in both groups, it would seem that initial perceptual analysis is equivalent in both high and low schizotypal groups. Any differences that give rise to inhibitory or facilitatory effects must therefore arise from disruptions in later selective inhibitory processes. The model developed to explain the findings (first reported in Beech *et al.* 1990) relies on two basic assumptions:

1. Spreading activation takes place prior to selective inhibitory processes, a proposal drawing on evidence that inhibition takes time to appear (Lowe 1985).

2. Spreading inhibition to related concepts is presumed to be not as great as spreading activation (S. P. Tipper, personal communication).

Fig. 4.1A shows how the inhibition effect found in low schizotypes and the facilitation effect in high schizotypes might be explained by the model. According to Fig. 4.1A low schizotypes' initial perceptual analysis produces an activation level of, say, 10 units in the semantic representation of the ignored stimulus DOG. Selective inhibition then begins to prevent response to, and awareness of, this irrelevant stimulus. The amount of inhibition = 12 units. The final output of the DOG representation (10–12) then produces 2 units of inhibition: if DOG has to be named it takes longer. It is assumed that 60 per cent of the initial activation and 50 per cent of the inhibition has spread close to the concept of CAT. Therefore the amount of priming associated with CAT is 10 x 0.6 = 6 units of excitation and 12 x 0.5 = 6 units of inhibition, so explaining the failure to find any semantic priming effects in low schizotypes to semantically related stimuli.

In Fig. 4.1B high schizotypes' initial perceptual analysis produces the same activation level of 10 units but there is a lower level of inhibition (**10 units**); this explains why there are no observed repeated priming effects in this group. Again it is assumed that 60 per cent of the initial activation and 50 per cent of the inhibition has spread closely to the concept of CAT. Therefore the amount of priming associated with CAT is 10 x 0.6 = 6 units of excitation and 10 x 0.5 = 5 units of inhibition. The final output is one unit of facilitation to semantically related material.

Shortcomings of the model

The assumptions made in the above model rely on the notion that the automatic activation of information occurs as an all-or-none phenomenon and is not subject to the influence of subsequent or preceding conscious attentional processes. However, it has been argued that conscious attention modulates the automatic activation of information and that automatic processing may be subject to some attentional control dictated by the information relevant to the task in hand (Cohen *et al.* 1990). Evidence from masked priming studies (using both repetition and semantic priming procedures) shows that, depending on the task performed by participants, responses may be either facilitated or inhibited (Dagenbach *et al.* 1989; Besner *et al.* 1990; Carr and Dagenbach 1990; Friedrich *et al.* 1991). Here it is suggested that information about the orthographic (perceptual), phonological, and semantic features of the priming stimuli is activated simultaneously and automatically. However, the requirements of the priming task determine which type of information is then focused upon by conscious attentional processes. For example, phonological information would be needed for any task requiring a verbal response, but a lexical decision task would also emphasize semantic;

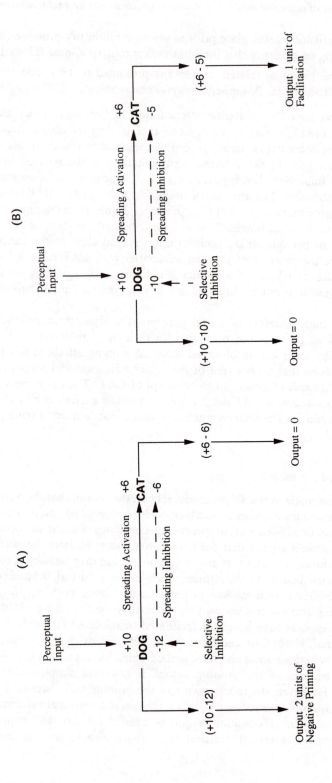

Fig. 4.1. Model of inhibitory and facilitatory processes: for (A) low schizotypy and (B) high schizotypy subjects.

a word naming task would emphasize letter recognition (i.e. orthographic information). In each case, the less relevant information (orthographic or semantic, respectively) would potentially interfere with the relevant information and thus need to be consciously suppressed. Cohen *et al.* (1990) have suggested that the suppression of irrelevant information might in some instances reduce the ability to facilitate relevant information, resulting in the inhibitory masked priming effects mentioned earlier.

The evidence for this revised view of automatic processing comes largely from masked priming studies, so its application to the negative priming paradigm is somewhat indirect. Further, the effects of task requirements on automatic processes involved in negative priming may be minimal because the to-be-ignored information is obviously not given conscious attention. None the less, it is important to note that negative priming is reduced in high schizotypes only when stimuli are analysed by primarily automatic processes (i.e. at 100 ms stimulus presentation). Thus, it is possible that there are individual differences in the impact of task requirements on the automatic activation of information that play some part in the subsequent activation of inhibitory mechanisms (Neely 1977). Thus, the proposal that high schizotypes (and, by extension, schizophrenics) show no apparent disruptions to pre-attentive (primarily automatic) processes may apply only under certain task conditions.

Some indication that different task requirements produce different effects on automatic or pre-attentive processing comes from other priming studies on schizophrenia; for example Kwapil *et al.* (1990). The latter's findings suggested that pre-attentive activation of information might in fact be heightened in schizophrenia. In their study the task was word naming, which would have encouraged participants to focus attention on the orthographic nature of the stimuli. Interestingly, and unexpectedly, Kwapil *et al.* found no differences in inhibition between schizophrenics and controls, indicating that the alteration to pre-attentive processing may indeed have impacted on inhibitory mechanisms for the schizophrenic group. A dynamic association between pre-attentive processes and inhibition would be consistent with previous comments that the inhibition of irrelevant information is thought to occur at the interface between pre-attentive analysis of this information and the more conscious application of selective attentional mechanisms (Dixon 1981).

Towards revising the model

An unexpected result found in some of the work reported here concerns the relationship between schizotypy and attended priming. In both of the studies concerned—Williams (1995) and Beech *et al.* (1991)—*attended repetition* and *attended semantic priming* conditions were part of the experimental design. These were included to see whether there was the usual pattern of attended priming effects, viz faster reaction times to words that were identical or semantically related to words that had been previously presented; these conditions also helped to make it less obvious what the true nature of the experimental task was. In the Beech *et al.* study there was a large positive priming effect in the *attended repetition* condition and a smaller but still significant effect in the *attended semantic* condition, for both the high and the low schizotypal groups. In the Williams study the Low and the Physical Anhedonia subgroups showed these effects. However, although the Ideational/Perceptual Disturbance and Cognitive Disorganization/Social Anhedonia subgroups showed the expected facilitation effects in the *attended semantic priming* condition, in the *attended repetition* condition an inhibition effect was found.

Drawing on the recent evidence, described above, for the effects of conscious influences over automatic processes involved in priming (Dagenbach *et al.* 1989; Seidenberg and McClelland 1989; Besner *et al.* 1990; Friedrich *et al.* 1991) it is suggested that these influences might operate differentially for those exhibiting high levels of positive traits, as against those with low general schizotypy, or a strong presence of physical anhedonia. This could depend on the task, so that inhibitory effects might not have been observed in the Beech *et al.* study because of the nature of the test requirements. Here it will be recalled that in the Williams task the requirements were such that attention would be allocated to orthographic information, and in the Beech *et al.* study to semantic information. The characteristics of the stimuli (the inclusion of lower frequency and abstract words) used in the Williams study may have also further directed attentional resources to orthographic information (Seidenberg and McClelland 1989). Therefore, the simultaneous automatic activation of 'less relevant' semantic information might have interfered with the computation from orthography to phonology (pronunciation) for individuals in the Ideational/Perceptual Disturbance and Cognitive Disorganization/Social Anhedonia subgroups, delaying response times.

The possibility that different attentional foci may produce differential priming effects in relation to schizotypal features indicates that the original 'reduced inhibition' model described at the beginning of this chapter was only a first approximation. The Williams findings would suggest that the model needs to be expanded to incorporate differences in unconscious or pre-attentive processing, as well as in selective inhibitory processes.

CONCLUSIONS

In various studies we have found that clusters of schizotypal subjects who showed elevated scores on the more positive schizotypal features, i.e. ideational, perceptual, and cognitive disorganization, show weakened inhibition or even a facilitation effect in experiments designed to measure cognitive inhibition. In contrast, low schizotypy scorers show expected inhibition effects. A cluster of subjects who showed elevated scores on the negative schizotypal feature of Physical Anhedonia also showed inhibitory effects, suggesting that weakened inhibitory processes are associated with positive schizotypal features. More specifically, as regards the content of the positive symptoms of schizophrenia, we found that material that should have been actively suppressed actually seemed to facilitate the recognition of subsequently presented, semantically related, material in high schizotypes.

Investigation of inhibitory processes in schizophrenic subjects found that facilitatory effects were observed in two clusters of patients: again those with more positive symptoms, viz Reality Distortion and Disorganization clusters. A third group, identified as Episodic—in that this group reported intermittent episodes of primarily positive symptoms—also showed a lack of measured cognitive inhibition, suggesting the latent presence of positive symptoms. In contrast, a fourth group with primarily negative symptoms (psychomotor poverty) showed the presence of intact inhibitory processes. Taken together the findings from these four schizophrenic groups suggest that weakened inhibitory processes are associated with the more positive features of the disorder.

Investigation of the effects of neuroleptics on inhibitory processes suggest that, although these do increase the ability of non-psychotic subjects to effectively screen out distracting information, neuroleptics do not normalize performance in schizophrenic subjects.

Finally in this chapter, we described a model of how hallucinatory experiences may arise. From the observation that distracting information, rather than being unavailable for further processing, in highly schizotypal normal subjects and schizophrenics facilitates a chain of semantic activation, leading to intrusions of 'irrelevant' information into consciousness. Initially this theory was based on a comparatively simple model of information processing involving preconscious spreading activation. However, in that form the model does not take into account conscious task requirements that may play a part in the process of attention. We suggest that any future work in the area should take account of this.

REFERENCES

Allport, D. A. (1980). Attention and performance. In *Cognitive psychology: new directions* (ed. G. Claxton), pp. 112–53. Routledge and Kegan Paul, London.

Andreasen, N. C. (1981). *Scale for the assessment of negative symptoms (SANS)*. University of Iowa, Iowa City.

Andreasen, N. C. (1984). *Scale for the assessment of positive symptoms (SAPS)*. University of Iowa, Iowa City.

Andreasen, N. C. and Olsen, S. (1982). Negative versus positive schizophrenia. Definition and validation. *Archives of General Psychiatry*, 39, 789–94.

Balota, D. A. and Chumbley, J. I. (1984). Are lexical decisions a good measure of lexical access? The role of word frequency in the neglected decision stage. *Journal of Experimental Psychology: Human Perception and Performance*, 10, 340–57.

Beech, A., Baylis, G. C., Smithson. P., and Claridge, G. (1989). Individual differences in schizotypy as reflected in measures of cognitive inhibition. *British Journal of Clinical Psychology*, 28, 117–29.

Beech, A. and Claridge, G. (1987). Individual differences in negative priming: Relations with schizotypal personality traits. *British Journal of Psychology*, 78, 349–56.

Beech, A., Powell, T., McWilliam, J., and Claridge, G. (1989). Evidence of reduced 'cognitive inhibition' in schizophrenia. *British Journal of Clinical Psychology*, **28**, 109–16.

Beech, A., Powell, T. J., McWilliam, J., and Claridge, G. S. (1990). The effect of a small dose of chlorpromazine on a measure of 'cognitive inhibition'. *Personality and Individual Differences*, **11**, 1141–5.

Beech, A., McManus, D., Baylis, G., Tipper, S., and Agar, K. (1991). Individual differences in cognitive processes: Towards an explanation of schizophrenic symptomatology. *British Journal of Psychology*, **82**, 417–26.

Besner, D., Smith, M. C., and MacLeod, C. M. (1990). Visual word recognition: A dissociation of lexical and semantic processing. *Journal of Experimental Psychology: Learning, Memory and Cognition*, **16**, 862–9.

Broadbent, D. E. (1958). *Perception and communication*. Pergamon Press, London.

Broadbent, D. E. (1971). *Decision and stress*. Academic Press, London.

Bullen, J. G. and Hemsley, D. R. (1984). Psychoticism and visual recognition thresholds. *Personality and Individual Differences*, **5**, 735–9.

Bullen, J. G. and Hemsley, D. R. (1987). Schizophrenia: A failure to control the contents of consciousness. *British Journal of Psychology*, **26**, 25–33.

Carr, T. H., and Dagenbach, D. (1990). Semantic priming and repetition priming from masked words: Evidence for a centre-surround attentional mechanism in perceptual recognition. *Journal of Experimental Psychology: Learning, Memory and Cognition*, **16**, 341–50.

Claridge, G. S. and Broks, P. (1984). Schizotypy and hemisphere function. I. Theoretical considerations and the measurement of schizotypy. *Personality and Inidividual Differences*, **5**, 633–48.

Cohen, J. D., Dunbar, K., and McClelland, J. L. (1990). On the control of automatic processes: A parallel distributed account of the Stroop Effect. *Psychological Review*, **82**, 407–528.

Corteen, R. S. and Wood, B. (1972). Automatic responses to shock-associated words in an unattended channel. *Journal of Experimental Psychology*, **94**, 308–13.

Dagenbach, D., Carr, T. H., and Wilhelmsen, A. (1989). Task-induced strategies and near-threshold priming: Conscious influences on unconscious perception. *Journal of Memory and Language*, **28**, 412–43.

Dixon, N. F. (1981). *Preconscious processing*. Wiley, New York.

Friedrich, F. J., Henik, A., and Tzelgov, J. (1991). Automatic processes in lexical access and spreading activation. *Journal of Experimental Psychology: Human Perception and Performance*, **17**, 792–806.

Frith, C. D. (1979). Consciousness, information processing and schizophrenia. *British Journal of Psychiatry*, **134**, 225–35.

Frith, C. D. (1981). Schizophrenia: An abnormality of consciousness? In *Aspects of consciousness, II* (ed. G. Underwood and R. Stevens). Academic Press, London.

Kwapil, T. R., Hegley, D. C., and Chapman, L. J. (1990). Facilitation of word recognition by semantic priming in schizophrenia. *Journal of Abnormal Psychology*, **3**, 215–21.

Liddle, P. F. (1987). The symptoms of chronic schizophrenia. A re-examination of the positive-negative dichotomy. *British Journal of Psychiatry*, **151**, 145–51.

Lowe, D. G. (1979). Strategies, context, and the mechanism of response inhibition. *Memory and Cognition*, **7**, 382–9.

Lowe, D. G. (1985). Further investigations of inhibitory mechanisms in attention. *Memory and Cognition*, **13**, 74–88.

Mackay, D. G. (1973). Aspects of the theory of comprehension. Memory and attention. *Quarterly Journal of Experimental Psychology*, **25**, 22–7.

Marcel, A. J. (1980). Conscious and unconscious recognition of polysemous words:

locating the selecting effects of prior verbal context. In *Attention and performance, VIII.* (ed. R. S. Nickerson), pp. 435–57. Erlbaum Hillsdale, New Jersey.

Marcel, A. J. (1983). Conscious and unconscious perception: Experiments on visual masking and word recognition. *Cognitive Psychology*, 15, 283–300.

Marchbanks, G., and Williams, M. (1971). Factors affecting word selection by schizophrenic patients. *British Journal of Social and Clinical Psychology*, 10, 241–52.

May, C. P., Kane, M. J., and Hasher, L. (1995). Determinants of negative priming. *Psychological Bulletin*, 118, 35–54.

Merritt, R. D., Balogh, D. W., and Leventhal, D. B. (1986). Use of a meta-contrast and para-contrast procedure to assess visual information processing of hypothetically schizotypic college students. *Journal of Abnormal Psychology*, 95, 74–80.

Neely, J. H. (1977). Semantic priming and the retrieval from lexical memory: Roles of inhibitionless spreading activation and limited-capacity attention. *Journal of Experimental Psychology: General*, 106, 226–54.

Neill, W. T. (1977). Inhibitory and facilitatory processes in attention. *Journal of Experimental Psychology: Human Perception and Performance*, 3, 444–50.

Neill, W. T. and Westberry, R. L. (1987). Selective attention and the suppression of cognitive noise. *Journal of Experimental Psychology: Learning, Memory and Cognition*, 13, 327–34.

Posner, M. I. and Boies, S. J. (1971). Components of attention. *Psychological Review*, 78, 391–408.

Rawlings, D. and Claridge, G. (1984). Schizotypy and hemisphere function-III. Performance asymmetries on tasks of letter recognition and local-global processing. *Personality and Individual Differences*, 5, 657–63.

Saccuzzo, D. P., Hirt, M., and Spencer, T. J. (1974). Backward masking as a measure of attention in schizophrenia. *Journal of Abnormal Psychology*, 83, 512–22.

Schvaneveldt, R. N., Meyer, D. E., and Becker, C. A. (1976). Lexical ambiguity, semantic context and visual word recognition. *Journal of Experimental Psychology: Human Perception and Performance*, 2, 243–56.

Schneider, K. (1959). *Clinical psychopathology* (trans. M. W. Hamilton). Grune Stratton, New York.

Schwartz-Place, E. J., and Gilmore, G. C. (1980). Perceptual organisation in schizophrenia. *Journal of Abnormal Psychology*, 89, 409–18.

Seidenberg, M. S. and McClelland, J. L. (1989). A distributed developmental model of word recognition. *Psychological Review*, 96, 523–68.

Tipper, S. P. (1984). Negative priming in visual selective attention. Unpublished D. Phil thesis. University of Oxford.

Tipper, S. P. (1985). The negative priming effect: Inhibitory priming by ignored objects. *Quarterly Journal of Experimental Psychology: Human Experimental Psychology*, 37, 571–90.

van der Heijden, A. H. C. (1981). *Short-term visual information forgetting*. Routledge and Kegan Paul, London.

Underwood, G. (1976). Semantic interference from unattended messages. *British Journal of Psychology*, 67, 327–38.

Williams, L. M. (1995). Further evidence of a multidimensional personality disposition to schizophrenia in terms of cognitive inhibition. *British Journal of Clinical Psychology*, 34, 193–213.

Williams, L. M. (1996). Cognitive inhibition and schizophrenic symptom subgroups. *Schizophrenia Bulletin*, 22, 139–51.

Wishner, J. and Wahl, B. (1974). Dichotic listening in schizophrema. *Journal of Consulting and Clinical Psychology*, 4, 538–46.

5
Semantic activation and preconscious processing in schizophrenia and schizotypy

JULIE L. EVANS

INTRODUCTION

Over a century ago, James (1890) proposed that certain forms of psychopathology could be seen as 'disruptions in the stream of conscious experience'. He elaborated upon the idea by stipulating two essential criteria for normal thought. First, that within each personal consciousness thought is sensibly continuous. Second, that thought is 'interested in some parts of objects to the exclusion of others'. In other words, some kind of inhibitory mechanism allows the normal individual to ignore sensory data that are ambiguous or irrelevant. It appears that both the above criteria are found in the schizophrenic individual, at different levels.

Similar observations have been recorded over the intervening years. For example, Kraepelin (1913) noted that his schizophrenic patients found it impossible to 'keep their attention fixed for any length of time' due to 'mental intrusions'. More recently, Chapman (1966) found that patients complained of difficulty in concentrating on a single item; for example 'I attend to everything at once and as a result I do not attend to anything'. Again, it appears that normal thought processes are disrupted by a clamour of irrelevant thoughts and percepts.

While there is no doubt that the information processing facilities of schizophrenics are in some ways aberrant, there is no general agreement as to the exact nature of the disturbance. Attempts to establish the locus and content of schizophrenic cognition has met with many problems, not least of which is the difficulty of studying cognitive function reliably in patient samples. Despite these many obstacles researchers in this area have attempted to find 'a single cognitive dysfunction from which the various abnormalities resulting in a diagnosis might be derived' (Hemsley 1988). However, many problems occur in tandem with this line of research: heterogeneity of symptomatology; disagreement as to what constitutes a diagnosis of schizophrenia; and a lack of consensus over what constitutes core symptoms of the disorder.

Earlier research in this area was hampered partially by a viewpoint that was descriptive rather than explanatory and which proceeded from the 'abnormal'. Deficits were emphasized and a medical perspective was applied that split the mechanisms of information processing clearly into the arenas of normal and not normal. Any theory of pathological cognition has to account for several observations:

1. Disturbances in information processing are not manifest from birth, in terms of

symptoms, in those who eventually suffer from psychosis—indeed this develops after two decades or so.

2. Individuals suffering from symptoms such as hallucinations do not suffer from them constantly, even when unmedicated.

3. Family studies have shown (for example Kety 1988) that relatives of psychotic patients, whilst eligible for a diagnosis of schizotypal personality disorder, do not themselves suffer from hallucinations and other positive symptoms.

4. Individuals who score highly on personality scales measuring schizotypy show performance similarities to schizophrenic patients on some cognitive tasks (for example, see Beech *et al.* 1989*b*; Lubow *et al.* 1992). Yet, the same individuals do not suffer from schizophrenic symptoms.

From these considerations it is clear that an explanation of schizophrenic cognition must proceed from a perspective of non-pathological information processing and must assume a graded progression from 'normal' to 'abnormal' within the same cognitive architecture.

Over the last thirty years, virtually every stage of information processing has been reported to be dysfunctional in schizophrenics. One pertinent question relating to this vast body of research is whether deficits shown in one area, i.e. short-term memory recall, indicate a basic deficiency at that stage or are a consequence of problems occurring at an earlier information processing stage, perhaps pre-attentively. Failure to take into account the different subtypes of schizophrenia whilst carrying out studies can also result in erroneous conclusions being drawn. For example. Marshall (1973) gave a group of schizophrenics two tasks to complete: card sorting and choice reaction time. From these data he concluded that schizophrenics had a deficit in response selection. Neufeld (1977) attempted a replication of this experiment but analysed his data according to subtypes. He found that the slowness in response selection was only found in the paranoid group and not in all of the schizophrenics.

Course of illness is also a confounding factor. If schizophrenics are not matched for duration of illness and severity of symptomatology, then any results may simply be temporary state effects, rather than being fundamental to the disorder. George and Neufeld (1985) justifiably point out that, drug effects apart, it is difficult to decide what is a symptom and what is a deficit. For example, if hallucinations interfere with a laboratory task designed to test selective attention, does that show a deficit in selective attention? If this is the case, can it really be concluded that selective attention is fundamentally disrupted in schizophrenics? Another weakness of work in this area is the focus on global explanations without attempts to relate models and data to specific symptoms. The experiential aspects of symptoms and their heterogeneity over time within an individual have largely been ignored, except for some notable exceptions (for example J. Chapman 1966).

The result of this narrow research focus has been a plethora of findings couched in experimental terms that bear little relation to the syndrome under investigation and have little explanatory power. As Anscombe (1987) points out, 'the neat lawns of cognitive psychology seem far removed from the jungle of paranoid symptomatology'. What many of the researchers fail to do is relate their findings to the cognitive processes of change that result in and maintain the symptoms of schizophrenia; although there are some notable exceptions, discussed below.

More recently, some researchers have abandoned their attempt to explain the entire syndrome of schizophrenia and have instead focused upon understanding particular symptoms such as hallucinations and delusions. This approach has as its starting point relevant models of non-pathological cognition. For example, Bentall and co-workers (1985, 1990) look at the stages and processes by which we form beliefs and uses this as a starting point to explore the formation of abnormal beliefs (delusions). Slade and Bentall (1988) also attempt to understand auditory hallucinations by looking at the conditions which affect the experience of hallucinations in non-clinical subjects. This approach has a two-fold advantage: first, it provides an explanation of the graded process of change discussed above; secondly, it allows researchers to adopt a continuum approach to the study of these cognitive changes, thereby making the use of non-clinical groups to study clinical symptoms a more logical proposition.

Accompanying this newer trend is the application of paradigms and explanations that predict superior performance in schizophrenics and schizotypal subjects, even though the underlying mechanism of the effect may be deviant. The work in question mostly attempts to explain positive symptom aspects of schizophrenia; examples from the area of selective attention are 'negative priming' (for example Beech and Claridge 1987; Beech *et al.* 1989a) and 'latent inhibition' (for example Baruch *et al.* 1988), which are discussed elsewhere in this book.

Some experimenters have drawn upon theories concerning the role of semantic activation (Maher 1983; Maher and Ross 1984) and preconscious processing in relation to the positive symptoms of schizophrenia. Activation of stored memories and their consequent experience in consciousness, have long been of interest in the field of psychology, and the mechanism and limitations of this activation have been extensively studied by cognitive psychologists (for example Meyer and Schvaneveldt 1971; Collins and Loftus 1975; Neely 1976, 1991).

Psychopathologists (for example Frith 1979; Maher 1983; Maher and Ross 1986) have been more concerned with studies of these same mechanisms mediating experiences that are involuntary, alien, intrusive, and unwanted, and found in those suffering from psychotic disorders as hallucinations, for example voices. In his seminal paper, Frith (1979) proposed that the positive symptoms of schizophrenia could be understood as the lessening of the suppression of preconscious activation. As a consequence, irrelevant, but automatically activated, items of knowledge become available to conscious awareness, and are then interpreted as voices. Delusions may arise as an attempt to explain these anomalous experiences. The inability to exclude preconscious information would prove particularly detrimental in ambiguous situations or upon presentation of ambiguous stimuli.

If normal thought and inner speech are a result of knowledge activation in memory, then there are three possible explanations for the disruption of the above processes in schizophrenia. First, the memory store itself is grossly damaged, producing the kind of cognitive deficits seen in patients with neuropsychological problems. However, evidence for this in schizophrenic patients is sparse and rather contradictory (see McKenna *et al.* (1994) for a recent review). Secondly, the process of knowledge activation is somehow aberrant, though not always dysfunctional, in clinical groups and highly schizotypal subjects. Thirdly, there is a progressive change in the sensory processing experiences of schizophrenic patients, which causes important changes in the structures of memory over time. This chapter will discuss the mechanism of action related to the latter two explanations and review evidence relating to differences in the activation of memory and its consequences in clinical and non-clinical populations.

BACKGROUND

One of the major characteristics of normal representations of knowledge is their instantiation within networks of related ideas acquired through experience with the real world. Knowledge may be activated by the processing of external stimuli or via the mechanism of spreading activation from a related knowledge area; at the same time, irrelevant information may be actively inhibited. Successful use of the networks, therefore, and the knowledge contained within them require processes of both inhibition and activation. An impairment of the inhibitory and activational processes could result in a 'leaking' of irrelevant themes in normal discourse and thought, experienced as hallucinations in schizophrenic patients.

Problems in the activation of related knowledge can also have greater long-term effects upon an individual. We carry with us a set of expectancies—a rough blueprint or set of procedural rules of what should happen in a given situation, based upon prior experience, sometimes encapsulated within schemas. These expectancies influence our behaviour and also our perception of that event.

This type of interactive operation has been given different names in psychology, depending upon the particular context and the level of explanation in which it takes place: 'pigeonholing' (Broadbent 1977); stereotyping (Tajfel 1982); and concept formation (Bruner *et al.* 1956; Rosch 1975). All these operations are tools that enable us to make sense and structure of a world that is full of potential 'noise' and ambiguity; they also reduce demands on an information processing system with limited conscious resources. Knowledge stored in semantic memory is an essential part of these operations, but only if it is accurate and up to date. If our view of the world becomes subtly distorted, we may readjust the way our knowledge is organized. We modify our expectancies and schemas if the old ones no longer explain or are continuous with our everyday experience; consequently, we change the connections and relationships between knowledge stored and activated in long-term memory.

For example, some small change in an individual's sensory processing may result in other people's faces looking different and strange. The behaviour towards others may change as an attempt is made to confirm or deny this feeling; he or she may stare excessively at people in close proximity; for example on public transport, in work, etc. This kind of behaviour may result in others initially moving away, feeling uncomfortable, or staring back because the other person is behaving in a socially unacceptable manner. After some time, the individual may actually *enter* social situations with the *set idea* that others will look at him (and they will because he *is* acting strangely!) and then selectively filter and seek out events or stimuli that confirm these expectancies. The final consequence would be a further strengthening of 'appropriate' memories and associations and the ignoring of any other, more rational, explanations for the experience. A good example of this process comes from the report of a patient in a study by Jorgensen and Jensen (1994) in which the phenomenology of the schizophrenic's predelusional state of mind was investigated:

First I heard a whistle, then a distant mumble and finally more voices talking about me. It was like a dream or rather a nightmare. I did not understand what was going on and could not make it stop, but soon it became very clear to me. I was being examined by the Mafia.

This patient clearly describes the progression of a changed sensory experience, causing initially fear and confusion, but finally being resolved by adopting another expectancy set (which could be labelled here a delusion), that can explain the anomalous experience. The two processes, of altered experience and expectancies stored in long-term memory that direct behaviour, form a parasitic relationship with each other; the end result is a full-blown paranoid delusion. Garety (1991) illustrates this attentional bias effect in a case study she describes; here the schizophrenic patient was found to be more likely to interpret ambiguous speech in a hostile way, because this was more contiguous with her particular delusion. Anscombe (1987) proposes that in schizophrenia, the capturing of attention is externally controlled, which results in a radically changed experience of the world. He also suggest that schizophrenics are at 'the mercy of their preattentive analysers', which in turn are directed by schemas in long-term memory. Pre-attentive analysers, he continues, are heavily biased to perceiving threatening stimuli in the environment, because 'it is no doubt important to attend to the eternally beautiful and the eternally true. But it is more important not to be eaten!' (Fodor 1985). The latter statement could certainly be applied to the formation of paranoid delusions. While the initial dysfunction may have been perceptual, the parallel processes that are currently held to be representative of cognitive mechanisms result in a virus-like spread of the original deficit.

Maher (1970, 1974, 1988a, b, c, 1990, 1993) emphasizes the role of anomalous experience as a starting point for more cognitive symptoms in schizophrenia, i.e. delusions. Indeed, he categorically states that delusions are the consequence of normal cognitive processes invoked to explain aberrant sensory experiences and that anomalous experience presents a problem to be explained for the person experiencing it. Explanations of altered experiences bring relief, he says, even if the explanation is not fully adequate to the situation:

A partially defective or incomplete explanation is better than no explanation at all ...

[and once established] dissonant new data are disturbing and *will be either ignored or reinterpreted to fit the explanation*. Data that are consistent with the explanation give relief and are therefore sought after.

In other words, these individuals will adopt an attentional bias, as a result of changes in long-term memory, that filters out anything that is not confirmatory evidence.

Many reports by schizophrenics of their early pre-psychotic experiences lend support to Maher's thesis that the perceptual experience of the individual is different. Several good examples have come from patients in a study by Jorgensen and Jensen (1994):

1. 'The world had changed and I thought of my self as a film actor . . .'
2. 'It all seemed a bit unrealistic. I could not decide whether I myself or my parents had changed. But I observed them more carefully than before and still something slipped my attention. I could not concentrate on anything and this was new to me. It was like a dream you know. You participate but you do not know what to do any more you cannot make it stop.'
3. 'For some time I thought the world had changed and that bewildered me. I felt my friends had become hostile to me and sometimes even planned to poison me. But you cannot decide . . .'

There is also confirmation of Maher's idea that delusional explanations of anomalous experience have positive benefits for the experiencer: 'It is so comfortable to become paranoid when you have insoluble problems. Everything around you becomes so simple and I have the key for understanding the world.' According to Jorgensen and Jensen (1994) the formation of beliefs to rationalize a highly altered world-experience brings to the person a sense of freedom and the ability to cope with the complexity of their new world.

Indeed, the beneficial aspects of what we would now call positive symptoms have been reported, but largely ignored, by most researchers since Esquirol described some patients who actually liked having hallucinations, as it made them feel more important, privileged, and protected. In a recent study, Miller *et al.* (1993) investigated hallucinations in fifty psychotic patients (12 medicated, 38 not) using semi-structured interviews. They attempted to elicit details of 12 phenomenological characteristics of hallucinations and also the patients' attitudes towards their experiences. The authors discovered that 52 per cent of their subjects reported positive aspects of their hallucinations, with 12 per cent wanting to keep their hallucinations; a further 20 per cent also wanted to do so if they could control when their hallucinations occurred. Some comments on these positive aspects of auditory hallucinations are organized by the authors under different themes, as follows:

1. Soothing: 'In a way if I can keep it low, it's relaxing, like having a radio on.'
2. Companionship: 'Recently I'd ask all the time to hear it. I was lonely, I wanted some friends.'

3. Defensive/Protective: 'I hallucinate shooting my dad instead of actually shooting him. It helped vent my feelings towards dad; I'm not in prison ... The voice was like my guardian angel, if my father was getting ready to do something to me, they'd wake me up.'

4. Performance: 'When I do greeting cards sometimes the voices make out the verses. They're helpful, they never interfere ...'

These comments reinforce the theory that altered sensory experiences which occur in schizophrenia generate explanations, the results of which cause long-term changes in memory. However, as can be seen by the examples quoted above, in some cases the process does not always produce negative reactions in the person experiencing them.

EVIDENCE IN SCHIZOPHRENICS

Several researchers have demonstrated specifically that schizophrenics have no problems in the area of fast automatic processing of information; it is the controlled serial type of processing that seems to be disrupted (for example Neuchterlein and Dawson 1984; Granholm *et al.* 1991). Indeed Callaway and Nagdhi (1982) conclude that 'in schizophrenics only the controlled serial system seems disordered. The automatic parallel system remains normal or may even appear supernormal.' Several researchers have demonstrated superior performance in schizophrenic patients in tasks relating to automatic activation of semantic memory compared with psychiatric and normal control groups (Manshreck *et al.* 1988; Kwapil *et al.* 1990, Spitzer *et al.* 1993a, 1993b, 1994).

   Manshreck *et al.* used a small group of thought disordered (TD) and non-thought disordered (NTD) schizophrenics, comparing their performance with non-psychotic and normal control groups in a semantic priming task. Subjects were asked to respond in a lexical decision task (LDT), to three categories of pairs of letter strings:

(1) associated word pairs, for example BREAD—BUTTER;

(2) non-associated word pairs, for example WATER—BUTTER;

(3) word non-word pairs, for example BREAD—UMPUL.

The authors predicted that the TD group would demonstrate greater semantic priming because of greater intrusions into speech and thought, which they held to be caused by semantic activation that was of a greater magnitude and lasted longer. The semantic priming effect was calculated by subtracting the mean reaction time (RT) for the associated word pairs from the mean RT for the non-associated word pairs. Manshreck *et al.* found that the schizophrenic group not only demonstrated a larger priming effect, but usually were also faster than the two control groups. They concluded that their data supported the theory that schizophrenics either have a disruption in the processes of inhibition that are required to terminate the active state of the semantic network in normal cognition, or that the activated associations decay less rapidly. The consequence of either explanation, according to Manshreck *et al.* is an increased potential for the intrusion of irrelevant and redundant activations into thought and language, which is not present under very controlled experimental conditions. The authors claim that 'the language anomalies that contribute to the diagnosis of thought disorder in schizophrenia are related to deviations in the processes that mediate associational activation and/or inhibition'. Outside the laboratory, super- or over-active automatic activation of knowledge in long term memory, which is not suppressed within the information processing system, results in the erroneous 'leaking' of these preconscious activations into conscious awareness.

However, other researchers (Chapin *et al.* 1992; Spitzer *et al.* 1993*a*, 1994) highlight the very small numbers involved in Manschreck *et al.*'s study and plead caution with regard to the generalization of these findings, especially concerning the faster reaction times of the TD schizophrenics.

Kwapil *et al.* used a different technique to demonstrate enhanced semantic activation in a group of schizophrenic patients. Because of problems with medication, generally slowing down performance on cognitive tasks, Kwapil *et al.* used accuracy measurements in an LDT. Along with appropriate clinical and non-clinical control groups, schizophrenics performed a priming task with associated, non-associated, and neutral conditions. Subjects were presented with pairs of letter strings and asked to make a lexical decision to the second of those letter strings. However, while the prime word was clearly visible, the overall accuracy of the associated and neutral items for each subject was attenuated to 50 per cent. This was titrated on an individual basis, being achieved by the deactivation of a portion of the pixels of light that composed the words on the screen. Facilitation was measured as the difference score between the number of correct recognitions of targets preceded by an associated prime and the number of correct recognitions of targets preceded by a neutral prime. Inhibition was calculated in the same way by subtracting the accuracy score for associated items from the score for non-associated items.

Kwapil *et al.* (1990) demonstrate that the mean facilitation effect for the schizophrenic group (18.4 s) was twice that of the clinical (9.4 s) and non-clinical (7.3 s) groups. There were no differences between the groups in terms of inhibition. While Kwapil *et al.* agree that their data support other findings and theories related to elevated semantic priming effects in those suffering from schizophrenia, they are not able to distinguish between several explanations for the effect. They state that 'It is unclear whether these [sic] are accounted for by a stronger activation or a delayed activation of associates, a greater persistence of associates, or a defect in the inhibition of associates.'

A study that attempts to distinguish between theories of greater activation or weakened inhibition of semantic knowledge has been carried out by Spitzer, *et al.* (1994). Earlier studies (Spitzer *et al.* 1993*b*) discovered a tendency for normal subjects to suppress phonologically related word associations under certain boundary conditions. They discovered that, unlike semantic priming, at a short stimulus onset asynchrony (SOA) of (200 ms) phonological priming had an inhibitory effect upon target recognition and a facilitative effect at a long SOA (700 ms). Spitzer *et al.* (1994) relate this to findings that suggest a failure in schizophrenic patients of fast-acting inhibitory processes which have been held to be responsible for positive symptoms (for example Frith 1979; Beech and Claridge 1987; Bullen and Hemsley 1987; Hemsley 1992). In their study, Spitzer *et al.* made two main predictions that:

1. TD patients would show a larger semantic priming effect compared with non-TD and control patients (thereby directly replicating the findings of Manshreck *et al.* (1988)).

2. TD patients, unlike controls, would demonstrate a phonological priming effect (especially at short SOAs, because of weakened automatic inhibitory processes) which are not present in the other subjects.

Their data essentially replicated the earlier findings of Manshreck *et al.* of a greater semantic priming effect in the TD group compared with controls; but did so in a larger sample (36 as opposed to 12). However, Manshreck *et al.*'s finding of faster reaction times in TD patients in the related condition and compared with all other groups, was not replicated. In fact, Spitzer *et al.* found that the RTs of the patients were significantly greater than those of controls, which indicates that the greater semantic priming in the TD group may be an artefact. The authors refute this explanation by pointing out that the data in their study are in line with three other studies (Kwapil *et al.* 1991; Spitzer *et al.* 1993*a,b*). The latter two studies showed (a) semantic priming in schizophrenic patients under short SOAs (200 ms) when it was not present in controls; and (b) the same effect in TD patients compared with non-TD and control patients. The authors claim that their results show that 'activation spreads faster and further through a presupposed network (for example from *lemon* via *sour* to *sweet*) in schizophrenic patients than it does in normals. They also point out that if the differences between the groups were due to similar differences in RTs, the pattern of these differences would be similar. However, the major differences in priming are between the TD and non-TD groups, with no significant difference between the latter and the controls. But, the pattern of overall RTs is very different: controls were much faster (700 ms) than non-TDs (1050 ms) and TD patients (1187 ms).

Regarding the phonological priming, the main result was that there is no phonological inhibition in the TD patients compared with the other groups, as predicted. That is, TD patients showed an average of 39 ms phonological priming), compared with the non-TD group (–17 ms) and the healthy control group (–8 ms). Taken in conjunction with the previous findings that in normal subjects phonological inhibition occurs at short SOAs, then the authors claim that 'the phenomenon is most likely due to an automated process'. Interestingly enough, none of the patients on examination showed evidence of any clang associations.

Spitzer *et al.* (1994) conclude that they are unable to decide from their study whether thought disorder in schizophrenics is a consequence of 'the activation or disinhibition of semantic associational networks, which can be detected using the semantic priming phenomenon'. They conclude that this line of investigation needs to be followed up, especially regarding the time course of inhibition and activation. While the experiments described above provide firm evidence for the 'supernormal' automatic processing in schizophrenics suggested by Callaway and Naghdi (1982), the experiments do not directly test the hypothesis that positive symptoms are a consequence of *preconscious* intrusions into conscious awareness, as proposed by Frith (1979) and Maher (1983), for example. Spitzer *et al.*'s findings do provide evidence for some kind of dysfunction in the automatic inhibitory processes, thought to be a normal concomitant of semantic activation. Schizophrenic patients displaying positive symptomatology are thought to possess a superfluous awareness of preconscious activation, due to either faster activation or an inefficient inhibitory mechanism. A consequence of this dysfunction has been held to be responsible for the enhanced semantic priming demonstrated by schizophrenic patients in highly controlled laboratory conditions; the same mechanism in uncontrolled conditions is thought to be responsible for positive symptoms.

One of the problems of experimentally demonstrating enhanced preconscious processing in schizophrenic patients is the arduous and lengthy procedures involved in threshold assessment. Research in this area has therefore looked to other non-clinical groups (such as highly schizotypal individuals) to investigate more directly the link between preconscious processing and cognitive changes relating to positive symptoms. These will be discussed in the next section.

PRECONSCIOUS PROCESSING AND SCHIZOTYPY

Because of the problems encountered with cognitive experimental studies using clinical groups, many researchers now utilize alternative subject groups to investigate aspects of schizophrenia and associated disorders (Launay and Slade 1981 Claridge 1987; Chapman *et al.* 1975, 1978; Chapman and Chapman 1987; Raine 1991). As Claridge (1987) states, 'psychotic characteristics are not the prerogative of classically diagnosable psychotic patients but form, instead, part of the array of psychological and biological features that impart individual variation to the human species'. The background and evidence for this type of research is outlined elsewhere in this book. It is sufficient to note here that there are healthy individuals who share similar, but diluted, cognitive and personality characteristics with schizophrenic patients. Furthermore, these individuals can be selected on the basis of their high scores on the schizotypy scales described in Chapter 2.

Maher (1983) states explicitly that he believes that 'the pathology of schizophrenia involves an inability to exclude from intrusion into consciousness, material from either external stimuli or internally stored associations . . . these are normally excluded because of their irrelevance to ongoing activity'. Whereas the feature to which Maher refers may be disruptive in the actual clinical state, it could be argued that an 'enhanced' preconscious activation of knowledge could be advantageous and facilitatory under certain boundary conditions, even in schizophrenics, as the experiments discussed in the previous section would suggest.

A very direct test of enhanced preconscious activation that could be expected to produce similar effects is what cognitive psychologists call Semantic Activation Without Conscious Identification (SAWCI). The involuntary activation of stored memories and their consequent experience in consciousness has been studied by cognitive psychologists in indirect and sometimes controversial ways. A typical paradigm that has been used with some success is to present a subject with a stimulus which they are not able to consciously report (thereby stimulating preconscious activation of memories) and record the effect of this upon a stimulus of which the subject is conscious. What is being observed in this type of paradigm is the effect of the first (unconscious) stimulus upon the second (conscious) one. The results are normally measured in an indirect way such as facilitation or inhibition. In the visual mode of presentation, the paradigm most used is a priming task where subjects have to make a lexical decision.

In view of our seemingly limited capacity to process information, it is a generally accepted view by cognitive psychologists that not all stimuli impinging on our sense receptors are available for our conscious inspection. The central question concerning the fate of these stimuli is directed at the *appropriate level of analysis they reach within the information processing system* (i.e. graphemic, phonemic, or semantic), while still remaining *unavailable* to conscious awareness. The LDT provides a way of testing the assumption that undetected stimuli do activate stored knowledge. When using supraliminal stimuli in an LDT, the facilitated recognition of the target by the prime is thought to operate via some mechanism of automatic spreading activation in semantic memory. If the first stimulus is undetected and the facilitation effect is still observed, then this demonstrates that the undetected stimulus was able to activate semantic knowledge and release that information into the information processing system without the knowledge ever becoming available to consciousness.

Problems have occurred using this technique to investigate SAWCI, mainly that of ensuring that the prime is undetectable to the subject. However, more recent studies have shown definitively that SAWCI can be reliably demonstrated, but only if the correct procedure is followed while assessing an individual's threshold of detectability, and if the equipment used is capable of presenting stimuli at such minimal exposure times (for example 10 ms). (See Dagenbach *et al.* 1989); Kemp-Wheeler and Hill (1988); Greenwald *et al.* (1989); and Merikle and Reingold (1990) for reviews of this area.)

To summarize, the theoretical implications underpinning SAWCI are that, in normal cognition, not all activated semantic knowledge is available to consciousness, but that, once activated, this knowledge may facilitate detection or recognition of semantic associates. What is occurring with the SAWCI effect is a dissociation between the activation of knowledge and a person's awareness of that knowledge. An analogous example is the demonstration of prosopagnosic patients showing implicit knowledge of familiar faces (De Haan *et al.* 1992)

Applied to schizophrenia, the argument would be that positive symptomatology, but not negative, entails a greater than normal awareness of the preconscious activation of knowledge. By extrapolation, we would expect that normal subjects high on schizotypal features, thought to correspond to the positive symptomatology of schizophrenia, would show a similar effect. Here it should be noted that recent studies suggest that a 'positive symptom' component can be isolated in schizotypy scales (see Chapter 2); these are the scales of interest in the experiments described below.

RECENT EXPERIMENTAL EVIDENCE

The author has carried out a number of experiments (Evans 1992) using the SAWCI priming paradigm, with two aims. First, to establish that SAWCI can be demonstrated using the procedure adopted and, secondly, to investigate individual differences in the effect as related to schizotypy. A small preliminary experiment—replicating one of Marcel's (1983)—asked subjects to perform a LDT after an initial threshold assessment. In the threshold assessment, subjects were presented with a blank card or a card with a word on it. All words were matched for frequency and word length with those used in the experimental trials; stimuli were presented tachistoscopically. Subliminality of the stimuli was said to be achieved when the subject was unable to distinguish between the two stimuli. A descending staircase method was used and appropriate signal detection measures taken (see Kemp-Wheeler and Hill (1988) for details of this procedure). Subjects then went on to complete the LDT, where they were presented with three categories of letter strings: related, unrelated, and word—non-word pairs, the prime in each case being presented 10 per cent below assessed threshold. Schizotypal status was measured using the CSTQ (Bentall *et al.* 1989).

Analysis of the data showed a highly significant priming effect, which was not correlated with signal detection measures of sensitivity. Correlating the amount of priming (i.e. mean RT for unrelated words minus mean RT for related words) with schizotypy showed a significant relationship with STA ($r = 0.59$) and a nearly significant relationship with the Launay-Slade Hallucination Scale (LSHS). However, other scales of interest, Pereptual Abberation (PAb) and Magical Ideation (Mgl), did not show the expected correlation. Although the number of subjects (12) involved here was small, it did fulfil the first aim of the experiment, which was to demonstrate the SAWCI effect. Concerning the personality variables, the prediction of positive correlations between schizotypy and priming was partially upheld, prompting further investigation with larger subject groups.

The second experiment used an identical procedure to the first, but stimuli were presented on an oscilloscope fitted with a fast phosphor screen. This enabled subject time of the experiment to be radically reduced. Subjects again completed the CSTQ. Of 25 subjects, all showed a reliable priming effect (mean 32 ms) and again, there was no correlation between signal detection measures of prime sensitivity. As predicted from the first experiment, there was a significant relationship between the amount of priming and subjects' schizotypy, this time with the PAb scale ($r = 0.50$; $p < 0.02$). Correlations with other scales of interest (STA, LSHS, and Mgl) were in the same direction but non-significant.

Before uncritically accepting these results as evidence of the effects sought, a possible source of artefact in the data needs to be considered. It could be argued that, on some trials, some subjects may have slipped over their threshold, the primes becoming clearly visible; it might have been these trials that were responsible for the overall priming effect found (B. Rosner, personal communication). A further experiment was therefore carried out, to see if subliminal and supraliminal priming differed in priming magnitude, as would be expected according to Rosner's argument. Results showed that the mean magnitude of priming (22 ms) was no greater when the prime was clearly visible than when it was not visible at all. It can be concluded with some certainty, then, that the priming shown in the earlier experiments was not artefactual, but did come from a number of undetectable primes. Regarding personality measures in this experiment, none of the scales correlated significantly with the amount of supraliminal priming. However, the correlation with PAb approached significance and, interestingly, was of *negative* sign ($r = -0.50$).

Using a somewhat larger sample, these effects were further examined, with the following results. In the subliminal, but *not* the supraliminal, priming condition significant priming was observed, with the majority of subjects (18 out of 20) showing an effect. Concerning the relationship with schizotypy, these replicated and strengthened the findings of the previous experiments. For subliminal priming there were significant positive correlations between the amount of priming and several scales of 'positive' schizotypy—STA, PAb, HOP, and LSHS—with a similar, but non-significant, trend in the same direction for STA. Supraliminal priming showed a significant relationship with STA, but in the opposite, negative direction ($r = -0.53$, $P < 0.02$). The latter result therefore showed further, this time sigificant, evidence that when primes are presented above the conscious threshold the performance of highly schizotypal subjects is actually disrupted rather than facilitated.

DISCUSSION

The purpose of this chapter was to present a review of the theories and evidence that positive symptoms in schizophrenia implicate mechanisms concerned with semantic activation and the structure of long-term memory. The proposal was that the occurrence of hallucinations and other positive symptoms is related to the 'leaking' of preconscious activations, which normally need to be suppressed, into current awareness. This kind of process is assumed to operate on a network that is altered in terms of structure or associative connections, consequent upon changes in the individual's sensory experience in real-world situations. Evidence for the former seems to have been reliably demonstrated by a number of researchers (for example Manschreck *et al.* 1988; Kwapil *et al.* 1990; Spitzer *et al.* 1993*a,b*, 1994). However, none of those studies is able to distinguish between explanations of the effects found, according to over-activation or to dysfunction in inhibitory processes in the semantic network.

It was suggested here that the same processes that are responsible for clinical symptoms are also responsible for the superior semantic priming found in the schizophrenic groups, but that evidence for this is only found in highly controlled environments, such as laboratory settings. Even then, several difficulties attend the use of patents in studies involving complex cognitive tasks, and in experiments reported here a direct test of the preconscious theory was carried out in healthy individuals who were assessed for their schizotypal profile. The rationale for these studies was that highly schizotypal subjects would also have greater access to preconscious activation, but in a diluted and, compared with schizophrenics, 'non-harmful' form. These healthy schizotypes would therefore also show superior performance on tasks where successful completion required use of preconscious activation.

Using the priming paradigm to investigate individual differences in SAWCI, it was demonstrated, as predicted, that the higher the individual's rating on 'positive' schizotypy, the greater the degree of subliminal priming. In contrast, supraliminal primes, with longer exposure time, resulted in more information flooding the network and consequently more partial activation of large bits of knowledge. In the latter case, active inhibition is required to generate the correct output; this may be weakened in high schizotypes, accounting for the negative correlations found between the priming effect and schizotypy in the supraliminal condition.

Although it is argued that schizophrenics and healthy schizotypes are cognitively similar, there are several ways in which they might differ from each other. Perhaps the schizophrenic inherits an information processing system that is simply more dysfunctional, in terms of its tendency towards activation of semantic knowledge. Changes in associative connections might then be formed at an earlier developmental stage and feed back into the cognitive system, with an escalating effect. Alternatively, the *content* of information stored, and therefore available for later activation, might be more negative in the schizophrenic or potential schizophrenic. Or both might be true, differences between the schizotype and the schizophrenic being due to the former growing up in a more protected, tolerant environment. The deleterious effects of the schizotype's unusual information processing system might then never emerge, or, if it does become apparent, it might do so more adaptively, for example as creative forms of expression (see Chapter 12 for some further discussion).

Regardless of how factors influence preconscious activations to produce 'state', as opposed to 'trait', effects, the essential alteration—that of enhanced access to the products of these activations—should be found in all people who might be assumed to share the same genotype. This includes, among others, high schizotypes, schizophrenics, and the relatives of such individuals. The data reported in this chapter go some way towards demonstrating a trait effect in the first group and support the proposal of a link between the cognitive processing styles of highly schizotypal individuals and those suffering from clinical psychosis. It would therefore seem worth trying to replicate the findings in other target groups. Finally, the work also emphasizes the importance and usefulness of applying paradigms developed in normal cognitive psychology to the study of pathological cognition.

REFERENCES

Anscombe, R. (1987). The disorder of consciousness in schizophrenia. *Schizophrenia Bulletin*, **13**, 241–260.

Baruch, J., Hemsley, D. R., and Gray, J. A. (1988). Latent inhibition and 'psychotic proneness' in normal subjects. *Personality and Individual Differences*, **9**, 771–83.

Beech, A. and Claridge, G. (1987). Individual differences in negative priming: relations with schizotypal personality traits. *British Journal of Psychology*, **78**, 349–56.

Beech, A., Baylis, G. C., Smithson, P., and Claridge G. (1989*a*). Individual differences in schizotypy as reflected in measures of cognitive inhibition. *British Journal of Clinical Psychology*, **28**, 117–29.

Beech, A. R., Powen, J. J., McNill on, J., and Claridge, G. (1989*b*). Evidence of reduced 'cognitive inhibition' in schizophrenia. *British Journal of Clinical Psychology*, **28**, 109–16.

Bentall, R. P. (1990). The illusion of reality: A review and integration of psychological research on hallucinations. *Psychological Bulletin*, **107**, 82–95.

Bentall, R. P. and Slade, P. D. (1985). Reality testing and auditory hallucinations: A signal detection analysis. *British Journal of Clinical Psychology*, **27**, 303–24.

Broadbent, D. E. (1977). The hidden pre-attentive processes. *American Psychologist*, **32**, 109–18.

Bentall, R. P., Claridge. G., and Slade. P. D. (1989). The multidimensional nature of schizotypal traits: a factor analytic study with normal subjects. *British Journal of Clinical Psychology*, **28**, 363–75.

Bruner, J. S., Goodnow, J. J, and Austin, J. G. (1956). *A study of thinking*. Wiley London.

Bullen, J. and Hemsley, D. (1987). Schizophrenia: a failure to control the contents of consciousness? *British Journal of Clinical Psychology*, **26**, 25–33.

Callaway, E. and Naghdi, S. (1982). An information-processing model for schizophrenia. *Archives of General Psychiatry*, **39**, 339–47.

Chapin, K., Vann, L., Lycaki, H., Josef, N., and Meyendorff, E. (1989). Investigation of the associative network in schizophrenia using the semantic priming paradigm. *Schizophrenia Research*, **2**, 355–60.

Chapman, J. (1966). The early symptoms of schizophrenia. *British Journal of Psychiatry*, **112**, 225–51.

Chapman, L. J. and Chapman, J. P. (1987). The search for symptoms predictive of schizophrenia. *Schizophrenia Bulletin*, **13**, 497–503.

Chapman, L. J., Chapman, J. P., and Raulin, M. (1975). Scales for physical and social anhedonia. *Journal of Abnormal Psychology*, 85, 374–82.

Chapman, L. J., Chapman, J. P., and Raulin, M. L. (1978). Body-image aberration in schizophrenia. *Journal of Abnormal Psychology*, 87, 399–407.

Claridge, G. (1987). 'The schizophrenias as nervous types' revisited. *British Journal of Psychiatry*, 151, 735–43.

Collins, A. M. and Loftus, E. F. (1975). A spreading-activation theory of semantic processing. *Psychological Review*, 82, 407–28.

Dagenbach, D., Carr, T., and Wilhemsen, A. (1989). Task-induced strategies and near-threshold priming: conscious influences on unconscious perception. *Journal of Memory and Language*, 28, 412–43.

De Haan, E., Bauer, R., and Greeve, K. (1992). Behavioural and physiological evidence for covert face recognition in a prosopagnosic patient. *Cortex*, 28, 77–95.

Evans J. L. (1992). Schizotypy and preconscious processing. Unpublished D.Phil thesis. University of Oxford.

Fodor, J. A. (1985). Précis of the modularity of mind. *Behavioural and Brain Sciences*, 8, 1–5.

Frith, C. D. (1979). Consciousness, information processing and schizophrenia. *British Journal of Psychiatry*, 134, 225–35.

Garety, P. (1991). Reasoning and delusions. *British Journal of Psychiatry*, 159, 14–18.

George, L. and Neufeld, R. J. (1985). Cognition and symptomatology in schizophrenia. *Schizophrenia Bulletin*, 11, 264–85.

Granholm, E., Arsenow R. F., and Marder S. R. (1991). Controlled information processing resources and the development of automatic detection responses in schizophrenia. *Journal of Abnormal Psychology*, 100, 22–30.

Greenwald, A. G., Klinger, M. R., and Liu, T. J. (1989). Unconscious processing of dichoptically masked words. *Memory and Cognition*, 17, 35–47.

Hemsley, D. R. (1988). Psychological models of schizophrenia. In *Adult abnormal psychology* (ed. E. Miller and P. J. Cooper), pp. 101–27. Churchill Livingstone, London.

Hemsley, D. R. (1993). Perception and cognition in schizoprenia. In *Schizophrenia: origins, processes, treatment and outcome.* (eds R. L. Cromwell and C. R. Snyder), pp. 135–50. Oxford University Press.

James, W. (1890). *The principles of psychology.* McMillan, London.

Jorgensen, P. and Jensen, J. (1994). How to understand the formation of delusional beliefs: A proposal. *Psychopathology*, 27, 64–72.

Kemp-Wheeler, S. M. and Hill, A. B. (1988). Semantic priming without awareness: some methodological considerations and replications. *Quarterly Journal of Experimental Psychology*, A40, 671–92.

Kety, S. (1988). Schizophrenic illness in the families of schizophrenic adoptees: Findings from the Danish Study. *Schizophrenia Bulletin*, 14, 217–22.

Kraepelin, E. (1913). *Dementia praecox and paraphrenia* (Translated R. M. Barclay, 1971, from Kraepelin's textbook, 8th edn). Kreiger Huntington, New York.

Kwapil, T. R., Hegley, D. C., Chapman, L. J., and Chapman, J. P. (1990). Facilitation of word recognition by semantic priming in schizophrenia. *Journal of Abnormal Psychology*, 99, 215–21.

Launay, G. and Slade, P. D. (1981). The measurement of hallucinatory predisposition in male and female prisoners. *Personality and Individual Differences*, 2, 221–34.

Lubow, R. E., Ingberg-Sachs, Y., Zalstein-Orda, N., and Gewirtz, J. C. (1992). Latent inhibition in law and high 'psychotic-prone' normal subjects. *Personality and Individual Differences*, 13, 563–72.

McKenna P., Mortimer, A., and Hodges, J. (1994). Semantic memory and schizophrenia.

In *The neuropsychology of schizophrenia* (ed. A. S. David and J. Cutting), pp. 163–78. Erlbaum, Hove.

Maher B. A. (1970). The psychology of delusions. Paper presented at the meeting of the American Psychological Association, Miami Beach, Florida.

Maher, B. A. (1974). Delusional thinking and perceptual disorder. *Journal of Individual Psychology*, 30, 98–113.

Maher, B. A. (1983). A tentative theory of schizophrenic utterance. In *Progress in experimental personality research* (ed. B. A. Maher and W. B. Maher), Vol. 12. Academic Press, New York.

Maher, B. A. (1988a). Anomalous experience and delusional thinking: the logic of explanations. In *Delusional beliefs*, (ed. T. F. Oltmanns and B. A. Maher). Wiley, New York.

Maher, B. A. (1988b). Delusions as the product of normal cognitions. In *Delusional beliefs* (ed. T. F. Oltmanns and B. A. Maher). Wiley, New York.

Maher, B. A. (1988c). Language disorders in psychoses and their impact on delusions. In *Psychopathology and philosophy* (ed. M. Spitzer, E. Uehlein, and G. Oepen). Springer-Verlag, Berlin.

Maher, B. A. (1990). The irrelevance of rationality in adaptive behaviour. In *Philosophy and psychopathology* (ed. M. Spitzer and B. A. Maher). Springer-Verlag, New York.

Maher, B. and Ross, J. S. (1984). Delusions. In *Comprehensive handbook of psycholopathology* (ed. H. E. Adams and P. Suther). Plenum, New York.

Maher, B. A. and Spitzer, M. (1993). Delusions. In *Comprehensive handbook of psychopathology (2nd edn)* (ed. P. Sutker and P. Adams). Plenum, New York.

Manschreck, T., Maher, B., Milavetz, J., and Jones, D. (1988). Semantic priming in thought disordered schizophrenic patients. *Schizophrenia Research*, 1, 61–6.

Marcel, A. J. (1983). Conscious and unconscious perception: experiments on visual masking and word recognition. *Cognitive Psychology*, 15, 197–237.

Marshall, W. L. (1973). Cognitive functioning in schizophrenia: stimulus analysing and response selection processes. *British Journal of Psychiatry*, 123, 33–40.

Merikle, P. and Reingold, R. (1990). Recognition and lexical decision without detection: unconscious perception? *Journal of Experimental Psychology, Human Perception and Performance*, 16, 574–83.

Meyer, D. E. and Schvaneveldt, R. W. (1971). Facilitation in recognising pairs of words: evidence of a dependence between retrieval operations. *Journal of Experimental Psychology*, 90, 227–34.

Miller, L. J., O'Connor, E, and DiPasquale, T. (1993). Patients' attitudes towards hallucinations. *American Journal of Psychiatry*, 150, 584–88.

Neely, J. H. (1976). Semantic priming and retrieval from lexical memory: evidence for facilitatory and inhibitory processes. *Memory and Cognition*, 4, 648–54.

Neely, J. H. (1991). Semantic priming effects in visual word recognition: a selective review of current findings and theories. In *Basic processes in reading: visual word recognition* (ed. D. Besner and G. W. Humphreys) Erlbaum, Hillsdale, New Jersey.

Neuchterlein, K. and Dawson, M. (1984). Information processing and attentional functioning in the developmental course of schizophrenic disorders. *Schizophrenia Bulletin*, 10, 160–203.

Neufeld, R. W. (1977). Components of processing deficit among paranoid and nonparanoid schizophrenics. *Journal of Abnormal Psychology*, 86, 60–4.

Raine, A. (1991). The Schizotypal Personality Questionnaire (SPQ): a scale for the assessment of schizotypal personality based on DSM-IIIR criteria. *Schizophrenia Bulletin*, 17, 555–64.

Rosch, E. (1975). Cognitive representation of semantic categories. *Journal of Experimental Psychology, General*, 104, 192–233.

Slade, P. D. and Bentall, R. P. (1988). *Sensory deception: A scientific analysis of hallucination.* Croom Helm, London.

Spitzer, M., Braun, U., Hermle, L., and Maier S (1993a) Associative semantic network dysfunction in thought-disordered schizophrenic patients: direct evidence from indirect semantic priming. *Biological Psychiatry*, 34, 864–77.

Spitzer, M., Braun, U., Naier, S., Hermule, L., and Maher, B. A. (1993b). Indirect semantic priming in schizophrenic patients. *Schizophrenia Research*, 11, 71–80.

Spitzer, M., Weisker, I., Winter, M., Maier, S., Hermle, L., and Maher, B. A. (1994). Semantic and phonological priming in schizophrenia. *Journal of Abnormal Psychology*, 103, 485–94.

Tajfel, H. (1982). *Social identity and inter-group relations.* Cambridge University Press.

6
Brain, self, and others: the neuropsychology of social cognition

PAUL BROKS

INTRODUCTION

The general aim of this chapter is to explore the neuropsychology of social cognition from the converging perspectives of autism and schizophrenia and to consider the relevance of work in this area to an understanding of schizotypy. I will argue that the cardinal features of both schizophrenic states and autism are shaped by abnormalities of social cognition and that the two conditions arise from the workings of a common underlying brain system, the key component of which is the amygdala. Broadly speaking, autism can be characterized as a condition involving impoverished comprehension of the mental states of others (and in extreme form failure to comprehend that others exist at all). The schizophrenias may be characterized by *distortions* in the perceptions of others' mental states and/or a dysfunctional conception of one's own mental states.

I shall not be much concerned with the question of whether 'schizophrenia' constitutes a disease entity. On this issue my views coincide with those of Claridge (1995) in so far as I would argue that neither biomedical nor psychological models alone provide a sufficient explanatory framework for understanding schizophrenia or the variants of 'normal' personality associated with it. To recruit a rather ungainly hybrid from the health psychology movement, I believe that schizophrenia can best be understood within a *biopsychosocial* frame of reference. In taking such a view I am neither accepting the biomedical model of schizophrenia nor entirely rejecting it. I think it is a mistake to set the dimensional model in contradistinction to the biomedical model—they are not necessarily mutually exclusive and both are relevant to an understanding of schizophrenia/schizotypy. More important than sterile debate about 'biomedical versus psychological' models is to identify a conceptual framework that offers a better insight into the explanatory mechanisms linking biology to behaviour and experience. This applies as much to the dimensional model as to the medical. With biopsychosocial thinking as a general background, the position I take is much influenced by recent attempts to place the question of social cognition within a neurobiological context. I shall begin by very briefly outlining my understanding of the biopsychosocial model before going on to describe theoretical developments in the neuropsychology of social cognition

The biopsychosocial approach grew from a dawning appreciation in the 1960s and 1970s that it is not possible to give a full account of the characteristics of physical health and disease without reference to psychosocial factors. Two issues in particular have bedeviled biomedical models of disease, the first being that there is great difficulty in defining absolute distinctions between disease and health *in purely biological terms*. It was recognized that health and illness have subjective dimensions and that social factors are relevant to an understanding of the disease concept. Secondly, there are problems defining the range of application of the biomedical model—in particular with regard to whether mental illness should fall within its remit. Engel (1977) defined two responses to this latter dilemma, *reductionist* and *exclusionist*: the first embracing the view that all mental disease was ultimately reducible to physical disorder in the conventional sense of there being a 'fault with the biological machinery'; the second maintaining that the concept of disease is irrelevant to an understanding of mental disorder.

The biopsychosocial model supersedes the biomedical model by reconceptualizing the notions of health and illness. In essence, it assumes a systems approach which acknowledges the interrelatedness of the social and biological domains (Engel 1977; Schwartz 1982). An individual's psychological condition is construed as the product of biological and social forces and there are assumed to be multidirectional cause and effect relationships binding social, psychological, and biological systems. Because physical diseases are themselves recognized as having psychosocial components, there no grounds for excluding behavioural and mental disorders nor, for the same reason, is it feasible to take a crude reductionist approach to mental illness.

This territory—the polarization of opinion between reductionism and exclusionism and disputes over the definition of disease—will be familiar to anyone who has taken an interest in the development of the concept of schizotypy and, in particular, ideas about the schizotypal nervous system. As a putative feature of brain organization underlying forms of normal personality structure which, in interaction with the social environment, might predispose to schizophrenia, the schizotypal nervous system lends itself naturally to biopsychosocial analysis. The schizotypy debate has often been framed in biopsychosocial terms without direct reference to parallel debates in the health psychology movement. I make explicit reference to the biopsychosocial model here in part simply to draw attention to the common ground that exists between the prevailing model of health psychology and the theoretical underpinnings of the concept of schizotypy. But, of more immediate concern, I think it appropriate to set an introduction to the emerging, interdisciplinary field of 'social neuropsychology' firmly within the biopsychosocial frame. The neuropsychology of social cognition is a topic which, inescapably, demands a synthesis of ideas from the 'bio', the 'psycho', and the 'social' perspectives, its fundamental objective being to achieve an understanding of the ways neural, cognitive, and social systems integrate and interact to produce adaptive social behaviour. A complete understanding of schizotypy, I believe, depends ultimately upon the success of this enterprise.

BACKGROUND TO RECENT DEVELOPMENTS IN THE NEUROPSYCHOLOGY OF SOCIAL COGNITION

There is a massive, theoretically informed literature on what might be considered the classical domains of interest within neuropsychology: perception, attention, memory, language, and motor-executive function (McCarthy and Warrington 1990; Kolb and Whishaw 1996). By contrast, until recently, little progress had been made towards an understanding of the social aspects of neuropsychological disorder. Although assessment in clinical neuropsychology usually does include evaluation of such things as mood, temperament, and social behaviour, for the most part this is done either in a qualitative fashion on the basis of clinical interview, or using psychometric measures transposed from the general psychiatric field. In contrast, there are hundreds of psychometric tests available for the assessment of non-social aspects of cognitive function (Lezak 1995). Why this imbalance between assessment of cognitive function and the evaluation of socioaffective status? After all, impairments of social competence can be catastrophic, often far outweighing the consequences of other cognitive disabilities. There has traditionally been a tendency to think about social behaviour and related concepts such as mood, emotion, and temperament as being vague and intractable and, certainly, they are difficult to pin down in the clinic room. Using psychometric instruments to tap into cognitive functions like memory or verbal comprehension is a relatively straightforward matter but it is not so easy to manipulate demands on temperament or social skill, or to quantify the patient's response. More fundamentally, what has been lacking is a *conceptual framework* for thinking about social cognition and behaviour within the neuropsychological context. There is a clear contrast here with what has been happening elsewhere in neuropsychology. Increasingly, clinical assessment procedures are *theory driven*, being derived more or less directly from theoretical developments in cognitive and experimental neuropsychology.

The intellectual climate has begun to change and recent years have seen a growth of interest in the neurobiological bases of social behaviour and experience. Factors contributing to this change of climate are diverse, although, interestingly, the influence of academic social psychology has been negligible. Social psychologists with an interest in social-cognitive theory have generally shown no interest in the neuropsychological perspective. There is a strong contrast here with the significant impact made by mainstream cognitive psychology on neuropsychological thinking over the past 25 years or so (see, for example, Ellis and Young (1988)).

AN EVOLUTIONARY PERSPECTIVE

A major influence on the growth of interest in the neuropsychology of social cognition has been the development of evolutionary thinking in psychology. In a seminal paper Humphrey (1976) distinguished between social and technical intelligence and, contrary to received wisdom, argued that social primate and hominid evolution was driven largely by advances in the former rather than the latter:

Thus social primates are required by the very nature of the system they create and maintain to be calculating beings; they must be able to calculate the consequences of their own behaviour, to calculate the likely behaviour of others, to calculate the balance of advantage and loss—and all this in a context where the evidence on which their calculations are based is ephemeral, ambiguous and liable to change, not least as a consequence of their own actions. In such a situation, 'social skill' goes hand in hand with intellect, and here at last the intellectual faculties required are those of the highest order.' (p. 309)

The 'Machiavellian Intelligence' hypothesis of primate brain evolution was subsequently developed by Byrne and Whiten (1988) who argued that what distinguishes primate social groups from other species is the sophistication with which primates develop and manipulate social knowledge about one another. Against the background of relatively static group-hierarchical structures, the success of an individual's interactions with other group members depends on the exercise of more dynamic abilities to gauge the intentions, desires, and beliefs of other individuals and to act appropriately on the basis of such cognitions. As Humphrey (1976) observed, 'In a complex society such as those we know exist among higher primates, there are benefits to be gained for each individual member both from preserving the overall structure of the group and at the same time from exploiting and out-manoeuvring others within it (p. 309). The ability to engage in such activity (playing 'social chess' to call on Humphrey's apt metaphor) depends on social-information processing and abstract reasoning of a high order, served by a highly evolved neurocognitive machinery. Humphrey goes as far as to suggest that, 'the chief role of creative intellect is to hold society together.' In indirect support of the Machiavellian Intelligence hypothesis, Dunbar (1993) has demonstrated a close correlation in primates between group size and neocortex ratio (i.e. the ratio of neocortex volume to the volume of the rest of the brain).

There are good grounds for arguing that the neurocognitive machinery subserving primate social cognition constitutes an innate brain module or, in Fodor's (1983) terms, a relatively special-purpose computational system. Brothers (1990, 1992) is persuasive in making a case for the existence of such a module, and we will return to consider her ideas below. But first let us consider some developments in cognitive and developmental psychology which have also contributed significantly to the growth of interest in social neuropsychology.

THEORIES OF THEORY OF MIND

Nourished by an intellectual climate allowing freedom to theorize using mentalistic (or 'intentional') terms and, informed by philosophical analyses of the place of intentionality in cognitive theory (especially Dennett 1978), psychologists have in recent years devoted substantial efforts to the analysis of metacognition, or the ability of human beings and other animals to 'think about thinking'. The technical term *intentionality* represents a key concept in social cognition, so it will be worth taking a moment to explain what it means. The notion of intentionality has been used by philosophers to forge a primary distinction between the mental and the physical. Intentional states refer to mental *attitudes*, including the everyday sense of intention (i.e. having one's mind fixed on a purpose) but going beyond this to include other mental states that are *about* something (beliefs, wishes, desires, fears, etc.). Without going into detailed philosophical argument we may note that this *aboutness* of intentional terms gives them a certain logical property, so-called *logical* or *referential opacity*, which renders them resistant to purely behavioural analysis and therefore of interest to philosophers who want to demarcate the boundaries of mental and physical (for further discussion see Whiten and Perner (1991)). Of more direct concern for the present discussion is the function that intentional states serve as the primary currency of social interaction, in particular the role they play in our (and the social primates') understanding of the mental lives of other individuals. In his influential development of the notion of intentionality, Dennett (1978) examines three ways in which we might endeavour to make sense of the behaviour of complex systems (such as people). In predicting the behaviour of a chess-playing computer, Dennett suggests, we may adopt a *Design Stance*, a *Physical Stance*, or an *Intentional Stance*. The Design Stance would lead us to explore the functional design of the computer. If one knew the exact design of the computer (including the design of the relevant program) one could predict its designed response to any move, by analysing the computational instructions of the program. Adopting the Physical Stance implies forming a prediction of the computer's behaviour on the basis of its actual physical state as an object, alongside available knowledge of the laws of nature. Although workable *in principle* this, as Dennett points out, would be, 'a pointless and herculean labor'. In fact, the Design Stance would be pretty hopeless too, given the complexity of chess programs. From the Design Stance they are usually unfathomable even to their own designers! This leaves the Intentional Stance, which means treating the computer rather like an intelligent human opponent who is liable to honour the rules of chess and opt for rational rather than reckless moves. In other words, we act as if we *ascribe* knowledge, beliefs, and desires to the computer. This tendency to use mental state ascriptions to explain and predict behaviour lies at the root of interpersonal interaction and forms the fabric of social life. It is hard to conceive of a mental life without the capacity to 'psychologize' in this way but autism, it has been suggested, involves just such a defect.

Theory of mind theories of autism

We must, then, assume that these children have come into the world with innate inability to form the usual biologically provided affective contact with people, just as other people come into the world with innate physical or intellectual handicaps. Kanner (1943)

This quotation from the first clinical account of the autistic syndrome by

Leo Kanner has a surprisingly contemporary feel given recent developments in psychological and neuropsychological thinking about the brain basis of socioaffective function in general and autism in particular. Since that first account there have been alternative ideas about autism having psychogenic origins and for a time in the 1950s and 1960s the psychoanalytic view that autism arose as a consequence of cold, emotionless parenting was predominant. But such ideas are now generally discredited. Kanner's original view was clearly that what is lacking in the autistic individual is some basic biological mechanism whose normal function is to allow socioaffective contact with other people. This view now commands widespread support. It is now not only generally accepted that autism is a behaviourally defined developmental disorder of brain function (Bauman and Kemper 1994); a number of theorists have also been working towards the view that the biological basis consists in the developmental failure of (or damage to) particular neurocognitive mechanisms whose dedicated function is to facilitate interaction with other people (for example Brothers 1990; Allman and Brothers 1994; Baron-Cohen 1995).

In terms of diagnostic criteria, the autistic syndrome is characterized by *impaired social interaction* (for example lack of reciprocity, lack of empathy; inability to comprehend the mental states of others); *impaired communication* (for example delayed/impaired language acquisition, impaired nonverbal communication, impoverished pragmatic skills); and a *lack of behavioural flexibility/imagination* (for example motor stereotypies, ritualistic behaviour, limited and obsessional interests, lack of spontaneous pretend play). Besides these criterial features, other behavioural abnormalities commonly, but not universally, occur. These include sensory-perceptual abnormalities, mental retardation, specific language learning disorder, clumsiness, and hyperactivity. (For a comprehensive introduction to autism in all its aspects see Trevarthen *et al.* (1996).)

The 'Theory of mind theory' of autism has been in the ascendancy since the mid-1980s, overshadowing in its influence all other cognitive approaches to the disorder. In essence, the theory holds that autistic children fail to develop a *theory of mind* (ToM), thus preventing them from grasping the notion that other people have mental states such as *beliefs* and *intentions* (Baron-Cohen *et al.* 1985; Leslie and U. Frith 1988). The term *theory of mind* as used in this sense was coined by Premack and Woodruff (1978) who were interested in chimpanzees' abilities to form representations of mental states which might be used to predict the behaviour of others. In that context they conceived of ToM not as the exercise of conscious, self-reflective thinking, but as the operation of an innately endowed cognitive mechanism automatically serving a specific function in enabling individuals to interact adaptively with other members of their group. To use another term that has gained common currency, autistic people are said to lack *mindreading* skills. As summarized by Happé (1994), the ToM theory of autism holds that:

... the triad of behavioural handicaps in autism socialization, communication, imagination result from an impairment of the fundamental human ability to 'mind-read'. Normal children, from around the age of 4 years, understand (however implicitly) that people have beliefs and desires about the world, and that it is these mental states (rather than the physical state of the world) which determine a person's behaviour. The 'theory of mind' explanation of autism suggests that autistic people lack this ability to think about thoughts, and so are specifically impaired in certain (but not all) social, communicative and imaginative skills. (p. 38)

As Trevarthen *et al.* (1996) observe, the ToM approach is both intellectually sophisticated and seductive, driven as it is by philosophy of mind and supported by evidence from a series of ingenious experimental studies which expose the limitations of autistic children in their conception of the beliefs of others. Typical experimental tasks take the form of a narrative. The classic 'Sally-Anne' false-belief task serves as an illustration. The child participating in the experiment is invited to watch as two dolls are used to act out the following scenario. One of them (Sally) has a basket, the other (Anne) has a box. Sally also has a marble which she puts into her basket, before going out. While Sally is away Anne removes the marble from the basket and puts it into her own box. Sally returns and wants to play with her marble, at which point the child is asked: 'Where will Sally look for her marble?' The correct answer should, of course, be 'in the basket', because that is where Sally would *believe* it to be. Failing to take Sally's belief into account, most autistic children fail this test. Non-autistic children of similar age but intellectually *less* able were generally found to have no difficulty reading Sally's mind to arrive at the correct answer (Baron-Cohen, *et al.* 1985).

SCHIZOPHRENIA AS A DISORDER OF SOCIAL COGNITION

My central contention will be that the brain circuitry which underlies social information processing represents a common frame of reference for understanding autistic spectrum disorders and schizophrenia and that, by extension, it is therefore also relevant to an understanding of schizotypy. In this, I shall be elaborating on the ideas put forward by C. Frith (1992, 1994) that autism and schizophrenia, although distinct disorders, share a common cognitive defect. Frith's suggestion is that the faulty mechanism in each case is the one whose function is to support 'mentalization' or 'second-order representations', which is necessary in order to achieve an understanding that other people have mental states.

As we have seen, there is evidence that autistic people lack the capacity to develop an adequate 'theory of mind'. Whereas the autistic deficit is most likely inborn (or perhaps in some cases early-acquired) people with schizophrenia generally function quite adequately until their first breakdown. As Frith puts it:

The autistic person has never known that other people have minds. The schizophrenic knows well that other people have minds, but has lost the ability to infer the contents of these minds: their beliefs and intentions. They may even lose the ability to reflect on the contents of their own mind. (C. Frith 1992, p. 121)

While noting similarities between autism and some of the 'negative' signs of schizophrenia (social withdrawal, stereotyped behaviour, and impoverished communication) Frith uses the notion of a failure of second-order representation to explain positive symptoms such as passivity experiences (thought insertion and delusions of control) and hallucinations. In an earlier paper (C. Frith 1987) it was suggested that passivity experiences arise from a defect in central monitoring, in particular affecting the capacity to be aware of the intention to make a response (motor or verbal) before the response is made. As a result, a person would not know what they were going to say or do until after they had said or done it, with the effect that the action might be perceived as orginating from some external agent. In a development of this model it is suggested that the failure of central monitoring is itself the consequence of a failure of the mechanism that enables us to form representations of our own mental states. In particular, the problem is said to reside in a 'failure of decoupling'. According to Leslie (1987) mental states (beliefs, intentions, etc.) require second-order representations, *metarepresentations*, to keep them distinct from first-order representations of the physical world. 'Decoupling' refers to the creation of a distinction between first-and second-order representations. This is necessary because, unlike first-order representations of the world, the content of a second-order proposition is neither true nor false. Compare, for example, the first-order proposition, 'The kitten is in the garden' with the content of the second-order proposition 'Jonathan believes that the kitten is in the garden'. In the first case it is either true or false (according to circumstances in the physical world) that the kitten is in the garden. In the second, as the content of a metarepresentation, *the kitten is in the garden* stands in relation to Jonathan's *belief* about the world rather than the world itself, a relation which holds whether or not the belief itself coincides with reality. According to Frith, if the decoupling process is faulty, the contents of second-order representations may become detached from the rest of the propositions in which they are embedded and consequently perceived as a representation of the real world, thereby giving rise to delusional thinking. For example, consider an intention to take a shower structured in the form of the metarepresentation, 'I am planning to take a shower'. Detached from the rest of the proposition 'I am planning to . . .' the content *take a shower* might take on an imperative quality and be experienced as a delusion of control. 'I know that it's time to fix an appointment with the dentist' becomes, *it's time to fix an appointment with the dentist* (thought insertion), and so on.

What may be relevant to an understanding of schizotypy is that the capacity to decouple first- from second-order representations is not an all-or-nothing phenomenon. In normal development children progress through a series of stages towards a fully fledged 'representational mind' (Perner 1991). Different stages of development are associated with different levels of awareness regarding goals and intentions, self and other. For example, it is not until around 18 months that infants develop an awareness of their own goals. Before that age their tendency to produce perseverative behaviours in relation to desired goals, regardless of the outcome of their actions, suggests that they have a poor conception of the notions of success and failure. However, an awareness of *intentions* seems to arrive somewhat later, between 3 and 5 years of age. Among other forms of evidence it has been shown, for example, that children below the age of five are unable to distinguish between an intended movement of the lower leg and reflex movements resulting from a tap on their knee (Shultz *et al.* 1980). Aspects of the ability to represent the mental states of other people also develop at different rates. An appreciation that others may hold false beliefs develops around the age of four years but higher-order abilities (for example the ability to comprehend that someone holds a false belief about someone else's beliefs) do not emerge until between seven and nine (Perner and Wimmer 1985).

Frith identifies three important stages in the development of the 'representational mind':

(1) awareness of our goals;

(2) awareness of our own intentions and other mental states; and

(3) awareness of other people's mental states.

He suggests that schizophrenia involves disorders of awareness which mirror these states, producing different classes of signs and symptoms. For example, loss of awareness of one's own goals may be associated with grandiosity (positive feature) or depersonalization and lack of will (negative features). Loss of one's own intentions may lead to delusions of control and thought insertion (positive) or poverty of thought and loss of affect (negative). Finally, loss of awareness of others' intentions may cause delusions of persecution and third-person hallucinations (positive) or derealization and social withdrawal (negative). As for the neural substrate of these signs and symptoms, Frith hypothesizes a disconnection between areas of the frontal cortex believed to be involved in the generation of willed action, and posterior regions of the brain. He does, however, allude to the possible significance of Brothers' model of 'the social brain' (Brothers 1990) which incorporates the prefrontal zones (C. Frith 1994). I will return to consider this model in more detail below.

Conceivably, I would suggest, schizotypy relates to the establishment and consolidation of such metarepresentational skills. An individual may be more or less prone to schizotypal experiences according to the integrity of function of their 'theory of mind mechanisms'. Even assuming that theory of mind problems have been satisfactorily solved at each developmental stage, it may be the case that, in schizotypal individuals, the underlying mechanisms function less reliably, or perhaps that they are 'calibrated' somewhat differently, allowing more finely tuned social perceptions and cognitions under some circumstances, but not others.

AN OPERATIONAL DEFINITION OF SOCIAL COGNITION

The suggestion is, then, that autism and schizophrenia might both be construed as disorders of social cognition. Before turning to consider the neurobiological bases of social-information processing, we should perhaps step back and take in a broader view of the notion of social cognition, particularly as it might be understood from the neuropsychological perspective. The study of social cognition will, I believe, come to represent an important area of common ground for social scientists and neuroscientists. But, as suggested above, current interest in the neuropsychology of social cognition has roots rather separate from the intellectual traditions of social psychology. Although it would be an interesting exercise to trace parallels and points of convergence between social psychology and neuroscience I shall, for present purposes, limit discussion to those aspects of social cognition which seem to me most directly relevant to an understanding of autistic spectrum disorders, schizophrenia, and mental and behavioural disorders associated with acquired neurological lesions. With this in mind, I offer the following operational definition of social cognition as:

(1) The perception of the dispositions and intentions of other individuals (a succinct definition owing to Leslie Brothers);

(2) the construction and maintenance of a viable concept of self;

(3) the production and regulation of behaviour in social contexts.

Although the components of this tripartite definition are each relevant to an understanding of autism, schizophrenia, and acquired neurological disorder, for reasons to be developed below I would suggest that component (1) is most directly relevant to autism, while components (1) and (2) are most relevant to an understanding of schizophrenia. Acquired neurological disorder may give rise to impairment of (1), (2), and (3), although the most commonly observed effects are at level (3).

From a neuropsychological perspective three general claims are worth examining, namely, that:

1. Some neuropsychological abnormalities (i.e. behaviours and experiences arising as a consequence of brain damage) are defined by their social context.

2. Disorders of social cognition/behaviour can be selective (i.e. occur independently of other disorders of cognition).

3. There are functional systems of the brain dedicated to social-information processing.

The first of these claims seems uncontentious and there are good grounds to accept the second. Various behavioural tendencies arising from brain damage may be entirely normal in some circumstances but abnormal in other social contexts. The exhibited behaviours themselves may be asocial or social in nature. To take an example of an asocial behaviour, it is biologically normal for people to break wind from time to time but, mostly, this is done in private or in public circumstances where the act is likely to go unnoticed. It would be taken as a sign of abnormality if one displayed an apparent lack of concern for social propriety by breaking wind ad lib at, say, a business lunch or a job interview. Scratching one's private parts is another example. As my colleague Tony Coughlan has noted (Coughlan 1996) there may be different reasons why such changes in behaviour emerge following some forms of brain damage. Among other possibilities, it may be that the person has forgotten the usual rules—a loss of 'social semantic memory', that they know the rules but fail to self-monitor, or that they have developed a cavalier disregard for social convention. Sexual disinhibition, again not uncommon following brain damage, provides an example of disinhibited *social* behaviour. There are, of course, situations in which sexual behaviours ranging from mild flirtatiousness to explicitly sexual physical advances are appropriate but if, as a result of brain damage, a person habitually and indiscriminately makes unsolicited sexual advances towards others regardless of the circumstances, this is considered to be abnormal. Note that in each case the behaviours themselves are not abnormal; rather it is the social circumstance in which they occur that defines them as such.

Such behavioural changes are usually linked with disorders of the frontal lobes and there is a broad agreement that different forms of 'frontal syndrome' are identifiable. A *disinhibited* syndrome, associated with orbital lesions and characterized by impulsivity, emotional lability, euphoria, and jocularity, has been termed the *pseudopsychopathic* syndrome. An *apathetic* syndrome, associated with dorsolateral lesions and characterized by indifference, apathy, psychomotor retardation, irritability, and poor anger control, has been termed the *pseudodepressive* syndrome (Blumer and Benson 1975). While there is some consensus on the behavioural syndromes, it is fair to say that the anatomical correlates are less firmly established. Beyond the orbital/dorsolateral distinction it has become increasingly apparent that laterality effects need to be taken into account, with 'pseudopsychopathic' states being more often associated with right-sided lesions and 'pseudodepressive' with left. It should also be noted that, in many cases, patients exhibit a combination of symptoms which seem to straddle the two categories. Presented below are outlines of two cases involving frontal-lobe damage which illustrate some abnormalities of socioaffective functioning characteristic of the 'frontal syndromes'. They are pertinent to the first two of the three general claims about the neuropsychology of social cognition outlined above. 'NK's' case is perhaps more typical of the pseudodepressive syndrome and 'SP' leans more towards a pseudopsychopathic presentation, although it can be seen that there is some degree of overlap. Coded initials have been used and some case details have been changed to preserve anonymity, but the clinical and behavioural details are faithful.

'NK'

NK, a 44-year-old motorway maintenance engineer sustained frontal brain injury when, as a bystander to a high-speed road traffic accident he was hit by flying debris; a fragment of metal penetrated his skull and lodged itself deep within the left frontal lobe. No other injuries were sustained. Despite the immediate loss of some brain matter from the hole in his skull, there was only fleeting loss of consciousness, as is sometimes the case with penetrating missile wounds. NK was taken to hospital where he subsequently underwent surgery to remove the foreign body from his brain, a process also involving removal of some adjacent brain substance. Even within a few days of surgery there were good indications that NK had survived his ordeal with intellectual and memory functions broadly intact. He found his own way from the ward to my office in an adjoining corridor and presented himself for assessment in a courteous and cooperative manner. He was, I thought, rather 'flat' emotionally but otherwise his manner was appropriate to the situation (in any case, one was inclined to think, he could be forgiven for appearing a little stunned given his recent traumatic experience). Six months following the accident he scored at average levels on the Wechsler Adult Intelligence Scale (Revised), (WAIS-R), consistent with estimates of his premorbid ability.

NK had been known as a devoted family man who worked hard to support his wife and four children (two of whom were now grown up and living away from home). He had a network of good friends and had enjoyed an active social life up to the time of the accident. On discharge from hospital he returned to live with his wife and teenage daughters. As routine daily life normalized in the weeks and months that followed it became apparent to family and friends that NK had changed. In terms of his temperament, his interests, and his attitudes to family and social life in general, he was no longer the person they had known. Previously placid and easy going, he was now prone to 'fly off the handle' at the slightest provocation, for example if one of his daughters put on a record he did not like. He would spend hours working on his car or doing other routine mechanical tasks but admitted, 'I haven't got so much time for people these days'. He was no longer inclined to go out with friends for a drink: 'I don't see the point', he would say. Part of the problem was that he could no longer appreciate his friends' sense of humour—'Jokes aren't funny anymore'. Somewhat reluctantly, he would go out with his wife and other couples occasionally, but did not particularly enjoy it and would sometimes cause embarrassment through the ill-judged remarks he was liable to make. On one occasion he and his wife were invited to dinner. Their hosts had recently spent a lot of money on redecorating their house and were eager to solicit the approval of the guests. Looking around the room, and impervious to the others' embarrassment, NK simply remarked, 'It's ghastly'. In his own terms, he conceded that he no longer felt 'sympathetic' to people, by which he meant that he was unaffected by others' distress. Television images of the horrors of the war in Bosnia left him unmoved. Of a major national news story about the callous abduction and murder of a young child, NK said that he understood that this was a dreadful thing to have happened and that the perpetrators deserved the severest punishment but, again, he felt no emotional response. There were occasions formerly when he had been moved to tears by news stories of this sort. His lack of emotional resonance with others also affected NK's appreciation of films and television drama. He had no difficulty describing characters or following stories but it was just 'people doing things', devoid of emotional content. In fact, all activities demanding some degree of emotional engagement had become flat and uninteresting, including listening to music and watching sport, both of which NK had been fairly passionate about before his injury.

'RP'

'RP' was a 38-year-old business manager who suffered a severe closed head injury in an accidental fall from the roof of his house. Severe bleeding deep into the frontal regions of his brain required surgical intervention but, within three weeks of the accident he was well enough to undergo some preliminary neuropsychological evaluation, at which stage he was fully alert and mobile. Initial indications were that intellectual functions and personality were grossly intact. He presented as pleasant and cooperative and seemed generally to be in a somewhat upbeat mood. At 6 months post-injury, psychometric testing established that his WAIS-R Verbal IQ was 123 which falls in the 'superior' range, and was consistent with estimates of his premorbid ability. Performance IQ was not far below, at 113 ('high average'). He and his wife described their marital relationship as strong. They had recently celebrated their fifth wedding anniversary. They had no children. RP had enjoyed an active social life centring largely around his sporting interests: golf and sailing.

In the months following the accident RP and those around him became aware of the gradual emergence of changes in his personal interests, motivation, and social behaviour. He remained socially active and people began to remark that he seemed to have 'loosened up' somewhat, becoming less reserved and more extraverted in his behaviour. He seemed to have a keener sense of humour, sometimes producing uncharacteristically witty remarks. In the early stages of his rehabilitation his wife light-heartedly remarked that these were 'changes for the better'. However, in due course, less welcome characteristics began to emerge. He began impulsively to spend considerable amounts of money on music CDs, heavy metal music in particular, which he would play loudly, often quite late into the night. Also, to his wife's distaste, he got into the habit of bringing home pornographic magazines and videos. These, he said, were interests he had previously 'contained'. He had always harboured a secret liking for heavy metal music but had felt that it did not suit the more sober image he liked to project. As for pornography, he had previously refrained because he knew his wife would disapprove. Now his attitude was 'If I like it, I'll do it'. To his wife's discomfiture he also developed an interest in trying to track down former girlfriends, 'just to get in touch for old time's sake'.

On his eventual return to part-time employment he found both the work and his colleagues 'boring'. Intellectually he was clearly capable of performing his former role but now lacked the motivation to actually get things done. Because of increasing absenteeism and generally poor work performance he was finally released by his employers. His marriage also failed. Within a year and a half of the accident he and his wife had separated.

In the light of such cases, the first two general claims about the neuropsychology of social cognition (that some neuropsychological abnormalities are defined by their social context, and that they can occur independently of other disorders of cognition) are not difficult to defend. It is usually the case that brain disease or injury sufficient to cause socioaffective dysfunctions *does* cause impairment of other cognitive functions. This is because the sorts of brain insult which most commonly give rise to socioaffective disturbance (including head injury, viral infection, and anterior haemorrhage) tend to cause relatively diffuse damage, encroaching upon different brain regions with diverse functions. But it is also clear that socioaffective changes of the frontal syndrome type can occur in the presence of broadly intact intellectual, perceptual, and memory functions. The two cases described above provide good examples of this. Eslinger and Damasio (1985) and Damasio (1994) also present compelling case-study evidence of frontal lobe damage having catastrophic effects on the ability to make real-life social judgements despite intact general intellectual abilities and good abstract social reasoning. It is the third claim—that there are brain circuits dedicated to social information processing—that has yet to be firmly established. But evidence converging from a number of different research directions is contributing to a growing belief among neuroscientists that such circuits do indeed exist and, because there has up to now been no generally accepted neuropsychological model of social behaviour and cognition, the implications for an understanding of the brain bases of personality and psychopathology may be far reaching.

THE SOCIAL BRAIN

What are the neural bases of social cognition and, in particular, what might a 'theory of mind mechanism' consist of? Some interesting and plausible speculations on the neurobiological bases of ToM have been offered by Baron-Cohen and Ring (1994) and Baron-Cohen (1995). Their model arises from an integration of Baron-Cohen's own work on the cognitive precursors of theory of mind and a neurobiological theory of social cognition developed by Brothers (1990, 1992). Because of its wider relevance to the present discussion, it is worth outlining the Brothers theory of 'The Social Brain' before returning to consider the views of Baron-Cohen and Ring on its relevance to the development of a 'theory of mind mechanism' (ToMM).

Leslie Brothers has been an influential proponent of the idea that there is a brain module dedicated to social cognition (Brothers 1990, 1992). According to Brothers' theory, social cognition ('the processing of any information which culminates in the accurate perception of the dispositions and intentions of other individuals') is mediated by a distributed brain system comprising as principal components: the *superior temporal sulcus* (STS)—concerned with various aspects of face perception; the *amygdala*, which is concerned with the regulation of emotional response; and the *orbitofrontal cortex* (OFC)—concerned with the regulation of social interactions. Some evidence in support of this theory will now be briefly reviewed before turning to examine its significance for understanding conditions such as autism and schizophrenia.

The STS and face processing

Faces are special objects in the social world. As Brothers (1992) states,

Brains are not neutral with respect to the content of information being processed: as far as primate brains are concerned, all visual stimuli are not created equal. Because of the selective pressure imposed by the demands of social living, it has probably been important to refine the circuitry for detecting and identifying faces, for example. (p. 409)

In line with this view, it has been established that within minutes of birth babies preferentially track moving human faces as opposed to other complex stimuli. This strongly suggests an innate predisposition to attend to faces (Goren *et al.* 1975; Johnson *et al.* 1991). Single cell recordings from macaque monkeys have implicated the STS in a range of face-processing functions, including identity perception (for example Bayliss *et al.* 1985; Desimone 1991), gaze direction (for example Perrett *et al.* 1985; Campbell *et al.* 1990) and orientation of head (Perrett *et al.* 1985).

The amygdala and emotional response

The amygdala, situated within the anterior portion of the medial temporal lobes, is a component of the so-called limbic brain. It is connected with a variety of cortical and subcortical regions and can be viewed as forming a sort of interface between the information processing activities of the neocortex and the activities of subcortical structures (hypothalamus and brainstem) involved in the regulation of autonomic and endocrine functions. As such, it is well placed to function as the key component of the brain's emotion-regulation system, integrating emotional, motivational, and cognitive processes (Le Doux 1995). Relevant to Brothers' putative social brain module, the STS is known to be interconnected with the lateral nucleus of the amygdala, and the amygdala in turn is richly connected with orbitofrontal cortex (Amaral *et al.* 1992). Brothers also cites evidence from neurophysiological studies in monkeys that the amygdala plays a role in face perception (Leonard *et al.* 1985), observations since confirmed by Nakamura *et al.* (1992). Recent studies also provide convincing evidence that damage to the amygdala in humans causes impairment in the processing of social signals from the face (Adolphs *et al.* 1994; Young *et al.* 1995). In our own work with 'DR', a woman who underwent partial bilateral amygdala surgery in an attempt to control severe epilepsy, we found that she not only showed impairments in identifying emotional expressions, but also in judging direction of gaze and recognizing faces that have become familiar since the time of her operations. In contrast, she performs well in face matching and other visual cognitive tasks and is able to recognize faces that were familiar before the date of her surgery (Young *et al.* 1995). It has since become clear that, with regard to the evaluation of emotional expressions, the amygdala plays a special role in the identification of fear (for example Adolphs *et al.* 1995). It has been suggested that congenital or early-acquired damage to the amygdala is necessary to produce face-processing impairments in humans (Hamann *et al.* 1996) but, against this, we have recently found that patients with damage to the amygdala sustained in middle age as a result of herpes simplex encephalitis also show selective impairments of emotion perception; this suggests that late-acquired damage can be sufficient to produce abnormalities in social-information processing (Broks *et al.* submitted). The point is relevant when we come to consider the possible role of amygdala dysfunction in autism and schizophrenia. To anticipate our discussion, it will be suggested that autism is related to congenital or early-acquired damage to the amygdala, but later-onset amygdala dysfunction may be sufficient to promote social-cognitive abnormalities underlying schizophrenia.

Orbitofrontal cortex and the regulation of social behaviour

As we have already noted, it is well established that damage to the frontal regions of the brain can cause impairments of social behaviour largely independent of any other perceptual or cognitive dysfunction. Brothers (1990) cites the case reported by Eslinger and Damasio (1985). Patient 'EVR', a 35-year-old man, underwent surgery for resection of an orbitofrontal meningioma (a tumorous growth, usually benign) which necessiated total removal of the right orbital cortex and part of the left. His intelligence remained above average and he showed no impairment in other standard neuropsychological tests, but he showed a dramatic loss of social competence in terms of his ability to judge and respond to social situations appropriately. By all accounts of his premorbid personality and behaviour his ability to gauge social situations had been exemplary. As summarized by Brothers

EVR has lost the ability to respond appropriately to social situations, apparently as a result of having lost access to the internal cues which the behaviour of others should generate. Nor does he seem to form an accurate appraisal of the motivations and attitudes others are likely to have in the imagined future. (p. 37)

Brothers highlights, 'a remarkable dissociation between his fund of abstract knowledge about social situations, which is fully intact as elicited by verbal testing, and his capacity to evaluate real-life social situations'. The consequences for EVR's personal and professional life have been severe.

THEORY OF MIND MECHANISMS AND THE SOCIAL BRAIN

The relevance of the social brain to an understanding of autism and psychosis was anticipated by Brothers (1990). She conceives of autism as 'an inborn selective absence of social cognition', the central feature of which is 'a lack of ability to perceive the inner world of other persons, or to convey one's own state to others' (pp 33–34). Paranoid psychosis, she suggests, can be characterized as a disorder driven by distortions in the perception of intentional states—i.e. other people's intentions and motivations. 'The distortion is often an exaggerated sense of emotional or psychological relatedness between one's inner life and that of others ("people are reading my mind" . . .) . . . the paranoid person is beset by "intentions"—benevolent, hostile, erotic—in almost disembodied form' (p. 38).

According to Leslie (1987) the ability to form representations of mental states develops in the second year of life. There is a growing appreciation that this ability may indeed rest on an innate, modular neurocognitive system which, using Leslie's terminology, has come to be referred to as the ToMM. In a development of Leslie's work, Baron-Cohen (1995) argues that ToMM depends on the existence of three developmentally earlier modules for which he cites various forms of evidence, including neuropsychological and developmental:

(1) ID (the Intentionality Detector);

(2) EDD (the Eye-Direction Detector);

(3) SAM (the Shared Attention Mechanism).

ID is described as, 'a perceptual device that interprets motion stimuli in terms of the primitive volitional mental states of goal and desire'. EDD is said to have three basic functions: detection of the presence of eyes or eye-like stimuli; computation of the direction of gaze; and formation of inferences about the organism's perception of the object under gaze, i.e. interpreting gaze as 'seeing'. The role of SAM is to build so-called *triadic representations* which 'specify the relations among an Agent, the Self, and a (third) Object. (The Object can be another Agent, too.) Included in a triadic representation is an embedded element which specifies that Agent and Self are both attending to the same object.' For example: [John-sees-(I-see-the girl)].

The speculative neurobiological model of ToMM put forward by Baron-Cohen and Ring (1994) and Baron-Cohen (1995) proposes that STS-amygdala circuitry subserves the EDD mechanism as well as some aspects of SAM, since shared attention also depends on information from gaze direction. Some of the neurophysiological and neuropsychological evidence implicating the STS and amygdala in eye-direction detection has been cited above. The OFC suggests itself as the seat of ToMM on the grounds that the effective exercise of social judgement requires a viable theory of mind mechanism. We have already discussed some evidence on the catastrophic social effects of OFC lesions (Eslinger and Damasio 1985). OFC lesions in rhesus monkeys have also been shown to lead to changes in social behaviour and loss of social status (Butter and Snyder 1972). In addition, Baron-Cohen and Ring point to a study which found that patients with OFC lesions performed poorly in an explicit ToM test (Price *et al.* 1990).

They also cite a study of their own using single photon emission computerized tomography (SPECT) to look at brain activation (in terms of increased blood flow) during a cognitive task designed to trigger mentalistic thinking. Healthy adult volunteers were required to distinguish mental-state words (for example *know, imagine, hope*) from non-mentalistic terms played through headphones and, in a control task, discriminate words describing parts of the body or body functions (for example *teeth, blood, walk*). Attention to mental-state terms was associated with increased activation in the OFC (especially on the right) relative to other frontal areas.

AUTISM AND SCHIZOPHRENIA AS NEUROPSYCHOLOGICAL DISORDERS: FRAMEWORK FOR A CAUSAL MODEL

Neuropsychology is a bridge discipline spanning biological and psychological levels of description. When considering causal models of mental and behavioural disorder (or for that matter *any* psychological phenomenon, 'disordered' or otherwise) it is important to keep a clear view of the different levels of description which might be called upon within neuropsychology and its hinterlands. To avoid conceptual confusion, this is especially the case when considering psychologically complex conditions such as autism and schizophrenia. The central thrust of this chapter is that autism and schizophrenia are essentially disorders of social cognition, with the fullest explanatory account of signs and symptoms to be found at the neuropsychological and cognitive levels of analysis. But it would be difficult to sustain this argument in the absence of supportive evidence at other levels of analysis, in particular the neuroanatomical and neurophysiological levels.

Citing the theoretical model of Morton and U. Frith (1994), Happé (1994) points out that the neurodevelopmental disorders, including autism, may be understood in terms of causal models expressed at three levels of explanation: biological, cognitive, and behavioural. Different relations between these levels will obtain for different clinical conditions. For example, some conditions may have a unitary biological origin but cause various effects at the cognitive and behavioural levels (for example the chromosomal disorder, Fragile X syndrome). Others (perhaps attention deficit disorder (ADD)) may be associated with various biological causes, diverse cognitive effects, but a single behavioural manifestation—extreme distractibility in the case of ADD. Autism, it is suggested, may have different basic biological causes, a *single* cognitive deficit (for example a ToM deficit), and various behavioural manifestations (disorders of communication, socialization, and imagination). This analysis is undoubtedly helpful in conceptualizing the developmental disorders but, arguably, a complete explanation of neuropsychological disorders in general (acquired as well as developmental) requires *five* levels of description, as follows. (Note that *functional anatomy* is used below in a sense largely interchangeable with *neuropsychology*):

(1) *aetiology*—referring to biological root cause;

(2) *neuropathology*—referring to the specification of structural damage or neurochemical abnormality;

(3) *functional anatomy*—referring to the specification of functional brain systems implicated;

(4) *psychology*—referring to specification of the associated cognitive or socio-affective deficit;

(5) *manifest behaviour*—referring to clinical signs/symptoms.

By way of example, consider the relatively straightforward case of cerebrovascular accident, the hierarchical analysis of which might unfold as follows:

(1) *aetiology*—vascular disease;

(2) *neuropathology*—right temporal lobe infarction;

(3) *functional anatomy*—visual memory system dysfunction;

(4) *psychology*—impaired visuospatial memory function;

(5) *manifest behaviour*—person mislocates objects, forgets routes, etc.

(At the level of psychological analysis impairments may be identified as *signs* which are not manifest as *symptoms*.)

In these terms, a causal map of autism might unfold in this way:

(1) *aetiology*—genetic cause or perinatal brain trauma;

(2) *neuropathology*—abnormal amygdala (or, say, malfunction of amygdala-STS circuitry);

(3) *functional anatomy*—social-cognitive system dysfunction;

(4) *psychology*—ToM defect (and/or other primary impairment of social perception and understanding);

(5) *manifest behaviour*—social/communicative/imaginative problems.

It is generally believed that the aetiological basis of autism is varied: genetic factors, viral infections, certain metabolic diseases, and perinatal brain trauma have all been considered relevant (see Gillberg and Coleman (1992) for a review). At the other end of the hierarchy (levels 4 and 5), the behavioural manifestations have been well described and there is no shortage of theoretical models concerning fundamental psychological deficits—the focus in the present discussion has been on ToM theories but, among other approaches, there are also influential theories addressing general executive function (Ozonoff *et al.* 1991), attention (Ashkoomoff and Courchesne 1992), as well as aspects of affective function (for example Hobson (1993)). As we have seen, with attention directed towards the brain's social information processing circuitry, efforts are currently being made to understand autism in terms of what I have referred to as Level 3 explanations (i.e. functional anatomy). What then of Level 2? What is the evidence that the brain structures putatively involved in social information processing can be directly implicated in autism, rather than indirectly implicated via psychological theory?

In fact there is now fairly widespread acceptance of the view that early pathology of the medial temporal lobes, and particularly the amygdala, underlies the development of autism. In a recent review, Bishop (1993) suggests that

as a working hypothesis, the notion of frontal lobe and limbic system dysfunction in autism seems promising, not just in guiding the search for neurobiological correlates of autism but also in suggesting ways to think about the puzzling range of psychological impairments seen in this condition.

There are various strands of evidence in support of this view, which include experimental work with animals, clinical neurological observation, brain imaging, and post-mortem studies (see Bachevalier 1994).

Primate studies in laboratory and naturalistic settings have demonstrated clearly that amygdala lesions cause catastrophic impairments of social functioning arguably analogous to autism in humans (Kling and Brothers 1992). Early lesions of the medial temporal lobes in monkeys cause abnormalities of facial and bodily expressiveness, and the development of stereotypic behaviours (Bachevalier 1994). Similarities have also been noted between autism and the behavioural effects of medial temporal-lobe damage in humans. Kluver-Bucy syndrome is associated with bilateral anterior temporal lesions and evidence from animal studies indicates that lesions of the amygdala are the critical factor (Weiskrantz 1956). Clinical features of Kluver-Bucy syndrome held in common with autism include profound socio-emotional disturbances and stereotypy (Hetzler and Griffin 1981). Post-mortem neuropathological studies of the brains of autistic people have found evidence of limbic system abnormalities in several structures, including the amygdala (Bauman and Kemper 1994).

It should be noted that other structures have also been implicated, in particular the vermis of the cerebellum (Courchesne *et al.* 1988), an observation which would not, at first sight, appear to fit with the with current conceptions of the social brain. Courchesne and his colleagues have suggested that an abnormal cerebellum might play a role in defective attentional control in autism, leading to stereotypic behaviour, but it is not easy to explain the full spectrum of autistic behaviours on this account. My own view is that the cerebellum may indeed be implicated in autism and that it may also form an important, as yet unacknowledged, component of the social brain. Briefly, I suggest that the cerebellum may contribute to the establishment of 'social dexterity' just as it plays a key role in motor-skill learning and, as recent studies suggest, other forms of 'cognitive dexterity' such as reading skill (Nicolson *et al.* 1995). In this way it may contribute to the autistic syndrome well beyond the generation of motor stereotypy.

As for integrating causal models of autism with causal models of schizophrenia, there is clearly some way to go. However, it is worth noting that there is evidence that schizophrenia is associated with structural and neurochemical abnormalities of the amygdala (Bogerts *et al.* 1985; Breier *et al.* 1992; Reynolds 1992). Also, at the neuropsychological level, both conditions share some interesting common features which fit with the general notion of social brain disorder. Specifically, both autism (for example Hobson 1988) and schizophrenia (for example Archer et al. 1994) have been associated with abnormalities in the judgement of facial expressions of emotion. It is now well established that this is also a characteristic of people with disease or surgery-related damage to the amygdala (Adolphs *et al.* 1995; Young *et al.* 1995) Our own studies also indicate that such impairments may arise from damage to the amygdala sustained in middle age through herpes simplex encephalitis (Broks *et al.* submitted). This leaves open the possibility that, whereas autism may depend on congenital or early-acquired amygdala dysfunction, late-acquired changes to amygdala function may cause changes in emotion perception, perhaps in some cases leading to psychopathological consequences. None of the patients we studied shows any signs of psychosis as far as we know (though we have yet to examine systematically for schizotypal traits), but it should be noted that all suffered sudden onset and severe damage. It is conceivable that a more gradual diminution of the integrity of function of the amygdala, where function is distorted rather than lost, and where ongoing adjustments to subtle changes in emotional perception and response are required, might have different consequences.

IMPLICATIONS FOR AN UNDERSTANDING OF SCHIZOTYPY

I am in general agreement with the model of schizotypy outlined by Claridge (1995, 1990) in which schizotypal experiences are understood to be the product of something referred to as the 'schizotypal nervous system'. What I have tried to offer in the present chapter is a somewhat different perspective on the cognitive and neurocognitive dimensions of the schizotypal nervous system than has previously been adopted. In summary, the key features of my proposal are as follows.

Although as clinical disorders they are quite distinct, schizophrenia and autism can be construed as disorders of social cognition in the sense that they are characterized by fundamental aberrations in the perception of self and/or others, reflecting the malfunction of an innate, modular, 'ToMM'. The ToMM itself is mediated via the operation of a distributed neural system functionally dedicated to social-information processing. This system is functionally dedicated and definable in the way that other complex functional systems of the brain are dedicated and definable—for example the 'motor system' or the 'visual system'. To draw a neurological analogy, Parkinson's disease and Huntington's disease are distinct clinical disorders, yet they are both categorized as motor disorders and both involve malfunction of various components (basal ganglia structures in particular) of a distributed brain system referred to as the motor system. I have suggested that the pivotal component of the brain's social cognitive system is the amygdala and that other key brain regions include the OFC, STS, and, possibly, the cerebellum. Other disorders, such as the frontal lobe syndromes, are also referrable to this system.

The approach I advocate does not negate previous biological or psychological approaches to the study of schizotypy; rather it suggests a more integrated approach in two senses. First, it holds promise of a closer integration of cognitive models and neuropsychological systems in so far as much current interest in the neuropsychology of social-information processing is yoked to fundamental research on the cognitive processes underlying ToM (cf. Brothers 1990; C. Frith 1994; Baron-Cohen 1995). Secondly, by identifying a distributed *functional system* of the brain with cognitive features of schizotypy/schizophrenia, there is the possibility that previously observed psychobiological aspects might eventually be understood in terms of a broader systemic understanding of their role in generating clinical signs and symptoms. For example, neither observations of anomalous autonomic arousal (Claridge 1972) nor reported variations in patterns of functional asymmetry (see Chapter 8) are necessarily lost to view by orienting to the 'social circuitry' of the brain. With regard to laterality, little is known as yet about functional asymmetries within the social brain module, other than evidence for asymmetries in face processing favouring the right hemisphere (Sergent *et al.* 1992) and evidence for differential hemispheric contributions to motivation and mood (see Davidson 1995). (As noted earlier, the characteristics of the frontal lobe syndrome depend to some extent on the laterality of the lesion.) It is perhaps worth noting that autism has also been linked with abnormal hemisphere function, with, perhaps, different forms of the disorder being associated with different patterns of asymmetry (for example Fein *et al.* 1984; Dawson *et al.* 1986; Shields *et al.* 1996). As regards autonomic arousal in schizophrenia/schizotypy I will merely observe that, given the key role of the amygdala in integrating higher cortical processes with autonomic and endocrine response, it is bound at some stage to be implicated in accounts of the schizotypal nervous system that take autonomic arousal as their primary focus. It is more than likely that a detailed understanding of the brain bases of social cognition (and associated disorders) will require an integration of knowledge about brain function along both 'horizontal' and 'vertical' axes; that is, taking account of both asymmetries of cerebral function and cortical—subcortical processes. In this regard, recognition of the dual role of the amygdala in mediating social cognition and physiological arousal processes, orchestrating cortical and subcortical activity, may constitute a clear signpost to the way forward.

Acknowledgements

Thanks to Jill Boucher and Andrew Mayes for hours of discussion about autism, brain function, and unrelated topics. Thanks also to Michael Evangeli who, at short notice, read and commented helpfully on the penultimate draft.

REFERENCES

Adolphs, R., Tranel, D., Damasio, H, and Damasio, A. (1994). Impaired recognition of emotion in facial expressions following bilateral damage to the human amygdala. *Nature*, 372, 669–72.

Adolphs R., Tranel, D., Damasio, H., and Damasio, A. (1995). Fear and the human amygdala. *Journal of Neuroscience*, 15, 5879–91.

Allman, J and Brothers, L. (1994). Faces, fear and the amygdala. *Nature*, 372, 613–14.

Amaral, D. G., Price, J. L., Pitkänen, A., and Carmichael, S. T. (1992). Anatomical organization of the primate amygdaloid complex. In *The amygdala: neurobiological aspects of emotion, memory, and mental dysfunction* (ed. J. P. Aggleton). Wiley-Liss, New York.

Archer, J., Hay, D. C., and Young, A. W. (1994). Movement, face processing and schizophrenia: evidence of a differential deficit in expression analysis. *British Journal of Clincial Psychology*, 33, 517–29.

Ashkoomoff, N. and Courchesne, E. (1992). A new role for the cerebellum in cognitive operations. *Behavioural Neuroscience*, **5**, 731–8.

Bachevalier, J. (1994). Medial temporal lobe structures and autism: A review of clinical and experimental findings. *Neuropsychologia*, **32**, 627–48.

Baron-Cohen, S. (1995). *Mindblindness: An essay on autism and theory of mInd*. M I T Press, Cambridge, Mass.

Baron-Cohen, S. and Ring, H. (1994). A model of the mindreading system: neuropsychological and neurobiological perspectives. In *Children's early understanding of mind: origins and development* (ed. C. Lewis and P. Mitchell), (pp. 183–207). Erlbaum, Hove.

Baron-Cohen, S., Leslie, A., and Frith, U. (1985). Does the autistic child have a 'theory of mind'? *Cognition*, **21**, 37–46.

Baron-Cohen, S., Ring, H., Moriarty, J., Shmitz, P. Costa, D., and Ell, P. Recognition of mental state terms: A clinical study of autism, and a functional neuroimaging study of normal adults. *British Journal of Psychiarty*. (In press.)

Bauman, M. L. and Kemper, T. L. (1994). Neuroanatomic observations of the brain in autism. In *The neurobiology of autism* (ed. M. L. Bauman and T. L. Kemper), pp. 119–45. J Johns Hopkins Press, Baltimore.

Bayliss, G. C., Rolls, E. T., and Leonard, C. M. (1985). Selectivity between faces in the responses of a population of neurons in the cortex in the superior temporal sulcus of the monkey. *Brain Research*, **342**, 91–102.

Bishop, D. V. M. (1993). Annotation: autism, executive functions and theory of mind: a neuropsychological perspective. *Journal of Child Psychology and Psychiatry*, **34**, 279–93.

Blumer, D. and Benson, D. F. (1975). Personality changes with frontal and temporal lobe lesions. In *Psychiatric aspects of neurological disease*, Vol. 1 (ed. D. F. Benson and D. Blumer). Grune and Stratton, New York.

Bogerts, B., Meetz, C., and Schonfeldt-Baush, R. (1985). Basal ganglia and limbic system pathology in schizophrenia: A morphometric study. *Archives of General Psychiatry*, **42**, 784–91.

Breier, A., Buchanan, R. W., Elkashef, A., Munson, R. C. Kirkpatrick, B., and Gellad, F. (1992). Brain morphology and schizophrenia. A magnetic resonance imaging study of limbic, prefrontal cortex, and caudate structures. *Archives of General Psychiatry*, **49**, 921–6

Broks, P., Young, A., Maratos, E., Calder, A., Coffey, P., Isaac, C., *et al. Human amygdala and recognition of fear*. (Submitted for publication.)

Brothers, L. A. (1990). The social brain: a project for integrating primate behaviour and neurophysiology in a new domain. *Concepts in Neuroscience*, **1**, (1), 27–51.

Brothers, L. A. (1992). Perception of social acts in primates: cognition and neurobiology. *Seminars in the Neurosciences*, **4**, 409–14.

Butter, C. and Snyder, D. (1972). Alterations in aversive and aggressive behaviors following orbital frontal lesions in rhesus monkeys. *Acta Neurobiologica*, **32**, 525–65.

Byrne, R. and Whiten, A. (eds). (1988) *Machiavellian intelligence*. Oxford University Press.

Campbell, R., Heywood, C., Cowey, A., Regard, M., and Landis, T. (1990). Sensitivity to eye gaze in prosopagnosic patients and monkeys with superior temporal sulcus ablation. *Neuropsychologia*, **28**, 1123–42.

Claridge, G. S. (1972) The schizophrenias as nervous types. *British Journal of Psychiatry*, **112**, 1–17.

Claridge, G. S. (1995). *Origins of mental illness* (new impression). Malor Books, Cambridge, Mass.

Claridge, G. S. (1990). Can a disease model of schizophrenia survive? In *Reconstructing schizophrenia* (ed. R.P. Bentall). Routledge, London.

Coughlan, A. K. (1996). Social and emotional changes following head injury. Paper presented at the Northern Neuropsychology Research Group symposium *Neuropsychology of social cognition*. St James's University Hospital, Leeds, UK, 16 May 1996.

Courchesne, E., Yeung-Courchesne, R., Press, G., Hesselink, J., and Jernigan, T. (1988). Hypoplasia of cerebellar vermal lobules VI and VII in autism. *New England Journal of Medicine*, 318, 1349–54.

Damasio, A. R. (1994). *Descartes' error*. Grosset/Putnam, New York.

Davidson, R. J. (1995). Cerebral asymmetry, emotion, and affective style. In *Brain asymmetry* (ed. R. J. Davidson and K. Hugdahl). M I T Press, Cambridge, Mass.

Dawson, G., Phillips, C., and Galpert, L. (1986). Hemispheric specialization and the language abilities of autistic children. *Child Development*, 57, 1440–53.

Dennett, D. C. (1978). *Brainstorms: philosophical essays on mind and psychology*. Bradford Books, Montgomery, VT.

Desimone, R. (1991). Face-selective cells in the temporal cortex of monkeys. *Journal of Cognitive Neuroscience*, 3, 51–67.

Dunbar, R. I. M. (1993). Coevolution of neocortical size, group size and language in humans. *Behavioral and Brain Sciences*, 16, 681–735.

Ellis, A. W. and Young, A. W. (1988). *Human cognitive neuropsychology*. Lawrence Erlbaum, Hove and London.

Engel, G. L. (1977). The need for a new medical model: a challenge for biomedicine. *Science*, 196, 129–36.

Eslinger, P. and Damasio A. R. (1985) Severe disturbance of higher cognition after bilateral frontal lobe ablation: Patient EVR. *Neurology*, 35, 1731–41.

Fein, D., Humes, E., Kaplan, D., and Waterhouse, L. (1984). The question of left hemisphere dysfunction in infantile autism. *Psychological Bulletin*, 95, 258–81.

Fodor, J. (1983). *The modularity of mind*. M I T Press, Cambridge Massachusetts.

Frith, C. D. (1987). The positive and negative symptoms of schizophrenia reflect impairment in the perception and initiation of action. *Psychological Medicine*, 17, 631–48.

Frith, C. D. (1992). *The cognitive neuropsychology of schizophrenia*. Erlbaum, Hove.

Frith, C. D. (1994). Theory of mind in schizophrenia. In *The neuropsychology of schizophrenia* (ed. A. S. David and J. C. Cutting), pp. 147–61. Erlbaum, Hove.

Gillberg, C. and Coleman, M. (1992). *The biology of the autistic syndromes* (2nd edn). MacKeith Press, London.

Goren, C., Sarty, M., and Wu, P. (1975). Visual following and pattern discrimination. *Pediatrics*, 56, 544–49.

Hamann, S. B., Stefanacci, L., Squire, L. R., Adolphs, R., Tranel, D. Damasio, H., and Damasio, A. (1996). Recognizing facial emotion. *Nature*, 379, 497.

Happé, F. (1994) *Autism: An introduction to psychological theory*. UCL Press, London.

Hetzler, B. E. and Griffin, J. L. (1981). Infantile autism and the temporal lobe of the brain. *Journal of Autism and Developmental Disorders*, 9, 153–7.

Hobson, R. P. (1993). *Autism and the development of mind*. Erlbaum Hove.

Hobson, R. P. (1988). Emotion recognition in autism Co-ordinating faces and voices. *Psychological Medicine*, 18, 911–23.

Humphrey, N. K. (1976). The social function of intellect. In *Growing points in ethology*, (ed. P. Bateson and R. Hinde pp. 303–21. Cambridge University Press.

Johnson, M., Dziurrawiec, S., Ellis, H., and Morton, J. (1991). Newborns preferential tracking of face-like stimuli and its subsequent decline. *Cognition*, 40, 1–19.

Kanner, L. (1943). Autistic disturbances of affective contact. *Nervous Child*, 2, 217–50

Kling, A. S. and Brothers, L. A. (1992). The amygdala and social behaviour. In *The amygdala: Neurobiological aspects of emotion, memory, and mental dysfunction* (ed. J. P. Aggleton), pp. 353–77. Wiley-Liss, New York.

Kolb, B. and Whishaw I. (1996). *Fundamentals of human neuropsychology* (4th ed.) W. H. Freeman, New York.

Le Doux, J. (1995). Emotion: clues from the brain. *Annual Review of Psychology*, **46**, 209–35.

Leonard, C. M., Rolls, E. T., Wilson, F. A. W., and Baylis, G. C. (1985). Neurons in the amygdala of the monkey with responses selective for faces. *Behavioral Brain Research*, **15**, 159–76.

Leslie, A. (1987) Pretence and representation: The origins of "theory of mind". *Psychological Review*, **94**, 412–26.

Leslie, A. and Frith, U. (1988). Autistic children's understanding of seeing, knowing, and believing. *British Journal of Developmental Psychology*, **6**, 315–24.

Lezak, M. D. (1995). *Neuropsychological assessment* (3rd ed). Oxford University Press.

McCarthy, R. A. and Warrington, E. K. (1990). *Cognitive neuropsychology: a clinical introduction.* Academic Press, San Diego.

Morton, J. and Frith U. (1994). Causal modelling: a structural approach to developmental psychopathology. In *Manual of developmental psychopathology*, Vol. I (ed. D. Cicchetti and D. J. Cohen). John Wiley, New York.

Nakamura, K., Mikami. A., and Kubota, K. (1992). Activity of single neurons in the monkey amygdala during performance of a visual discrimination task. *Journal of Neurophysiology*, **7**, 1447–63.

Nicolson, R. I., Fawcett. A. J. and Dean, P. (1995). Time estimation deficits in developmental dyslexia: Evidence for cerebellar involvement. *Proceedings of the Royal Society*, **259**, 43–7.

Ozonoff, S., Pennington, B. F., and Rogers, S. J. (1991). Executive function deficits in high-functioning autistic individuals: relationship to a theory of mind. *Journal of Child Psychology and Psychiatry*, **32**, 1081–105.

Perner, J. (1991). *Understanding the representational mind*. MIT Press, Cambridge, Mass.

Perner, J. and Wimmer, H. (1985). 'John thinks that Mary thinks that . . .': Attribution of second-order beliefs by 5–10 year old children. *Journal of Experimental Child Psychology*, **39**, 437–71.

Perrett, D., Smith, P., Potter, D., Mistlin, A., Head, A., Milner, A, and Jeeves, M. (1985). Visual cells in the temporal cortex sensitive to face view and gaze direction. *Proceedings of the Royal Society of London*, B223, 293–317.

Premack, D. and Woodruff, G. (1978). Does the chimpanzee have a theory of mind? *Behavioural and brain sciences*, **4**, 515–26.

Price, B., Daffen, K., and Stowe, R. (1990). The compartmental learning disabilities of early frontal damage. *Brain*, **113**, 1383–93.

Reynolds, G. P. (1992). The amygdala and the neurochemistry of schizophrenia. In *The Amygdala: neurobiological aspects of emotion, memory, and mental dysfunction* (ed. J. P. Aggleton). Wiley-Liss, New York.

Schwartz, G. E. (1982). Testing the biopsychosocial model: The ultimate challenge facing behavioural medicine? *Journal of Consulting and Clinical Psychology*, **50**, 1040–53.

Sergent, J., Ohta, S., and MacDonald, B. (1992). Functional neuranatomy of face and object processing. *Brain*, **115**, 15–36.

Shields, J., Varley, R., Broks, P., and Simpson, A. (1996). Hemispheric function in developmental language disorders and high-level autism. *Developmental Medicine and Child Neurology*, **38**, 473–86.

Shultz, T. R., Wells, D., and Sarda, M. (1980). The development of the ability to distinguish intended actions from mistakes, reflexes and passive movements. *British Journal of Social and Clinical Psychology*, **19**, 301–10.

Trevarthen, C., Aitken, K., Papoudi, D., and Roberts, J. (1996). *Children with autism*. Jessica Kingsley Publishers, London.

Weiskrantz, L. (1956). Behavioral changes associated with ablation of the amygdaloid complex in monkeys. *Journal of Comparative and Physiological Psychology*, **49**, 381–91.

Whiten, A. and Perner, J. (1991). Fundamental issues in the multidisciplinary study of mindreading. In *Natural theories of mind: evolution, development and simulation of everyday mindreading* (ed. A. Whiten), pp. 1–17. Basil Blackwell, Oxford.

Young, A., Aggleton, J., Hellawell, D., Johnson, M., Broks, P., and Hanley, R. (1995). Face processing impairments after amygdalotomy. *Brain*, **118**, 15–24.

7

Latent inhibition: relevance to the neural substrates of schizophrenia and schizotypy?

HELEN J. CASSADAY

INTRODUCTION

Schizophrenia may be marked by a loss of the 'selectivity which normal attention ordinarily exercises among the sensory impressions' (Bleuler 1911): an operational measure of such a marker might provide a handle on measuring predisposition to schizophrenia, together with related traits in the normal population. A measure appropriate for use in animals would allow investigation of the neural substrates of the presumed marker. Latent inhibition (LI) has recently emerged as one such possibility.

Selectivity in the learning mechanism ensures that outcomes are normally attributed to their most likely causes. One aspect of such selectivity is the reduced associability of familiar but ineffectual stimuli. Normal animals, rats and people alike, do not show learning when the stimulus that presently predicts an event has previously been without any consequences for the subject. This effect can be measured systematically: latent inhibition results from repeated presentation of a stimulus without effects (pre-exposure); the 'LI effect' refers to the *difference* in later learning with that stimulus, comparing pre-exposed and non-pre-exposed groups. Treatments abolishing LI in the laboratory rat are used to determine the particular neurotransmitter systems and brain structures necessary for its normal development (see Weiner 1990, for review). In tandem, research with human subjects indicates that the loss of LI may be a marker of an attentional deficit characteristic of human schizophrenia (cf. Bleuler 1911) and also reflect differences in selective learning associated with schizotypy. Thus the inability to filter out irrelevant stimuli may be a trait-related risk factor for schizophrenia. The fact that this (in)ability can be studied experimentally in an animal model raises the additional possibility that investigation of its neural substrates (in the rat) may inform biological theories of schizophrenia and schizotypy.

A measure of selectivity in the learning mechanism provides a *psychological* model of schizophrenic dysfunction. More typically, animal models have relied on the similarity of certain drug-induced states to schizophrenia: the drug (usually amphetamine) is then given to the animal with a view to identifying novel drugs which reverse the behavioural disturbances as anti-psychotics. In LI studies, the animal model relies on a behavioural link (the loss of LI) to bridge the gap between investigations of cognitive change in human subjects and its neural substrates in the rat. The loss of LI thus provides a potential neurocognitive correlate of both schizophrenia and of schizotypy in non-clinical populations.

There is good support for the view that schizotypy is a reliable discriminating measure (Jackson and Claridge 1991), and that such measures are related to schizophrenia (Chapman *et al.* 1994; also see Chapter 1). However, since the loss of LI is empirically associated with schizotypy (see below) inferences from the animal model about the biological correlates of schizotypy do not presume the relationship between schizophrenia and schizotypy. The fact that the degree of LI provides a marker for both suggests the possibility that they have at least some shared biological bases (see Claridge 1987, 1994*a*). So investigation of the neural substrates of LI might prove relevant to both schizophrenia and a dimension of biological variation associated with schizotypy.

The case for LI as a model for schizophrenia has a long history (Solomon *et al.* 1981; Weiner *et al.* 1981; Lubow *et al.* 1987; Lubow 1989; Solomon and Crider 1988; Feldon and Weiner 1991*a*). The basic model rests on a series of assumptions and observations, summarized below in overview. Recent moves also attempt to integrate the neuropsychology of LI with that of schizophrenia (Weiner 1990; Gray *et al.* 1991; J. A. Gray *et al.* 1995). The assumptions are as follows:

1. The loss of LI provides a potential model of an 'attentional' disorder characteristic of schizophrenia: an openness to environmental stimuli irrespective of their past significance.

2. LI is reduced or abolished in acute schizophrenia and, since the failure of LI is expressed as a relative *learning increment*, this change cannot be due to non-specific features of the disease process.

3. The symptoms of acute schizophrenia are associated with a disturbance in the dopamine (DA) system. The indirect DA agonist amphetamine can precipitate psychosis in some individuals and established antipsychotics are DA antagonists.

4. LI is abolished by amphetamine treatment in the rat and this effect can be reversed by treatment with known antipsychotic drugs. Treatment with antipsychotics can also enhance LI in the rat, and human subjects may show comparable effects.

5. The normal development of LI depends critically on the hippocampus and nucleus accumbens.

Whilst the loss of LI is a psychological model of schizophrenic dysfunction, not necessarily tied to dysfunction in particular neurotransmitter systems, its close ties with the amphetamine model and DA hypothesis of schizophrenia may prove a constraint on its success. The validity of the DA hypothesis is itself in question. However, the fact that LI can be demonstrated in human subjects and is absent in schizophrenics already gives the model a significant advantage over drug models which rely on reproducing the neurochemical changes of schizophrenia, rather than offering insights into the components of the psychological dysfunction *a priori*.

First, the paradigm itself requires explanation: the procedures used to demonstrate LI in control groups and to compare different subject populations are set out in the following two sections. An outline of the psychological mechanisms that may underlie LI then follows, to give a framework for interpreting the effects of experimental drug and lesion treatments and considering any relevance they may have for schizophrenia and schizotypy. This relevance depends on the adequacy of the (loss of) LI as a marker for schizophrenia and hence on the criteria used to assess the validity of the animal model.

LATENT INHIBITION PROCEDURES

The degree of LI is assessed by comparing the pre-exposed (PE) group with a non-pre-exposed (NPE) control in a follow-up test of associative learning. Experimental effects (of drug or lesion treatments or in different subject populations) can be measured in a simple 2 × 2 design. The degree of LI is assessed by comparing PE and NPE groups in each experimental condition. The strict control of pre-exposure to an alternative stimulus has not typically been incorporated into designs that include treatment or individual differences variables, because of the increase in subject numbers required (but see Tsaltas *et al.* 1984; Lipp and Vaitl 1992).

Effects on conditioning are determined by comparing NPE groups in the experimental and control conditions, since treatments such as amphetamine might increase learning or sensitivity to motivationally significant stimuli like shock (see J. A. Gray *et al.* 1995). Loss of LI due to an increase in learning in the PE group is most clearly interpretable if learning in the NPE group is reduced or unaffected. This is precisely the pattern of effects seen in schizophrenics and high schizotypes (Baruch *et al.* 1988*a,b*; N. S. Gray *et al.* 1992*a*; Lubow *et al.* 1992); it is also the trend seen after some drug treatments in the rat (Cassaday *et al.* 1993*a*). Analysis of the many studies with amphetamine done in Tel Aviv suggests that amphetamine in fact has no consistent effect on conditioning in NPE groups (see J. A. Gray *et al.* 1995). In such cases, the loss of LI cannot be due to non-specific effects on learning associated with the individual differences variable or treatment condition.

Within-subject designs compare each subject's learning after pre-exposure to one stimulus with learning about an alternative (non-pre-exposed) stimulus. Such procedures introduce a certain amount of noise, since stimuli inevitably differ in salience and this too affects learning, but they have the advantage that subjects now serve as their own control for the comparison of PE and NPE conditions, so that the effects of between-subjects variance are minimized.

Rat subjects

Many of the rat studies described below use the conditioned suppression procedure (Estes and Skinner 1941), with a 'pre-exposure' stage to set up LI (for example Weiner *et al.* 1984). We compare the disruption of drinking

(A)

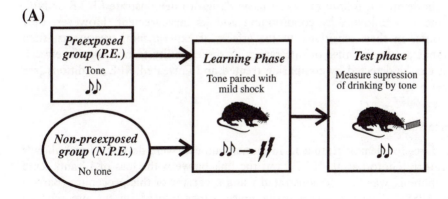

(B)

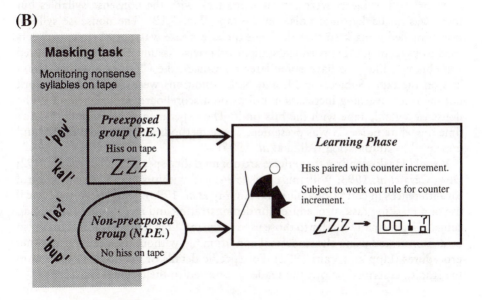

Fig. 7.1. Schematic representation of original procedures used to demonstrate latent inhibition in (A) rat and (B) human subjects. Further details are given in the text.

after the presentation of a tone (conditioned stimulus, CS) associated with shock (unconditioned stimulus, UCS), in groups pre-exposed or not pre-exposed to the tone (see Fig. 7.1A). Normal animals with past experience of the tone without consequence show reduced learning relative to controls, which do not have such pre-exposure. A variety of other procedures are also used to demonstrate LI in the rat, such as conditioned avoidance, also using an aversive UCS, and appetitive procedures, in which the pre-exposed stimulus later signals food. These procedures differ in detail but follow the same basic design to demonstrate LI: PE or NPE in stage 1 is followed by conditioning and its measurement. However, they may differ in their sensitivity to the effects of experimental treatments, such as amphetamine, because of differences in susceptibility to non-specific effects. These can be detected by comparing treated and untreated NPE conditions (see above).

Human subjects

Procedures for demonstrating LI in human subjects were developed in Lubow's laboratory (Ginton *et al.* 1975), and the link between the loss of LI and acute schizophrenia was first demonstrated using a variant of this procedure (Baruch *et al.* 1988*a*). The CS was a white noise, superimposed, in the pre-exposed condition, on a tape of nonsense syllables which the subjects were required to monitor. NPE subjects were set the same task with the nonsense syllables but there was no background noise on the tape (Fig. 7.1B). The nonsense syllable task provided a mask so that the pre-exposure phase was not obvious (subjects used to psychological experiments might otherwise assume that the pre-exposed stimulus was likely to have some later relevance): the CS-to-be sounded like a hiss on the tape. Subjects in PE and NPE conditions were then asked to work out the rule governing increases in points on a scoreboard while listening to the nonsense syllable tape with the hiss on it. The experimenter added a point each time the white noise CS was presented. These methods have been developed and improved by automation (Allan *et al.* 1995).

Visual LI tasks confirm that effects are not modality-specific (Lubow *et al.* 1992; De la Casa *et al.* 1993; Williams *et al.* 1994) and within-subjects designs control for differences in conditionability (N. S. Gray *et al.* 1995). Aside from the typical use of a masking task, procedures for demonstrating and measuring LI in human subjects are formally similar to those used in the rat. LI in human subjects may also be demonstrated using electrodermal conditioning, without the need for masking procedures (Lipp and Vaitl 1992). For specific details of the procedures used in the studies described below, the reader is referred to the original sources.

RESEARCH ON LATENT INHIBITION IN HUMAN SUBJECTS

Lubow and colleagues (Weiner *et al.* 1981, 1984, 1988; Lubow 1989) argued for the identity of the attentional processes necessary for normal LI and those dysfunctional in schizophrenia. After the demonstration of the loss of LI in acute schizophrenics (Baruch *et al.* 1988*a*; N. S. Gray *et al.* 1992*a*), it was important to determine the reliability and specificity with which reduced LI is related to the disturbances of acute schizophrenia.

The first possibility, that the loss of LI in acute schizophrenics was an artefact of medication, was dismissed by Baruch *et al.* (1988*a*): the loss of LI in human schizophrenia is seen in the acute but not the chronic phase of illness and

Baruch's acute schizophrenics were on higher levels of medication than those in the chronic phase of illness. If treatment with neuroleptics were to abolish LI, chronic schizophrenics might still show as much LI as controls because of the development of tolerance during treatment and the use of lower doses. The difficulty with this account is the conflict with the rat data, in that there is a consistent body of evidence that treatment with amphetamine blocks (Solomon *et al.* 1981; Weiner *et al.* 1981, 1984, 1988), and dopaminergic antipsychotics enhance, LI (Weiner *et al.* 1987; Christison *et al.* 1988; Solomon and Crider 1988; Feldon and Weiner 1991*a*). However, the fact that disruption of LI is also seen when normal animals are given higher doses of haloperidol (Dunn *et al.* 1993) suggests that the possibility that the loss of LI in acute schizophrenics is due to medication cannot be excluded. Such an effect of postsynaptic blockade is not inconsistent with the effects of amphetamine on LI, since it may be related to the normal mechanisms of tolerance, one aspect of which is the transient stimulation of DA release (Di Chiara and Imperato 1985). Consistent with the possibility that the loss of LI in schizophrenics *results from their drug treatment* is a recent study in which normal LI was found in drug-free schizophrenics (Williams *et al.* 1996*c*).

The study of unmedicated schizophrenics is problematic in that they are difficult to find and may then turn out to be too unwell to be tested. Unmedicated schizophrenics who are well enough to be tested may turn out to be atypical. We already know that there are subgroups of schizophrenics who show normal LI. In an early test of the hypothesis, Baruch found (counter to prediction) that paranoid schizophrenics show normal LI (Lubow *et al.* 1987) and it is consistently reported that LI is normal in chronic schizophrenics (Baruch *et al.* 1988*a*; N. S. Gray *et al.* 1992*a*). It now seems that this normalization of LI is not a result of medication: unmedicated patients ill for less than 12 months do not show LI, whereas those ill for more than 12 months at the time of testing show LI as usual (N. S. Gray *et al.* 1995). It follows that duration of illness at the point of diagnosis may explain normal LI in schizophrenics who evade medication (Williams *et al.* 1996*c*). N. S. Gray *et al.* caught cases at the point of diagnosis, through the normal systems of referral, and used independent criteria to determine the onset of illness retrospectively.

It is now well-established that LI may be reduced in normal subjects with high scores on the Eysenck P-scale or the more specific measure of schizotypy, the STA (Baruch *et al.* 1988*b*; Lipp and Vaitl 1992; Lubow *et al.* 1992; De la Casa *et al.* 1993; Allan *et al.* 1995). A recent study finds a significant negative correlation between measures of schizotypy and within-subjects LI (Morton *et al.* 1996). Such demonstrations provide a further point of continuity from animal to human studies and show that LI may also be absent in subjects without behavioural abnormalities. The finding that hyperactive children also show LI deficits (Lubow and Josman 1993) makes sense in that such children may be more likely to process non-salient irrelevant stimuli, but weakens the case for LI as a selective marker for *schizophrenic* attention dysfunction.

In addition to its association with personality variables, LI in human subjects may be abolished by a single 5 mg dose of amphetamine (N. S. Gray *et al.*

1992*b*). Whilst this finding is superficially consistent with the presumed role of DA in schizophrenia, the dose level involved is a mild treatment that does not induce signs of schizophrenic disturbance. In fact even regular amphetamine use is typically insufficient to induce psychosis (see Claridge and Healy 1994). Tobacco smoking is similarly associated with the loss of LI in human subjects (Allan *et al.* 1995). Whilst there is no evidence that smoking causes schizophrenia, there is strong evidence for an association between the two (reviewed by Lohr and Flynn 1992). Recently, it has been demonstrated that schizotypal personality traits are associated both with smoking regular tobacco (Williams *et al.* 1996*a*) and a history of cannabis use (Williams *et al.* 1996*b*), but again there are no longitudinal studies that allow analysis of whether personality predisposes to drug use or vice versa.

The fact that a range of non-schizophrenic groups do not show LI suggests that its loss is associated with an underlying disturbance, perhaps necessary but certainly not sufficient for the display of acute schizophrenic symptoms. We need more systematic investigation of LI in other adult psychiatric populations: the well-documented role of DA in the normal development of LI is consistent with the possibility that LI is modulated by arousal levels, and increased arousal is not specific to schizophrenia. Moreover, since in normal subjects, variables such as tobacco smoking have already been found to affect the size of the LI effect seen, it is critical that carefully matched controls are used in evaluating effects due to schizophrenia and schizotypy.

THE PSYCHOLOGICAL MECHANISMS UNDERLYING LATENT INHIBITION

If there is no normal LI effect in acute schizophrenia (Baruch *et al.* 1988*a*; N. S. Gray *et al.* 1992*a*), the best psychological account of this deficit may inform cognitive accounts of schizophrenia. The deficit cannot be attributed to a non-specific consequences of the disease process since the loss of LI shows itself as a relative *increase* in learning in the pre-exposed group.

Repeated stimulus presentations also result in habituation, already extensively studied in relation to schizophrenia; but the relationship between LI and habituation is controversial. There is evidence that habituation is necessary for normal LI, in that the orienting response provides an index of stimulus associability (Swan and Pearce 1988), but it does not follow that habituation and LI are one and the same thing. Habituation refers to the decline in the orienting response, both within and between stimulus presentations. The latter 'long-term' effect has been suggested to explain the decline in associability at the conditioning phase of an LI procedure. But, although there is some evidence for this proposed equivalence (Kaye and Pearce 1987), LI and long-term habituation have been found to differ, for example, in their sensitivity to contextual changes (Hall and Channel 1986). They are also affected in opposite ways by changes in stimulus salience (see reviews by Lubow (1989) and Hall (1991)).

LI is typically proposed as a model of attentional deficit, measured as selectivity in the learning mechanism (Lubow and Moore 1959; Mackintosh 1975). However, although schizophrenic deficits have been consistently described in attentional terms, attention is itself a poorly defined construct with several properties, including span, level, maintenance, and the capacity to shift. Related to the latter, it is selective. The normal development of LI restricts the range of stimuli likely to enter into subsequent associations and when LI is abolished, there is relatively little effect on learning of previous non-reinforcement of the stimulus in use. The loss of LI may thus result from an increased behavioural switching (Weiner 1990), but this would presumably constitute *increased* attention to current events when reinforcement contingencies change. Similarly, the loss of LI in human subjects may be related to the failure of the masking task or a greater capacity for controlled processing (Lubow and Gewirtz 1995; see below): this effect might also be described as *heightened* attention. It follows that 'attentional deficit' may not be the best description of what is measured by the (loss of) LI.

Recent accounts of the (loss of) LI and schizophrenia have been framed in terms of the lack of effect of 'memories of past regularities' (Hemsley 1977, 1993; Weiner 1990; Gray *et al.* 1991). In the rat studies, amphetamine has effects across a number of two-stage paradigms which are consistent with a failure to mediate when normal performance depends on an interaction between the stimulus presented and stored memories of past contingencies (see Weiner 1990). This deficit could also be described in terms of the 'output processes' of attention which are concerned with the retrieval of information from memory before responding (cf. Hemsley 1977, 1993). Retrieval processes also provide some account of normal LI in the rat (Kraemer and Roberts 1984; Kraemer and Spear 1992; Bouton 1993). The idea is that the association formed in pre-exposure ('this stimulus signals nothing') normally interferes with conditioning ('this stimulus signals something'), or with the expression of previous learning (measured in a transfer test).

The need for masking in most human LI paradigms has often been dismissed as a necessary methodological difference between rat and human studies, of little theoretical significance. However, just as the use of electric shock in rat studies may introduce problems of interpretation, masking makes the interpretation of the loss of LI in human subjects less than straightforward (Lubow and Gerwirtz 1995). Since the demonstration of LI depends on the use of an effective masking task, it follows that when LI is reduced this could be due to an impairment of processes necessary for LI, common to rat and human, or to a failure of the masking procedure in the pre-exposed human subjects. Systematic comparison of masking task load has in fact shown that masking modulates LI (see Lubow and Gewirtz 1995). This finding suggests that the need for masking in human studies should not be dismissed as a procedural detail and it has been written into Lubow and Gewirtz's (1995) theoretical account of LI, in terms of the switch from controlled to automatic processing of events without consequence (Schneider and Shiffrin 1977). With relatively ineffective masking, there may be increased controlled processing of the pre-exposed stimuli and hence no LI: in the original auditory procedure (Baruch *et al.* 1988*a*; Ginton *et al.* 1975), successful demonstration of LI requires that monitoring the nonsense syllables (the masking task) demands attentional resources to the extent that subjects have no subjective awareness of the hiss on the tape (the CS-to-be). There is evidence that such masking procedures are less effective for highly schizotypal subjects (De la Casa *et al.* 1993) and this suggests an account of schizophrenic attention dysfunction in terms of an impairment in the ability to switch from controlled to automatic processing (Lubow and Gewirtz 1995). It would follow from this analysis that LI tasks in animals do not measure the same underlying process as human LI tasks that rely on masking: fortunately, some do not (Lipp and Vaitl 1992).

THE NEURAL SUBSTRATES OF LATENT INHIBITION

Lesion studies

There have been a number of reports that damage to the septo-hippocampal system abolishes LI (Solomon and Moore 1975; Kaye and Pearce 1987; Clark *et al.* 1992; see Weiner 1990 for a review) and there is evidence that damage to nucleus accumbens is sufficient to disrupt LI (Tai *et al.* 1995). Recent theoretical syntheses put these data together to propose a neuropsychology of LI and, by inference, schizophrenia, supposing that the normal interaction between hippocampus and accumbens may be critical (Gray *et al.* 1991; Weiner 1990). However, there is a recent report that neurotoxic lesions to hippocampus, produced with ibotenic acid that spares fibres of passage, do not abolish LI (Honey and Good 1993), and some evidence that neurotoxic and conventional hippocampal lesions and conventional lesions to the nucleus accumbens may actually enhance LI (Reilly *et al.* 1993; Harrington and Purves 1995; Purves *et al.* 1995).

Whilst the data are at present contradictory in terms of the direction of effects, the rat studies suggest that the limbic system is critically involved in the normal development of latent inhibition. Superficially these findings appear consistent with the neuropathology believed to be associated with schizophrenia (Weiner 1990; Gray *et al.* 1991; Bogerts 1993; Bogerts *et al.* 1993; see also below). More lesion work will be required to establish which pathways are critical for the normal development of LI and what determines the direction of effects seen.

Pharmacological studies

In the rat, LI is disrupted by acute (Weiner *et al.* 1988) or chronic (Solomon *et al.* 1981; Weiner *et al.* 1984) treatment with the indirect DA agonist, amphetamine. Conversely, LI is enhanced by the typical neuroleptic haloperidol, given acutely (Weiner *et al.* 1987; Weiner and Feldon 1987) or chronically (Christison *et al.* 1988). These findings are compatible with the dominant DA theory of schizophrenia (Haracz 1982). The demonstration that LI is also reduced in normal subjects treated with amphetamine (N. S. Gray *et al.* 1992*b*) supports the view that the DA system is also critically involved in the normal development of LI in human subjects.

Whilst nicotine administration abolishes LI in the rat (Joseph *et al.* 1993), it seems likely that this effect is mediated by nictotine's action as an indirect DA agonist. Evidence for the role of the noradrenergic system in the development of LI is inconsistent (Tsaltas *et al.* 1984; Weiner 1990, for review). There is clearer evidence for a role of the serotonergic (5-HT) system in the development of LI. Solomon and co-workers first demonstrated that LI is abolished by treatments which deplete 5-HT (Solomon *et al.* 1978, 1980). Further studies have demonstrated that LI is also abolished by selective serotonergic lesions (Asin *et al.* 1980; Cassaday *et al.* 1993*b*) and that such effects are haloperidol reversible (Loskutova *et al.* 1990). LI is also abolished by treatment with the serotonergic drugs RU 24969 and ritanserin (Cassaday *et al.* 1993*a*). RU 24969 has the secondary effect of increasing extra-cellular DA in nucleus accumbens (Boulenguez *et al.* 1994; J. A. Gray *et al.* 1995) and ritanserin also activates DA neurons (Ugedo *et al.* 1989). The serotonergic system is well placed to modulate both the dopaminergic system (for example Barnes *et al.* 1987) and normal integration between the hemispheres (Doty 1989). So there is no necessary contradiction in the above data with either the DA model, the effects of amphetamine on LI (cf. Trulson and Jacobs 1979), or accounts of schizophrenia and schizotypy which stress the role of interhemispheric processes.

A MARKER FOR SCHIZOPHRENIC ATTENTION DYSFUNCTION?

How much should we reasonably expect of an animal model of schizophrenia? LI is shown by many species (Lubow 1989). This kind of phylogenetic continuity—the idea that the learning mechanism in rat and human is selective—is generally accepted and is a basic assumption of (animal) learning theory (for example Dickinson 1980). Far more contentious is the validity of an animal model of schizophrenia, since the central feature of schizophrenia is, by definition, thought disorder, related to disturbances in language and information processing which depend on the normal functioning of higher cortical areas. Such deficits have no obvious parallel in other species and the loss of LI therefore cannot provide an analogue of the entire spectrum of schizophrenic symptoms. At best it provides a marker of a fundamental change in information processing, assumed close, or identical, to the central underlying dysfunction(s) of schizophrenia. There are a number of established criteria for assessing the validity of animal models: whether the changes produced by the experimental treatment resemble the human condition modelled (face validity); how such changes relate to our theoretical understanding of the condition (construct validity); and the reliability with which the model is sensitive to established treatments for the condition and suggests effective new treatments (predictive validity).

Construct and face validity of the LI model

Amphetamine-treated rats bear little superficial resemblance to human schizophrenics. However, with the adoption of the marker approach, using animal models, one can duck face validity as a potential irrelevance: models with little obvious face validity can turn out to have high pharmacological predictive validity (see below).

Construct validity is more important (Willner 1984, 1991; Ellenbroek and Cools 1990). Initially it was assumed that a good model should resemble the clinical condition in aetiology, neurobiological mechanisms, symptomatology, and treatment (McKinney and Bunney 1969). However, this turned out to be a tall order in that the first two criteria are typically unknown, if not the subject of the study. In the case of LI, construct validity rests on the evidence that rats with hyperactive DA mechanisms fail to show LI and an identical failure to show LI is found in acute schizophrenics, marking an essential characteristic of the disease process (Feldon and Weiner 1991*b*). But the dopamine hypothesis is already at issue and it is not enough to focus on apparent similarities between the behavioural measures used in LI and the clinical symptoms of schizophrenia: construct validity requires theoretical analysis of both, with a theoretical integration, in so far as this is possible (Willner 1991). As we have seen, the theoretical interpretation of LI is controversial and the procedures used in animal and human studies may not measure the same underlying processes. Issues related to construct validity will naturally qualify the conclusions reached here.

Predictive validity: screening for novel antipsychotics

Many animal models also fail tests of predictive validity; that is they do not reliably discriminate between effective and ineffective therapeutic treatments. To take an example from the depression literature—a model plausibly based on behavioural despair—the Porsolt swim test (Porsolt 1979) turns out to have poor predictive validity as a screen for novel antidepressants, since swim-time is also increased by stimulants such as caffeine (Schechter and Chance 1979). Another model based on surgical intervention, 'the olfactory bulbectomized rat', turns out to have very good predictive validity in that the biochemical consequences of the surgery both resemble those associated with depression and are selectively reversed by antidepressant drugs (Van-Riezen and Leonard 1990).

For our purposes, LI enhancement should pick up known antipsychotics (see Feldon and Weiner 1991*a*; Dunn *et al.* 1993) and indicate new treatments for schizophrenia. But while, for example, the anti-psychotic potential of 5–HT3 antagonists (Costall *et al.* 1988) was supported by the LI model (Moran and Moser 1992; Warburton *et al.* 1994), there is little evidence that 5-HT3 antagonists are of benefit in schizophrenia. If the predictive validity of the LI model is good, it should not turn out to be enhanced by treatments without demonstrable antipsychotic effects.

It remains to be seen whether LI will discriminate novel non-dopaminergic antipsychotics. The angiotensin converting enzyme (ACE) inhibitor, ceronapril, has also been found to enhance LI, but only within a narrow dose range (Weiner *et al.* 1992). Information on the effectiveness of ACE inhibitors in the clinical management of schizophrenia is not available. However, it has been established that the novel antipsychotic, sertindole, both enhances LI in normal rats and antagonizes amphetamine-induced disruption of LI (Weiner *et al.* 1994).

CONCLUSIONS AND FUTURE DIRECTIONS

There are many threads to the argument that the loss of LI provides a valid model of schizophrenic attention deficit. Employing animal studies to investigate the associated neural substrates results in further testable predictions (Weiner 1990; Gray *et al.* 1991). Furthermore, the measurement of LI might mark a continuum of cognitive style, through levels of schizotypy to schizophrenia, with benign discontinuous effects (the loss of LI) being apparent before clinically significant signs of abnormality which meet diagnostic criteria for schizophrenia (see Claridge and Broks 1984; Claridge 1987, 1994*a*). This raises the possibility that the neural systems involved in LI may also be involved in schizotypy.

Do we have a neuropsychology of schizotypy?

Neuropsychology is not synonymous with neuropathology, but in the case of schizophrenia, there is evidence for structural changes in the brain as the disease progresses. Unfortunately, medication typically confounds interpretation of these changes. Leaving aside the debate over the pattern and consistency of pathology associated with schizophrenia, ventricular enlargement supports the view that something irreversible may happen to the schizophrenic brain after prolonged illness and medication. And there is even some intriguing overlap with the areas involved in the normal development of LI. For example, there is post-mortem evidence for a loss of neurons in nucleus accumbens in the brains of chronic schizophrenics (Pakkenberg 1990) and LI has been found to be abolished by restricted lesions to nucleus accumbens in the rat (Tai *et al.* 1995). This is not a tidy convergence of evidence since the loss of LI is claimed to provide a marker of *acute* rather than *chronic* schizophrenia (Baruch *et al.* 1988*a*; N. S. Gray *et al.* 1995).

It has nevertheless been suggested that the mesolimbic DA system, specifically the nucleus accumbens, may be the 'final common path' via which treatments abolishing LI act (Weiner 1990); and the research interest in LI has been driven by its sensitivity to dopaminergic drugs and limbic lesions. The effects of non-specific hippocampal lesions on LI are also well-documented and further work is needed to clarify the relationship between the septo-hippocampal system, associated fibre pathways, and nucleus accumbens function with respect to LI (Gray *et al.* 1991; J. A. Gray *et al.* 1995). Lesion studies on LI in the animal model may help to delineate the critical circuitry necessary for the normal development of LI but cannot reproduce the pathology characteristic of schizophrenia.

The schizophrenic brain will be characterized by atypical patterns of functioning and/or regions of incomplete cell loss or partial lesion, rather than complete (targeted) lesions to hippocampus, adjacent cortex, or accumbens. Malfunctioning in a *partially damaged* structure has, for example, been shown to have particularly deleterious effects after anoxic brain damage (Bachevalier and Mishkin 1989). However, if we can generalize from rat to human, and if all of the above data prove reliable, the fact that (chronic) *unmedicated* schizophrenics show normal LI (N. S. Gray *et al.* 1995; Williams *et al.* 1996c) suggests that the very brain structures necessary for LI in the rat are functioning *normally* in schizophrenia. The results of these studies also conflict with the evidence that LI is a reliable trait marker, since chronic schizophrenics presumably still have the associated schizotypal trait!

There is little evidence allowing us to map a neuropsychological continuum associated with schizotypy onto cognitive function, and schizophrenia is associated with discontinuous effects, including some brain damage. However, there is evidence that normal individual differences in hemisphere asymmetry are related to schizotypy (Chapter 8) and amphetamine effects on LI may be lateralized (N. S. Gray *et al.* 1992b). Differences in hemispheric asymmetry may co-occur with the lower-level dysfunctions related to schizophrenia, whether as asymmetric loss of cells in the limbic system (Bogerts *et al.* 1993) or as asymmetric loss of normal input from the brain stem (Doty 1989). However, there is no evidence to suggest that highly schizotypal 'normal' subjects are also characterized by this sort of neuropathology.

Do we have a neurochemical correlate of schizotypy?

The loss of LI offers a model only for the *acute* phase of schizophrenia, since it is well established that LI is normal in chronic schizophrenics (Baruch *et al.* 1988a; N. S. Gray *et al.* 1992a, 1995). The acute phase of illness may be transient and reversible (individuals may recover completely after an episode of illness), suggesting that it is associated with functional rather than structural disturbance. In this respect, too, the loss of LI after lesions in the rat needs explanation, in terms of the neurochemical consequences of the lesions. The abolition of LI by acute amphetamine administration, in both rat and human subjects, is consistent with the view that the LI model measures neurochemical abnormality, i.e. a functional and potentially reversible dysfunction.

There is some indirect evidence that neurochemical variation correlates with schizotypy, at least at the extremes. LI enhancement in normal subjects is most apparent in subjects with high schizotypy scores (Williams *et al.* 1994) and this suggests that the psychological effect of DA blockade may show a different dose-response relation in high and low schizotypes. If schizotypy scores are related to DA function, this might mediate the effect of schizotypy on LI, or the relationship might be indirect, both dimensions of variation in some way related to disturbance in a second functional system. The relationship between schizotypy and cigarette smoking would be consistent with the above (nicotine increases mesolimbic DA transmission (Grenhoff and Svensson 1989), if it were not for the demonstration that tobacco smoking and high STA scores correlate independently with the loss of LI in the normal population (Allan *et al.* 1995).

More information on the range of drugs affecting LI is needed. It is not clear how closely the pharmacology of LI in rats corresponds to the clinical pharmacology of schizophrenia. LI is abolished by a range of treatments, including chlordiazepoxide (CDP) and selective serotonergic compounds, which do not result in psychotic-like experiences in man (Feldon and Weiner 1989; Cassaday *et al.* 1993*a*). However, it is possible that such compounds abolish LI by a different mechanism: CDP abolishes LI when its administration is confined to the pre-exposure phase of the experiment, perhaps because it impairs the processing of novel stimuli (see Feldon and Weiner 1989).

In the human literature further dissociations arise. The dose of amphetamine (5 mg) shown to abolish LI in normal subjects (N. S. Gray *et al.* 1992*b*) is low and does not produce serious psychological disturbances. Similarly, the loss of LI in those with schizotypal personalities is not associated with schizophrenic-type symptoms (Baruch *et al.* 1988*b*; Lipp and Vaitl 1992). At best then, the loss of LI is associated with neurochemical disturbance that is necessary but not sufficient for the display of schizophrenic symptoms in the acute phase. Convincing demonstration that the two are necessarily related will require a larger data base in order to determine the correlation between the size of LI and level of positive symptomatology (cf. Baruch *et al.* 1988*b*; N. S. Gray *et al.* 1995).

What is being measured in LI procedures?

Given that there is disagreement over the theoretical interpretation of (the loss of) LI and its validity as a marker for schizophrenia, the focus of research on its neural substrates may be premature. Further work is also needed to clarify the psychological mechanisms associated with the loss of LI: as we have seen, it cannot, for example, be accounted for simply in terms of a failure of habituation.

Further specification of the nature of the deficit underlying the loss of LI may be possible when the theoretical interpretation of LI is clearer (for example Mackintosh 1975; Bouton 1993). We should compare the effects of treatments known to abolish LI (i.e. reduce the effects of stimulus pre-exposure) on learning reduced in other ways. Useful procedures include low compared with high UCS intensity (Killcross *et al.* 1994) and trace conditioning procedures: with increasing delay of UCS presentation, conditioning to the CS is reduced. DeVietti and co-workers suggest that LI may effectively reduce to a trace-conditioning phenomenon: pre-exposure to the CS-to-be may alter its associability because of a change in salience, so that only the onset and initial segments of the stimulus are effective in later conditioning (DeVietti *et al.* 1987).

LI tasks used in human subjects may measure something different again

(Lubow and Gewirtz 1995). A better understanding of normal LI may in turn have implications for theories of information processing in schizophrenia.

Where next?

The potential of the LI model lies in providing a behavioural marker which may be used, both in a range of psychiatric groups and normal subjects, to establish its specificity to schizophrenia; and, in animals, to establish the neural systems necessary for its normal development. LI might also be useful as a screen for novel antipsychotics, given that established antipsychotics reliably enhance LI. There is, however, a paradox in the logic in the development of a model within the DA hypothesis of schizophrenia, with a view to screening for better drugs. It seems that the DA hypothesis is wrong enough for better drugs to be needed but right enough to provide a first hurdle for the prospective animal model. Precisely this assumption has been challenged with respect to LI and the use of amphetamine, rather than, for example LSD, as the drug model for schizophrenia (Claridge 1994*b*). LI fails Claridge's test of validity in that, although it is affected by a number of other serotonergic treatments, it is not reliably abolished by LSD (see Cassaday *et al.* 1993*b*). As previously discussed, the interpretation of amphetamine and neuroleptic drug effects on LI in the terms of the model relies on the DA hypothesis of schizophrenia, which could well be wrong or incomplete; starting with a different drug model may therefore suggest different behavioural markers. In the case of LI, emphasis on the amphetamine model and DA hypothesis is paradoxical, given the early findings with schizophrenics: amphetamine psychosis resembles paranoid schizophrenia most closely, but LI was found to be normal in paranoid schizophrenia (Lubow *et al.* 1987).

Irrespective of the status of LI as a model for schizophrenia, plenty of evidence suggests that LI provides a sensitive (if indirect) measure of DA function. In schizophrenics, the degree of LI may reliably predict susceptibility to DA-related disturbances whether primary or secondary, as a consequence of medication. The general approach of using relatively simple paradigms from animal learning theory allows for both the development of animal models for investigating the relevant neural substrates, and the fractionation of the many and complex changes of schizophrenia into their (non-verbal) components. The results obtained with LI are to some extent compatible with the picture emerging from studies of Kamin's (1968) blocking effect (Jones *et al.* 1992*a,b*) and pre-pulse inhibition (Swerdlow *et al.* 1984; Geyer and Braff 1987). Further careful analysis of the information processing changes characteristic of (predisposition to) schizophrenia is now needed.

The link between schizotypy and LI has been directly demonstrated in a number of studies, including a latent inhibtion procedure that does not require the use of a masking task (Lipp and Vaitl 1992). The fact that LI is reduced in schizotypal normal subjects means that, irrespective of some of the problems with LI as a marker for schizophrenia, *including the possibility that in this case its loss is a result of medication*, the biological systems necessary for its normal development may have some relevance for schizotypy. Despite inconsistencies in the direction of effects reported, there is consensus that LI in some way depends on the DA system. Differences in DA function may therefore correlate with individual differences in schizotypy. The fact that the effect of haloperidol on LI in normal subjects depends on their levels of schizotypy already supports the view that variation in DA function is normally associated with schizotypy (Williams *et al.* 1994). If so, the highly schizotypal individual may, for example, show particular sensitivity to the activating effects of amphetamine and nicotine. Abnormalities of the normal U-shaped function relating performance to arousal have already been linked with schizophrenia and schizotypy (Claridge 1987, 1994*b*).

However, returning to the lesion studies, it is as yet difficult to reconcile the known neuropsychology of LI with its use as a trait marker for schizotypy. The brain differences correlated with normal variation are in organization (for example lateralization) and neurotransmitter function (for example DA, 5-HT turnover). Such differences may be associated with hyper-or hypo-function of affected brain structures, but not lesions. We do not know much about how brains may vary in association with human individual differences in the normal range (cf. Gray 1971). And we have yet to bridge the gap between the 'swiss cheese' neuropsychology of LI and the organizational neuropsychology of schizotypy.

Acknowledgements

H. J. C. was supported by Wellcome Trust Project Grant 036159. Thanks to Neil Ferguson for producing the figure, and to Louise Allan, Nicky Gray, Nick Rawlins, Nigel Wellman, and Jonathan Williams, for discussion of unpublished data.

REFERENCES

Allan, L. M., Williams, J. H., Wellman, N. A., Tonin, J., Taylor, E., Rawlins, J. N. P., and Feldon, J. (1995). Effects of tobacco smoking, schizotypy and number of pre-exposures on latent inhibition in healthy subjects. *Personality and Individual Differences*, **19**, 893–902.

Asin, K. E., Wirtshafter, D., and Kent, E. W. (1980). The effects of electrolytic median raphe lesions on two measures of latent inhibition. *Behavioural and Neural Biology*, **28**, 408–17.

Bachevalier, J. and Mishkin, M. (1989). Mnemonic and neuropathological effects of occluding the posterior cerebral artery in *Macaca mulatta*. *Neuropsychologica*, **27**, 83–105.

Barnes, J. C., Costall, B., and Naylor, R. J. (1987). Influence of medial raphe nucleus lesions on behavioural responding to dopamine infusion into the rat amygdala. *British Journal of Pharmacology (Suppl.)*, **91**, 428P.

Baruch, I., Hemsley, D. R., and Gray, J. A. (1988*a*). Differential performance of acute and chronic schizophrenics in a latent inhibition task. *Journal of Nervous and Mental Disease*, **176**, 598–606.

Baruch, I., Hemsley, D. R., and Gray, J. A. (1988*b*). Latent inhibition and 'psychotic proneness' in normal subjects. *Personality and Individual Differences*, **9**, 777–83.

Bleuler, E. (1911). *Dementia Praecox or the group of schizophrenias* (trans. J. Zinkin 1950). International Universities Press, New York.

Bogerts, B. (1993). Recent advances in the neuropathology of schizophrenia. *Schizophrenia Bulletin*, 19, 431–45.

Bogerts, B. Lieberman, J. A. Ashtari M., Bilder R. M., Degreef G., Lerner G., *et al.* (1993). Hippocampus-amygdala volumes and psychopathology in chronic schizophrenia. *Biological Psychiatry*, 33, 236–46.

Boulenguez, P., Joseph, M. H., Gray, J. A., and Mitchell, S. N. (1994). Dopamine release in the nucleus accumbens after systemic and intrahippocampal injections of 5HT-1 agonists which differentially affect attention in the rat. *British Journal of Pharmacology (Suppl.)*, 111, 153P.

Bouton, M. E. (1993). Context, time, and memory retrieval in the interference paradigms of Pavlovian learning. *Psychological Bulletin*, 114, 80–99.

Cassaday, H. J., Hodges, H., and Gray J. A. (1993a). The effects of ritanserin, RU 24969 and 8-OH-DPAT on latent inhibition in the rat. *Journal of Psychopharmacology*, 7, 63–71.

Cassaday, H. J., Mitchell, S. N., Williams, J. H., and Gray, J. A. (1993b). 5,7–Dihydroxytryptamine lesions in the fornix-fimbria attenuate latent inhibition. *Behavioral and Neural Biology*, 59, 194–207.

Chapman, L. J., Chapman, J. P., Kwapil, T. P., Eckblad, M., and Zinser, M. C. (1994). Putatively psychosis-prone subjects 10 years later. *Journal of Abnormal Psychology*, 103, 171–83.

Christison, G. W., Atwater, G. E., Dunn, L. A., and Kilts, C. D. (1988). Haloperidol enhancement of latent inhibition: relation to therapeutic action? *Biological Psychiatry*, 23, 746–9.

Claridge, G. (1987). 'The schizophrenias as nervous types' revisited. *British Journal of Psychiatry*, 151, 735–43.

Claridge, G. (1994a). Single indicator of risk for schizophrenia: probable fact or likely myth? *Schizophrenia Bulletin*, 20, 151–68.

Claridge, G. (1994b). LSD a missed opportunity. *Human Psychopharmacology*, 9, 343–51.

Claridge, G. and Broks, P. (1984). Schizotypy and hemisphere function I: Theoretical considerations and the measurement of schizotypy. *Personality and Individual Differences*, 5, 633–48.

Claridge, G. and Healy, D. (1994). The psychopharmacology of individual differences. *Human Psychopharmacology*, 9, 1–14.

Clark, A. J. M., Feldon, J., and Rawlins, J. N. P. (1992). Aspiration lesions of rat ventral hippocampus disinhibit responding in conditioned suppression or extinction, but spare latent inhibition and the partial reinforcement extinction effect. *Neuroscience*, 48, 821–9.

Costall, B., Naylor, R. J., and Tyers, M. B. (1988). Recent advances in the neuropharmacology of 5HT3 agonists and antagonists. *Reviews in the Neurosciences*, 2, 41–65.

De la Casa, L. G., Ruiz, G., and Lubow, R. E. (1993). Latent inhibition and recall/recognition if irrelevant stimuli as a function of pre-exposure duration in high and low psychotic-prone normal subjects. *British Journal of Psychology*, 84, 119–32.

DeVietti, T. L., Bauste, R. L., Nutt, G., Barrett, O. V., Daly, K., and Petree, A. D. (1987). Latent inhibition: A trace conditioning phenomenon? *Learning and Motivation*, 18, 185–201.

Di Chiara, G. and Imperato, A. (1985). Rapid tolerance to neuroleptic-induced stimulation of dopamine release in freely moving rats. *Journal of Pharmacology and Experimental Therapeutics*, 235, 487–94.

Dickinson, A. (1980). *Contemporary animal learning theory*. Cambridge University Press. pp. 1–25.

Doty, R. W. (1989). Schizophrenia: a disease of interhemispheric processes at forebrain and brainstem levels? *Behavioural Brain Research*, 34, 1–33.

Dunn, L. A., Atwater, G. E., and Kilts, C. D. (1993). Effects of antipsychotic drugs on latent inhibition: sensitivity and specificity of an animal behavioral model of clinical drug action. *Psychopharmacology*, 112, 315–23.

Ellenbroek, B. A. and Cools, A. R. (1990). Animal models with construct validity for schizophrenia. *Behavioural Pharmacology*, 1, 469–90.

Estes, W. K. and Skinner, B. F. (1941). Some quantitative properties of anxiety. *Journal of Experimental Psychology*, 29, 390–400.

Feldon, J. and Weiner, I. (1989). Abolition of the acquisition but not the expression of latent inhibition by chlordiazepoxide in rats. *Pharmacology, Biochemistry and Behaviour*, 32, 123–7.

Feldon, J. and Weiner, I. (1991a). The latent inhibition model of schizophrenic attention disorder: Haloperidol and sulpiride enhance rats' ability to ignore irrevelant stimuli. *Biological Psychiatry*, 29, 635–46.

Feldon, J. and Weiner, I. (1991b). An animal model of attentional deficit. In *Neuromethods*, 18, *Animal models in psychiatry, vol. 1* (ed. A. A. Boulton, G. B. Baker, and M. T. Martin-Iverson), pp. 313–61. Humana Press, New Jersey.

Geyer, M. A. and Braff, D. L. (1987). Startle habituation and sensorimotor gating in schizophrenia and related animal models. *Schizophrenia Bulletin*, 13, 643–69.

Ginton, A., Urca, G., and Lubow, R. E. (1975). The effects of preexposure to a non-attended stimulus on subsequent learning: Latent inhibition in adults. *Bulletin of the Psychonomic Society*, 5, 5–8.

Gray, J. A. (1971). The mind-brain identity theory as a scientific hypothesis. *Philosophical Quarterly*, 21, 247–54.

Gray, J. A., Feldon, J., Rawlins, J. N. P., Hemsley, D. R., and Smith, A. D. (1991). The neuropsychology of schizophrenia. *Behavioral and Brain Sciences*, 14, 1–84.

Gray, J. A., Joseph, M. H., Hemsley, D. R., Young. A. M. J., Warburton, E. C., Boulenguez, P., *et al.* (1995). The role of mesolimbic dopaminergic and retrohippocampal afferents to the nucleus accumbens in latent inhibition: implications for schizophrenia. *Behavioural Brain Research*, 71, 19–31.

Gray, N. S., Hemsley, D. R., and Gray, J. A. (1992a). Abolition of latent inhibition in acute but not chronic schizophrenics. *Neurology, Psychiatry and Brain Research*, 1, 83–9.

Gray, N. S., Pickering, A. D., Hemsley, D. R., Dawling, S., and Gray, J. A. (1992b). Abolition of latent inhibition by a single 5 mg dose of D-amphetamine in man. *Psychopharmacology*, 107, 425–30.

Gray, N. S., Pilowsky, L. S., Gray, J. A., Kerwin, R. W. (1995). Latent inhibition in drug naive schizophrenics: relation to duration of illness and dopamine D2 binding using SPET. *Schizophrenia Research*, 17, 95–107.

Grenhoff, J. and Svensson, T. H. (1989). Pharmacology of nicotine. *British Journal of Addiction*, 84, 477–92.

Hall, G. (1991). *Perceptual and associative learning*. Oxford Psychology Series (No. 18), pp. 29–107. Clarendon Press, Oxford.

Hall, G. and Channell, S. (1986). Context specificity of latent inhibition in taste aversion learning. *Quarterly Journal of Experimental Psychology*, 38B, 121–39.

Haracz, J. L. (1982). The dopamine hypothesis of schizophrenia: an overview of studies with schizophrenic patients. *Schizophrenia Bulletin*, 8, 438–69.

Harrington, N. R. and Purves, D. G. (1995). Bilateral electrolytic lesions of the nucleus accumbens enhance latent inhibition. *Journal of Psychopharmacology*, 9, A43.

Hemsley, D. R. (1977). What have cognitive deficits to do with schizophrenic symptoms? *British Journal of Psychiatry*, 130, 167–73.

Hemsley, D. R. (1993). A simple (or simplistic) cognitive model for schizophrenia. *Behaviour Research and Therapy*, 31, 633–45.

Honey, R. C. and Good, M. (1993). Selective hippocampal lesions abolish the contextual specificity of latent inhibition and conditioning. *Behavioral Neuroscience*, 107, 23–33.

Jackson, M. and Claridge, G. (1991). Reliability and validity of a psychotic traits questionnaire (STQ). *British Journal of Clinical Psychology*, 30, 311–23.

Jones, S. H., Gray, J. A., and Hemsley, D. R. (1992a). Loss of the Kamin blocking effect in acute but not chronic schizophrenics. *Biological Psychiatry*, 32, 739–55.

Jones, S. H., Gray, J. A., and Hemsley, D. R. (1992b). The Kamin blocking effect, incidental learning and schizotypy: A reanalysis. *Personality and Individual Differences*, 13, 57–60.

Joseph, M. H., Peters, S. L., and Gray, J. A. (1993). Nicotine blocks latent inhibition in rats: evidence for a critical role of increased functional activity of dopamine in the mesolimbic system at conditioning rather than preexposure. *Psychopharmacology*, 110, 187–92.

Kamin, L. J. (1968). 'Attention-like' processes in classical conditioning. In *Miami symposium on the prediction of behavior: aversive stimulation* (ed. M. R. Jones), pp. 9–33. University of Miami Press.

Kaye, H. and Pearce, J. M. (1987). Hippocampal lesions attenuate latent inhibition and the decline of the orienting response. *Quarterly Journal of Experimental Psychology*, 39B, 107–125.

Killcross, A. S., Dickinson, A., and Robbins, T. W. (1994). Amphetamine-induced disruptions of latent inhibition are reinforcer-mediated: implications for animal models of schizophrenic attentional dysfunction. *Psychopharmacology*, 115, 185–95.

Kraemer, P. J. and Roberts, W. A. (1984). The influence of flavour preexposure and test interval on conditioned taste aversions in the rat. *Learning and Motivation*, 15, 259–78.

Kraemer, P. J. and Spear, N. E. (1992). The effect of nonreinforced stimulus exposure on the strength of a conditioned taste aversion as a function of retention interval: Do latent inhibition and extinction involve a shared process? *Animal learning and Behavior*, 20, 1–7.

Lipp, O. V. and Vaitl, D. (1992). Latent inhibition in human Pavlovian differential conditioning: Effect of additional stimulation after preexposure and relation to schizotypal traits. *Personality and Individual Differences*, 13, 1003–12.

Lohr, J. B. and Flynn, K. (1992). Smoking and schizophrenia. *Schizophrenia Research*, 8, 93–102.

Loskutova, L. V., Luk'yanenko, F. Ya., and Il'yuchenok, R. Yu. (1990). Interaction of serotonin- and dopaminergic systems of the brain in mechanisms of latent inhibition in rats. *Neuroscience and Behavioral Physiology*, 20, 500–5.

Lubow, R. E. (1989). *Latent inhibition and conditioned attention theory*. Cambridge University Press, Cambridge/New York.

Lubow, R. E. and Gewirtz, J. C. (1995). Latent inhibition in humans: data, theory, and implications for schizophrenia. *Psychological Bulletin*, 117, 87–103.

Lubow, R. E. and Josman, Z. E. (1993). Latent inhibition deficits in hyperactive children. *Journal of Child Psychology and Psychiatry*, 34, 959–73.

Lubow, R. E. and Moore, A. U. (1959). Latent inhibition: the effect of non-reinforced preexposure to the conditional stimulus. *Journal of Comparative and Physiological Psychology*, 52, 415–19.

Lubow, R. E., Weiner I., Schlossberg, A., and Baruch, I. (1987). Latent inhibition and schizophrenia. *Bulletin of the Psychonomic Society*, 25, 464–7.

Lubow, R. E., Ingberg-Sachs, Y., Zalstein-Orda, N., and Gewirtz, J. C. (1992). Latent inhibition in low and high 'psychotic-prone' normal subjects. *Personality and Individual Differences*, 13, 563–72.

McKinney, W. T. and Bunney, W. E. (1969). Animal model of depression. I. Review of evidence: implications for research. *Archives of General Psychiatry*, 21, 240–8.

Mackintosh, N. J. (1975). A theory of attention: variations in the associability of stimuli with reinforcement. *Psychological Review*, 82, 276–98.

Moran, P. M. and Moser, P. C. (1992). MDL 73, 147EF, a 5-HT3 antagonist, facilitates latent inhibition in the rat. *Pharmacology, Biochemistry and Behaviour*, 42, 519–22.

Morton, N., Gray, N. S., Mellers, J. D. C., Toone, B. K., and Gray, J. A. (1996). Relationships between schizotypy, within-subject latent inhibition and prepulse inhibition *Schizophrenia Research*, 18, 229.

Pakkenberg, B. (1990). Pronounced reduction of total neuron number in mediodorsal thalamic nucleus and nucleus accumbens in schizophrenics. *Archives of General Psychiatry*, 47, 1023–8.

Porsolt, R. D. (1979). Animal model of depression. *Biomedicine*, 30, 139–40.

Purves, D., Bonardi, C., and Hall, G. (1995). Enhancement of latent inhibition in rats with electrolytic lesions of the hippocampus. *Behavioral Neuroscience*, 109, 366–70.

Reilly, S., Harley, C., and Revusky, S. (1993). Ibotenate lesions of the hippocampus enhance latent inhibition in conditioned taste aversion and increase resistance to extinction in conditioned taste preference. *Behavioral Neuroscience*, 107, 996–1004.

Schechter, M. D. and Chance, W. T. (1979). Non-specificity of 'behavioral despair' as an animal model of depression. *European Journal of Pharmacology*, 60, 139–42.

Schneider, W. and Shiffrin, R. M. (1977). Controlled and automatic human information processing: I. Detection, search and attention. *Psychological Review*, 84, 1–66.

Solomon, P. R., and Crider, A. (1988). Toward an animal model of schizophrenic attention disorder. In *Animal models of psychiatric disorder* (ed. P. Simon, P. Soubrie and D. Widlocher), Vol. 2, pp. 21–42. Karger, Basel.

Solomon, P. R., and Moore, J. W. (1975). Latent inhibition and stimulus generalization of the classically conditioned nictitating membrane response in rabbits (*Oryctolagus cuniculus*) following dorsal hippocamal ablation. *Journal of Comparative and Physiological Psychology*, 89, 1192–203.

Solomon, P. R., Kiney, C. A., and Scott, D. R. (1978). Disruption of latent inhibition following systemic administration of parachlorophenylalanine (PCPA). *Physiology and Behaviour*, 20, 265–71.

Solomon, P. R., Nichols, G. L., Kiernan, III, J. M., Kamer, R. S., and Kaplan, L. J. (1980). Differential effects of lesions in medial and dorsal raphe of the rat: Latent inhibition and septohippocampal serotonin levels. *Journal of Comparative and Physiological Psychology*, 94, 145–54

Solomon, P. R., Crider, A., Winkelman, J. W., Turi, A., Kamer, R. M., and Kaplan, L. J. (1981). Disrupted latent inhibition in the rat with chronic amphetamine or haloperidol-induced supersensitivity: Relationship to schizophrenic attention disorder. *Biological Psychiatry*, 16, 519–37.

Swan, J. A. and Pearce, J. M. (1988). The orienting response as an index of stimulus associability in rats. *Journal of Experimental Psychology: Animal Behaviour Processes*, 14, 292–301.

Swerdlow, N., Braff, D., Geyer, M., and Koob, G. (1984). Central dopamine hyperactivity in rats mimics abnormal acoustic startle response in schizophrenics. *Biological Psychiatry*, 21, 23–33.

Tai, C.-T., Cassaday, H. J., Feldon, J., and Rawlins, J. N. P. (1995). Both electrolytic and excitotoxic lesions of nucleus accumbens disrupt latent inhibition of learning in rats. *Neurobiology of Learning and Memory*, 64, 36–48.

Trulson, M. E. and Jacobs, B. L. (1979). Long-term amphetamine treatment decreases brain serotonin metabolism: Implications for theories of schizophrenia. *Science*, 205, 1295–7.

Tsaltas, E., Preston, G. C. Rawlins, J. N. P., Winocur, G., and Gray, J. A. (1984). Dorsal bundle lesions do not affect latent inhibition of conditioned suppression. *Psychopharmacology*, 84, 549–55.

Ugedo, L., Grenhoff, J., and Svensson, T. H. (1989). Ritanserin, a 5-HT2 receptor antagonist, activates midbrain dopamine neurons by blocking serotonergic inhibition. *Psychopharmacology*, 98, 45–50.

Van-Riezen, H. and Leonard, B. E. (1990). Effects of psychotropic drugs on the behavior and neurochemistry of olfactory bulbectomized rats. *Pharmacology and Therapeutics*, 47, 21–34.

Warburton, E. C., Joseph, M. H., Feldon, J., Weiner, I., and Gray, J. A. (1994). Antagonism of amphetamine-induced disruption of LI in rats by haloperidol and ondansetron: implications for a possible antipsychotic action of ondansetron. *Psychopharmacology*, 114, 657–64.

Weiner, I. (1990). Neural substrates of latent inhibition: The switching model. *Psychological Bulletin*, 108, 442–61.

Weiner, I. and Feldon, J. (1987). Facilitation of latent inhibition by haloperidol in rats. *Psychopharmacology*, 91, 248–53.

Weiner, I., Lubow, R. E., and Feldon, J. (1981). Chronic amphetamine and latent inhibition. *Behavioural Brain Research*, 2, 285–6.

Weiner, I., Lubow, R. E., and Feldon, J. (1984). Abolition of the expression but not the acquisition of latent inhibition by chronic amphetamine in rats. *Psychopharmacology*, 83, 194–9.

Weiner, I., Feldon, J., and Katz, Y. (1987). Facilitation of the expression but not the acquisition of latent inhibition by haloperidol in rats. *Pharmacology Biochemistry and Behavior*, 26, 241–6.

Weiner, I., Lubow, R. E., and Feldon, J. (1988). Disruption of latent inhibition by acute administration of low doses of amphetamine. *Pharmacology Biochemistry and Behavior*, 30, 871–8.

Weiner, I., Smith, A. D., Rawlins, J. N. P., and Feldon, J. (1992). A neuroleptic-like effect of ceronapril on latent inhibition. *Neuroscience*, 49, 307–15.

Weiner, I., Kidron, R., Tarrasch, R., Arnt, J., and Feldon, J. (1994). The effects of the new antipsychotic, sertindole, on latent inhibition in rats. *Behavioural Pharmacology*, 5, 119–24.

Williams, J. H., Wellman, N. A., Rawlins, J. N. P., Geaney, D. P., Cowen, P. J., and Feldon, J. (1994). Haloperidol increases latent inhibition in high schizotypal subjects. *Schizophrenia Research*, 11, 162.

Williams, J. H., Wellman, N. A., Allan, L. M., Taylor, E., Tonin, J., Feldon, J., and Rawlins, J. N. P. (1996a). Tobacco smoking correlates with schizotypal and borderline personality traits. *Personality and individual differences*, 20, 267–70.

Williams, J. H., Wellman, N. A., and Rawlins J. N. P. (1996b). Cannabis use correlates with schizotypy in healthy people. *Addiction*, 91, 869–77.

Williams, J. H., Wellman, N. A., Geaney, D. P., Cowen, P. J., Feldon, J., and Rawlins J. N. P. (1996c). Latent inhibition is not reduced in drug-free patients with schizophrenia. *Schizophrenia Research*, 18, 205.

Willner, P. (1984). The validity of animal models of depression. *Psychopharmacology*, 83, 1–16.

Willner, P. (1991). Methods for assessing the validity of animal models of human psychopathology. In *Neuromethods*, 18, *Animal models in psychiatry*, Vol. 1, (ed. A. A. Boulton, G. B. Baker, and M. T. Martin-Iverson), pp. 1–23. Humana Press, New Jersey.

8
Schizotypy and cerebral lateralization

A. J. RICHARDSON, OLIVER MASON, AND GORDON CLARIDGE

INTRODUCTION

The idea that psychosis might involve abnormalities of cerebral lateralization has stimulated considerable enthusiasm, an interest that has inevitably generalized to work on schizotypy. A review of the now vast literature on laterality in schizophrenia itself is clearly beyond the scope of this chapter (for reviews see Walker and McGuire 1982; Gruzelier 1991; Wexler *et al*. 1991). Only a summary overview of major themes will therefore be given, with discussion largely restricted to findings from studies using paradigms and techniques that have also been applied to the investigation of schizotypy. These mostly include the assessment of handedness and other sensori-motor asymmetries, neuropsychological measures, and divided visual field and dichotic listening paradigms. However, before considering such material, and its rationale, three points are worth making.

First, as will become evident in the ensuing sections, work in this area has become extremely complex—some would say uninterpretable. The reasons lie partly in the ambiguity of the concept of 'laterality' (with consequent difficulties in its measurement), compounded by the problem of applying these to the already poorly defined clinical construct of 'schizophrenia'.

Secondly, the emphasis that has been placed on the two cerebral hemispheres has tended to obscure the fact that, important though it undoubtedly is, the lateralization of brain functions is not the only dimension along which individuals can be expected to differ. Anterior/posterior comparisons are likely to prove equally crucial, while many functional asymmetries that have been attributed to 'hemispheric' differences may well reflect, instead, the operation of subcortical mechanisms (see Efron 1990). Indeed, as Broks argues in this volume (Chapter 6), physiological variations of primitive origin in the brain might contribute, in their own right, to important psychological features highly relevant to our understanding of schizotypy.

Thirdly, as a sobering caveat to any generalizations that might appear to be made here about brain differences in psychotic disorders, it is worth bearing in mind, that despite numerous claims, there is actually no evidence at present for a *consistent* neuropathology in schizophrenia (see Chua and McKenna (1995) for a recent meta-analysis).

THEORETICAL CONSIDERATIONS AND MEASUREMENT ISSUES

The nature and extent of functional asymmetries in many domains of higher-level processing are not yet well understood. Even what has come to be accepted as the 'standard' pattern of left-hemispheric specialization for language functions. and an apparent right-hemispheric dominance for aspects of visuospatial and attentional processing, can vary considerably among apparently normal individuals. This is particularly so with respect to sex and handedness, but also in relation to other factors, such as ability and personality traits (McGlone 1980; Bryden 1987; Glass 1987; O'Boyle and Hellige 1989).

More fundamentally, the issue of what exactly is specialized remains unresolved; as does the question of whether specialization is absolute or relative. Absolute specialization implies that each hemisphere has unique capabilities which the other cannot undertake; relative specialization suggests that one hemisphere may possess an advantage for a particular task or process, but that the other could undertake the same functions if required, albeit with some loss of efficiency. Evidence from clinical studies where major dysfunction often follows unilateral damage would tend to suggest that some functions are absolutely specialized. However, extreme caution is warranted in drawing inferences about normal function from such cases; for example, the deficits observed after unilateral damage could equally well reflect callosal inhibition of the intact hemisphere by the damaged hemisphere. In fact neither the study of commissurotomy patients nor research with normal subjects offers any support for a model of absolute cognitive lateralization (Cohen 1982). Similarly, functional imaging studies have shown that brain blood-flow increases bilaterally in both linguistic and spatial tasks, and that this far exceeds the small differences found between hemispheres that are presumed to reflect some degree of cognitive specialization (Gur *et al.* 1983). However, even if absolute specialization is rejected, and relative specialization taken to be the norm, there still remain several competing models that have been proposed for the nature and extent of hemispheric interactions (see Bradshaw 1989; Hellige 1993).

Another important distinction that has been drawn is between 'fixed structure' and 'dynamic process' asymmetries (Cohen 1982) 'fixed structure' asymmetries refer to capacities specialized to either hemisphere that are presumed to have their basis in anatomical differences between the two sides of the brain. But, even where such differences might be presumed to exist, there is considerable scope for functional variation. For example, the usual left-hemispheric advantages for language processing are generally assumed to bear some relation to the typical leftward structural asymmetries of perisylvian regions such as the planum temporale (Galaburda *et al.* 1987). However, a number of other factors may influence asymmetries of function. These include the nature of the stimulus, the type of processing involved, and the stage of processing. Furthermore, some specialization appears to be mediated by more dynamic influences, such as differences in physiological arousal between the hemispheres, and by attentional strategies (Kinsbourne 1977; Levy *et al.* 1983; Kim *et al.* 1990).

It is also important to note—as Hellige (1993) has emphasized—that these sources of variation probably represent several logically independent dimensions. Thus the direction of hemispheric asymmetry should be distinguished from its magnitude, while another dimension, just mentioned, is relative asymmetry of hemispheric arousal, which may have both trait and state components. Also important is the complementarity of hemispheric asymmetries, with possible disadvantages in the 'crowding out' of some functions by others, unless these are lateralized to opposite hemispheres (Levy 1969; Geschwind and Galaburda 1987; O'Boyle and Hellige 1989). Finally, there is the nature and extent of interhemispheric communication. Any or all of these effects may influence the performance asymmetries found in a particular individual, at any one time, on any given measure. Added to this, different measurement techniques introduce their own problems.

Very broadly, three types of asymmetry measure can be distinguished: behavioural, physiological, and anatomical. For reasons discussed above, consistent relationships between these cannot be assumed. Procedures allowing direct investigation of brain structure and physiological functions should in theory be amongst the most reliable of asymmetry measures and these have been widely used with schizophrenic patients. However, there are technical and interpretative problems associated with both post-mortem investigation and *in-vivo* imaging procedures. For example, with functional imaging a major limitation is that the interpretation of activity in particular brain regions is ambiguous unless it is known what those regions do. But, in any case, with some exceptions (Raine *et al.* 1992; Flaum and Andreasen 1995), such methods have rarely been employed in the study of healthy schizotypal subjects, and, even when they have, never, as far as we know, to test laterality theory directly.

In most schizotypy research, 'hemispheric specialization' has been inferred from various perceptual, cognitive, or motor asymmetries, i.e. behavioural laterality measures. Most of these have their own limitations and typically suffer from three major problems. First, they tend to have poor test-retest reliability. This compounds the second problem, which is poor concurrent validity: the correlations between different behavioural indices of laterality are often unsatisfactory (Hiscock *et al.* 1985), as are their associations with other types of asymmetry measure, for example structural (though see Raine *et al.* 1992). A third difficulty with behavioural indices is their susceptibility to extraneous influences of the kind referred to earlier, including such factors as stimulus familiarity, priming effects, and the subject's strategy or level of skill.

Careful attention to study design is therefore needed if performance asymmetries are to be properly interpreted as due to genuine information-processing differences between the hemispheres. Here a 'componential' approach (Hellige 1995) to theory and measurement is likely to be the most illuminating. Unfortunately, such sophistication is rarely the case in laterality research, especially in the fields of psychopathology and normal individual differences.

THEORIES OF LATERALIZATION IN SCHIZOPHRENIA

Conceptualizations of the nature of lateralized abnormalities in schizophrenia can roughly be grouped into three categories: left-hemisphere dysfunction, right-hemisphere dysfunction, and abnormalities of interhemispheric communication. In evaluating the relative worth of each of these theories it is worth bearing in mind that *a priori* it seems unlikely that any unilateral dysfunction model could possibly account for the full range of symptomatology encountered in schizophrenia, let alone psychosis as a whole. The heterogeneity of these disorders defies a unitary hypothesis in any domain: with respect to laterality, Gruzelier (1983, 1991), for example, has consistently argued for subgroups relating to opposite patterns of hemispheric asymmetry. More fundamentally, if psychosis involves any kind of early neurodevelopmental disturbance in cerebral lateralization—which has often been argued (Crow *et al.* 1989)—the effects of this are likely to be, at least to some extent, bilateral.

Left hemisphere

The majority of research into laterality and schizophrenia has evolved from the hypothesis that it primarily involves a disorder of left-hemispheric functions. A perhaps obvious idea—because of the prominence of language disorder in schizophrenia—it was given early impetus by the writings of Flor-Henry (1969). He had observed a resemblance between left temporal lobe epilepsy and schizophrenia, and suggested that the latter was similarly due to a left-hemisphere dysfunction; he proposed that a right-hemisphere dysfunction characterized the affective psychoses.

The continuing popularity of a left-hemisphere theory of schizophrenia has drawn upon a variety of evidence. On the anatomical front, the lateral ventricular enlargement earlier claimed for schizophrenia is now supposedly predominantly left-lateralized. Correspondingly, numerous studies have suggested reduced area or volume of the left temporal lobe and associated structures in schizophrenia (Crow *et al.* 1989, 1990; Bogerts *et al.* 1990; Rossi *et al.* 1990; Degreef *et al.* 1992). Here particular connections have been made to symptoms of hallucinations and thought disorder (Barta *et al.* 1990; Shenton *et al.* 1992). Others investigators have pointed to a significant reduction or reversal of the usual leftward asymmetry of the planum temporale in schizophrenia, an auditory association area known to be involved in language processing (Rossi *et al.* 1992; Falkai *et al.* 1995; Petty *et al.* 1995).

Against a simple left-hemispheric deficit model, many structural imaging studies have shown bilateral differences or no differences in relation to schizophrenia (Andreasen *et al.* 1982; Kleinschmidt *et al.* 1994; Menon *et al.* 1995). So, even with such direct anatomical measures, findings are inconsistent. This again emphasizes the heterogeneity of clinical schizophrenia and, as with other theories, raises the possibility that that some of the abnormalities that have been reported in schizophrenic patients may actually arise as a consequence of the illness and/or its treatment.

From functional brain imaging the picture is also difficult to interpret. Left-hemisphere over-activation in schizophrenia has been a fairly consistent finding (For example Gur *et al.* 1983), but it remains an open question whether this reflects primary left-hemisphere dysfunction, or whether it is secondary to abnormalities of interhemispheric and/or right-hemisphere function. Furthermore, essentially similar patterns of regional cerebral blood flow have been found in non-schizophrenic controls during performance on a range of neuropsychological tests (Berman and Weinberger 1990). This excessive left hemisphere activation has been found in medication-free patients challenged with spatial as well as verbal tasks (Gur *et al.* 1985); Gur *et al.* (1987 *a, b*) also reported a similar pattern under resting conditions, but this then reversed when the patients were placed on medication, which highlights the potential influence of symptoms and/or neuroleptic usage. Patterns of activation are also likely to differ according to symptom profiles (Gunther *et al.* 1991); if these are not considered, findings may again, therefore, remain equivocal.

Right hemisphere

Although less popular, right-hemisphere theories of schizophrenia have been proposed by a number of writers. Cutting (1990) argues that the aspects of language most disturbed in schizophrenia are those mediated by the right hemisphere, namely metaphor, humour, prosody, and even pragmatic or common-sense communications. He also maintains that the disorders of perception, attention, and self-identity in schizophrenia suggest right-hemisphere dysfunction. Venables (1983) has similarly noted parallels between attentional (and other) impairments in schizophrenia and those associated with right-parietal damage. As an explanation, he suggested that early limitations on right-hemisphere development may lead to a compensatory shift of visuospatial functions to the left hemisphere; this might then compromise the normal development of verbal ability, at least in some pre-schizophrenic individuals (especially males at risk for so-called 'process' schizophrenia). Consistent with this account are reports of left-hemisphere advantages for spatial processing in schizophrenia, which could reflect compensation for a relative right-hemisphere deficiency (Gur *et al.* 1983, 1985).

Whether or not a developmental 'crowding-out' hypothesis holds water, it certainly seems plausible that the excessive left-hemisphere activation sometimes reported for many schizophrenic patients is secondary to other influences, emanating from the right hemisphere. Oepen *et al.* (1987) have suggested surplus emotion 'spilling over' to the left hemisphere and disrupting its language functions. Alternatively it could reflect a failure of the pre-attentive filtering normally carried out by the right hemisphere, which is relatively specialized for the massive parallel processing required to select, group, and enhance relevant information, while inhibiting irrelevant information. If this early pre-attentive processing were defective, then perhaps, as Cromwell (1987) rather colourfully put it, 'the left hemisphere of the schizophrenic finds itself "up to its crotch in crocodiles ... while its major purpose is to drain the swamp" i.e. to perform the final homeostatic stages of information resolution'. A similar proposal is made by Rotenberg (1994), reviewing laterality research into schizophrenia from a psychophysiological perspective.

Interhemispheric communication

The third kind of model for disturbances of lateralization in schizophrenia proposes abnormalities of interhemispheric transfer or integration. Several studies have indicated specific problems with bimanual and other cross-hemispheric matching in schizophrenics, suggestive of difficulties with interhemispheric integration (Green 1978; Carr 1980; Dimond *et al.* 1980; Walker and Green 1982). Extending the investigation of this idea to cognitive functions, Green and his colleagues (Green *et al.* 1983) reported binaural deficits in auditory comprehension and recall in schizophrenic subjects relative to normal controls, as well as abnormal monaural asymmetries. They are also reported similar effects in genetically at-risk individuals, i.e. the children of schizophrenics (Hallett and Green 1983). However, other studies using the same paradigm have since produced inconsistent or negative results (Ditchfield and Hemsley 1990; Kwapil *et al.* 1992).

As a result of their findings, Green and his colleagues proposed a persuasive neurodevelopmental model to account for differences in risk for schizophrenia. This was based on the notion of delayed maturation of the corpus callosum having consequent effects on the development of hemisphere specialization for language functions (Birchwood *et al.* 1988). In general, and for obvious reasons, the corpus callosum—as the major channel of interhemispheric communication—has been the subject of investigation and source of evidence for theories of this third type. Some early reports claimed increased callosal width in schizophrenia (Bigelow and Rosenthal 1972; Bigelow *et al.* 1983), but findings have been inconsistent. In a careful and detailed review of these and other studies, Witelson (1987) concluded that although there may be some differences between schizophrenic and normal subjects, these are likely to be in the relative size of different callosal regions, with probable complex interactions with sex and handedness. Subsequently, Raine *et al.* (1990), using magnetic resonance imaging, confirmed a sex-dependent effect by showing thicker callosal width in female compared with male schizophrenics, a pattern opposite to that found in normal subjects. Finally, in a rare consideration of schizophrenic subtypes in relation to callosal morphology, Gunther *et al.* (1991) found increased callosal width in positive but not negative-symptom patients, suggesting that excessive interhemispheric connectivity may only be relevant to understanding the more 'active' manifestations of psychosis.

CONCLUSIONS ABOUT SCHIZOPHRENIA

The evidence reviewed above supports the idea that some form of unusual cerebral lateralization may be a feature of schizophrenia, though its exact nature remains unclear. It could be that some of the inconsistencies in the data can be reconciled by reference to different syndromes of the disorder. Gruzelier (1983, 1991), who has reviewed the literature on laterality and schizophrenia, endorses this option, claiming to have found a consistent pattern when subtype differences are taken into account. He maintains that paranoid, acute, reactive, and positive-symptom patients typically show asymmetries indicative of left-hemisphere over-activation or right-hemisphere deficits. Non-paranoid, chronic, process, and negative-symptom patients tend to show the opposite pattern, though on balance there is perhaps less evidence for abnormal asymmetries in relation to the negative than to the positive features of psychosis.

Some of the issues raised in patient research should be capable of being addressed—in some ways more easily—by looking at schizotypy, and its corresponding components, among clinically normal individuals. The value of this dimensional approach has been demonstrated in a range of studies, using methodologies drawn from the behavioural-laterality literature. For simplicity, this work will be considered here according to the kind of measurement techniques employed, and where appropriate in the context of findings from similar research into schizophrenia.

STUDIES OF SCHIZOTYPY

Handedness

Quinan (1930) was the first to suggest an increased incidence of sinistrality among schizophrenics, but subsequent investigations have proved inconclusive; this due, no doubt, to differences in diagnostic criteria and the classification of handedness. While higher rates of left-handedness in schizophrenic patients have been reported in a number of studies (for example Gur 1977; Chaugule and Master 1981; Manoach *et al.* 1988) others have proved negative (Lishman and McMeekan 1976), or even found the reverse (Taylor *et al.* 1980). The position is hardly clarified by large-scale population studies which can sample carefully in prospective designs and so avoid selection bias. Left-handers were over-represented among the 30 schizophrenics identified in the 1946 birth cohort (Cannon *et al.* 1996), but in David *et al.*'s (1995) sample of 50 000 conscripts, no such association emerged. Part of the problem lies in an over-simplistic approach to measuring hand usage and preference. If the important factor associated with schizophrenia is reduced or inconsistent lateralization, then handedness must be assessed across a range of tasks that may reveal this, and indeed by noting the *actual* (as opposed to reported) hand usage of patients. Green *et al.* (1989) had patients perform a number of tasks on two occasions and found an excess of mixed handers—*not* left-handers—in schizophrenic patients, relative to controls. They also found that 'ambiguous' handedness (meaning inconsistency on the same tasks on re-testing) was more common in the patient group: they suggest that this is evidence for some kind of neurodevelopmental 'arrest' of the usual process of establishing cerebral lateralization. Of course, it may alternatively or additionally be due to attentional deficits in some patients.

Given the great variety of symptoms and syndromes within schizophrenia, it is unlikely that unusual behavioural asymmetries associated with the disorder all have a single cause. To develop one aetiological strand, it may be that early brain injury provides a contributing factor to some patients' schizophrenia, reflected in handedness as a provoked shift away from full dextrality. This is suggested by the relationships between sinistrality and cognitive impairment, increased ventricular size (Katsanis and Iacono 1989; Faustman *et al*. 1991), and a range of negative symptoms such as poverty of speech content (Manschreck and Ames 1984; Manoach *et al*. 1988), as well as impairment of language and memory functions (Manschreck *et al*. 1996). In contrast, other schizophrenics may be left- or mixed-handed for genetic reasons, as it appears that in some such cases the offspring also exhibit a greater rate of left-handedness (Green et al. 1983). The pattern of symptoms and prognosis for familial sinistrals is unclear despite claims of milder or less chronic disorder (Gur 1977; Nasrallah *et al*). These claims are consistent, however, with Lishman and McMeekan's (1976) finding of a significant excess of left-handedness among young male delusional patients. It may be that the mixed or inconsistent handedness noted by Green *et al*. (1989) is most prevalent among positively, rather than negatively, symptomatic individuals, perhaps with a greater association among males.

Just such a conclusion is supported by the majority of schizotypy studies. Chapman and Chapman (1987) found that high scorers on 'Per-Mag' (the combined Perceptual Aberration and Magical Ideation scales) and Impulsive Nonconformity showed a raised incidence of mixed-handedness (defined as anything other than consistent right or left preference); while high scorers on Physical Anhedonia did not differ from controls. Similarly, Kim *et al*. (1992), using Raine's SPQ, found that mixed-handed adults had significantly higher scores than either left- or right-handers on the cognitive-perceptual factor. Kelley and Coursey's (1992) high schizotypy group (on a composite of positive scales) showed significantly higher rates of left-and mixed-handedness. Quite clearly it is the 'positive schizotypy' scales that produce significant results and not schizoidal or anhedonia scales. The only study not to do so (Overby 1992) used a crude single-question measure of handedness to which only 4 per cent responded with 'mixed'. This figure is so at odds with the usual proportion of 10–25 per cent that the measure can be deemed a failure.

Turning to our own laboratory, several data sets have been collected using the STA scale, with broadly consistent results: Richardson (1994) and Claridge *et al*. (submitted) found that STA schizotypy scores were significantly elevated in mixed-handers relative to consistent left- and right-handers. However, the

Claridge *et al.* data reveal an effect that cautions against a simple equation of schizotypy and mixed-handedness. The sample collected was large enough to compare individual groups of more or less consistently left-, mixed-, and right-handed subjects. Interestingly, mixed-handers with strong left-handed tendencies scored unusually *low* on the STA scale. The most schizotypal subjects were actually individuals who were right-handed (by writing hand), but who showed only a few signs of incomplete lateralization. The result could be seen to be consistent with Mason's (1995) finding that high Unusual Experiences scorers (on the O-LIFE) endorsed a significantly greater number of 'either' responses (these are traditionally ignored when scoring handedness inventories). The finding may be a weaker counterpart of the 'ambiguous' handedness in schizophrenics, reported by Green *et al.* (1989), and emphasizes again the need to be clear about what one means when referring to 'mixed-handedness' as a clinical and individual differences characteristic.

We can nevertheless conclude that, judged from handedness data, there are several small indicators of unusual lateralization in schizotypy and schizophrenia, beyond that of simple writing-hand preference. We must stress, however, that we do not believe that this is, *per se*, necessarily pathological or narrowly confined to schizotypy/schizophrenia, and certainly not in a purely clinical sense. Handedness differences are so widespread as to be considered rather general indicators of individual differences in brain/behaviour relations. Mason's (1995) finding is illustrative of the point. Using the O-LIFE questionnaire (see Appendix II) he identified a trend—though only a trend—towards increased positive schizotypy among mixed-handers. Equally interesting was the finding of a two-way association with another personality measure, viz. Openness to Experience (McCrae 1987, 1994). In males, mixed-handedness, and the STA and O-LIFE Unusual Experiences scales, were together associated with Openness to Experience. Openness—allegedly a trait of heightened receptivity to the environment—may well be something of a non-pathological counterpart to positive schizotypy, relevant to diverse phenomena, such as creativity (see Chapter 13) and the out-of-the-body experience (see Chapter 12).

Neuropsychological measures

Schizophrenia research has revealed abundant cognitive and neuropsychological deficits in patient samples and, in the tradition of neuropsychology, such impairments have been used to make inferences about the localization of brain dysfunction in schizophrenia. Although this approach has made a valuable contribution to research, there are some obvious caveats concerning its applicability to the study of functional psychosis, and especially to research on healthy schizotypal subjects. One of these concerns the psychometric limitations of many neuropsychological tests: ceiling effects generally render them unsuitable for use with both normal subjects and many schizophrenic patients. Even where this is not a problem, tests may still lack the sensitivity required to show differential deficits in these populations (Blanchard and Neal 1994). A more fundamental problem is that most neuropsychological tests draw their primary validation from the study of (previously normal) patients with acquired brain damage; it may not be safe to assume that the same structure—function relationships will hold in schizophrenic or schizophrenia-spectrum subjects.

Another difficulty of interpretation is that, although wide-ranging performance differences are routinely found during neuropsychological testing of patient subjects, it is rarely possible to distinguish those 'deficits' that may be intrinsic to the predisposition to schizophrenia from impairments arising from the deleterious effects of the illness itself, or from medication. A common procedure, even in studies of first-episode schizophrenia, is to delay neuropsychological testing until patients have been 'stabilized' on medication (Hoff *et al.* 1992). This may sometimes be unavoidable, and it may well be justifiable to argue that test results would be less reliable in patients who were floridly symptomatic, but the approach makes little sense if we want to know about schizophrenia rather than the effects of neuroleptics (see Williams *et al.* 1996). Moreover, medication may be a particularly serious confound in laterality research if drugs have asymmetric effects (Gur *et al.* 1987b)—a strong possibility, given the fact that asymmetries are being revealed in most, if not all, of the major neurotransmitter systems (Wittling 1995).

Where researchers do take the trouble to examine never-medicated schizophrenics, a different profile may emerge from that found in previously drugged patients. This was confirmed by Saykin *et al.* (1994), who compared three groups: never-medicated first-episode patients, unmedicated previously treated patients, and healthy controls. The deficits common to both patient groups that they did find were specific to verbal memory and learning. But it was notable that previously treated patients were more impaired relative to never-medicated patients on spatial cognition, fine motor-speed, and visual memory. The apparently primary language impairments in these untreated patients were interpreted as implicating left temporal-hippocampal systems.

'Left temporal-lobe dysfunction' has long been suggested as central to schizophrenia (Flor-Henry 1969) and there is evidence for this in both positive and negative-symptom patients. However, the latter typically show much more diffuse and bilateral impairments (for example Silverstein, 1991; Buchanan *et al.*, 1994). The more specific association appears to be between left temporal dysfunction and positive symptoms, for example thought disorder (Shenton *et al.* 1992) and hallucinations (Barta *et al.* 1990). With regard to the negative symptoms of schizophrenia, the frontal lobes, and particularly the dorsolateral pre-frontal cortex, have been more widely implicated (Weinberger 1987). Well-documented neuropsychological deficits here include perseverative tendencies, problems with spatial working memory, and general 'executive dysfunction'. In addition, attentional and associative impairments in these schizophrenic syndromes further suggest parietal dysfunction (for example Buchanan *et al.* 1994).

Turning to schizotypy, there is little evidence of the kinds of impairment routinely found in schizophrenia. Kelley and Coursey (1992) compared cognitive and neuropsychological function in high and low scorers on a composite measure of positive schizotypy, using four tests of motor performance and four WAIS-R IQ subtests, but could find no differences between groups on any of these measures. Similarly, LaPorte *et al.* (1994) examined verbal memory function and verbal intelligence in a large sample of college students assessed for psychosis-proneness using the Chapman Scales, and found no significant association between any dimensions of psychosis-proneness and these cognitive abilities. However, Lenzenweger and Korfine (1994) did report impairments on the Wisconsin Card Sorting Test for high scorers on the Chapmans' Perceptual Aberration scale; and Raine *et al.* (1990) reported the same for high scorers on his SPQ, relating these to reduced pre-frontal volume on MRI imaging. This appears to be the only study yet to use structural imaging in schizotypy, and no lateralized differences were reported here, but further investigations of a similar kind are clearly warranted.

From a more dynamic-process perspective, Gruzelier (1991, 1994) has proposed three syndromes of schizotypy which parallel his three-syndrome model of schizophrenia. He relates two of these syndromes to opposite asymmetries in hemispheric arousal: an 'Active', positive syndrome to a relative left > right asymmetry, and a 'Withdrawn', negative syndrome to the reverse pattern of right > left activation. (With his third syndrome, 'Unreality'—consisting of positive features of perceptual aberration and magical thinking—he predicts no consistent patterns of lateralization.) The findings of Gruzelier *et al.* (1995) were in keeping with his 'hemispheric imbalance' model for schizotypy. Scores for the three syndromes in a large sample of university students were obtained via factor analysis of Raine's SPQ and cognitive asymmetry was assessed by comparing recognition memory for words versus unfamiliar faces using a neuropsychological test that assesses temporo-parietal functions. As predicted, the equivalent of the active syndrome among these normal subjects was related to a word > face advantage, while the withdrawn syndrome was associated with the opposite cognitive asymmetry pattern.

Gruzelier and Richardson (1994) used the same word-face recognition memory test with normal subjects assessed for psychosis-proneness on the four subscales of the O-LIFE inventory (Mason *et al.* 1995; see also Chapter 2 and Appendix II). Although these scales are based on a different four-factor structure of psychosis-proneness from that proposed by Gruzelier, some parallels with the latter's model were still apparent. In males, Impulsive Nonconformity (with some resemblance to Gruzelier's Active syndrome) was associated with word > face superiority, while Introvertive Anhedonia (resembling a Withdrawn syndrome) was associated with face > word superiority. However, neither Unusual Experiences nor Cognitive Disorganization was associated with cognitive asymmetry.

Other studies using neuropsychological measures to investigate schizotypy in normal subjects are few. Jutai (1989) used the visual-search cancellation tasks of Weintraub and Mesulam (1985) to investigate right-hemisphere function in relation to Physical Anhedonia and Perceptual Aberration—Magical Ideation in normal subjects. High scorers on either scale showed some impairment of performance, but Per-Mag was particularly associated with problems in searching random rather than structured arrays, consistent with right-hemisphere attentional dysfunction. Other evidence that positive schizotypal traits may be associated with right-hemispheric dysfunction for visual processing was provided by Richardson and Stein (1993), who used a dot-localization task to assess visual-direction sense in relation to both dyslexia and schizotypy (assessed by the STA scale) in normal subjects. Like dyslexics, the high STA subjects were impaired at spatial localization, and made a particular excess of errors when leftward judgments were required. Richardson and Gruzelier (1994) used the same dot localization task in normal subjects assessed for both positive and negative syndromes of schizotypy. The positive syndromes were associated with the same pattern of performance observed for the STA scale, but performance was not impaired in relation to a negative syndrome, which was weakly associated with the opposite asymmetry. The association of positive schizotypy with dyslexia (Richardson 1994), and other evidence for visual-processing anomalies in both, are discussed in Chapter 9. Here it may simply be noted that, with regard to laterality, the common findings are broadly consistent with relative impairments of right-hemispheric visuospatial functions (see also Stein *et al.* 1989).

Divided visual field (DVF) and dichotic listening studies

These methods typically involve presenting information to one eye or ear so as to elicit a timed response. The accuracy or reaction time of that response is generally taken as an index of the controlling hemisphere's performance and can be compared with its neighbour. There are several problems in interpreting asymmetries and generally it may be safest to consider that differences arise both from 'fixed' and 'dynamic' asymmetries. Discrepancies in the overall level of performance between patients and normal subjects make even these interpretations hazardous.

Several fairly consistent observations can be made from the long list of DVF studies in schizophrenia. The majority have used tasks designed to target the left hemisphere, using letters and words, and many show relative deficits in right visual field (RVF) performance (Pic'l *et al.* 1979; George and Neufeld 1987). However, when 'right-hemisphere' tasks have been used, some studies have shown substantial deficits here too. The diagnosis may be critical as several studies have shown paranoid patients to differ from non-paranoid in both visual (Pic'l *et al.* 1979; Magaro and Chamrad 1983) and auditory (Overby *et al.* 1989) paradigms. These studies agree that the left-hemisphere deficit may be more pronounced in paranoid schizophrenics and the right-hemisphere deficit more pronounced in non-paranoids. Magaro and Chamrad (1983) found that the paranoid deficit was in processing faces when presented to the left visual field (LFV) / right hemisphere (RH), while the non-paranoid deficit was in processing letters presented to the RVF/left hemisphere (LH). Studies are by no means unanimous, however: Pic'l *et al.* (1979) demonstrated poor RH performance on a dot-counting task in non-paranoid patients.

Dichotic listening tasks have typically used verbal materials and so have examined a potential reduction in the usual right-ear advantage (REA) with similar findings to visual studies. While some studies show a reduction in REA in some schizophrenics (Green *et al.* 1983), it appears that this is state-dependent (Gruzelier and Hammond 1980) perhaps influenced by high levels of arousal. Green *et al.* (1994) found that only hallucinating patients showed a reduction in REA and suggested that a left-hemisphere abnormality is implicated in placing some patients at risk for auditory hallucinations.

Some of the DVF tasks have used faces as particularly effective stimuli for studying reductions in right-hemisphere superiorities. Schizophrenics often report particular difficulties with face recognition, illusions and hallucinations of faces, and self-perception of one's reflected face. Cutting (1981) found that acute schizophrenics were inferior at judging emotional expression, while Frith *et al.*'s (1983) results with schematic faces suggested an impairment in perception of the integrated gestalt. Normal studies using faces indicate that gestalt processing and emotional recognition are predominantly right-hemisphere skills. David (David and Cutting 1990; David 1995) has demonstrated that schizophrenics do not show the usual bias to use the left side of the face when making emotional judgments of 'chimeric' faces (in which half is happy and half is sad).

Overall, neither dichotic listening nor DVF studies have provided evidence for a single type of hemispheric imbalance or deficit and, as with other methods, it seems likely that several, perhaps overlapping, alterations of hemispheric function can be detected in different patients, depending on the nature of their disorder. We can tentatively conclude that some patients process verbal materials less efficiently in the left hemisphere (and/or more in the right), suggesting relative LH hypo-function. However some studies have also indicated right-hemisphere dysfunction, particularly in acute or positively symptomatic patients. The evidence from similar research in relation to schizotypy will therefore also be considered under these broad headings.

Schizotypy and language processing

DVF and dichotic listening techniques were a natural choice for initial investigations into lateralization in schizotypy, because of their previous widespread use in experimental psychopathology and normal individual-differences research. The first studies of schizotypy came from Broks and Rawlings in our own laboratory, and attempted to show that normal subjects with above average schizotypy had reduced or reversed asymmetries on various 'hemisphere' tasks involving language processing. Broks (1984) used a DVF technique to assess performance asymmetries for syllable identification. High STA subjects showed an attenuation of the expected RVF/LH advantage, to the point of symmetry in some subjects, though this effect was confined to males. Similarly, in a DVF letter identification task, Rawlings and Claridge (1984) found an unusual LVF/RH advantage in high STA subjects of both sexes, whereas low STA scorers showed the opposite, typical pattern. These results are all consistent with an association between STA schizotypy and a shift towards increased right-hemisphere activation for linguistic processing, at least for tasks involving the visual modality.

Parallel findings have emerged from some studies involving auditory language functions: Rawlings and Borge (1987) used the dichotic listening technique to assess performance asymmetries for auditory language-processing in a shadowing task, and found an absence of the expected (REA) in high STA subjects. Broks *et al.* (1984) assessed the comprehension of prose passages presented both binaurally and monaurally, as used in the study of schizophrenic patients by Green *et al.* (1983). High-Scoring STA subjects showed reduced or reversed lateral asymmetry compared with low scorers, and showed a superior left-ear performance, again compatible with an unusual right-hemisphere contribution to language function. It is interesting to note that the reduced asymmetry of highly schizotypal subjects typically arises from rather better performance in the 'normally' poorer-performing hemisphere. Whatever contributes to this relatively greater efficiency is clearly not present for most schizophrenics whose reduced asymmetry almost invariably results from poorer LH performance.

Other research also suggests an association between elevated right-hemisphere linguistic capacities and certain 'positive schizotypal' capacities. Brugger *et al.* (1993) found that believers in extra-sensory perception (ESP) showed no asymmetry on a DVF lexical decision task, while non-believers showed the expected RVF/LH advantage. Furthermore, as was found for high STA schizotypy scorers in the studies by Claridge and colleagues, this absence of asymmetry in ESP believers arose not from an impaired left-hemisphere performance, but rather from a significantly enhanced lexical-decision accuracy in the LVF/RH. It is unlikely that such a result is confined to, or particularly 'explains' (*sic*), ESP. But the difference is consistent with the larger picture of reduced asymmetry for linguistic processing in subjects scoring highly on scales developed separately from schizotypy research, that measure identical cognitive characterstics—in this case magical beliefs and experiences.

The evidence using verbal stimuli is not unanimous, however, and can be interpreted in a number of ways (Lencz *et al.* 1995). For example, Raine and his colleagues have favoured an 'arousal explanation' of findings in the area. Illustrating this, Raine and Manders (1988) employed a dichotic listening task in subjects subdivided on a composite measure of hallucinatory predisposition, perceptual aberration, and magical ideation. They explained an increased right-ear advantage found in high scorers as being due to increased left-hemisphere activation. Here they made use of an inverted-U model to account for their data, arguing that in normal subjects a certain increase in left-hemisphere activation may be facilitatory, leading to improved language performance. However, *over*-activation, as might occur in schizophrenics, could lead to overload and performance deficit.

Schizotypy and the right hemisphere

Other studies of schizotypy have moved away from a focus on language processing to explore, instead, attentional and other functions thought to involve differential hemisphere-processing. Rawlings and Claridge (1984) used a DVF paradigm with stimuli designed to elicit 'local' or 'global' processing of letter stimuli, and thereby putative left-or right-hemispheric advantages respectively (Martin 1979). Low STA subjects showed the expected RVF/LH advantage for local processing and LVF/RH advantage for global processing, as well as an overall superiority in the global condition. In contrast, the high STA subjects showed an unusual overall advantage for local processing; furthermore, their local processing showed a LVF/RH advantage, the opposite to that which would be predicted by laterality theory. The possible mechanisms which might underlie this unusual pattern of performance is unclear, but it is possible that anomalous visual processing may be a factor. The distinction between 'local' versus 'global' features of a stimulus may actually be misleading, as stimulus size—or 'spatial frequency'—may be more important (Hellige 1995). (Here the usual pattern of relative advantages is thought to reflect a right-hemisphere superiority for *low* spatial frequencies and a left-hemisphere superiority for *high* spatial frequencies (Kitterle and Christman 1991).) Hence it is possible that the poor global processing of high-scoring STA subjects reflects a relative insensitivity to low spatial-frequency information; this would be consistent with a disorder of transient visual processing, for which there is other evidence (see Chapter 9).

Another kind of contribution to the laterality literature on schizotypy has come from work where several experimental approaches have been married into a combined paradigm. As an example, Claridge *et al.* (1992) investigated visual field differences in a lateralized version of one of the negative priming procedures described in Chapter 4. As discussed there, negative priming occurs when a stimulus that was previously presented as a to-be-ignored distractor is then re-presented as a target to be named; naming takes longer than if there had been no prior distractor condition, but this effect is much reduced or even reversed in high schizotypes. In a lateralized version, it was found that high-scoring STA subjects again showed an absence of negative priming, but only in an LVF condition; normal priming was found where priming stimuli were presented first to the RVF. This suggests a special right-hemisphere involvement in the weakened cognitive inhibition that is supposedly responsible for the high schizotype's absence of negative priming. However, as with many other measures of lateralized performance and schizotypy, these effects were confined to males.

Of other studies using DVF tasks to investigate 'right-hemisphere' function in schizotypy, some that have been inspired by patient research indicate that responsiveness to face stimuli is particularly relevant in schizophrenia, and sensitive to hemisphere differences. This also seems true of schizotypy. Several items on schizotypy questionnaires explicitly enquire about alterations in face perception of self and others, though the phenomenology of this has not been investigated empirically. However, the emotional perception task developed by David (1989) to test right-hemisphere function in patients using split or 'chimeric' faces has been used in normal samples (Mason 1995). High scoring males on the STA and O-LIFE Unusual Experiences scales showed a reduction in the usual bias to the left side of the face (as presented), suggesting right hemisphere hypo-function. This finding remained when tachistoscopic presentation was used to ensure the absence of eye movements. Mirroring results from studies using verbal materials, schizotypal individuals tended to have quicker reaction times to decisions in the usually less-utilized hemisphere than less schizotypal subjects. Moreover, the difference in asymmetry between high and low scorers appeared to alter over time, suggesting that the difference arises from dynamic processes within the hemispheres.

CONCLUSIONS

From the findings reviewed here, it would seem that research into patterns of cerebral lateralization in normal individuals with schizotypal traits can help to address the question of whether laterality may be relevant in understanding the predisposition to psychotic disorder. But first it needs to be re-emphasized that psychosis (like laterality) cannot be regarded as a unitary construct; all the evidence points to multiple aetiologies, though these will prove difficult to elucidate while research continues to pay only lip-service to syndromal or dimensional models of disorder. Moreover, in addition to at least some degree of dimensionality within or across the domain of psychosis itself, the evidence also favours a continuity view of the relationship between psychosis and normal function (see Chapter 1); parallels for each of the syndromes proposed, even for schizophrenia alone, can also be discerned in the structure of personality traits in normal subjects.

Consistent with findings from schizophrenia research, studies of schizotypy using a wide range of techniques offer some support for the idea that positive, but not perhaps negative, schizotypal personality traits in normal subjects are associated with unusual patterns of cerebral lateralization. With regard to handedness, there is a rare consensus that positive schizotypy is associated with a shift away from non-right handedness—at least in the form of *inconsistent*, if not truly mixed, preference. Similarly, divided visual field and dichotic listening studies suggest a relationship between positive schizotypal traits and reduced asymmetry for language functions, though it is notable that this appears to arise from an unusually proficient right-hemisphere contribution to language processing, rather than to any left-hemisphere impairment. There seems to be a corresponding pattern—i.e. superior left-hemisphere performance in high schizotypes—on some 'right-hemisphere' tasks, such as attentional and visuospatial processing and emotional judgments of face stimuli.

These observations—of healthy schizotypes showing apparently enhanced performance patterns, albeit in association with departures from 'normal' patterns of cerebral laterality—seem contradictory to the main thrust of the patient work, particularly that adopting the classic neuropsychological approach—for the latter is largely dedicated to seeking evidence of organic *deficit*. The dilemma provides a striking illustration of the contrast, referred to in Chapter 1, between so-called 'quasi-dimensional' and 'fully dimensional' models of schizotypy, and the radically different perspectives these offer on the aetiology of psychosis. As they stand at present, the findings from cerebral laterality research could be compatible with both models. Although the picture in patient samples is certainly complicated by the artefactual effects on performance of neuroleptic medication (and possibly other secondary influences of the ill state), there does seem to be evidence of genuine structural pathology in some schizophrenic syndromes: an extrapolation to schizotypy might then require a *forme fruste* formulation of some of the dimensional aspects. On the other hand, many of the findings can be accommodated within a dynamic process/state, rather than structural/trait view of psychosis and psychosis-proneness. This, in turn, is compatible with a fully dimensional view and the notion, alluded to earlier, that an inverted-U relationship between arousal and performance could account for some of the apparent 'deficits' found in schizophrenics on tasks where healthy schizotypes perform optimally.

As for future research, it is clear that, like other experimental approaches, studies of laterality will benefit greatly from a syndromal approach in clinical investigations and from a multidimensional approach in work involving healthy subjects. In the latter, in particular, it would also be useful to bring to the study of schizotypy a number of additional techniques—viz. structural and functional brain imaging—that allow more direct study of the brain and which are especially suited to examining the many issues raised in the present chapter. Two such studies of normal schizotypy, both using MRI have already been reported. Raine *et al.* (1992) have described reduced pre-frontal area volume among high scorers on Raine's own schizotypy scale. Then, following on from this, Flaum and Andreasen (1995) have reported correlations between various structural indices and several of the Chapman scales: the relationships observed were mostly only trends, though always in the direction predicted by the authors, and with one significant (negative) association—between hippocampal volume and Perceptual Aberration. Neither of these investigations considered the cerebral-laterality question and it would be of considerable interest to extend their remit to do so. Here the examination of the temporal lobes, and particularly the planum temporale, would be well worth doing, given the recent intriguing convergence of data from schizophrenia research and from studies of dyslexic individuals, who show both abnormal asymmetry of the areas in question (Galaburda *et al.* 1985; Hynd *et al.* 1990) and evidence of positive schizotypal traits (Richardson, 1994; and see Chapter 9).

Nevertheless, as noted at the beginning of this chapter, the horizontal arrangement of the brain is not by any means the only view that it is possible to take of central nervous functioning and, over the years, interest among experimental psychopathologists in hemisphere organization has waxed and waned. The topic now seems to be in the ascendant again, with cerebral lateralization re-emerging as a perspective on the brain that might have a peculiar significance for the understanding of psychotic disorder. With better experimental techniques and more sophisticated theories—that integrate the study of the abnormal into the investigation of normal individual differences—it might finally be possible to construct a sensible account of the aetiology of the psychoses, including schizophrenia.

REFERENCES

Andreasen, N. C., Dennert, J. W., Olsen, S. A., and Damasio, A. R. (1982). Hemispheric asymmetries and schizophrenia. *American Journal of Psychiatry*, 139, 427–30.

Barta, P. E., Pearlson, G. D., Powers, R. E., Richards, S. S., and Tune, L. E. (1990). Reduced volume of superior temporal gyrus in schizophrenia: relationship to auditory hallucinations. *American Journal of Psychiatry*, 147, 1457–62.

Berman, K. F. and Weinberger, D. R. (1990). Lateralisation of cortical function during cognitive tasks: regional cerebral blood flow studies of normal individuals and patients with schizophrenia. *Journal of Neurology Neurosurgery and Psychiatry*, 53, 150–60.

Bigelow, L. and Rosenthal, R. (1972). Schizophrenia and the corpus callosum. *Lancet*, 1, 694.

Bigelow, L. B., Nasrallah, A. A., and Rauscher, F. P. (1983). Corpus callosum thickness in chronic schizophrenia. *British Journal of Psychiatry*, 142, 284–7.

Birchwood, M. J., Hallett, S. E., and Preston, M. C. (1988). *Schizophrenia: an integrated approach to research and treatment*. Longman, London.

Blanchard, J. J. and Neale, J. M. (1994). The neuropsychological signature of schizophrenia: generalized or differential deficit? *American Journal of Psychiatry*, 151, 40–8.

Bogerts, B., Ashtari, M., Degreef, G., Alvir, J. M. J., Bilder, R. M., and Lieberman, J. A. (1990). Reduced temporal limbic structure volumes on magnetic resonance images in first episode schizophrenia. *Psychiatry Research*, 35, 1–13.

Bradshaw, J. L. (1989). *Hemispheric specialisation and psychological function*. Wiley, Chichester.

Broks, P. (1984). Schizotypy and hemisphere function—II. Performance asymmetry on a verbal divided visual field task. *Personality and Individual Differences*, 5, 649–56.

Broks, P., Claridge, G. S., Matheson, J., and Hargreaves, J. (1984). Schizotypy and hemisphere function—IV. Story comprehension under binaural and monaural listening conditions. *Personality and Individual Differences*, 5, 665–70.

Brugger, P., Gamma, A., Muri, R., Schafer, M., and Taylor, K. I. (1993). Functional hemispheric asymmetry and belief in ESP: towards a 'neuropsychology of belief'. *Perceptual and Motor Skills*, 77, 1299–308.

Bryden, M. P. (1987). Handedness and cerebral organisation: data from clinical and normal populations. In *Duality and unity of the brain: unified functioning and specialisation of the hemispheres* (ed. D. Ottoson), pp. 55–70. MacMillan, London.

Buchanan, R. W., Strauss, M. E., Kirkpatrick, B., Holstein, C., Breier, A., and Carpenter, W. T. Jr (1994). Neuropsychological impairments in deficit vs nondeficit forms of schizophrenia. *Archives of General Psychiatry*, 51, 804–11.

Cannon, M., Jones, P. B., Murray, R. M., and Wadsworth, M. E. J. (1996). Hand preference and hand skill in schizophrenic patients: findings from the 1946 Birth Cohort. *Schizophrenia Research*, 18, 212–13.

Carr, S. A. (1980). Interhemispheric transfer of stereognostic information in chronic schizophrenics. *British Journal of Psychiatry*, 136, 53–8.

Chapman, J. P. and Chapman, L. J. (1987). Handedness of hypothetically psychosis-prone subjects. *Journal of Abnormal Psychology*, 96, 89–93.

Chaugule, V. B. and Master, R. S. (1981). Impaired cerebral dominance and schizophrenia. *British Journal of Psychiatry*, 139, 23–4.

Chua, S. E. and McKenna, P. J. (1995). Schizophrenia—a brain disease? A critical review of structural and functional cerebral abnormality in the disorder. *British Journal of Psychiatry*, 166, 563–82.

Claridge, G., Clark, K., and Beech, A. R. (1992). Lateralisation of the 'negative priming' effect: relationships with schizotypy and with gender. *British Journal of Psychology*, 83, 12–23.

Claridge, G., Clark, K., Davis, C., and Mason, O. (Submitted.). Schizophrenia risk and handedness: a mixed picture.

Cohen, G. (1982). Theoretical interpretations of lateral asymmetries. In *Divided visual field studies of cerebral organisation* (ed. J. G. Beaumont), pp. 87–105. Academic Press, New York.

Cromwell, R. L. (1987). An argument concerning schizophrenia: the left hemisphere drains the swamp. In *Individual differences in hemispheric specialisation* (ed. A. Glass), pp. 349–56. Plenum, New York.

Crow, T. J. (1990). Temporal lobe asymmetries as the key to the aetiology of schizophrenia. *Schizophrenia Bulletin*, 16, 433–43.

Crow, T. J., Ball, J., Bloom, S. R., Brow, R., Bruton, C. J., Colter, N., *et al.* (1989). Schizophrenia as an anomaly of development of cerebral asymmetry: a postmortem study and a proposal concerning the genetic basis of the disease. *Archives of General Psychiatry*, 46, 1145–50.

Cutting, J. (1981). Judgement of emotional expression in schizophrenics. *British Journal of Psychiatry*, 139, 45–56.

Cutting, J. (1990). *The right cerebral hemisphere and psychiatric disorders*. Oxford University Press.

David, A. (1989). Perceptual asymmetry for happy—sad chimeric faces: effects of mood. *Neuropsychologia*, 27, 1289–1300.

David, A. (1995). Spatial and selective attention in the cerebral hemispheres in depression, mania and schizophrenia. *Brain and Cognition*, 12, 67–79.

David, A. and Cutting, J. C. (1990). Affect, affective disorder and schizophrenia: A neuropsychological investigation of right hemisphere function. *British Journal of Psychiatry*, 156, 23–38.

David, A., Malmberg, A., Lewis, G., Brandt, L., and Allebeck, P. (1995). Are there neurological and sensory risk factors for schizophrenia? *Schizophrenia Research*, 14, 247–51.

Degreef, G., Ashtari, M., Bogerts, B., Bilder, R. M., Jody, D.N., Alvir, J.M.J., and Lieberman, J. A. (1992). Volumes of ventricular system subdivisions measured from magnetic resonance images in first-episode schizophrenic patients. *Archives of General Psychiatry*, 49, 531–37.

Dimond, S. J., Scammell, R. E., Pryce, I. G., Huws, D., and Gray, C. (1980). Some failures on intermanual and cross-lateral transfer in chronic schizophrenics. *Journal of Abnormal Psychology*, 89, 505–9.

Ditchfield, H. and Hemsley, D. R. (1990). Interhemispheric transfer of information and schizophrenia. *European Archives of Psychiatry and Neurological Science*, 239, 309–13.

Efron, R. (1990). *The decline and fall of hemispheric specialisation*. Erlbaum, New Jersey.

Falkai, P., Bogerts, B., Schneider, T., Greve, B., Pfeiffer, U., Pilz, K., *et al.* (1995) Disturbed planum temporale asymmetry in schizophrenia. A quantitative post-mortem study *Schizophrenia Research*, 14, 161–76.

Faustmann, W. O., Moses, J. A., Ringo, R. L., and Newcomer, J. W. (1991). Left-handedness in male schizophrenic patients is associated with increased impairment on the Luria-Nebraska Neuropsychological Battery. *Biological Psychiatry*, 30, 326–34.

Flaum, M. and Andreasen, N. C. (1995). Brain morphology in schizotypal personality as assessed by magnetic resonance imaging. In *Schizotypal personality* (ed. A. Raine, T. Lencz, and S. A. Mednick), pp. 385–405. Cambridge University Press.

Flor-Henry, P. (1969). Psychosis and temporal lobe epilepsy: a controlled investigation. *Epilepsia*, 10, 365–95.

Frith, C. D., Stevens, M., Johnstone, E. C., Owens, D. G., and Crow, T. J. (1983). Integration of schematic faces and other complex objects in schizophrenia. *Journal of Nervous and Mental Disease*, 171, 34–9.

Galaburda, A. M., Sherman, G. F., Rosen, G. D., Aboitiz, F., and Geschwind, N. (1985). Developmental dyslexia: four consecutive patients with cortical anomalies. *Annals of Neurology*, 18, 222–33.

Galaburda, A. M., Corsiglia, J., Rosen, G. D., and Sherman, G. F. (1987). Planum temporale asymmetry: reappraisal since Geschwind and Levitsky. *Neuropsychologia*, 25, 853–68.

George, L. and Neufeld, R. W. (1987). Attentional resources and hemispheric functional asymmetry in schizophrenia. *British Journal of Clinical Psychology*, 26, 35–45.

Geschwind, N. and Galaburda, A. M. (1987). *Cerebral lateralization: biological mechanisms, associations and pathology*. MIT Press, Cambridge, Mass.

Glass, A. (ed.) (1987). *Individual differences in hemispheric specialisation*. Plenum, New York.

Green, M. F., Satz, P., Smith, C., and Nelson, L. (1989). Is there atypical handedness in schizophrenia? *Journal of Abnormal Psychology*, 98, 57–61.

Green, M. F., Hugdahl, K., and Mitchell, S. (1994). Dichotic listening during auditory hallucinations in patients with schizophrenia. *American Journal of Psychiatry*, 151, 357–62.

Green, P. (1978). Defective interhemispheric transfer and schizophrenia. *Journal of Abnormal Psychology*, 87, 472–80.

Green, P., Hallett, S., and Hunter, H. (1983). Abnormal interhemispheric integration and hemispheric specialisation in schizophrenics and high-risk children. In *Laterality and psychopathology* (ed. P. Flor-Henry and J. H. Gruzelier), pp. 433–70. Elsevier, Amsterdam.

Gruzelier, J. H. (1983). A critical assessment and integration of lateral asymmetries in schizophrenia. In *Hemisyndromes: psychobiology, neurology and psychiatry* (ed. M. S. Myslobodsky), pp. 265–326. Academic Press, New York.

Gruzelier, J. H. (1991). Hemispheric imbalance: syndromes of schizophrenia, premorbid personality, and neurodevelopmental influences. In *Handbook of schizophrenia. Vol. 5: Neuropsychology, psychophysiology and information processing* (ed. S. R. Steinhauer, J. H. Gruzelier, and J. Zubin), pp. 559–650. Elsevier, London.

Gruzelier, J. H. (1994). Syndromes of schizophrenia and schizotypy, hemispheric imbalance and sex differences: implications for developmental psychopathology. *International Journal of Psychophysiology*, 18, 167–78.

Gruzelier, J. H. and Hammond, N. V. (1980). Lateralised deficits and drug influences on the dichotic listening of schizophrenic patients. *Biological Psychiatry*, 15, 759–79.

Gruzelier, J. and Richardson, A. (1994). Patterns of cognitive asymmetry and psychosis proneness. *International Journal of Psychophysiology*, 18, 217–25.

Gruzelier, J., Burgess, A., Stygall, J., Irving, G., and Raine, A. (1995). Patterns of cognitive asymmetry and syndromes of schizotypal personality. *Psychiatry Research*, 56, 71–9.

Gunther, W., Petsch, R., Steinberg, R., Moser, E., Streck, P., Heller, H., *et al.* (1991). Brain dysfunction during motor activation and corpus callosum alterations in schizophrenia measured by cerebral blood flow and magnetic resonance imaging. *Biological Psychiatry*, 29, 535–55.

Gur, R. (1977). Motoric laterality imbalance in schizophrenia. *Archives of General Psychiatry*, 34, 33–7.

Gur, R. E., Skolnick, B. E., Gur, R.C., Karoff, S., Rieger, W., Ohrist, W.D., *et al.* (1983). Brain function in psychiatric disorders. *Archives of General Psychiatry*, 40, 1250–4.

Gur, R. E., Gur, R. C., Skolnik, B. E., Caroff, S., Obrist, W. D., Resnick, S., and Reivich, M. (1985). Brain function in psychiatric disorders, III: regional cerebral blood flow in unmedicated schizophrenics. *Archives of General Psychiatry*, 42, 329–34.

Gur, R.E., Resnick, S., Alavi, A., Gur, R.C., Caroff, S., Dann, R., *et al.* (1987*a*). Regional brain function in schizophrenia. I. A Positron Emission Tomography study. *Archives of General Psychiatry*, 44, 119–25.

Gur, R. E., Resnick, S. M., Gur, R. C., Alavi, A., Caroff, S., Kushner, M., and Reivich, M. (1987*b*) Regional brain function in schizophrenia, II: Repeated evaluation with Positron Emission Tomography. *Archives of General Psychiatry*, 44, 126–9.

Hallett, S. and Green, P. (1983). Possible defects of interhemispheric integration in children of schizophrenics. *Journal of Nervous and Mental Disease*, 171, 421–5.

Hellige, J. B. (1993). *Hemispheric asymmetry: what's right and what's left.* Harvard University Press.

Hellige, J. B. (1995). Hemispheric asymmetry for components of visual information processing. In *Brain asymmetry* (ed. R. J. Davidson and K. Hugdahl), pp. 99–122. MIT Press, Cambridge, Mass.

Hiscock, M., Antoniuk, D., Prisciak, K., and von Hessert, D. (1985). Generalized and lateralized interference between concurrent tasks performed by children: effects of age, sex and skill. *Developmental Neuropsychology*, 1, 29–48.

Hoff, A. L., Riordan, H., O'Donnell, D. W., Morris, L., and DeLisi, L. E. (1992). Neuropsychological functioning of first-episode schizophreniform patients. *American Journal of Psychiatry*, 149, 898–903.

Hynd, G. W., Semrud-Clikeman, M., Lorys, A. R., Novey, E. S., and Eliopoulos, D. (1990). Brain morphology in developmental dyslexia and attention deficit disorder/hyperactivity. *Archives of Neurology*, 47, 919–26.

Jutai, J. W. (1989). Spatial attention in hypothetically psychosis-prone college students. *Psychiatry Research*, 27, 207–15.

Katsanis, J. and Iacono, W. G. (1989). Association of left-handedness with ventricle size and neuropsychological performance in schizophrenia. *American Journal of Psychiatry*, 146, 1056–8.

Kelley, M. P. and Coursey, R. D. (1992). Lateral preference and neuropsychological correlates of schizotypy. *Psychiatry Research*, 41, 115–35.

Kim, H., Levine, S. C., and Kertesz, S. (1990). Are variations among subjects in lateral asymmetry real individual differences or random error in measurement?: Putting variability in its place. *Brain and Cognition*, 14, 220–42.

Kim, D., Raine, A., Triphon, N., and Green, M. F. (1992). Mixed handedness and features of schizotypal personality in a non-clinical sample. Journal of *Nervous and Mental Disease*, 180, 133–5.

Kinsbourne, M. (1977). Hemi-neglect and hemisphere rivalry. In *Advances in neurology*, Vol. 18 (ed. E. Weinstein and R. Friedland), pp. 41–9. Raven, New York.

Kitterle, F. L. and Christman, S. (1991). Hemispheric processing of sine wave gratings. In *Cerebral lateralization* (ed. F. L. Kitterle), pp. 201–25. Erlbaum, New York.

Kleinschmidt A., Falkai P., Huang Y., Schneider T., Furst, G., and Steinmetz H. (1994). In-vivo morphometry of planum temporale asymmetry in first-episode schizophrenia. *Schizophrenia Research*, 12, 9–18.

Kwapil, T. R., Chapman, L. J., and Chapman, J. P. (1992). Monaural and binaural story recall by schizophrenic subjects. *Journal of Abnormal Psychology*, 101, 709–16.

LaPorte, D. J., Kirkpatrick, B., and Thaker, G. K. (1994). Psychosis-proneness and verbal memory in a college student population. *Schizophrenia Research*, 12, 237–45.

Lencz, T., Raine, A., Benishay, D. S., Mills, S., and Bird, L. (1995). Neuropsychological abnormalities associated with schizotypal personality. In *Schizotypal personality* (ed. A. Raine, T. Lencz, and S. A. Mednick), pp. 289–328. Cambridge University Press.

Lenzenweger, M. F. and Korfine, L. (1994). Perceptual aberrations, schizotypy, and the Wisconsin Card Sorting Test. *Schizophrenia Bulletin*, 20, 345–57.

Levy, J. (1969). Possible basis for the evolution of lateral specialisation of the human brain. *Nature*, 224, 614–15.

Levy, J., Heller, W., Banich, M. T., and Burton, L. A. (1983) Are variations among right-handed individuals in perceptual asymmetries caused by characteristic arousal differences between hemispheres? *Journal of Experimental Psychology: Human Perception and Performance*, 9, 329–59.

Lishman, W. A., and McMeekan, E. R. L. (1976). Hand preference patterns in psychiatric patients. *British Journal of Psychiatry*, 129, 158–66.

McCrae, R. (1987). Creativity, divergent thinking and openness to experience. *Journal of Personality and Social Psychology*, 52, 1258–65.

McCrae, R. (1994). Openness to experience: expanding the boundaries of Factor V. *European Journal of Personality*, 8, 251–72.

McGlone, J. (1980). Sex differences in human brain organisation: a critical survey. *Behavioural and Brain Sciences*, 3, 215–27.

Magaro, P. A. and Chamrad, D. L. (1983). Hemispheric preference of paranoid and nonparanoid schizophrenics. *Biological Psychiatry*, 18, 1269–85.

Manoach, D. S., Maher, B. A., and Manschreck, T. C. (1988). Left-handedness and thought disorder in the schizophrenias. *Journal of Abnormal Psychology*, 97, 97–9.

Manschreck, T. C., and Ames, D. (1984). Neurological features and psychopathology in schizophrenic disorders. *Biological Psychiatry*, 19, 703–19.

Manschreck, T. C., Maher, B. A., Redmond, D. A., Miller, C., and Beaudette, S. M. (1996). Laterality, memory and thought disorder in schizophrenia. *Neuropsychiatry, Neuropsychology and Behavioural Neurology*, 9, 1–7.

Martin, M. (1979). Hemispheric specialisation for local and global processing. *Neuropsychologia*, 17, 33–40.

Mason, O. (1995). Schizotypy: questionnaire and experimental studies. Unpublished D. Phil. thesis. University of Oxford.

Mason, O., Claridge, G., and Jackson, M. (1995). New scales for the assessment of schizotypy. *Personality and Individual Differences*, 18, 7–13.

Menon, R. R., Barta, P. E., Aylward, E. H., Richards, S. S., Vaughn, D. D., Tien, A. Y., et al. (1995). Posterior superior temporal gyrus in schizophrenia: grey matter changes and clinical correlates. *Schizophrenia Research*, 16, 127–35.

Nasrallah, H.A., McCalley-Whitters, M., and Kuperman, S. (1982). Neurological differences between paranoid and non-paranoid schizophrenia: Part 1. Sensory-motor lateralization. *Journal of Clinical Psychiatry*, 43, 305–6.

O'Boyle, M. W. and Hellige, J. B. (1989). Cerebral hemisphere asymmetry and individual differences in cognition. *Learning and Individual Differences*, 1, 7–35.

Oepen, G., Fünfgeld, M., Höll, T., Zimmermann, P., Landis, T., and Regard, M. (1987). Schizophrenia—and emotional hypersensitivity of the right cerebral hemisphere. *International Journal of Psychophysiology*, 5, 261–4.

Overby, L. A. III (1992). Handedness patterns of psychosis-prone college students. *Personality and Individual Differences*, 15, 261–5.

Overby, L. A., Harris, A. E., and Leek, M. R. (1989). Perceptual asymmetry in schizophrenia and affective disorder: Implications from a right hemisphere task. *Neuropsychologia*, 27, 861–70.

Petty, R. G., Barta, P. E., Pearlson, G. D. McGilchrist, I. K., Lewis, R. W., Tien, A. Y., et *al.* (1995). Reversal of asymmetry of the planum temporale in schizophrenia. *American Journal of Psychiatry*, **152**, 715–21.

Pic'l, A. K., Magaro, P. A., and Wade, E. A. (1979). Hemispheric functioning in paranoid and nonparanoid schizophrenia. *Biological Psychiatry*, **14**, 891–903.

Quinan, C. (1930). The principal sinistral types: An experimental study, particularly as regards their relation to the so-called psychopathic states. *Archives of Neurology and Psychiatry*, **24**, 35–47.

Raine, A. and Manders, D. (1988). Schizoid personality, interhemispheric transfer, and left hemisphere overactivation. *British Journal of Clinical Psychology*, **27**, 333–47.

Raine, A., Harrison, G. N., Reynolds, G. P., Sheard, C., Cooper, J. E., and Medley, I. (1990). Structural and functional characteristics of the corpus callosum in schizophrenics, psychiatric controls, and normal controls. A magnetic resonance imaging and neuropsychological evaluation. *Archives of General Psychiatry*, **47**, 1060–4

Raine, A., Sheard, C., Reynolds, G. P., and Lencz, T. (1992). Pre-frontal structural and functional deficits associated with individual differences in schizotypal personality. *Schizophrenia Research*, **7**, 237–47.

Rawlings, D. and Borge, A. (1987). Personality and hemisphere functions: Two experiments using the dichotic shadowing technique. *Personality and Individual Differences*, **8**, 438–88.

Rawlings, D. and Claridge, G. S. (1984). Schizotypy and Hemisphere Function—III. Performance asymmetries on tasks of letter recognition and local/global processing. *Personality and Individual Differences*, **5**, 657–64.

Richardson, A. J. (1994). Dyslexia, handedness and syndromes of psychosis-proneness. *International Journal of Psychophysiology*, **18**, 251–63.

Richardson, A. J. and Gruzelier, J. (1994). Visual processing, lateralization and syndromes of schizotypy. *International Journal of Psychophysiology*, **18**, 227–39.

Richardson, A. J. and Stein, J. F. (1993). Dyslexia, schizotypy and visual direction sense. *Annals of the New York Academy of Sciences*, **682**, 400–1.

Rossi, A., Stratta, P., D'Albenzio, L., Tartaro, A., Schiazza, G., di Michele, V., *et al.* (1990). Reduced temporal lobe areas in schizophrenia: preliminary evidences from a controlled multiplanar magnetic resonance imaging study. *Biological Psychiatry*, **27**, 61–8.

Rossi, A., Stratta, P., Mattei, P., Cupillari, M., Bozzao, A., Gallucci, M. and Casacchia, M. (1992). Planum temporale in schizophrenia: a magnetic resonance study. *Schizophrenia Research*, **7**, 19–22.

Rotenberg, V. S. (1994). An integrative psychophysiological approach to brain hemisphere functions in schizophrenia. *Neuroscience Biobehavioural Review*, **18**, 487–95.

Saykin, A. J., Shtasel, D. L., Gur, R. E., Kester, D. B., Mozley, L. H., Stafiniak, P., and Gur, R. C. (1994). Neuropsychological deficits in neuroleptic naive patients with first-episode schizophrenia. *Archives of General Psychiatry*, **51**, 124–31.

Shenton, M. E., Kikinis, R., Jolesz, F. A., Pollak, S. D., LeMay, M., Wible, C. G., *et al.* (1992). Abnormalities of the left temporal lobe and thought disorder in schizophrenia. A quantitative magnetic resonance imaging study. *New England Journal of Medicine*, **327**, 604–12.

Silverstein, M. L., Marengo, J. T., and Fogg, L. (1991). Two types of thought disorder and lateralized neuropsychological dysfunction. *Schizophrenia Bulletin*, **17**, 679–87.

Stein, J. F., Riddell, P. M., and Fowler, M. S. (1989). Disordered right hemisphere function in developmental dyslexia. In *Brain and reading. Werner Gren Symposium*, Vol. 54 (ed. C. von Euler.), pp. 139–57. Macmillan, London.

Taylor, P. J., Dalton, R, and Fleminger, J. J. (1980). Handedness in schizophrenia. *British Journal of Psychiatry*, **136**, 375–83.

Venables, P. H. (1983). Cerebral mechanisms, autonomic responsivity and attention in schizophrenia. In *Theories of schizophrenia and psychosis* (ed. G. W. Spaulding), 31st Nebraska Symposium on Motivation, pp. 144–83. University of Nebraska Press, Lincoln.

Walker, E. and Green, M. (1982). Soft signs of neurological dysfunction in schizophrenia: An investigation of lateral performance. *Biological Psychiatry*, 17, 381–6.

Walker, E. and McGuire, M. (1982). Intra-and interhemispheric information processing in schizophrenia. *Psychological Bulletin*, 92, 701.

Weinberger, D. R. (1987) Implications of normal brain development for the pathogenesis of schizophrenia. *Archives of General Psychiatry*, 44, 660–9.

Weintraub, S. and Mesulam, M. (1985). Mental state assessment of young and elderly adults in behavioural neurology. In *Principles of behavioural neurology* (ed. M. Mesulam), pp. 71–123. F. A. Davis, Philadelphia.

Wexler, B. E., Giller, E. L. Jr, and Southwick, S. (1991). Cerebral laterality, symptoms, and diagnosis in psychotic patients. *Biological Psychiatry*, 29, 103–16.

Williams, J. H., Wellman, N. A., Geaney, D. P., Cowen, P. J., Feldon, J., and Rawlins, J. N. P. (1996). Latent inhibition is not reduced in drug-free patients with schizophrenia. *Schizophrenia Research*, 18, 205.

Witelson, S. F. (1987). Individual differences in the anatomy of the corpus callosum: Sex, hand preference, schizophrenia and hemisphere specialization. In *Individual differences in hemispheric specialization* (ed. A. Glass). Plenum, New York.

Wittling, W. (1995). Brain asymmetry in the control of autonomic-physiologic activity. In *Brain asymmetry* (ed. R. J. Davidson, R. J., and K. Hugdahl), pp. 305–58. MIT Press, Cambridge, Mass.

Part III Schizotypy in non-psychotic disorder

9

Dyslexia and schizotypy

A. J. RICHARDSON

INTRODUCTION

Research into the nature and possible causes of dyslexia and schizophrenia has produced two huge sets of literature which, until very recently, no one has seen reason to connect. However, the proposal made here is that there may actually be important shared features in the predisposition to both these disorders. This idea arose from the author's findings of a strong association between dyslexia and certain aspects of schizotypy, following studies of personality traits in dyslexic adults, and these results will be summarized here. However, other findings from research in both fields will also be discussed, because these show that the similarities between dyslexia and the schizophrenia spectrum extend beyond phenomenology to experimental, epidemiological, and genetic evidence, supporting the idea of common factors at a neurobiological level.

Given its context, it is assumed that the reader of this chapter will be more familiar with the concept of schizotypy and the associated literature than with the field of dyslexia research, so more emphasis has been placed on the latter. An overview of the clinical syndrome of dyslexia is first presented, noting the very wide range of features associated with reading difficulties. It is hoped that some of the parallels with schizophrenia and schizotypy may be apparent from this, but explicit discussion of these is postponed until later in the chapter. The evidence for biological factors in the predisposition to dyslexia is then briefly discussed, and the idea that this predisposition may also be expressed in the domain of personality. Two questionnaire studies are reported which revealed a strong association between dyslexia and 'positive', but not 'negative', schizotypal traits, and discussion of these is followed by a review of other evidence for an association between dyslexia and the schizophrenia spectrum. In this, two themes in particular will be apparent: first, the issue of 'unusual cerebral lateralization' and its possible significance (though this is discussed in more detail in relation to schizotypy in Chapter 8); and second, various abnormalities of sensory (and cognitive) function common to dyslexia and schizotypy, which may reflect a more fundamental disorder of rapid temporal processing. Abnormalities of temporal coding are a major focus of current research into the biological basis of dyslexia, and it is suggested that similar abnormalities may also underlie some features of schizophrenia and schizotypy. Finally, a novel but intriguing genetic and biochemical hypothesis is discussed which could explain some of the links between dyslexia and the schizophrenia spectrum.

In summarizing, consideration is given to the implications of a dyslexia-schizotypy relationship for schizotypal trait measures as indices of risk for actual psychosis; this involves some discussion of the differences between dyslexia and schizotypy. Suggestions are also made for future research, with the proposal that a perspective on schizotypy and schizophrenia from the viewpoint of dyslexia research might help to shed further light on the nature and origins of psychiatric illness.

THE DYSLEXIA SYNDROME

Developmental dyslexia refers to specific difficulties in learning to read and write, relative to general ability, which cannot be attributed to lack of motivation or opportunity nor to other emotional or social causes. Diagnosis requires a clear discrepancy between written language skills and general ability, but, in addition, dyslexia typically involves a particular pattern of problems with short-term memory, sequencing, orientation, and direction (Miles 1994). Prevalence estimates range from 5 to 10 per cent of schoolchildren (Benton and Pearl 1978), there is clear evidence for a genetic predisposition (DeFries et al. 1987), and three to four males are affected for every female (James 1992). A wide range of additional features are associated with dyslexia, including a variety of 'soft neurological signs', poor motor coordination, non-right-handedness, and autoimmune disorders (Geschwind and Galaburda 1987; Tonnessen et al. 1993). Clinically, there is some overlap with other disorders; developmental speech and language problems inevitably lead on to dyslexic difficulties, and although in overt cases dysphasia would be the primary diagnosis (Denckla 1993), more subtle problems with spoken language are common in dyslexic individuals. Attention-deficit-hyperactivity-disorder (ADHD) also often occurs with dyslexia, with 30–50 per cent overlap in both directions (Conners 1990; Dykman and Ackerman 1991), but again these are separable conditions. Furthermore, in a major epidemiological survey, Yule et al. (1974) showed that specific reading difficulties (dyslexia) could also be distinguished from general reading backwardness by the excess of males affected, a relative lack of associated organic problems, and ironically, a poorer prognosis. Dyslexia occurs at similar rates across cultures (Tarnopol and Tarnopol 1976), and problems persist into adulthood (Miles 1986; Kinsbourne et al. 1991). All of these features suggest a relatively distinct syndrome with a neurobiological basis.

In terms of cognitive profile, dyslexia is more often associated with deficits in verbal relative to performance IQ, as might be expected, but the reverse pattern is also found. There is considerable variability between dyslexic subjects on IQ subtest profiles, but particular problems with sequencing and auditory short-term memory are characteristic, with demonstrable deficits persisting into adulthood (Miles 1986). Equally pervasive are deficits in rapid naming (Denckla and Rudel 1976) and poor phonological skills, i.e. problems segmenting spoken language into its constituent sounds, with a relative insensitivity to rhyme and alliteration

(Bradley and Bryant 1983). Impairments of low-level visual processing are also evident in most individuals with dyslexia (Stein 1991; Willows *et al* 1993), but these are not readily detected on routine clinical screening, nor via standard cognitive and neuropsychological measures.

In view of the clinical heterogeneity of dyslexia, many have sought to identify subtypes (for example Ingram *et al.* 1970; Boder 1973; Mattis *et al.* 1975). However, this approach has been less successful than similar efforts to identify syndromes of schizophrenia and schizotypy, and overall there appears to be no evidence for clear and consistent subgroups within dyslexia (Hooper and Willis 1989). Although the commonest proposed distinction has been between 'auditory-linguistic' and 'visuospatial' problems, sometimes related to left- versus right-hemisphere deficits (Bakker 1979), the fact is that in most cases visual and phonological problems occur together (Lovegrove 1991; Stein 1991; Slaghuis *et al.* 1993); and there are current speculations that auditory-linguistic and visual problems in dyslexia may even have a common basis, as discussed further below.

Many maintain that the fundamental problem in dyslexia lies in linguistic processing, and specifically in phonological coding (Snowling 1987). However, it is clear that a 'phonological deficit' hypothesis can in no way account for the full range of findings related to dyslexia, as there is abundant evidence of problems in skills quite independent of phonological processing. Atrocious handwriting is a common feature, as well as forgetfulness, distractibility, clumsiness, and being accident-prone and absent-minded. Augur (1985) summarized the clinical evidence to derive a list of 21 classic dyslexic problems, and though many of these related in some way to reading and phonological skills, a surprisingly large number implicated motor difficulties (clumsiness, problems in tying shoelaces, hopping and skipping, clapping, riding a bicycle, rhythm, and throwing and catching a ball). Others suggested central attentional problems or rate-limiting weaknesses in information processing: examples here included problems in carrying out several instructions simultaneously, high distractibility, and rapid tiring under continuous load. Data from the UK 1970 National Birth Cohort Study support the picture of motor coordination as a fundamental weakness. Haslum (1989) used multivariate analysis on scores from 17 000 children for 87 variables assessed at age five, to discover which might predict dyslexia at age ten. She identified just six independent factors: three concerned parental attitudes and education, one was reading disorder in a sibling, and the remaining two were catching a ball after clapping, and walking backwards. A similarly broad range of impairments persists into adulthood: Kinsbourne *et al.* (1991) found a very wide range of deficits on neuropsychological testing in dyslexic adults, and these were by no means confined to the language domain. Particularly striking were their deficits in tasks where performance could not be expected to depend in any way on reading or educational experience, such as neuromotor performance and simple temporal-order judgements in both visual and auditory domains.

Attempting to account for the wide range of problems found in the dyslexia syndrome, Nicolson and Fawcett (1990) proposed a general deficit in the automatization of skills. Pointing out that even well-remediated dyslexics show a distinct lack of fluency in written language skills, with abnormal susceptibility to interference from other tasks, they suggested that 'incomplete mastery' characterizes many other features of dyslexic performance, such as problem with learning to ride a bicycle or tie shoelaces, and general clumsiness. 'Automatization' of a skill involves a reduction in the need for conscious attentive control of performance, leading to greater speed and efficiency and a decreased likelihood of breakdown under stress, as well as the ability to perform a concurrent task with minimal interference. Fawcett and Nicolson (1992) compared dyslexics and controls on single and dual tasks; and while controls showed little or no impairment under dual-task conditions, dyslexics showed marked impairment even on a simple balancing task, suggesting that their near-normal single-task performance was achieved by 'conscious compensation'. In cognitive tasks, deficits in dyslexia extend down to the level of impairments on choice, but not simple reaction time, again consistent with a general automatization deficit (Nicolson and Fawcett 1994). This is certainly better able to account for the wide range of features associated with dyslexia than a simple phonological deficit hypothesis, but still leaves open the question of its biological basis. Nicolson et al. (1995) have hypothesized that cerebellar dysfunction may be a factor, which could be consistent with proposals of a general impairment of temporal processing, to be discussed below.

DYSLEXIA: EVIDENCE FOR A BIOLOGICAL BASIS

Genetic studies have shown substantial heritability for reading difficulties (DeFries et al. 1987), but have so far shed little light on possible biological mechanisms. By contrast, post-mortem studies have revealed various microscopic abnormalities of neuronal organization in dyslexic brains which are regarded as aetiologically significant. Early reports suggested these were particularly concentrated in left perisylvian regions (Galaburda et al. 1985), but their distribution appears to be widespread and bilateral, and varies between individual cases (which could help to explain some of the clinical heterogeneity). Their cause is unknown, but these abnormalities occur during the second trimester and could reflect abnormal autoimmune influences on the developing brain. Neuroanatomical evidence has also provided some support for Orton's (1937) hypothesis that unusual cerebral lateralization may be important in the predisposition to dyslexia. Observing an excess of non-right-handedness in dyslexics, he proposed a failure to develop the normal left-hemispheric dominance for language functions. Post-mortem and imaging studies have now shown that the usual structural asymmetries are more often reduced or reversed in dyslexic subjects (Hynd and Semrud-Clikeman 1989), and particular significance has been attached to the fact that dyslexic brains typically show an unusual symmetry (rather than the usual leftward asymmetry) of the planum temporale, an auditory association area important in language processing (Galaburda et al. 1985; Lubs et al. 1988). This planum symmetry appears to distinguish dyslexic from ADHD children (Hynd *et al.* 1990) and has also been related to poor phonological skills (Larsen *et al.* 1990), but since 'abnormal' symmetry of the planum is found in approximately 25 per cent of the population (Galaburda *et al.* 1987), it can by no means provide a sufficient explanation for dyslexic problems, though it could represent an important risk factor.

More recently, attention has focused on the so-called 'magnocellular hypothesis', that dyslexia involves a neurodevelopmental disorder which specifically affects a subset of large neurones responsible for very rapid temporal processing in the nervous system (Livingstone *et al.* 1991; Stein 1994). There is compelling evidence of low-level visual deficits in dyslexia for tasks involving very rapid temporal coding (Lovegrove *et al.* 1990; Stein 1991; Willows *et al.* 1993). Recent findings point to similar deficits in aspects of auditory temporal resolution, which may underlie dyslexics' poor phonological processing (Tallal *et al.* 1993; McAnally 1994; McAnally and Stein 1996; Baldeweg *et al.* 1997); and deficits in precise neural timing could also account for motor abnormalities in dyslexia (Wolff 1993). In the visual system the subcortical 'magnocellular' pathway provides the main substrate for such rapid temporal processing (Merigan and Maunsell 1993), so it is significant that abnormalities specific to the magnocellular layers of the lateral geniculate nucleus were reported post-mortem in dyslexic brains (Livingstone *et al.* 1991). Similar anomalies may also affect the medial geniculate nucleus, a subcortical relay for auditory information (Galaburda *et al.* 1994). Thus both anatomical and experimental evidence indicate that dyslexia may involve a multi-modal disorder of rapid temporal processing which is of neurodevelopmental origin. Although further investigation is clearly required, this hypothesis is compatible with the otherwise puzzlingly diverse range of features associated with dyslexia, from linguistic problems, unstable visual perception, and poor motor coordination to a more general difficulty in the automatization of skills; in addition, as Stein (1994) has argued, it is even possible that hemispheric specialization may depend on a left-hemisphere advantage for temporal processing, which fails to develop in dyslexics.

DYSLEXIA AND SCHIZOTYPAL PERSONALITY

A biological basis to dyslexia seems to be beyond doubt, even if its precise nature is not yet clear, and it seems possible that this could also help to determine some primary aspects of temperament or personality. Orton, one of the earliest investigators, did suggest this (cited in Geschwind 1982), but most research into personality factors in dyslexia has tended rather to focus on characteristics such as anxiety, depression, and low self-esteem, and to interpret these as understandable secondary consequences of reading problems (Critchley 1970; Miles 1994). There are obvious difficulties in distinguishing 'primary' from 'secondary' traits beyond a theoretical level, but a few have suggested that there may be traits which stem from the same constitutional factors that underlie dyslexic-type difficulties. Rourke and

Fisk (1981, 1988) proposed that different types of socio-emotional disturbance might be intrinsically associated with different subtypes of learning disability. They related language disabilities to 'externalizing' behaviours such as conduct disorder or aggression, and visuospatial and arithmetical deficits to 'internalizing' disturbances such as anxiety, withdrawal, and depression, proposing that these may reflect left- and right-hemisphere dysfunction respectively. Both Spreen (1989) and Duane (1989) have argued that the same biological mechanisms which induce reading disabilities may also play a role in engendering psychiatric disorder, and Duane (1991) tentatively suggested that both might be related to incomplete lateralization, as shown by a shift away from right-handedness.

Dyslexics' self-reports indicate that a rather wide range of unusual perceptual and cognitive features may relate to reading difficulties; and it was these which prompted an initial investigation by the author into personality traits in adult dyslexia (Richardson and Stein 1991, 1993a). Many dyslexic subjects report various unusual visual perceptions, including distortions of size constancy and colour, a heightened or labile sensitivity to light, visual instability (objects appearing to move or shimmer), symptoms of glare or blurring, poor depth and distance judgments, and problems distinguishing figure from ground. These features are of course consistent with the growing body of experimental research showing significant low-level visual deficits in dyslexia (Stein 1991; Willows *et al.* 1993). Also predictable, in view of the well-documented auditory-linguistic deficits of dyslexics, are their own reports of problems with pronunciation, word-finding, and the comprehension of rapid or degraded speech. However, in addition, and analogous to the visual problems they report, dyslexics often complain of other auditory perceptual anomalies, including over-sensitivity to environmental sounds, problems with auditory localization, and other distortions which make it difficult to distinguish sounds against background noise. It should be emphasized that these problems are not confined to the processing of language, and, experimentally, very low level auditory perceptual abnormalities have been found in dyslexia (McAnally 1994; McAnally and Stein 1996). Other reported perceptions are more unusual, involving experiences of synaesthesia, distortions in the perception of time, powerful feelings of intuition or precognition, and even out-of-body experiences (see Richardson and Stein 1993a).

Many dyslexic subjects also report attentional problems, ranging from an unusual distractibility to 'over-absorption', consistent with the high concordance between reading difficulties and clinical attentional disorders. But perhaps the most common complaint is a general 'disorganization'. De Hirsch and Jansky (1980) noted the pervasiveness of organizational problems in dyslexia, which encompass perception, language, attention, and motor behaviour. They construed this as a failure of 'gestalt' processing, i.e. 'a general instability in apprehending part-whole and figure-ground relationships', with consequent problems for structuring both internal and external events. This interpretation has descriptive rather than explanatory value, but it does serve to capture the very wide range of domains over which 'disorganization' is experienced. It is also consistent with Wolff's (1993) proposal that dyslexics' motor coordination problems may reflect a specific difficulty in *assembling* components of behaviour into coherent, 'temporally ordered larger ensembles'. Finally, analogous perhaps to their perceptual style, dyslexic subjects typically report that their thinking is non-linguistic, and correspondingly 'divergent' or lateral, rather than convergent, linear, and sequential. Their strategies of reasoning and problem-solving therefore often seem unstructured and idiosyncratic, even when these are highly successful.

All of these features suggested a rather unusual perceptual and cognitive style which it would be difficult to explain away as being entirely the *result* of reading and writing problems. In view of the obvious surface similarities to various aspects of the schizotypal personality profile it seemed possible that trait measures of this kind might capture and quantify some of the characteristics reported by dyslexics; and this proposal formed the basis for two investigations of schizotypy or psychosis-proneness in adult dyslexic subjects.

Results from an initial investigation using the STA scale in dyslexia were reported by Richardson and Stein (1993*a*), but as this study was then extended (Richardson 1993), details relating to the larger sample are provided here. The dyslexic group comprised 66 adults (36 males and 30 females; mean age 23.5 years; age range 17–53). All were independently diagnosed by psychologists on the basis of a significant discrepancy between general ability and written language skills, but most had pursued education up to or beyond 18, and all could read well enough to take part in a questionnaire study. Controls had no history of reading or spelling problems, and were matched as closely as possible for age, sex, and occupation or education; in many cases more than one control was found for each dyslexic subject, yielding a group of 111 controls (65 males and 46 females; mean age 24.1 years; age range 17–55). All subjects completed a self-report inventory of personality measures, comprising the four Eysenck scales—Lie, Extraversion, Neuroticism and Psychoticism—(Eysenck and Eysenck 1975) and the two Claridge scales—STA and STB—designed to assess Schizotypal and Borderline personality traits respectively (Claridge and Broks 1984; see Appendix 1). The dyslexic group showed highly elevated scores on STA schizotypy (dyslexics: $X = 19.7$, SD = 6.3; controls: $X = 13.1$, SD = 7.1; $P < 0.001$), which held for both males and females. They also showed a much smaller but significant elevation on the STB borderline scale (dyslexics: $X = 8.5$, SD = 3.8; controls: $X = 7.0$, SD = 4.0; $P = 0.023$), though on subdivision by sex this was significant only in males. No group differences were found for any of the Eysenck scales.

STA schizotypy scores were so much higher in dyslexics that it seemed worth attempting to illuminate this by examining each group's responses to individual scale items. The STA measures a fairly broad spectrum of positive schizotypal traits, and the relative heterogeneity of its content allowed Hewitt and Claridge (1989) to factor analyse the *items* from the scale. This yielded three main factors, identified as Magical Ideation, Unusual Perceptual Experiences, and Paranoid Ideation/Social Anxiety. Comparison of endorsement frequencies for each item between dyslexic and control groups showed a significant difference for 19 of the

Table 9.1   Examples of STA items endorsed by significantly more dyslexics than controls

Item	Percentage Endorsement (dyslexic, control)
Does your own voice ever seem distant, far away?	(63, 19)
Do everyday things sometimes seem unusually large or small?	(56, 14)
Have you ever felt when you looked in a mirror that your face seemed different?	(75, 40)
Do you ever suddenly feel distracted by distant sounds that you are not normally aware of?	(75, 41)
Does your sense of smell sometimes become unusually strong?	(46, 19)
Are your thoughts sometimes so strong that you can almost hear them?	(60, 31)
Have you ever thought you heard people talking only to discover that it was in fact some nondescript noise?	(50, 25)
Do things sometimes feel as if they were not real?	(73, 49)
Do you ever become over-sensitive to light or noise?	(67, 45)
Do you often have vivid dreams that disturb your sleep?	(46, 25)
When in a crowded room do you often have difficulty in following a conversation?	(46, 27)
When in the dark do you often see shapes and forms even though there's nothing there?	(46, 28)

37 scale items, examples of which are shown in Table 9.1. Using the three-factor classification of Hewitt and Claridge (1989), seven of these nineteen items related to unusual perceptual experiences and four to magical ideation, with one item common to both; only two items related to social anxiety/paranoia, and the remaining six were non-specific, though these also generally showed highest loadings on unusual perceptual experiences and magical ideation.

Dyslexics' high schizotypy scores thus reflected their high endorsement of STA items relating to unusual aspects of perception and cognition, in keeping with their spontaneous reports of such experiences. Importantly, they differed least from controls on items relating to social anxiety/paranoid ideation, making it less likely that their high STA scores simply reflected more general emotional problems, secondary to their dyslexia. Moreover, no group differences were found for Eysenck's Neuroticism, which indexes traits more relevant to anxiety and depression and which does correlate with STA schizotypy (Bentall *et al.* 1989). This further supports the idea that the STA may index personality traits that are primary to dyslexia, i.e. which reflect the expression of some of the same biological factors that predispose people to reading difficulties.

These results showed that one measure of schizotypy—Claridge's STA scale—does appear to capture and quantify some aspects of dyslexics' perceptual and cognitive style. However, since the development of this scale the field of schizotypy research has undergone a considerable expansion; and so has the number of scales used to assess what has become a *range* of traits thought to index 'psychosis-proneness' in normal subjects. In parallel with the idea of different syndromes or dimensions of clinical schizophrenia with potentially different aetiologies (Liddle 1987; Gur *et al.* 1991), interest has focused on the multi-dimensional nature of schizotypy. As discussed in Chapters 2 and 3, the broader concept of psychosis-proneness involves at least three and probably four dimensions (Claridge *et al.* 1996), with a possible further addition of paranoia/ suspiciousness. The four-factor model derived from the Oxford-Liverpool studies involves a primary positive factor of 'Unusual Experiences', a clear negative factor of 'Introvertive Anhedonia' and two additional positive factors; one of these, 'Impulsive Nonconformity' includes disinhibited, borderline, or antisocial traits while the other, 'Cognitive Disorganization', relates to attentional problems, low self-esteem, and social anxiety. Claridge's STA scale loads most heavily on the Unusual Experiences factor, though it also loads significantly on Cognitive Disorganization; however, it does not tap the negative, anhedonic, or 'schizoid' aspects of psychosis-proneness, nor the antisocial, impulsive dimension. In view of the strong relationship found between dyslexia and STA schizotypy, which relates to only two of these four factors, it seemed worth investigating dyslexia in relation to a dimensional model of psychosis-proneness.

A further study was therefore conducted with 50 dyslexic and 82 control subjects, using the Combined Schizotypal Traits Questionnaire (CSTQ) from the Oxford-Liverpool studies (Bentall *et al.* 1989; Claridge *et al.* 1996). This includes ten scales assessing different aspects of psychosis-proneness, in addition to the four scales from Eysenck's EPQ. Results have been reported and discussed elsewhere (Richardson 1994a), so these will simply be summarized here. For the individual scales, dyslexics showed very significantly higher scores on Claridge's STA ($P < 0.001$) as well as the Chapmans' Hypomania scale ($P < 0.001$) and Magical Ideation ($P < 0.002$); they also scored more highly on Eysenck's Psychoticism scale ($P < 0.001$), which was not the case in the previous study. Much smaller elevations were found for the Nielsen-Petersen Schizophrenism scale, tapping attentional problems ($P < 0.03$), as well as Eysenck's Extraversion ($P < 0.05$), and the Launay-Slade Hallucination scale, assessing proneness to perceptual distortions ($P < 0.05$). Of the four factors derived from scores on all the scales, dyslexia was associated only with the perceptual/cognitive dimension of 'Unusual Experiences' ($P < 0.002$), indexing traits which resemble 'positive' symptomatology in the clinical domain. Though the STA scale also loads on the second positive factor, reflecting attentional problems, social anxiety, and emotional sensitivity, dyslexics showed only a trend towards higher scores on this dimension ($P < 0.08$). No association was found with the two dimensions which are *not* indexed by the STA, namely Impulsive Nonconformity and Introvertive Anhedonia.

The relationship between dyslexia and STA schizotypy was therefore confirmed, and the dimensional analysis showed that this association reflects 'Unusual Experiences' in particular, involving perceptual aberrations and associated odd beliefs. The lack of association with Cognitive Disorganization may seem surprising in view of self-reported attentional problems, but Neuroticism is a strong element on this factor, and in neither study did dyslexics show higher scores on this scale. However, their higher scores on the Hypomania scale were noteworthy, and clinical impressions suggested that this scale may relate to attentional problems in dyslexic subjects, though unfortunately no formal ratings of ADHD were available. Hyperactivity itself might be expected to show in Impulsive Nonconformity, for which no group difference was found, but in fact dyslexia more often involves attentional disorder without overt hyperactivity (Dykman and Ackerman 1991, Hynd *et al.* 1991) which may none the less involve a somewhat 'manic' profile. It may also be relevant that a strong correlation has been noted between hypomanic characteristics and artistic and other creative abilities (Andreasen 1980; see also Chapter 13), as many dyslexics do show superior abilities in these domains.

As the STA indexes only positive schizotypal traits, an important aim in using a wider range of scales was to find out if dyslexia might be associated with a negative, anhedonic, withdrawn syndrome of schizotypy; these findings suggest that it is not. However, a cautionary note should be sounded here, since these dyslexic subjects may not be fully representative of the dyslexic population: most had pursued education and were relatively successful in this, and all were willing to be identified as dyslexic and participate in research. As such, they may well differ in personality traits from those dyslexics who have been less successful, go undiagnosed, or seek to conceal their problems. This may have a bearing on the lack of associations found here between dyslexia and emotional vulnerability (as indexed by Neuroticism, the STB borderline scale and the Cognitive Disorganization factor on which these load), 'externalizing' behaviour (Impulsive Nonconformity), and the more negative, schizoid traits indexed by Introvertive Anhedonia. Further studies are required to determine whether these findings will generalize, but it is notable that Kinsbourne *et al.* (1991) found no evidence for qualitative differences in terms of underlying neurological predisposition between subjects severely affected with dyslexia and those who were well remediated or more mildly affected.

DYSLEXIA AND SCHIZOTYPY: OTHER SHARED FEATURES

The strong association between dyslexia and positive schizotypal traits suggests that there may be important shared features in the predispositions to dyslexia and schizophrenia spectrum disorders, and invites consideration of other evidence which could illuminate this relationship. The clinical profile associated with dyslexia was discussed earlier and, as may have been apparent, many of the same features are found in members of the schizophrenia spectrum. Speech and language problems, generally interpreted as evidence for 'left-hemisphere' impairment, are one common factor; like dyslexic subjects, schizophrenic patients and their relatives often show poor verbal abilities and deficits in auditory short-term memory (Gruzelier *et al.* 1979; Kremen *et al.* 1994; Saykin *et al.* 1994). Language and communication deficits are evident in children with schizophrenia-spectrum disorder (Caplan 1994), and problems with both receptive language (including phonological deficits) and expressive language have been well-documented in schizophrenia itself (Flor-Henry 1976; Taylor and Abrams 1983). Written language skills are less often assessed, but Scarone *et al.* (1983) found schizophrenic patients poor at copying and spelling; and Thomas *et al.* (1993) found they made more errors relative to controls in a written language task, despite showing no impairment of syntactic complexity. In addition, data from the UK National Child Development Study showed significant reading deficits in pre-schizophrenic individuals at ages 7, 11, and 14 (Crow *et al.* 1995), and a history of language-delay and reading problems in schizophrenic patients has also been noted in retrospective studies (DeLisi *et al.* 1991). Most significant, however, is the fact that high-risk studies have repeatedly shown an excess of dyslexia in the children of schizophrenic subjects (Marcus 1974; Rieder and Nichols 1979; Erlenmeyer-Kimling *et al.* 1984; Fish 1987), giving firm support to the idea that there may be important shared features in the predisposition to both disorders.

Speech and language abnormalities in both dyslexia and the schizophrenia spectrum have of course been explicitly linked with the issue of unusual cerebral lateralization; and in view of the reduced planum temporale asymmetry found in dyslexia, it is particularly interesting that abnormal asymmetries of this region are also found in schizophrenic patients (Falkai *et al.* 1995; Petty *et al* 1995; Rossi *et al.* 1992; see also Chapter 8). In schizophrenia, these unusual temporal lobe asymmetries have been associated with positive symptoms of hallucinations and thought disorder (Barta *et al.* 1990; Shenton *et al.* 1992). In the schizotypy domain it is precisely the equivalent positive, symptom-like traits of perceptual aberration and magical ideation which dyslexics show, suggesting that an abnormal symmetry of brain structures important for language processing may be one common feature contributing to the association between dyslexia and schizotypy.

In contrast with findings from schizophrenic patients and their relatives, however, no actual impairments of language have been reported in normal schizotypal subjects. LaPorte *et al.* (1994) found no deficits in verbal memory in high scorers on the Chapman psychosis-proneness scales, and Kelley and Coursey (1992) reported no differences in neuropsychological test performance between high and low scorers on a composite (positive) schizotypy measure. Similarly, the high STA subjects studied by Claridge and colleagues (Broks 1984; Broks *et al.* 1984; Broks *et al.* 1984; Rawlings and Claridge 1984) showed normal or superior performance overall on language-related tasks, although they did show reduction or reversal of the usual performance asymmetries Thus there is no evidence that schizotypy in normal subjects is associated with the verbal *deficits* characteristic of both dyslexia and the clinical schizophrenia spectrum. However, this is perhaps less surprising given that these studies typically involve high-achieving university students. Moreover, the measures so far used with these groups are not sufficiently sensitive to detect, for example, impairments in phonological coding, and the use of written language tasks in particular would be required to find out whether normal schizotypal subjects do show dyslexic tendencies. MRI studies in normal subjects would also be of interest, to find out whether planum symmetry might in fact be associated with positive schizotypal traits. As noted earlier, its prevalence in the general population is such that this feature cannot be sufficient for either dyslexia or schizophrenia, though it could be a trait marker for both, and it remains possible that if such symmetry leads to increased bilaterality of language functions, this may actually be advantageous in some circumstances.

The idea of reduced cerebral lateralization as a feature common to dyslexia and positive schizotypy is also supported by other evidence. In relation to schizotypy, this is discussed in Chapter 8 and needs only a brief summary here. It is notable that mixed hand preference is associated both with dyslexia (Richardson 1994a, 1995b) and with positive schizotypy in normal subjects (Chapman and Chapman 1987; Kelley and Coursey 1992; Kim et al. 1992), particularly for scales assessing unusual perceptual experiences (Richardson 1994a). In dyslexia, behavioural measures of cognitive asymmetry have provided little evidence for Orton's original hypothesis, that dyslexics lack the usual left-hemisphere dominance for language functions, but it does seem that dynamic, attentional factors may operate to produce abnormal patterns of lateralization (Moscovitch 1987; Obrzut 1988). Kershner and Morton (1990) found dyslexic subjects had particular problems in *switching* attention between left and right hemispheres according to task demands, and their model of 'bilateral excessive activation' is consistent with deficiencies in the normal homeostatic regulation of relative hemispheric arousal. Functional imaging supports this picture: dyslexic subjects typically activate the same left-hemisphere regions as controls during language-related tasks, but activation tends to be excessive, extending over a more diffuse area, and is often bilateral (Naylor et al. 1990; Gross-Glenn et al. 1991). No such studies have yet been conducted with normal schizotypal subjects, but in schizophrenia there is similar evidence for excessive left-hemispheric or bilateral excessive activation (Gur et al. 1987), particularly in relation to positive symptoms (Gunther et al. 1991). On the basis of other evidence, Claridge (1995, 1987) has suggested that a basic feature of the schizotypal nervous system may be an inherent 'instability' of physiological reactivity, reflecting some aspect of altered homeostasis in the mechanisms governing arousal. The similarities indicated by the experimental evidence suggest that this kind of lability may perhaps also be a feature of the dyslexic nervous system, at least with respect to the lateralization of cognitive functions.

Another feature common to both dyslexia and the schizophrenia spectrum is an association with attentional disorders. In schizophrenia itself, attentional dysfunction is clearly central to the illness, but as a trait marker, attentional deficits are also a highly consistent finding in studies of relatives (Cornblatt and Erlenmeyer-Kimling 1985; Asarnow et al. 1995), and the high clinical overlap between dyslexia and ADHD has already been noted. Experimentally, dyslexia and ADHD are both associated with deficits on most 'attentional' tasks, but in a comparative review Conners (1990) noted that dyslexics' performance appears particularly vulnerable either when tasks involve very rapid timing, or when the information load increases (compatible with 'magnocellular' and 'automatization' hypotheses of dyslexia). Moreover, while ADHD children show particular impairment of 'frontal' attentional functions, deficits in dyslexia are apparent at earlier stages of processing and particularly for selective visual attention, implicating parietal systems. Other evidence suggests parietal dysfunction in dyslexia, particularly for 'right hemisphere' tasks (Stein *et al.* 1989); while Kershner and Micallef (1991) proposed that a primary deficit in right-hemispheric attentional capacities could underlie the poor word-decoding in dyslexia which is usually attributed to left-hemisphere impairment. In schizophrenia, several researchers have made the parallel proposal that apparent 'left-hemisphere dysfunction' may in fact follow from a primary right-hemispheric attentional deficit (Venables 1984; Cromwell 1987; Cutting 1990).

With regard to schizotypy, abnormalities in selective attention have been demonstrated with the negative priming paradigm (see Chapter 4); in a lateralized version of this task, high-scoring STA subjects showed an absence of negative priming in the LVF/RH, suggesting a failure of inhibition specific to right-hemispheric attentional processes (Claridge *et al.* 1992). Positive schizotypal traits were also associated with right hemispheric visuospatial deficits in studies by Richardson and Stein (1993*b*) and Richardson and Gruzelier (1994) discussed below, with impairments similar to those found in dyslexia. It may also be relevant that Wilkins and Venables (1992) found normal subjects scoring highly on either schizophrenism or physical anhedonia had an unusual difficulty in *switching* attention between visual and auditory modalities in a reaction-time task, which may parallel the kind of attentional impairments found in dyslexia by Kershner and Morton (1990).

Impaired motor control in dyslexia was noted earlier, and this is particularly apparent for complex tasks requiring bimanual coordination (Wolff 1993). Similar problems of neuromotor coordination and integration have been the single most consistent finding from high-risk studies of the offspring of schizophrenics (Erlenmeyer-Kimling *et al.* 1984). Fish (1987) coined the term 'pandysmaturation' to describe a constellation of motor and visuomotor problems apparent from early infancy in children at genetic risk for schizophrenia. Most significant is that she found such early deficits in visuospatial and visuomotor skills were actually associated with dyslexia in these children in later years (Fish and Hagin 1973; Fish 1987).

A further parallel can be drawn with the 'automatization deficit' hypothesis of dyslexia (Nicolson and Fawcett 1990), as exactly the same proposition was made by Asarnow *et al.* (1995), reviewing retrospective and cross-sectional studies of schizophrenic children. In early childhood, prior to the onset of symptoms, most of these children (like dyslexics) show language delay and poor visuomotor coordination, which may not be apparent at later ages. Asarnow *et al.* (1995) therefore proposed that schizophrenic children are simply slow to automatize these skills, and attributed this to their 'limited information-processing capacities' as revealed by a wide range of experimental evidence. Similar wide-ranging deficits are apparent in dyslexia, although with no global impairment of intellectual abilities, and an automatization deficit does appeal in explaining the broad nature of these deficits. However, as noted earlier, it does little to identify possible biological mechanisms in either case.

Turning now to visual function, there is very good evidence for deficits in dyslexia, implicating the fast magnocellular (transient) system. Thus, dyslexic subjects show reduced sensitivity to flicker and motion, increased visible persistence, anomalies of backward masking, poor spatial localization, and impaired visual search (Lovegrove *et al.* 1990; Riddell *et al.* 1990; Solman and May 1990; Cornelissen *et al.* 1995; Iles *et al.* 1996), as well as reduced and delayed flicker visual evoked potentials (Livingstone *et al.* 1991; Lehmkuhle *et al.* 1993; Stein 1994) and, consistent with the role of the magnocellular system in eye-movement control, impaired pursuit and vergence eye movements (Adler-Grinberg and Stark 1978; Stein and Fowler 1988). The most direct evidence was the finding of abnormalities specific to the magnocellular layers of the lateral geniculate nucleus in dyslexic brains post-mortem (Livingstone *et al.* 1991). Magnocellular impairment could help to explain some of the visual perceptual anomalies that dyslexics report, and it is perhaps significant that these perceptual distortions and associated odd beliefs were largely responsible for the very strong association between dyslexia and positive schizotypy. To find out whether magnocellular dysfunction might also be a feature of schizotypy, it seemed worthwhile to examine visual function in relation to schizotypy in normal subjects, using tasks on which dyslexics show impaired performance.

Richardson and Stein (1993*b*) therefore used a dot-localization task to examine visual direction sense in adult dyslexics and controls assessed for STA schizotypy, and found similar deficits in both high-scoring STA and dyslexic subjects, with both showing a particular excess of errors for leftward judgements. Richardson and Gruzelier (1994) used the same task in normal subjects assessed for three syndromes of schizotypy, and further showed that poor visual-direction sense was associated with positive, but not negative, schizotypal traits. These results are consistent with impaired visual transient and right-hemisphere function in positive schizotypy, as in dyslexia. However, a much more direct measure of magnocellular function—and probably the best behavioural measure—is sensitivity to coherent motion in random dot patterns (Schiller *et al.* 1990). Reduced visual motion sensitivity in dyslexia was shown by Cornelissen *et al.* (1995), and, using the same task, Richardson (1994*b*, 1995*a*) found similar deficits in normal subjects scoring highly on STA schizotypy. In further studies (Gruzelier and Richardson 1995; Richardson and Gruzelier 1996), visual motion sensitivity was assessed in relation to the three schizotypy syndromes proposed by Gruzelier (1991). Consistent with findings for the STA scale, only an 'Unreality' syndrome, involving unusual perceptual experiences and magical ideation, was associated with poor performance. In addition, Richardson *et al.* (1996) found impaired motion sensitivity in neuroleptic-free schizophrenic patients, with deficits comparable with those of a dyslexic group.

These results are consistent with magnocellular visual dysfunction as a trait marker for schizophrenia, and such dysfunction could also underlie the visual backward masking deficits and eye movement abnormalities widely found in schizophrenic patients, their relatives, and normal individuals with schizotypal traits (Siever 1985; Holzman 1987; Merritt and Balogh 1989, 1990; Siever *et al.* 1989). The increased susceptibility to backward, but not forward, visual masking found in the schizophrenia spectrum is most explicable in terms of abnormal transient (magnocellular) processing, as noted by Balogh and Merritt (1987) and Schuck and Lee (1989). Further evidence for this in schizophrenic (and manic) patients was provided by Green *et al.* (1994*a,b*); while other selective deficits in visual function in schizophrenia (O'Donnell *et al.* 1996) are consistent with magnocellular impairment. Dysfunction of the fast magnocellular/transient system could therefore be a biological feature common to dyslexia and the schizophrenia spectrum and, if so, this might help to explain some of the other common features. However, it should be noted that in dyslexia the evidence generally points to reduced or delayed magnocellular responses, while in the schizophrenia spectrum, although many of the findings are similar, what has usually been postulated is an *overactivity* of the system. This certainly requires clarification, as experimental findings to date have yielded a very inconsistent picture; but as Claridge (1985, 1987) has emphasized, one of the most striking features of schizophrenia is an extreme *variability* of psychophysiological responses, not just between individuals but *within the same individual*, suggesting a dissociation of physiological systems which are normally yoked in an homeostatic, self-regulating manner. If such instability is characteristic of the schizotypal nervous system, it could be that the transient system in these individuals is not consistently 'over-active' or 'under-active,' but simply unstable. Transient (magnocellular) and sustained (parvocellular) visual channels normally show reciprocal inhibitory interactions (Breitmeyer 1984), and if these were subject to abnormal variability, then either system might be prone to veer to unusual extremes of activity. Repeated and systematic assessment of individuals would be needed to find out if such instability is a factor in either dyslexic or schizophrenia-spectrum subjects.

There could also be parallels between this kind of low-level visual dysfunction and the well-documented abnormalities in 'sensory gating' in schizophrenia which are apparent across many sensory modalities (Venables 1977; Siegel *et al.* 1984). As noted earlier, the 'magnocellular' hypothesis of dyslexia has recently evolved into the broader proposition of a multi-modal disorder of temporal coding in the nervous system, which may underlie auditory as well as motor abnormalities in dyslexia (Galaburda and Livingstone 1993; Stein 1994). Any generalized dysregulation of neural timing could obviously also have wider implications for attentional capacities, the automatization of skills, and the integrity of many other aspects of 'higher' cognitive function. However, our understanding of the neural basis of these functions remains extremely limited, and, as any global concept of 'temporal coding' is too vague to be useful, further validation of the hypothesis needs to be sought at the level of sensory and motor function, with attention to precisely what kinds of temporal information may cause processing problems. In dyslexia this is already under investigation, but in view of the many common features, a similar approach could also prove fruitful in the study of schizophrenia and schizotypy.

DYSLEXIA AND SCHIZOTYPY: A POSSIBLE GENETIC BASIS FOR THE ASSOCIATION?

The evidence discussed above shows that the strong phenomenological relationship between dyslexia and schizotypal traits is backed up by many similarities in clinical and experimental findings. These point to common factors at the level of biological predisposition, and a possible genetic basis for the association is suggested by the excess of dyslexia in the relatives of schizophrenic subjects (Marcus 1974; Rieder and Nichols 1979; Erlenmeyer-Kimling *et al.* 1984; Fish 1987). There is a substantial genetic component to liability for both dyslexia (DeFries and Decker 1982) and schizophrenia (Gottesman 1991), but environmental factors play an equally large role, with vulnerability being best explained by a diathesis-stress model. In both cases, the data generally suggest a dimensional, polygenically determined predisposition, though in each condition there is also some evidence for the influence of major genes (Vogler and DeFries 1986; Gottesman and Bertelsen 1989). Moreover, the potential complexity of gene expression is such that many of the models used to interpret data from family studies may be inadequately simplistic (Roberts and Claridge 1991). The heterogeneity of both dyslexia and schizophrenia is another problem found when attempting to form genetic models, but, since phenotypic homogeneity does not guarantee genetic homogeneity and vice versa, this is by no means the only confound in attempting to disentangle genetic contributions to these conditions. In the absence of clear 'endophenotypic' information in both fields, i.e. the identification of traits which are intermediate between the genotype and phenotype (Gottesman 1991), attempts to identify candidate genes using linkage analysis have generally been plagued with failures of replication, and much of the search for endophenotypes has been guesswork. There are independent suggestions that the genetics of dyslexia and schizophrenia may relate to the genetics of cerebral lateralization (Annett 1985; Crow 1991), but equally little is known of what *this* may involve. Sex differences in the expression of schizophrenia and lateralization have induced speculations of an X-chromosomal locus (Crow 1988), but in dyslexia the inheritance patterns do not support this, and in both conditions the data could equally reflect sex-dependent modulation of a polygenically determined liability threshold, or even different underlying disorders in males and females (DeFries and Decker 1982; Goldstein *et al.* 1989). In dyslexia, recent suggestions of linkage to a site in the HLA region of chromosome 6 (Cardon *et al.* 1994) have aroused interest, as this could have a bearing on the complex associations between dyslexia and autoimmune disorders (Tonnessen *et al.* 1993), but this too requires replication.

Very recently, an intriguing, if speculative, hypothesis has been put forward by Horrobin *et al.* (1995) to account for the associations between dyslexia and the schizophrenia spectrum: specifically, they propose genetic interactions between the two, with implications for membrane-phospholipid metabolism. There is already substantial evidence for an abnormality of membrane phospholipids in schizophrenia (Horrobin et al 1994). The fatty acids of these phospholipids are essential to the normal structure of cell membranes, and changes in their composition can therefore affect the functioning of membrane-bound and membrane-associated proteins and normal cell-signalling responses (Nunez 1993). In the central nervous system, two essential fatty acids (EFAs) are particularly important: arachidonic acid (AA) and docosahexaenoic acid (DHA), together making up 15 per cent of the dry weight of the brain (Horrobin 1996). Via their prostaglandin derivatives, EFAs can influence dopaminergic function (Schwartz *et al.* 1982; Davidson *et al.* 1988), and AA is an important second messenger at NMDA receptors, giving EFA deficiency a plausible role in explaining some aspects of schizophrenic symptomatology. AA also mediates the normal 'flushing' (a dramatic vasodilation response) which follows a large oral dose of niacin: this is absent in around 30 per cent of schizophrenic patients (Rybakowski and Weterle 1991). There is now direct evidence of reduced AA and DHA in red-cell membranes in schizophrenia (Glen *et al.* 1994), probably reflecting excessive levels of a cytosolic phospholipase A2 enzyme (cPLA2) which displaces both of these EFAs from cell membranes (Gattaz *et al.* 1990). Recently, a potential genetic basis for these abnormalities in schizophrenia has been identified, involving the promoter region of a cPLA2 gene on chromosome 1 (Hudson *et al.* 1996).

In dyslexia, evidence for a phospholipid abnormality was put forward by Stordy (1995), who found an impairment of dark adaptation in dyslexic adults, which normalized following DHA supplementation. Horrobin *et al.* (1995) have therefore proposed that dyslexia may involve a relatively mild deficiency of DHA and AA, arising from either a defect in their incorporation into cell membranes, or perhaps an increased rate of loss, as in schizophrenia. They hypothesize that in dyslexia this defect arises from a different genetic abnormality to the one already identified in schizophrenia. If this is so, it follows that a wide variety of clinical outcomes could result from the possible combinations of both a 'dyslexia' gene and a 'schizophrenia' gene, each independently acting to reduce AA and DHA concentrations in cell membranes. The presence of *both* defects would clearly cause a greater abnormality than either one alone, and they propose that this is the case in 'unequivocal' clinical schizophrenia. In the case of either gene alone, other enzyme systems may be able to compensate to some extent, so that although this may cause an abnormal flux in the cycling of these fatty acids into and out of cell membranes, with consequent abnormalities for cell signalling, their overall concentrations could still be maintained above a critical level. This would therefore lead to a milder clinical picture—possibly dyslexia on the one hand, or schizoaffective or bipolar disorder on the other.

The authors acknowledge the highly speculative nature of this hypothesis, but their proposal is plausible in helping to explain at least some aspects of a dyslexia—schizotypy association. Unfortunately, there has been almost no research to date into the biochemistry of dyslexia, so the evidence for EFA deficiency in dyslexia is as yet limited to Stordy's (1995) observations; but she had also found that mothers of dyslexic children were more likely to have had a diet deficient in EFAs during pregnancy than mothers of non-dyslexics. In addition there is one anecdotal report (Baker 1985) of the case of a dyslexic boy in whom biochemical investigation did reveal EFA deficiency. In view of the relationship between dyslexia and attentional disorders, it is also of interest that EFA deficiency (including low levels of both AA and DHA) was recently confirmed in children with attention-deficit hyperactivity disorder (Stevens *et al.* 1995), supporting the proposal made by Colquhoun and Bunday (1981) on the basis of clinical observations.

As yet, it is not clear either exactly how the impairment in dark adaptation found by Stordy (1995) may relate to the other visual deficits that have been documented in dyslexia, i.e. to a 'magnocellular hypothesis', let alone to other dyslexic symptoms, but this clearly warrants investigation. There is already good evidence, however, that DHA in particular is crucial for normal visual (and cognitive) development (Neuringer *et al.* 1994; Makrides *et al.* 1995), and it is an attractive speculation that EFA deficiency may perhaps particularly affect fast 'magnocellular' systems. If so, the hypothesis of abnormal phospholipid metabolism could be compatible with the generalized disorder of 'rapid neural timing' that has been postulated in both dyslexia and the schizophrenia spectrum (Stein 1994), but considerably more research is needed to explore this possibility.

As Horrobin and colleagues have emphasized (Horrobin *et al.* 1994, 1995; Horrobin 1996), a major strength of their hypothesis of phospholipid abnormalities in schizophrenia is that it could potentially explain a whole range of disparate observations about the disorder which are difficult to reconcile under other current theories. While the details of these and the putative role of EFAs in accounting for them cannot be given here, suffice it to note that many, if not most, of these features of schizophrenia have also been described in relation to dyslexia. They include neurodevelopmental anomalies which are not confined to the brain but show also in minor physical anomalies and dermatoglyphic irregularities; the prevalence of 'soft neurological signs' and particularly motor abnormalities; the role of viral infections and other stressors, including dietary factors, especially during prenatal development; an association with obstetric complications and low birth weight; and relationships with inflammatory and other immune disorders in affected individuals and their relatives. In addition, the EFA membrane theory is entirely compatible with the major environmental component to liability observed in both disorders, and the apparent absence of selective pressure against the genes which may be involved.

One final observation is perhaps of particular interest with regard to a 'membrane hypothesis' of schizophrenia, dyslexia, and related disorders: the evidence that females have lower EFA requirements than males (Pudelkewicz *et al.* 1968; Huang *et al.* 1990). A sex bias in favour of males is found in a wide range of developmental disorders, including both dyslexia and early-onset schizophrenia, but also language disorders, stuttering, attention-deficit hyperactivity disorders, and autism; and all of these conditions show significant clinical overlap. No satisfactory explanation has yet been found for the fact that males are so much more vulnerable to this wide range of (overlapping) developmental disorders, but it seems at least plausible that a sex-specific vulnerability to EFA deficiency may be a contributory factor. A membrane hypothesis of psychiatric and other disorders may not yet be widely accepted, but it is eminently testable, and seems to offer more promise than many other current lines of investigation.

SUMMARY, EVALUATION, AND CONCLUSIONS

Questionnaire studies have shown a strong association between dyslexia and certain aspects of schizotypy or psychosis-proneness. Specifically, dyslexia is associated with the primary positive factor of 'Unusual Experiences', involving milder versions of the clinical symptoms of hallucinations and delusions. It is not associated with the other positive factors of 'Cognitive Disorganization' and 'Impulsive Nonconformity'; nor with a negative dimension of schizotypy involving anhedonia and withdrawal. (These last three dimensions are probably more likely than 'Unusual Experiences' to reflect traits which could be secondary to reading failure.) In addition, a wide range of experimental and epidemiological evidence supports a relationship between dyslexia and schizophrenia-spectrum disorders, strongly suggesting shared features in terms of biological predisposition. Common characteristics at this level may include unusual cerebral lateralization, with potential implications for language processing, and anomalies of visual function, which could form part of a general disorder of rapid temporal processing affecting not only other sensory modalities, but motor function, attention, and other aspects of cognition. The genetic evidence also bears out an association of dyslexia with the schizophrenia spectrum, and, though precise mechanisms remain to be elucidated, it seems probable that either common or separate, but interactive, genetic factors may help to explain the pattern of aggregation of these and other related disorders within families. A novel but promising hypothesis which could account for much of the evidence reviewed here is that dyslexia and schizophrenia both involve similar and interactive abnormalities of membrane-phospholipid metabolism (Horrobin *et al.* 1995).

Despite their significant common features, dyslexia and schizophrenia are of course also clearly separable conditions. By definition, the primary problem in dyslexia lies with the acquisition of literacy skills, and, despite the damage this can do to emotional well-being and self-esteem (which may well account for some increase in diagnosable psychiatric problems; see for example Saunders and Barker (1972)), many if not most dyslexics appear remarkably well-adjusted in terms of their social skills and interactions. They seem more akin to the 'happy schizotypes' identified by McCreery (see Chapter 12). In distinguishing dyslexia from schizophrenia itself, it may therefore be most significant that the studies reported here found no association between dyslexia and *negative* schizotypal traits involving anhedonia or withdrawal; so it seems probable that the traits most likely to predict risk of actual breakdown into psychotic illness are in precisely this domain of personal social interactions, involving an odd, aloof, asocial, and 'schizoid' profile (Rado 1953; Meehl 1962; Kendler *et al.* 1995). Consistent with this, De Hirsch and Jansky (1980) noted the many similarities between dyslexic and schizophrenic children, but were explicit about the superior social adjustment of the former.

The fundamental difference . . . is their capacity for relationships; they are available; they form affect bonds. Although social techniques are sometimes crude—a few suffer from a degree of social dyspraxia—they have friends, and their response to remedial therapy is much more positive than that of schizophrenic or borderline youngsters.

It has always been recognized that negative rather than positive symptoms are associated with a more severe, poor-prognosis form of schizophrenic illness, and if dyslexics do not show these features in the domain of personality, this may also help to explain why most do not themselves develop any actual psychiatric disorder. However, this is not to say that the positive schizotypal traits that they *do* show may not form an important part of the risk for psychosis. Both positive and negative schizotypy assessed using questionnaire measures have been shown to predict risk for schizophrenia over a ten-year follow-up (Chapman *et al.* 1994). Moreover, although family studies often suggest that negative traits may predominate in individuals genetically liable to schizophrenia (for example Kendler *et al.* 1995), it should be borne in mind that the more florid, positive aspects of schizotypy, such as perceptual distortions or bizarre beliefs, are likely to be more difficult to assess accurately in relatives of a schizophrenic proband.

To acknowledge that schizotypal traits do index a predisposition to psychosis is not of course equivalent to regarding these as necessarily 'pathological' in themselves. As Claridge has persuasively argued, both in this volume (see Chapter 1) and elsewhere (Claridge 1995, 1987; Claridge and Beech 1995), these traits may, instead, simply form part of normal individual variation in personality. In extreme form they may represent an increased vulnerability to psychiatric illness, but additional factors are required to precipitate this. Thus schizotypal traits are quite compatible with healthy adjustment, and may indeed confer some advantages, perhaps most notably with regard to creative ability, as has often been suggested (Heston 1966; Karlsson 1978; Andreasen 1987; and see Chapter 13).

Dyslexia too may be construed either as a pathological condition or as a facet of normal individual variation; in support of the latter view, it is clear that dyslexia would not be recognized as a disability in societies where literacy is not essential to full participation in society. Moreover, by definition those affected have no generalized deficits in intellectual capacity, so there must also be some advantages to the dyslexic profile which compensate for deficiencies in skills important for decoding written language. Superior visuospatial, mechanical, and artistic abilities are often cited (Gordon 1980; Geschwind and Galaburda 1987), and it is possible that even some of the 'deficits' identified in dyslexia may have advantages under certain circumstances. For example, the same factors that lead to confusion of letters such as *p*, *d*, *q* and *b*, could also underlie an exceptional ability in recognizing objects despite their rotation in space. In design, mechanics, engineering, architecture, physics, chemistry, and aspects of mathematics, the ability to identify shape and form independent of orientation or direction of view can be of great value, whereas in learning to read it may be a potential handicap.

Another example relevant to both dyslexia and schizophrenia is the 'failure of automatization' postulated in both cases. While this may create obvious problems for rote learning and the forming of rigid associations, it could also lead to more cognitive flexibility and a greater capacity for novel associations, with advantages for originality and creativity in thinking or problem-solving. This is already being raised in relation to schizotypy (see Chapter 13); but it is suggested here that some of the psychological features which may connect creativity with schizotypy may also be common to dyslexia. It is notable that both Albert Einstein and Isaac Newton had serious difficulties in learning to read and write (Thompson 1969), while Newton is additionally reputed to have suffered from psychosis (Karlsson 1978). This might perhaps not be entirely coincidental.

Related to the issue of deficits versus differences is the debate over whether dyslexia or schizotypy should be viewed in categorical or dimensional terms (Claridge and Beech 1995; see Chapter 1, this volume). The relevance of this distinction may diminish somewhat if another aetiological perspective is adopted, as it seems to the present writer that much of the apparent controversy may arise from confusion between different levels of description. The membrane-phospholipid hypothesis of Horrobin *et al.* (1995) provides a model for discussing this. They have posed two different genes with interactive effects—one predisposing to dyslexia, and one already implicated in schizophrenia, with ten different alleles (Hudson *et al.* 1996). At the genetic level some categorization may therefore be possible, but, as the authors point out, assuming the simplest case for the 'dyslexia' gene (i.e. a single allele of which an individual receives no, one, or two copies), combinations of these two genes alone could give rise to 300 possible genotypes. At the biochemical level, however, the nature of gene action is such that individual differences are likely to be dimensional (see also Roberts and Claridge 1991). Dimensional variations could include the quantities of specific enzymes present, their level of activity, and resulting concentrations of particular EFAs in cell membranes. Numerous additional factors would influence these dimensional biochemical 'traits' (other enzymes may either compensate for or exacerbate any original abnormality, while factors such as diet, viral exposure and psychological stressors can also affect EFA metabolism), and to some extent these biochemical variables may be reflected in behavioural traits which are also dimensional. However, a reduction in the EFA concentration of cell membranes beyond some critical threshold may lead to clear (categorical?) behavioural abnormalities as cell signalling is disrupted beyond compensation, and prolonged deficiency might also give rise to structural, qualitative changes in brain organization. Adding the further variations that could arise from individual differences in the timing of such a critical deficiency (for example whether this occurs prenatally, or in early childhood, adolescence, or later life) the complexity of possible outcomes becomes simply enormous, and it is clear that any resulting disorder could not be satisfactorily described in categorical versus dimensional terms. None the less, this kind of picture would not be inconsistent with the well-recognized heterogeneity of both dyslexia and the schizophrenia spectrum; and it is likely that a better understanding of the biological mechanisms underlying these and other developmental disorders may well show that our current diagnostic classifications have little aetiological validity.

To conclude, further investigation of schizotypal traits in dyslexia certainly seems warranted, but the use of unselected population samples would be the best way to assess whether the relationship found here between dyslexia and positive schizotypy can be generalized. In addition to assessing schizotypy in dyslexic individuals, it would be useful to take the converse approach and examine reading, spelling, and phonological skills in non-dyslexic subjects assessed for schizotypy. It would also be helpful to establish the incidence of dyslexia in patients with schizophrenia or related disorders and in their relatives; the patterns of aggregation of these disorders within families (ideally explored in conjunction with genetic and biochemical markers) could yield information about the nature and extent of common or interactive genetic factors. Experimental studies of schizophrenic and schizotypal subjects could further help to determine what psychophysiological features are common to dyslexia and the schizophrenia spectrum. Here it seems likely that low-level aspects of rapid temporal coding in visual and auditory perception are promising lines of investigation. It may, furthermore, be particularly illuminating to examine these in conjunction with biochemical measures of membrane-phospholipid metabolism.

REFERENCES

Adler-Grinberg, D. and Stark, L. (1978). Eye movements, scan paths and dyslexia. *American Journal of Optometry and Physiological Optics*, 55, 557–70.

Andreasen, N. J. C. (1980). Mania and creativity. In *Mania: An evolving concept* (ed. R. H. Belmaker and H. M. Van Praag), pp. 377–86. Spectrum, Jamaica, New York.

Andreasen, N. J. C. (1987). Creativity and mental illness: Prevalence rates in writers and their first degree relatives. *American Journal of Psychiatry*, 144, 1288–92.

Annett, M. (1985). *Left, right, hand and brain: The right shift theory*. Erlbaum, Hillsdale, New Jersey.

Asarnow, R. F., Brown, W., and Strandburg, R. (1995). Children with a schizophrenic disorder: neurobehavioral studies. *European Archives of Psychiatry and Clinical Neuroscience*, 245, 70–9.

Augur, J. (1985). Guidelines for teachers, parents and learners. In *Children's written language difficulties* (ed. M. Snowling), pp. 147–69. NFER-Nelson, Windsor.

Baker, S. M. (1985). A biochemical approach to the problem of dyslexia. *Journal of Learning Disabilities*, 18, (10), 581–4.

Bakker, D. J. (1979). Hemispheric differences in reading strategies: two dyslexias? *Bulletin of the Orton Society*, 29, 84–100.

Baldeweg, T., Richardson, A. J., Watkins, S., Foale, C., and Gruzelier, J. H. (1997). An automatic frequency discrimination deficit in dyslexia: A mismatch negativity study. (Submitted.)

Balogh, D. W. and Merritt, R. D. (1987). Visual masking and the schizophrenia spectrum. *Schizophrenia Bulletin*, 13 679–98.

Barta, P. E., Pearlson, G. D., Powers, R. E., Richards, S. S., and Tune, L. E. (1990). Reduced volume of superior temporal gyrus in schizophrenia: relationship to auditory hallucinations *American Journal of Psychiatry*, **147**, 1457–62.

Bentall, R. P., Claridge, G. S., and Slade, P. D. (1989). The multidimensional nature of schizotypal traits: A factor analytic study with normal subjects. *British Journal of Clinical Psychology*, **28**, 363–75.

Benton, A. L. and Pearl, D. (1978). *Dyslexia: An appraisal of current knowledge*. Oxford University Press, New York.

Boder, E. (1973). Developmental dyslexia: A diagnostic approach based on 3 atypical reading-spelling patterns. *Developmental Medicine and Child Neurology*, **15**, 663–87.

Bradley, L. and Bryant, P. E. (1983). Categorising sounds and learning to read. A causal connection. *Nature*, **301**, 419–21.

Breitmeyer, B. G. (1984). *Visual masking: An integrative approach*. Oxford University Press, New York.

Broks, P. (1984). Schizotypy and hemisphere function—II. Performance asymmetry on a verbal divided visual field task. *Personality and Individual Differences*, **5**, 649–56.

Broks, P., Claridge, G. S., Matheson, J., and Hargreaves. J (1984) Schizotypy and hemisphere function—IV. Story comprehension under binaural and monaural listening conditions. *Personality and Individual Differences*, **5**, 665–70.

Caplan, R. (1994). Communication deficits in childhood schizophrenia spectrum disorders. *Schizophrenia Bulletin*, **20**, (4), 671–83.

Cardon, L. R., Smith, S. D., Fulker, D. W., Kimberling, W. J., Pennington, B. F., and DeFries, J. C. (1994). Quantitative trait locus for reading disability on chromosome 6. *Science*, **266**, 276–9.

Chapman, J. P. and Chapman, L. J. (1987). Handedness of hypothetically psychosis-prone subjects. *Journal of Abnormal Psychology*, **96**, 89–93.

Chapman, L. J., Chapman, J. P., Kwapil, T. R., Eckblad, M., and Zinser, M. C. (1994). Putatively psychosis-prone subjects 10 years later. *Journal of Abnormal Psychology*, **103** (2), 171–83.

Claridge, G. S. (1995). *The origins of mental illness* (new impression). Malor Books, Cambridge, Mass.

Claridge, G. S. (1987). 'The schizophrenias as nervous types' revisited. *British Journal of Psychiatry*, **151**, 735–43.

Claridge, G. S and Beech, A R (1995) Fully and quasi-dimensional constructions of schizotypy. In *Schizotypal Personally* (ed. A. Raine, T. Lencz, and S. A. Mednick, pp. 192–216. Cambridge University Press.

Claridge, G. S. and Broks, P. (1984). Schizotypy and hemisphere function—I. Theoretical considerations and the measurement of schizotypy. *Personality and Individual Differences*, **5**, 633–48.

Claridge, G. S., Clark, K. H., and Beech, A. R. (1992). Lateralization of the 'negative priming' effect: Relationships with schizotypy and with gender. *British Journal of Psychology*, **83**, 13–23.

Claridge, G., McCreery, C., Mason, O. Bentall, R., Boyle, G., Slade, P., and Popplewell, D. (1996). The factor structure of 'schizotypal traits: A large replication study. *British Journal of Clinical Psychology*, **35**, 103–15.

Colquhoun, I. and Bunday, S. (1981). A lack of essential fatty acids as a possible cause of hyperactivity in children. *Medical Hypotheses*, **7**, 673–9.

Conners, C. K. (1990). Dyslexia and the neurophysiology of attention. In *Perspectives on dyslexia*, Vol. 1 (ed. G. Th. Pavlidis), pp. 163–95. John Wiley & Sons, Chichester.

Cornblatt, B. and Erlenmeyer-Kimling, L. (1985). Global attentional deviance as a marker of risk for schizophrenia: Specificity and predictive validity. *Journal of Abnormal Psychology*, **94**, 470–86.

Cornelissen, P. L., Richardson, A. J., Mason, A. J. S., and Stein, J. F. (1995). Contrast sensitivity measured at photopic luminance levels and coherent motion detection in dyslexics and controls. *Vision Research*, **35**, 1483–94.

Critchley, M. (1970). *The dyslexic child*. Heinemann, London.

Cromwell, R. L. (1987). An argument concerning schizophrenia: The left hemisphere drains the swamp. In *Individual differences in hemispheric specialisation* (ed. A. Glass), pp. 349–56. Plenum, New York.

Crow, T. J. (1988). Sex chromosomes and psychosis: The case for a pseudoautosomal locus. *British Journal of Psychiatry*, **153**, 675–83.

Crow, T. J. (1991). The search for the psychosis gene. *British Journal of Psychiatry*, **158**, 611–14.

Crow, T. J., Done, D. J. and Sacker, A. (1995). Childhood precursors of psychosis as clues to its evolutionary origins. *European Archives of Psychiatry and Clinical Neuroscience*, **245**, 61–9.

Cutting, J. (1990). *The right cerebral hemisphere and psychiatric disorders*. Oxford University Press.

Davidson, B., Kustiens, N. P., Patton, J., and Cantrill, R. C. (1988). Essential fatty acids modulate apomorphine activity at receptors in cat caudate slices. *European Journal of Pharmacology*, **149**, 317–22.

DeFries, J. C. and Decker, S. N. (1982). Genetic aspects of reading disability: The Colorado Family Reading Study. In *Reading disability: Varieties and treatments* (ed. R. N. Malatesha and P. G. Aaron), pp. 255–79. Academic Press, New York.

DeFries J. C., Fulker, D. W., and La Buda, M. C. (1987). Evidence for a genetic aetiology in reading disability of twins. *Nature*, **329**, 537–9.

De Hirsch, K. and Jansky, J. J. (1980). Patterning and organizational deficits in children with language and learning disabilities. *Bulletin of the Orton Society*, **30**, (Reprint No. 92).

DeLisi, L. E., Boccio, A. M., Riordan, H., Hoff, A. L., Dorfman, A., McClelland, J. *et al.* (1991). Familial thyroid disease and delayed language development in first admission patients with schizophrenia. *Psychiatry Research*, **38**, (1), 39–50.

Denckla, M. B. (1993). A neurologist's overview of developmental dyslexia. *Annals of the New York Academy of Sciences*, **682**, 23–6.

Denckla, M. B. and Rudel, R. (1976). Rapid automatized naming (RAN): Dyslexia differentiated from other learning disabilities. *Neuropsychologia*, **14**, 471–9.

Duane, D. D. (1989). Neurobiological correlates of learning disorders. *Journal of the American Academy of Child and Adolescent Psychiatry*, **28**, 314–18.

Duane, D. D. (1991). Summary. In *The reading brain: The biological basis of dyslexia* (ed. D. B. Gray and D. D. Duane), pp. 161–92. York Press, Parkton, Maryland.

Dykman, R. A. and Ackerman, P. T. (1991). Attention deficit disorder and specific reading disability: Separate but often overlapping disorders. *Journal of Learning Disabilities*, **24**, 96–103.

Erlenmeyer-Kimling, L., Marcuse, Y., Cornblatt, B., Friedman, D., Rainer J. D., and Rutschmann, J. (1984). The New York High Risk Project. In *Children at risk of schizophrenia: A longitudinal perspective* (ed. N. F. Watt, L. C. Anthony, and J. E. Rolf), pp. 169–89. Cambridge University Press, New York.

Eysenck, H. J. and Eysenck, S. B. G. (1975). Manual of the Eysenck Personality Questionnaire. Hodder and Stoughton, London.

Falkai, P., Bogerts, B., Schneider, T., Greve, B., Pfeiffer, U., Pilz, K.,*et al.* (1995). Disturbed planum temporale asymmetry in schizophrenia. A quantitative post-mortem study. *Schizophrenia Research*, **14**, (2), 161–76.

Fawcett, A. J. and Nicolson, R. I. (1992). Automatisation deficits in balance for dyslexic children. *Perceptual and Motor Skills*, 75, 507–29.

Fish, B. (1987). Infant predictors of the longitudinal course of schizophrenic development. *Schizophrenia Bulletin*, 13, 395–409.

Fish, B. and Hagin, R. (1973). Visual-motor disorders in infants at risk for schizophrenia. *Archives of General Psychiatry*, 28, 900–4.

Flor-Henry, P (1976). Lateralised temporal-limbic dysfunction and psychopathology. *Annals of the New York Academy of Sciences*, 280, 777–97.

Galaburda, A. M. and Livingstone, M. (1993). Evidence for a magnocellular deficit in developmental dyslexia. *Annals of the New York Academy of Sciences*, 682, 70–82.

Galaburda, A. M. Sherman, G. F., Rosen, G. D., Aboitiz, F., and Geschwind, N. (1985). Developmental dyslexia: Four consecutive patients with cortical anomalies. *Annals of Neurology*, 18, 222–33.

Galaburda, A. M., Corsiglia, J., Rosen, G. D., and Sherman, G. F. (1987). Planum temporale asymmetry: Reappraisal since Geschwind and Levitsky. *Neuropsychologia*, 25, 853–68.

Galaburda, A. M., Rosen G. D., and Menard M. T. (1994). Aberrant auditory anatomy in developmental dyslexics. *Proceedings of the National Academy of Sciences*, 91, 8010–13.

Gattaz, W. F., Hubner, C. V. K., Nevalainen, T. J., Thuren, T., and Kinnunen, P. K. (1990). Increased serum phospholipase A2 activity in schizophrenia: a replication study. *Biological Psychiatry*, 28, (6), 495–501.

Geschwind, N. (1982). Why Orton was right. *Annals of Dyslexia*, 32, 13–30 (Reprint No. 98).

Geschwind, N. and Galaburda, A. M. (1987). *Cerebral lateralization: Biological mechanisms, associations and pathology*. MIT Press; Cambridge, Mass.

Glen, A. I. M., Glen, E. M. T., Horrobin, D. F., Vaddadi, K. S., Spellman, M., Morse-Fisher, N., *et al.* (1994). A red cell membrane abnormality in a subgroup of schizophrenic patients: Evidence for two diseases. *Schizophrenia Research*, 12, 53–61.

Goldstein, J. M., Tsuang, M. T. and Faraone, S. U. (1989). Gender and schizophrenia: Implications for understanding the heterogeneity of the illness. *Psychiatry Research*, 28, 243–53.

Gordon, H. W. (1980). Cognitive asymmetry in dyslexic families. *Neuropsychologia*, 18, 645–56.

Gottesman, I. I. (1991). *Schizophrenia genesis*. Freeman, New York.

Gottesman, I. I. and Bertelsen, A. (1989). Confirming unexpressed genotypes for schizophrenia: Risks in the offspring of Fisher's Danish identical and fraternal discordant twins. *Archives of General Psychiatry*, 46, 867–72.

Green, M. F., Neuchterlein, K. H. and Mintz, J. (1994a). Backward masking in schizophrenia and mania. I. Specifying a mechanism. *Archives of General Psychiatry*, 51, 939–44.

Green, M. F., Neuchterlein, K. H., and Mintz, J. (1994b). Backward masking in schizophrenia and mania. II. Specifying the visual channels. *Archives of General Psychiatry*, 51, 945–51.

Gross-Glenn, K., Duara, R., Barker, W., Loewenstein, D., Chang, J., Yoshii, F., *et al.* (1991). Positron emission tomographic studies during serial word-reading by normal and dyslexic adults. *Journal of Clinical and Experimental Neuropsychology*, 13, 531–44.

Gruzelier, J. H. (1991). Hemispheric imbalance: Syndromes of schizophrenia, premorbid personality, and neurodevelopmental influences. In *Handbook of schizophrenia, Volume 5: Neuropsychology, psychophysiology and information processing* (ed. S. R. Steinhauer, J. H. Gruzelier, and J. Zubin), pp. 599–650. Elsevier, London.

Gruzelier, J. H. and Richardson, A. J. (1995). Psychosis-proneness: Syndromes, hemisphere asymmetry and perceptual (magnocellular) functions. *Schizophrenia Research*, 15, 119–20.

Gruzelier, J. H., Mednick, S., and Schulsinger, F. (1979). Lateralised impairments in the WISC profiles of children at genetic risk for psychopathology. In *Hemisphere asymmetries of function in psychopathology* (ed. J. Gruzelier and P. Flor-Henry), pp. 105–10. Elsevier/North Holland Biomedical Press, Amsterdam.

Gunther, W., Petsch, R., Steinberg, R., Moser, E., Streck, P., Heller, H., *et al.* (1991). Brain dysfunction during motor activation and corpus callosum alterations in schizophrenia measured by cerebral blood flow and magnetic resonance imaging. *Biological Psychiatry*, 29, (6), 535–55.

Gur, R. E., Mozley, P. D., Resnick, S. M., Levick, S., Erwin, R., Saykin, A. J, and Gur, R. C. (1991). Relationships among clinical scales in schizophrenia. *American Journal of Psychiatry*, 148, 472–8.

Gur, R. E., Resnick, S., Alavi, A., Gur, R. C., Caroff, S., Dann, R., *et al.* (1987). Regional brain function in schizophrenia. I. A Positron Emission Tomography Study. *Archives of General Psychiatry*, 44, 119–25.

Haslum, M. N. (1989). Predictors of dyslexia? *Irish Journal of Psychology*, 10, 622–30.

Heston, L. L. (1966). Psychiatric disorders in foster home reared children of schizophrenic mothers. *British Journal of Psychiatry*, 112, 819–25.

Hewitt, J. K. and Claridge, G. S. (1989). The factor structure of schizotypy in a normal population. *Personality and Individual Differences*, 10, (3), 323–9.

Holzman, P. S. (1987). Recent studies of psychophysiology in schizophrenia. *Schizophrenia Bulletin*, 13, 49–76.

Hooper, S. and Willis, W. G. (1989). Learning disability subtyping: Neuropsychological foundations, conceptual models and issues in clinical differentiation. Springer, New York.

Horrobin, D. F. (1996). Schizophrenia and membrane lipids. In *Lipids and human behaviour* (ed. M. Hillibrand and R. T. Spitz). American Psychological Association. (In press.)

Horrobin, D. F., Glen, A. I. M., and Vaddadi, K. (1994). The membrane hypothesis of schizophrenia. *Schizophrenia Research*, 13, 195–207.

Horrobin, D. F., Glen, A. I. M., and Hudson, C. J. (1995). Possible relevance of phospholipid abnormalities and genetic interactions in psychiatric disorders: The relationship between dyslexia and schizophrenia. *Medical Hypotheses*, 45, 605–13.

Huang, Y. S., Horrobin, D. F., Watanabe, Y., Bartlett, M. E., and Simmons, V. A. (1990). Effects of dietary lineloic acid on growth and liver phospholipid fatty acid composition in intact and gonadectomized rats. *Biochemical Archives*, 6, 47–54.

Hudson, C. J., Kennedy, J., Skorecki, K., and Horrobin, D. F. (1996). A possible genetic basis for schizophrenia. *Schizophrenia Research*. (In press.)

Hynd, G. W. and Semrud-Clikeman, M. (1989). Dyslexia and brain morphology. *Psychological Bulletin*, 106, 447–82.

Hynd, G. W., Semrud-Clikeman, M., Lorys, A. R., Novey, E. S., and Eliopoulos, D. (1990). Brain morphology in developmental dyslexia and attention deficit disorder/hyperactivity. *Archives of Neurology*, 47, 919–26.

Hynd, G. W., Lorys, A. R., Semrud-Clikeman, M., Nieves, N., Huettner, M. I. S., and Lahey, B. B. (1991). Attention-deficit disorder without hyperactivity: a distinct behavioural and neurocognitive syndrome. *Journal of Child Neurology*, 6, (Suppl.), 35–41.

Iles, J., Walsh, V., and Richardson, A. J. (1996). Extension of the mLGN hypothesis of dyslexia? Applied Vision Association Meeting, Reading, UK, April.

Ingram, T. S., Mason, A. W., and Blackburn, I. (1970). A retrospective study of 82 children with reading disability. *Developmental Medicine and Child Neurology*, 12, 271–81.

James, W. H. (1992). The sex ratios of dyslexic children and their sibs. *Developmental Medicine and Child Neurology*, 34, 530–3.

Karlsson, J. L. (1978). *Inheritance of creative intelligence*. Nelson-Hall, Chicago.

Kelley, M. P. and Coursey, R. D. (1992). Lateral preference and neuropsychological correlates of schizotypy. *Psychiatry Research*, 41, 115–35.

Kendler, K. S., McGuire, M., Gruenberg, A. M., and Walsh, D. (1995). Schizotypal symptoms and signs in the Roscommon Family Study. Their factor structure and familial relationship with psychotic and affective disorders. *Archives of General Psychiatry*, 52, (4), 296–303.

Kershner, J. and Micallef, J. (1991). Cerebral laterality in dyslexic children: Implications for phonological word decoding deficits. *Reading and Writing: An Interdisciplinary Journal*, 3, 395–411.

Kershner, J. and Morton L. (1990). Directed attention dichotic listening in reading disabled children: A test of four models of maladaptive lateralization. *Neuropsychologia*, 28, 181–98.

Kim, D., Raine, A., Triphon, N., and Green, M. F. (1992). Mixed handedness and features of schizotypal personality in a non-clinical sample. *Journal of Nervous and Mental Disease*, 180, 133–5.

Kinsbourne, M., Rufo, D. T., Gamzu, E., Palmer, R. L., and Berliner, A. K. (1991). Neuropsychological deficits in adults with dyslexia. *Developmental Medicine and Child Neurology*, 33, 763–75.

Kremen, W. S., Seidman, L. J., Pepple, J. R., Lyons, M. J., Tsuang, M. T, and Faraone, S. V. (1994). Neuropsychological risk indicators for schizophrenia: a review of family studies. *Schizophrenia Bulletin*, 20, (1), 103–19.

LaPorte, D. J., Kirkpatrick, B., and Thaker, G. K. (1994). Psychosis-proneness and verbal memory in a college student population. *Schizophrenia Research*, 12, (3), 237–45.

Larsen, J. P., Hoien, T., Lundberg, I., and Odegaard, H. (1990). MRI evaluation of the size and symmetry of the planum temporale in adolescents with developmental dyslexia. *Brain and Language*, 39, 289–301.

Lehmkuhle, S., Garzia, R. P., Turner, L., Hash, T., and Baro, J. A (1993). A defective visual pathway in children with reading disability. *New England Journal of Medicine*, 328, (14), 989–96.

Liddle, P. F. (1987). The symptoms of chronic schizophrenia. A re-examination of the positive-negative dichotomy. *British Journal of Psychiatry*, 151, 145–51.

Livingstone, M. S., Rosen, G. D., Drislane, F. W., and Galaburda, A. M. (1991). Physiological and anatomical evidence for a magnocellular defect in developmental dyslexia. *Proceedings of the National Academy of Sciences (USA)*, 88, 7943–7

Lovegrove, W. (1991). Spatial frequency processing in dyslexic and normal readers. In *Vision and visual dyslexia* (ed. J. F. Stein), pp. 148–54. Macmillan Press, London.

Lovegrove, W. J., Garzia, R. P., and Nicholson, S. B (1990). Experimental evidence for a transient system deficit in specific reading disability. *Journal of the American Optometric Association*, 61, 137–46.

Lubs, A. L., Smith, S., Kimberling, W., Pennington, B., Gross-Glenn, K., and Duara, R. (1988). Dyslexia subtypes: Genetics, behaviour and brain imaging. In *Language, communication and the brain* (ed. F. Plum), pp.139–47. Raven Press, New York.

McAnally, K. (1994). Auditory temporal coding in dyslexia. 23rd International Conference of the Rodin Remediation Academy, Malta, 20–24 September.

McAnally, K. and Stein, J. F. (1996). Auditory temporal coding in dyslexia. *Proceedings of the Royal Society of London (B)*, 263, 961–5.

Makrides, M., Newmann, M., Simmer, K., Pater, J., and Gibson, R. (1995). Are long-chain polyunsaturated fatty acids essential nutrients in infancy? *The Lancet*, **345**, 1463–8.

Marcus, J. (1974). Cerebral functioning in offspring of schizophrenics: A possible genetic factor. *International Journal of Mental Health*, **3**, 57–73.

Mattis, S., French, J. H., and Rapin, I. (1975). Dyslexia in children and young adults: Three independent neuropsychological syndromes. *Developmental Medicine and Child Neurology*, **17**, 150–63.

Meehl, P. E. (1962). Schizotaxia, schizotypy, and schizophrenia. *American Psychologist*, **17**, 827–38.

Merigan, W. H. and Maunsell, J. H. R. (1993). How parallel are the primate visual pathways? *Annual Review of Neurosciences*, **16**, 369–402.

Merritt, R. D. and Balogh, D. W. (1989). Backward masking spatial frequency effects among hypothetically schizotypal individuals. *Schizophrenia Bulletin*, **15**, 573–83.

Merritt, R. D. and Balogh, D. W. (1990). Backward masking as a function of spatial frequency: A companson of MMPI identified schizotypic and control subjects. *Journal of Nervous and Mental Disease*, **178**, 186–93.

Miles, T. R. (1986). On the persistence of dyslexic difficulties into adulthood. In *Dyslexia: Its neuropsychology and treatment* (ed. G. Th. Pavlidis and D. F. Fisher), pp. 149–63. Wiley, New York.

Miles, T. R. (1994). Dyslexia: The pattern of difficulties. Blackwell, Oxford.

Moscovitch, M. (1987). Lateralization of language in children with developmental dyslexia: A critical review of visual half-field studies. In *Duality and unity of the brain* (ed. D. Ottoson), pp. 324–46. Macmillan Press, London.

Naylor, C. E., Wood, F. B., and Flowers, D. L. (1990). Physiological correlates of reading disability. In *Perspectives on dyslexia*, Vol. 1 (ed. G. Th. Pavlidis), pp. 141–62. John Wiley & Sons, Chichester.

Neuringer, M., Reisbeck, S., and Janowsky, J. (1994). The role of n-3 fatty acids in visual and cognitive development. *Journal of Pediatrics*, **125**, 539–47.

Nicolson, R. I. and Fawcett, A. J. (1990). Automaticity: A new framework for dyslexia research? *Cognition*, **30**, 159–82.

Nicolson, R. I. and Fawcett, A. J. (1994). Reaction times and dyslexia. *Quarterly Journal of Experimental Psychology (A)*, **47**, (1), 29–48.

Nicolson, R. I., Fawcett, A. J., and Dean, P. (1995). Time estimation deficits in developmental dyslexia: evidence of cerebellar involvement. *Proceedings of the Royal Society of London (B): Biological Sciences*, **259**, (1354), 43–7.

Nunez, E. A. (ed.) (1993). Fatty acids and cell signalling. *Prostaglandins, Leukotrienes, and Essential Fatty Acids*, **48**, 1–122.

O'Donnell, B. F., Swearer, J. M., Smith, L. T., Nestor, P. G., Shenton, M. E., and McCarley, R. W. (1996). Selective deficits in visual perception and recognition in schizophrenia. *American Journal of Psychiatry*, **153**, 687–92.

Obrzut, J. (1988). Deficient lateralization in learning disabled children. In *Brain lateralization in children* (ed. D. L. Molfese and S. J. Segalowitz), pp.567–89. Guilford Press, New York.

Orton, S. T. (1937). Reading, writing and speech problems in children. Norton, New York.

Petty, R. G., Barta, P. E., Pearlson, G. D., McGilchrist, I. K., Lewis, R. W., Tien, A. Y., *et al.* (1995). Reversal of asymmetry of the planum temporale in schizophrenia. *American Journal of Psychiatry*, **152**, (5), 715–21.

Pudelkewicz, C., Seufert, J., and Holman, R. T. (1968). Requirements of the female rat for linoleic and linoenic acids. *Journal of Nutrition*, **64**, 138–47.

Rado, S. (1953). Dynamics and classification of disordered behaviour. *American Journal of Psychiatry*, **110**, 406–21.

Rawlings, D. and Claridge, G. S. (1984). Schizotypy and Hemisphere Function—III. Performance asymmetries on tasks of letter recognition and local/global processing. *Personality and Individual Differences*, 5, 657–64.

Richardson, A. J. (1993). Dyslexia and Schizotypal Personality. D. Phil Thesis. University of Oxford.

Richardson, A. J. (1994*a*). Dyslexia, handedness and syndromes of psychosis-proneness. *International Journal of Psychophysiology*, 18, (3), 251–63.

Richardson, A. J. (1994*b*). Reduced motion sensitivity is associated with dyslexia, mixed-handedness and schizotypal traits in normals. Rodin Academy 23rd International Conference, Malta, 20–24 September.

Richardson, A. J. (1995*a*). Syndromes of psychosis-proneness and dyslexia: relations with hemisphere function and visual processing. *Schizophrenia Research*, 15, 132.

Richardson, A. J. (1995*b*). Handedness and visual motion sensitivity in adult dyslexics. *Irish Journal of Psychology*, Special Issue on Dyslexia, 16, 229–47.

Richardson, A. J. and Gruzelier, J. (1994). Visual processing, lateralization and syndromes of schizotypy. *International Journal of Psychophysiology*, 18, (3), 227–39.

Richardson, A. J. and Gruzelier, J. (1996). Visual motion sensitivity in relation to schizotypy syndromes. (In preparation.)

Richardson, A. J. and Stein, J. F. (1991). Personality characteristics of adult dyslexics. International Conference of the Rodin Remediation Academy, Berne, August.

Richardson, A. J. and Stein, J. F. (1993 *a*). Personality characteristics of adult dyslexics. In Studies in Visual Information processing (ed. R. Groner and S. Wright), pp. 411–23 Elsevier/North Holland.

Richardson, A. J. and Stein, J. F. (1993*b*). Dyslexia, schizotypy and visual direction sense. *Annals of the New York Academy of Sciences*, 682, 400–1.

Richardson, A. J., Gruzelier, J. H., and Puri, B. K. (1996). Reduced visual motion sensitivity in neuroleptic-free patients with schizophrenia. *Schizophrenia Research*, 18, 217–18.

Riddell, P., Fowler, M. S., and Stein, J. F. (1990). Inaccurate visual localisation in dyslexic children. *Perceptual and Motor Skills*, 70, 707–18.

Rieder, R. O. and Nichols, P. L. (1979). The offspring of schizophrenics: 3. Hyperactivity and neurological soft signs. *Archives of General Psychiatry*, 36, 665–74.

Roberts, D. and Claridge, G. (1991). A genetic model compatible with a dimensional view of schizophrenia. *British Journal of Psychiatry*, 158, 451–6.

Rossi, A., Stratta, P., Mattei, P., Cupillari, M., Bozzao, A., Gallucci, M., and Casacchia, M. (1992). Planum temporale in schizophrenia: a magnetic resonance study. *Schizophrenia Research*, 7, (1), 19–22.

Rourke, B. P. and Fisk, J. L. (1981). Socio-emotional disturbances of learning disabled children: The role of central processing deficits. *Bulletin of the Orton Society*, 31, 77–88.

Rourke, B. P. and Fisk, J. L. (1988). Subtypes of learning disabled children: Implications for a neurodevelopmental model of differential hemispheric processing. In *Brain lateralization in children* (ed. D. L. Molfese and S. J. Segalowitz), pp. 547–65, Guilford Press, New York.

Rybakowski, J and Weterle, R. (1991). Niacin test in schizophrenia and affective illness. *Biological Psychiatry*, 29, 834–6.

Saunders, W. A. and Barker, M. G. (1972). Dyslexia as a cause of psychiatric disorder in adults. *British Medical Journal*, 4, 759–61.

Saykin, A. J., Shtasel, D. L., Gur, R. E., Kester, D. B., Mozley, L. H., Stafiniak, P., and Gur, R. C. (1994). Neuropsychological deficits in neuroleptic naive patients with first-episode schizophrenia. *Archives of General Psychiatry*, 51, (2), 124–31.

Scarone, S., Gambini, O., and Pieri, E. (1983). Dominant hemisphere dysfunction in chronic schizophrenia: Schwartz test and short aphasia screening test. In *Laterality and psychopathology* (ed. P. Flor-Henry and J. Gruzelier), pp. 129–42. Elsevier Science Amsterdam.

Schiller, P. H., Logothetis, N. K., and Charles, E. R. (1990). Functions of the colour-opponent and broad-band channels of the visual system. *Nature*, 343, 68–70.

Schuck, J. R. and Lee, R. G. (1989). Backward masking, information processing and schizophrenia. *Schizophrenia Bulletin*, 15, 491–500.

Schwartz, R. D., Uretsky, N. J., and Bianchine, J. R. (1982). Prostaglandin inhibition of apomorphine-induced circling in mice. *Pharmacological Biochemical Behaviour*, 17, (6), 1233–7.

Shenton, M. E., Kikinis, R., Jolesz, F. A., Pollak, S. D., LeMay, M., Wible, C. G., *et al.* (1992). Abnormalities of the left temporal lobe and thought disorder in schizophrenia. A quantitative magnetic resonance imaging study. *New England Journal of Medicine*, 327, (9), 604–12.

Siegel, C., Waldo, M., Mizner, G., Adler, L. E, and Freedman, R. (1984). Deficits in sensory gating in schizophrenic patients and their relatives. *Archives of General Psychiatry*, 41, 607–12.

Siever, L. J. (1985). Biological markers in schizotypal personality disorder. *Schizophrenia Bulletin*, 11, 564–75.

Siever, L. J., Coursey, R. D., Alterman, I. S., Zahn, T., Brody, L., Bernad, P., *et al.* (1989). Clinical, psychophysiological, and neurological characteristics of volunteers with impaired smooth pursuit eye movements. *Biological Psychiatry*, 26, (1), 35–51.

Slaghuis, W. L., Lovegrove, W. J., and Davidson, J. A. (1993). Visual and language processing deficits are concurrent in dyslexia. *Cortex*, 29, (4), 601–15

Snowling, M. (1987). *Dyslexia. A cognitive developmental perspective*. Blackwell, New York.

Solman, R. T. and May, J. G. (1990). Spatial localization discrepancies: A visual deficiency in poor readers. *American Journal of Psychology*, 103, 243–63.

Spreen, O. (1989). The relationship between learning disability, emotional disorders, and neuropsychology: some results and observations. *Journal of Clinical and Experimental Neuropsychology*, 11, 117–40.

Stein, J. F. (ed.) (1991). *Vision and visual dyslexia*. Macmillan Press, London.

Stein, J. F. (1994). Developmental dyslexia, neural timing and hemispheric lateralization. *International Journal of Psychophysiology*, 18, 241–9.

Stein, J. F. and Fowler, M. S. (1988). Disordered vergence eye movement control in dyslexic children. *British Journal of Opthalmology*, 72: 162–6.

Stein, J. F., Riddell, P. M., and Fowler, M. S. (1989). Disordered right hemisphere function in developmental dyslexia. In *Brain and reading* (ed. C. von Euler), Wenner Gren Symposium Vol. 54, pp. 139–157. Macmillan, London.

Stevens, L. J., Zentall, S. S., Deck, J. L., Abate, M. L., Watkins, B. A., Lipp, S. R., and Burgess, J. R. (1995). Essential fatty acid metabolism in boys with attention-deficit hyperactivity disorder. *American Journal of Clinical Nutrition*, 62, 761–8.

Stordy, B. J. (1995). Benefit of docosahexaenoic acid supplements to dark adaptation in dyslexia. *Lancet*, 346, 385.

Tallal, P., Miller, S., and Fitch, R. H. (1993). Neurobiological basis of speech: A case for the preeminence of temporal processing. *Annals of the New York Academy of Sciences*, 682, 27–47.

Tarnopol, L. and Tarnopol, M. (1976). *Reading disabilities: An international perspective*. University Park Press, Baltimore.

Taylor, M. and Abrams, R. (1983). Cerebral hemisphere dysfunction in the major psychoses. In *Laterality and psychopathology* (ed. P. Flor-Henry and J. Gruzelier), pp. 143–52. Elsevier Science, Amsterdam.

Thomas, P., Leudar, I., Newby, D., and Johnston, M. (1993). Syntactic processing and written language output in first onset psychosis. *Journal of Communication Disorders*, 26, (4), 209–30.

Thompson, L. J. (1969). Language disabilities in men of eminence. *Bulletin of the Orton Society*, 29, 113–20.

Tonnessen, F. E., Lokken, A., Hoien, T., and Lundberg. I. (1993). Dyslexia, left-handedness, and immune disorders. *Archives of Neurology*, 50, (4), 411–16.

Venables, P. H. (1977). Input dysfunction in schizophrenia. In *Contributions to the psychopathology of schizophrenia* (ed. B. Maher) pp. 1–56, Academic Press, New York.

Venables, P. H. (1984). Cerebral mechanisms, autonomic responsiveness, and attention in schizophrenia. In *Nebraska Symposium on Motivation* (ed. W. D. Spaulding and J. K. Cole), pp. 47–92. University of Nebraska Press, Lincoln.

Vogler, G. P. and DeFries, J. C. (1986). Multivariate path analysis of cognitive ability measures in reading-disabled and control nuclear families and twins. *Behavioural Genetics*, 16, 89–106.

Wilkins, S. and Venables, P. H. (1992). Disorder of attention in individuals with schizotypal personality. *Schizophrenia Bulletin*, 18, (4) 717–23.

Willows, D. M., Kruk, R. S., and Corcos, E. (eds) (1993). *Visual processes in reading and reading disability*. Erlbaum, London.

Wolff, P. H. (1993). Impaired temporal resolution in developmental dyslexia. *Annals of the New York Academy of Sciences*, 682, 87–103.

Yule, W., Rutter, M., Berger, M., and Thompson, J. (1974). Over and under achievement in reading: Distribution in the general population. *British Journal of Educational Psychology*, 44, (1), 1–12.

10

Schizotypy and obsessive-compulsive disorder

SIMON ENRIGHT AND ANTHONY BEECH

CURRENT STATUS OF OBSESSIVE-COMPULSIVE DISORDER

Background

Within the two most widely used systems of diagnostic classification, the primary diagnosis of Obsessive-compulsive disorder (OCD) is inextricably bound to the anxiety disorders: ICD-9 (World Health Organization 1977) lists the disorder under the general heading of 'Neurotic, stress-related and somatoform disorders'; DSM-IV (American Psychiatric Association 1994) records OCD as an 'Anxiety state' under the general heading of 'Anxiety disorders'. The diagnostic criteria on Axis I of DSM-IV include the presence of recurrent, persistent, and unwanted thoughts, impulses, or images (obsessions), and/or the performance of repetitive, often seemingly purposeful, ritualistic behaviours (compulsions). These obsessions and compulsions are seen as intrusive, forcing themselves on the patient against his or her will (ego-dystonic), and at some point in the illness most patients make some effort to resist them. The ego-dystonic nature of the illness, the attempt to resist, and interference with daily function are not only mandatory for the diagnosis but are also clinically important in differentiating it from other diagnoses, such as obsessive-compulsive personality disorder, the schizophrenias, and phobic disorders.

Despite these apparently straightforward diagnostic criteria, in actual clinical practice diagnosis is not always easy or obvious. For example, Rasmussen (1985) reported that many patients were originally referred to a dermatologist because of dermatitis caused by excessive hand-washing. But for these physical symptoms, he believes, many would never have eventually received psychiatric help. Patients are also more inclined to seek help for other psychiatric symptoms such as depression, phobias, and panic disorders which can occur concurrently (Jenike *et al.* 1986; Mellman and Uhde 1987). The embarrassment and consequent secretiveness that many patients report may explain why two studies (Pollit 1957; Rasmussen and Tsuang 1986) found an average of seven years between onset of OCD and the patient seeking treatment.

Though the diversity of clinical presentation of OCD may seem wide, the great majority of sufferers fall into one of four major symptom clusters. These have been found to be consistent across cultures and time (Akhtar *et al.* 1975; O'Kasha *et al.* 1968; Rasmussen and Tsuang 1984). The two most common presentations take the form of washing and cleaning, and checking rituals, making up between 69 and 94 per cent of clinical cases (Akhtar *et al.* 1975; Dowson 1977; Norshirvani *et al.* 1991). Much less common is pure obsessional thinking (16 per cent, reported by Norshirvani *et al.*) and obsessional slowness (3 per cent reported by Ratnasuriya *et al.* (1991)). The problem of compulsive washing and cleaning is more frequently found in women (Norshirvani *et al.* 1991). The pattern of the illness is illustrated by a patient of the first author who feared passing germs on to her young children and therefore washed her hands up to hundred times a day. Frequently this hand-washing extended up to the elbows and involved a set number of specific patterns of movement and rubbing at different anatomical points on the arms. It was common for the patient's hands to become sore and chapped, and to bleed. The continuation of washing under these circumstances was often associated with a great deal of pain.

Compulsive checking routines are found to occur at equal frequencies in men and women (Marks 1987). A clinical example is a patient who checked that all electrical appliances were unplugged before going to bed. This was done in a set routine. However, at some point in this routine the patient may have become convinced that he had missed one of the earlier items. Instead of simply returning to that single item, he felt compelled to start the routine again from the beginning. This process would be repeated many times and would often include the man getting up in the middle of the night.

Pure obsessional thinking is also described as obsessional ruminating. There are no reported gender differences. It involves a recurrent thought or image which constantly assails the patient in the absence of any compulsive activity. An example of this was the mother who constantly imagined herself causing harm to her child. Some of these images related to hitting the child, acts of sexual abuse, and attempts to flush the child down the toilet.

Primary obsessional slowness is characterized by the length of time it takes to complete simple daily acts such as cleaning one's teeth or going to the toilet. It is more commonly associated with men (80 per cent of cases, Norshirvani *et al.* 1991). An illustration of this was a man who spent over an hour on the toilet. For most of the time he was simply trying to convince himself, beyond any doubt, that he had finished. At that point he would use an entire roll of toilet paper until he had cleaned himself to his own satisfaction.

What may be clear from these illustrations is that OCD is often severely disruptive and distressing. It can have a major impact upon a person's life and family, and it is often only when this disruption becomes intolerable that treatment is sought. Despite the increasing publicity for the disorder in the form of popular books (for example Rapoport 1990; Toates 1990; DeSilva and Rachman 1992; Foa and Wilson 1993), and recent television coverage, many patients are still amazed to find that others have similar problems.

Prevalence

OCD was, until recently, thought to be the least common of the anxiety disorders. Rudin (1953) and Woodruff and Pitts (1964) estimated that the incidence in the general population was approximately 0.05 per cent. Black (1974), and Beech and Vaughan (1978) noted that various studies had suggested that these patients represent between 0.1 and 4.6 per cent of all psychiatric contacts. Results of more recent demographic surveys now suggest that OCD may be among the most common of psychiatric disorders. Robins *et al.* (1984) report a lifetime prevalence in the general population of between 2 and 3 per cent. Karno *et al.* (1988) found an incidence of between 1.9 and 3.3 per cent across five US communities of over 18 500 people. Bland *et al.* (1988), reporting on epidemiological assessments in Canada, estimate a lifetime prevalence of 3 per cent.

OCD as an anxiety disorder

One of the potential difficulties in establishing a diagnostic classification for OCD is the high co-morbidity with other anxiety disorders (Pitman *et al.* 1987). This makes it possible that those aspects of OCD often labelled as evidence of significant anxiety may in fact be due to the coexistence of other anxiety disorders (OADs). Indeed, such co-morbidity has been a major justification for including OCD with OADs.

There appears to be a particularly high concomitance with phobia. Kringlen (1965) noted that 80 per cent of his sample of 91 obsessional patients reported phobic symptoms; Videbech (1975) reported a figure of 50 per cent; and Ingram (1961) quoted a figure of 25 per cent. Rasmussen and Tsuang (1986) found that 27 per cent of obsessional patients had a lifetime history of simple phobia. Lo (1967) noted that 35 per cent of his patients had significant phobias in childhood. Indeed, Rachman and Hodgson (1980) point out that OCD and phobias have a number of features in common: increased autonomic response and subjective discomfort in the presence of specific stimuli or situations; extensive avoidance behaviour, with the primary aim of reducing anxiety; and a positive response to behavioural intervention, particularly exposure.

Despite these similarities a number of important distinctions can be made between obsessional and phobic behaviour. OCD is characterized by continual preoccupation with disturbing and repetitive thoughts and compulsive behaviour, whereas phobic patients show little or no distress when not in contact with the phobic stimuli. Obsessional patients invariably report dysphoric mood, increased general tension, self-doubt, ambivalence, and increased social disruption. Ritual-istic behaviour in obsessional patients is common in the absence of the specific focal stimuli or prompt. However, phobia is invariably triggered by a particular external stimulus or situation.

Other categories of anxiety disorder have also been commonly reported in obsessional patients. Rasmussen and Tsuang (1986) interviewed 100 OCD patients and found social phobia in 18 per cent, separation anxiety in 18 per cent, while 13 per cent had a history of panic disorder. Pitman *et al.* (1987) noted that of 16 OCD patients, 14 also satisfied the criteria for generalized anxiety disorder, 9 for panic disorder, and 10 for phobic disorder. Relatives have also been reported as exhibiting an increased prevalence of anxiety neuroses

(Rosenberg 1967). This high concurrence raises the possibility that those aspects of OCD often labelled as evidence of significant anxiety may in fact be due to other anxiety disorders coexisting with OCD.

The similarities mentioned above are, however, more than outweighed by the differences between OCD and OAD patients. The sex distribution for OCD is roughly equal, whereas in anxiety states females outnumber males in the order of two to one. The age of onset of OADs is also much earlier than for OCD (Karno *et al.* 1988). Although the treatment methods for OCD and OADs have similarities, outcome studies suggest that behavioural interventions with OCD patients are much less successful. Beech and Vaughan (1978) note that claims for the success of behavioural therapy with obsessional patients have been grossly exaggerated, with insufficient follow-up periods and inadequate objective data. This criticism is still pertinent 18 years on. Salkovskis (1989) reports that cognitive-behavioural treatment failures, including those who drop out of treatment, account for over half of all obsessional clients. Where treatment is effective it is often difficult and protracted. This contrasts markedly with the relatively straightforward and effective cognitive-behavioural treatments for OADs.

There also appear to be important differences in the biochemistry of OCD and OADs. Conventional anxiolytics such as benzodiazapines and beta-blockers appear largely ineffective with OCD symptoms, which usually have a selective responsivity to serotonergic medication (Montgomery 1990). Unlike OADs, OCD symptoms are not made worse with the administration of anxiogenic compounds (Gorman *et al.* 1985; Rasmussen *et al.* 1987). The response to placebo compounds is strikingly high in anxiety states and remarkably low in OCD (Montgomery 1990).

Steketee *et al.* (1987) compared OCD and OAD groups regarding demographic, familial, and intrapersonal characteristics. OCD subjects demonstrated greater poverty and unemployment, more psychiatric symptoms (specifically depression and interpersonal discomfort), and increased feelings of inadequacy, hostility, and guilt. The authors concluded that OCD was functionally more debilitating than OADs. Cameron *et al.* (1986) compared the symptom pattern and severity in a mixed group of 316 OAD subjects to test the validity of the disorders as discrete syndromes. Their results supported the grouping of these conditions within the general diagnostic category of anxiety disorders, 'with the possible exception of obsessive-compulsive disorder' (p. 1135).

Reed (1985) has argued forcibly that anxiety plays no central role in the aetiology of the disorder. He states that:

it is an over-simplification to regard it as predominant or at the core of the compulsive experience. And where it can be identified it seems to be as a result rather than a cause of compulsive activity, being in many cases elevated rather than reduced by that activity. (p. 137)

Although, undoubtedly, anxiety is associated with OCD in the majority of patients, whether this anxiety is primary, secondary, or at times a consequence of a concomitant anxiety disorder remains unclear. However, regardless of any definitive conclusion, the presence of anxiety in OCD is in no way incompatible with the possible association of OCD and the schizophrenias, as discussed in the next section.

THE RELATIONSHIP BETWEEN OCD AND SCHIZOPHRENIA

Background

The proposition that some severe obsessional patients express focal delusions leads logically to the suggestion that there may be some relationship between OCD and the schizophrenias, since delusions are one of the central features of the latter (Schneider 1959). Arguments about a putative relationship between OCD and the schizophrenias have been around since Westphal (1878) first suggested that the entire 'obsessive compulsive syndrome' was a variant or prodrome of schizophrenia. They appear to have a number of demographic features in common, both having a similar age of onset (early 20s) and reduced marriage and fertility rates. Historically, both have responded poorly to psychological and physical treatments. Additionally, both groups share an increased incidence of other neuroses and personality disorders. Baer *et al.* (1990) found that 52 per cent of 96 OCD patients also met the DSM-IIIR (American Psychiatric Association 1987) criteria for at least one personality disorder. Rasmussen and Tsuang (1984) noted that in the overwhelming majority of their obsessional patients a chronic waxing and waning course was observed. The fact that OCD is reportedly worsened by stress, with a course generally characterized by exacerbation and remission, led Rasmussen and Tsuang to suggest a syndrome model for OCD analogous to that proposed for schizophrenia.

For many clinicians the single most important and striking factor that differentiates OCD from OAD patients is the nature of the cognitive experience: the everyday intrusion into conscious thinking of such intense, repetitive, personally abhorrent, absurd, and alien thoughts leading to endless repetition of specific acts or to the rehearsal of bizarre and irrational mental and behavioural rituals. These repetitive thoughts are often evoked by stimuli that are more abstract than those seen in OAD patients—for example untidiness, contamination, and danger— while the fear is one of vague consequences, often unconnected to the eliciting stimuli (Marks 1987).

The majority of OCD patients remain aware of the senselessness and futility of their obsessional thoughts and behaviours. However, for others the intensity and fixity of the irrational belief appears to have more in common with delusional states. These symptoms have tended to be categorized rather parsimoniously as 'over-valued ideas' (Foa 1979). Such features have led other authors to suggest the creation of separate diagnostic categories for these more apparently deluded OCD patients. These include: 'obsessive compulsive disorder with psychotic features' (Insel and Akiskal 1986); 'schizoanancastic' (Shakhlamov 1988); 'schizo-obsessive' (Jenike *et al.* 1986); 'obsessive compulsive psychosis'

(Robinson *et al.* 1976; Weiss *et al.* 1975); and 'obsessive psychosis' (Solyom *et al.* 1985).

OCD as a prodrome of schizophrenia

Arguments have raged about obsessional patients being at greater risk of becoming schizophrenic. In 1969 Goodwin *et al.* reviewed the available studies and concluded that any findings of high co-morbidity of OCD and schizophrenia were based on poor diagnosis and that obsessional patients were not at any increased risk of developing schizophrenia, compared with the general population. Black (1974) concurred with this finding. He reviewed the available studies and reported that in a total sample of over 300 patients, the chance of OCD developing into schizophrenia ranged from 0 to 3.3 per cent. Similarly, Rachman and Hodgson (1980) reported that not one out of a sample of 83 obsessional patients went on to develop schizophrenia.

However, more recent evidence suggests that there may be an increased incidence of schizophrenia in patients originally diagnosed as exhibiting OCD, although there may still be some problems with diagnostic specificity in these studies. Of nine studies, reviewed by Insel and Akiskal (1986), the mean incidence of schizophrenia in a follow-up of obsessional patients was 4.42 per cent (ranging from 0 to 12.3 per cent). This compares with a 1 per cent incidence of schizophrenia in the general population. Eisen and Rasmussen (1993) report that, out of 475 patients originally with a DSM-IIIR diagnosis of OCD, 40 met the diagnostic criteria for schizophrenia, delusional disorder, or schizotypal personality disorder. Jorgensen and Parnas (1990), analysing the correlation between background, pre-morbid, and clinical variables following onset of illness in 129 schizophrenic mothers, found an association between positive symptoms and pre-morbid obsessional traits. Finally, although there would also appear to be some strong evidence of a raised incidence of OCD symptoms in pre-morbid schizophrenics, it should be noted that such patients show a generally raised incidence of neurotic and personality disorder symptoms.

Co-morbidity of schizophrenia and OCD

Rosen (1957) reviewed 848 schizophrenics and found that 3.5 per cent exhibited marked OCD symptoms. Fenton and McGlashan (1986) reported that 13 per cent of 163 chronic schizophrenic patients exhibited prominent obsessional symptoms and that the presence of OCD in schizophrenia is a powerful predictor of poor prognosis. This latter finding was supported by Hwang and Hollander (1993), who contended that a significant subgroup of schizophrenic patients suffer from severe and persistent obsessive compulsive features. These patients may also have a more pervasive 'neuropsychiatric dysfunction', a worse clinical course, and a poorer treatment outcome than comparable non-OCD schizophrenic patients.

Experimental evidence

Flor-Henry *et al.* (1979) suggest similarities in psychophysiology between OCD and schizophrenia. They investigated neuropsychological and power-spectral EEG characteristics of 10 unmedicated OCD patients and tentatively concluded that OCD reflects dominant frontal dysfunction, with a loss of normal inhibitory process in that zone. They comment that:

The formal characteristics and associations of the obsessional syndrome suggest that it is much closer to syndromes of psychosis than neurosis. (p. 127)

Ciesielski *et al.* (1981) noted that the evoked potentials during cognitive processing of six out of eight OCD patients paralleled those reported in psychotic patients. This result was replicated by Beech *et al.* (1983) and became more evident as the cognitive complexity of the task increased.

Fransella (1974) used repertory grid methods and reported that the results of OCD patients overlapped significantly with those of thought-disordered schizophrenic patients, but had little in common with neurotic patients. Related to this are the findings of abnormalities on the Wisconsin Card Sorting Test (WCST) in OCD subjects. The WCST assesses subjects' ability to form, maintain, and shift cognitive sets, including the capacity to use feedback to modify inappropriate but previously rewarded responses. Harvey (1986) and Head *et al.* (1989) found that OCD patients demonstrated greater total errors compared with normal control subjects and marked perseverative errors similar to those seen in schizophrenic subjects (Fey 1951; Malmo 1974; Heaton *et al.* 1978).

Despite these observations, many authors have expressed scepticism concerning a significant relationship between OCD and the schizophrenias. Black (1974) suggests that, 'there is no close affinity between OCD and schizophrenia' (p. 53), while Rachman and Hodgson (1980) opine: 'It would be unwise to suggest obsessional illness and schizophrenia are closely linked' (p. 87). We have no difficulty in acquiescing with these conclusions. It is not being suggested here that OCD is functionally the same as or simply a less severe form of schizophrenia. However, we next intend to review a literature and present psychometric and experimental evidence for the proposition that some of the processes that underlie schizophrenic symptomatology, particularly positive symptoms, may also be evident in OCD.

OCD AND SCHIZOTYPY

A number of studies attest to the increased incidence of clinical schizophrenic-like (schizotypal) features in OCD patients. Insel and Akiskal (1986), Joffe *et al.* (1988), and Solyom *et al.* (1985) report figures around 17 per cent for OCD patients exhibiting concomitant schizotypal personality disorder (SPD). Jenike *et al.* (1986) report that 30 per cent of their OCD patients expressed significant schizotypal features. Stanley *et al.* (1990) reported a figure of 28 per cent; of those, eight per cent reached the full criteria for SPD. Maina *et al.* (1993)

reported concomitant Axis II personality disorders (DSM-IV) in 44 of a sample of 48 OCD subjects. SPD was most commonly associated with chronic OCD problems.

Lewis *et al.* (1991) described three monozygotic twin pairs concordant for OCD, but discordant for schizophrenia in two, and for schizoaffective disorder in one, of the cases. Follow-up found that the non-psychotic twin in each case exhibited SPD. These authors concluded that OCD and the schizophrenia-spectrum disorders can coexist and may in some cases be inherited together.

There is also evidence that the concomitance of OCD and schizophrenic-like features is associated with a more complex and severe subtype of OCD and predicts a less optimistic therapeutic outcome. Jenike *et al.* (1986) examined 43 treatment-resistant OCD patients, finding that 26 of the 29 non-schizotypal patients improved at least moderately, whereas only one of the 14 schizotypal patients improved at all. In addition, the number of schizotypal features characteristic of each patient was highly inversely correlated with treatment outcome. A similar finding has been reported by Minichiello *et al.* (1987) evaluating behavioural and drug treatment outcome in 29 OCD patients, 10 of whom also met the diagnostic criteria for SPD. Of the 19 non-SPD patients 16 improved at least moderately. Only one patient with concomitant OCD and SPD showed any improvement.

Further evidence of a putative link between schizophrenia spectrum disorders and OCD is reported by Markowitz *et al.* (1991). They studied the efficacy of fluoxetine (a serotonin-uptake inhibitor commonly used in the treatment of OCD) in 22 patients with SPD or Borderline Personality Disorder (BPD). They found that use of the drug in patients with these two spectrum disorders produced significant reductions in self-injury and in scores on the Hopkins Symptoms Checklist (Derogatis *et al.* 1974). Raine *et al.* (1992) found increased perseverative errors on the WCST (also reported by Lenzenweger and Korfine (1994)), as well as reduced pre-frontal activity in magnetic-imaging studies of patients suffering from SPD. Both of these findings have also been reported in OCD patients (Harvey 1986; Insel 1992).

Although OCD is not diagnostically related to schizophrenia, there may be, as previously suggested, some common ground at a functional level. The hypothesis becomes particularly plausible in the light of increasing evidence for dimensional theories of psychotic disorders, as elaborated in this book. This suggests the possibility of a dimensional link between OCD and schizophrenia, via SPD and schizotypy. Further evidence for this, from our own work, is discussed below. The next sections of the present chapter describe our research, in which we have attempted to investigate OCD within such a framework, from two points of view: (a) whether OCD patients have higher scores on various questionnaires designed to measure schizotypal characteristics; and (b) the extent to which the experimental evidence for putative dysfunctional mechanisms underlying schizophrenic symptomatology is mirrored in OCD.

Psychometric evidence

In an initial study (Enright and Beech, 1990) we compared 16 OCD and 15 mixed OAD patients on the Combined Schizotypal Traits Questionnaire (CSTQ). As described in Chapter 2, the latter consists of 18 scales, 15 of which—reproduced for ease of reference in Table 10.1—purport to measure various aspects of psychosis-proneness. With the exception of the Eysenck P-scale and the two measures of anhedonia. OCD patients proved to have significantly higher scores on all of the scales shown in the table. A similar result was obtained in a subsequent study (Enright *et al.* 1994) on larger samples of 37 OCD and 62 OAD patients. The findings obtained for individual scales, *vis-à-vis* their significance for obsessional disorder, deserve comment here.

The higher scores of OCD patients on the Launay-Slade Hallucinatory Scale are not unexpected, as the test could be viewed as a measure of frequent intrusive thoughts, as well as of hallucinatory experiences. The result for the STA—a more general measure of schizotypy—offers some support for previous reports, referred to earlier, of the high prevalence of schizotypal features in OCD (Jenike *et al.* 1986; Minichiello *et al.* 1987). Notably, the mean STA score for OCD patients in our samples was very close to that reported by Jackson and Claridge (1991) in a group of (partially remitted) schizophrenics. In contrast, the mean score of the OAD patients was well within the range established for the STA in non-clinical subjects.

In the obsessional group, significantly higher scores for STB, together with elevated Hypomanic Personality, suggest emotional instability, particularly of mood; this is in line with Walker and Beech's (1969) emphasis on the importance of unstable mood in the mechanism of OCD. The findings are also consistent with

Table 10.1   Psychosis-proneness scales included in the CSTQ

Launay-Slade Hallucinatory Scale
Perceptual Aberration
Magical Ideation
Schizotypal Personality (STA)
Borderline Personality (STB)
Hypomanic Personality
Eysenck Psychoticism (P) Scale
Schizophrenism
Social Anhedonia
Physical Anhedonia
Schizoidia Scale
Delusions of Persecution
Delusions of Contrition
Delusions of Grandiosity
Delusions of Disintegration

studies showing an increased incidence of mixed personality disorders in OCD (Baer *et al.* 1990; Mavissakalian *et al.* 1990).

All four of the Foulds and Bedford delusional scales showed consistently higher scores in the OCD group. These scales—more clinical than the other parts of the CSTQ—indicate the presence of significantly greater symptomatology associated with the upper (psychotic) levels of the hierarchy of mental illness proposed by Foulds and Bedford (1975). That is to say, OCD patients reported significantly more delusions of both an integrated and disintegrated kind. The result is particularly interesting since Foulds and Bedford postulate that the anxiety disorders are contained specifically within a lower level (level two) of the hierarchy.

The pattern of results for these individual scales—including the higher scores on Magical Ideation and Perceptual Aberration—suggested that the psychotic features associated with OCD were confined to so-called 'positive' symptomatology. This was confirmed in further analysis of our data. There we compared our OCD and OAD patient groups for factor scores derived from the principal components analyses of the CSTQ reported by Bentall *et al.* (1989). The latter authors had shown that, depending on whether or not the delusional scales were included in the analysis, either three or four factors could explain their CSTQ data (see also Chapter 2, this volume). Using both factor solutions as the basis for our own analysis, we found that it was the components of what Bentall *et al.* called 'positive psychotic symptoms' and 'cognitive disorganization/anxiety' that maximally discriminated the OCD and OAD patients.

We concluded from these data that they provided further support for the idea that OCD and the schizophrenia spectrum disorders might be linked indirectly along a dimension of schizotypy, expressed particularly through those components concerned with cognitive functioning. This led us to suppose further that such similarities might be further elucidated experimentally, using paradigms that purport to examine cognitive processes relevant to the aetiology of schizophrenia. One such paradigm is that of negative priming (NP).

Information processing studies

The negative priming paradigm, and its relevance to schizophrenia, has been discussed in detail by Williams and Beech in Chapter 4. Briefly, interest lies in its use as a procedure to examine the role of active inhibition in selective attention, and in a clinical context to test the theory that such inhibition is weaker in schizophrenics and schizotypal individuals. This, in turn, has been held to result in, or reflect, a relative failure to 'limit the contents of consciousness' (Frith 1979) and to be responsible for some of the positive symptoms of schizophrenia.

Evidence for a similar breakdown in the selective processes of obsessionals may be inferred from the research of Steketee *et al.* (1985) who report that 92 per cent of obsessional washers' fears and 60 per cent of checkers' fears were generated by associations with external stimuli. This survey was based on clinical interview aimed at identifying the strength of the association, high or low, between the

OCD patients' fear responses and circumscribed external cues. The problems of a compulsive washer who is washing, having just retrieved the milk bottles from the front doorstep, would therefore be recorded as 'high' external stimulation, whereas the problems of a person compelled to retrace their car journey for fear of having knocked down a cyclist, in the absence of dents in the car or loud bangs on the journey, would be recorded as 'low' external stimulation. It has been argued elsewhere (Enright 1996) that the sole analysis of such obvious associations is likely to grossly underestimate the extent to which external stimuli trigger OCD symptoms, since in reality many associations will be very subtle, idiosyncratic, and non-logical.

None the less, it can be proposed that a majority of obsessional symptoms appear to be related to a failure to inhibit unwanted associations triggered by external stimuli. This problem might therefore be investigated using an NP task. If OCD can also be distinguished from the other categories of anxiety disorder using these methods, then it suggests that there might also be a fundamental difference in mechanisms of information processing. This might then warrant reconsideration of the alignment of OCD in the current systems of diagnostic classification.

The NP paradigm used in our experiments consisted of the following four basic experimental conditions.

1. *Priming Distractor:* the word or letter to be ignored became the target in the next trial.
2. *Control:* the ignored stimulus was unrelated to the target in the next trial.
3. *Repeated Distractor:* the ignored stimulus was the same throughout the list and unrelated to the subsequent target.
4. *Neutral Distractor:* the ignored stimulus was a series of crosses or a slash.

A derived measure of NP exhibited by a subject was calculated by subtracting the mean reaction time (RT) for the control condition from the mean RT of the priming distractor condition. Procedural and other details of these experiments can be found in the original papers.

Pilot study

Enright and Beech (1990) first used the adapted Stroop NP technique (Stroop 1935) with colour words to demonstrate cognitive information processing differences between OCD and a heterogeneous group comprised of subjects drawn from the other categories of anxiety disorder. Most significant was the pattern of results. Whereas OAD subjects exhibited similar amounts of NP to those of low-schizotypal non-clinical subjects studied by Beech *et al.* (1989a), the NP results of OCD subjects were much closer to those exhibited by highly schizotypal and schizophrenic subjects (Beech *et al.* 1989a, 1989b). These comparisons are shown in Fig. 10.1.

In the light of these results it seemed important to attempt to replicate and consolidate such findings using other NP procedures, previously utilized with highly

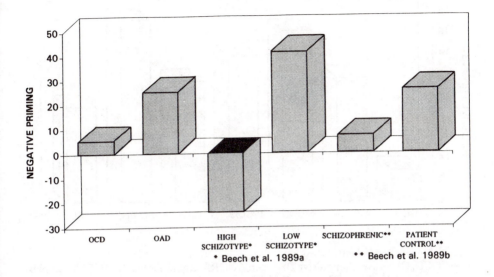

Fig. 10.1. A comparison of NP data from the pilot study with other studies.

schizotypal subjects. Additionally, there is experimental evidence (Ciesielski *et al.* 1981; Beech *et al.* 1983) that OCD subjects can be increasingly differentiated from normal controls as the cognitive complexity of the experimental task increases. Subsequent NP experimentation therefore sought to utilize tasks of increasing cognitive complexity. Lastly, in order to investigate the specificity of the reduced NP effect to OCD amongst the anxiety disorders, it was necessary to compare OCD separately with groups of subjects drawn from each of the OAD subcategories. Three further experiments were therefore carried out, involving 37 obsessive-compulsive subjects and 62 subjects with other anxiety disorders. The latter group contained the following number in each of the following DSM-IIIR categories: 10 Agoraphobia, 12 Monophobia, 11 Panic Disorder, 10 Generalized Anxiety Disorder, 9 Social Anxiety, and 10 Post-Traumatic Stress Disorder.

The negative priming paradigm using letters

Allport *et al.* (1985) were the first to describe NP effects using a letters task with normal subjects. The experimental procedure involved reading aloud consecutive single red letters whilst ignoring single green letters presented simultaneously and slightly overlapping. On a theoretical basis, it was assumed that the demands of information processing on this task related principally to the physical analysis of the letter which enables recognition. There is evidence that this level of analysis occurs at an early basic phase in the processing of sensory information and it was therefore assumed that the task reflected a relatively simple cognitive demand

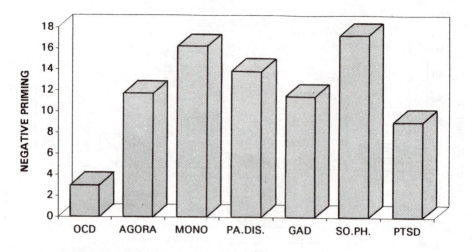

Fig. 10.2.   Derived NP letters task.

Key: OCD, Obsessive-Compulsive Disorder; AGORA, Agoraphobia; MONO, Monophobia; PA. DIS., Panic Disorder; GAD, Generalized Anxiety Disorder; SO. PH., Social Phobia; PTSD, Post-Traumatic Stress Disorder

(Lindsay and Norman 1977). Using this task we found evidence of reduced NP in OCD subjects (Enright and Beech 1993*a*). OCD subjects clearly exhibited the least priming (see Fig. 10.2) However, in comparing amounts of NP in OCD and OAD subjects, significant differences were limited to only three OAD subgroups, namely Monophobia, Panic disorder, and Social Phobia.

The adapted Stroop negative priming task

Results using the adapted Stroop priming task from the pilot study were replicated with this much larger experimental sample (Enright and Beech 1993*a*). Since the processing of colour and colour words is assumed to be cognitively more complex than the recognition of letters, this task represented a greater information processing demand for the same subjects that were used in the previous experiment. As shown in Fig. 10.3, the OCD group exhibited the least amount of NP, being significantly different from four of the OAD subgroups, namely Agoraphobia, Generalized Anxiety Disorder, Social Phobia, and Post-Traumatic Stress Disorder.

Repetition and semantic negative priming

This experiment involved a more complex semantic processing of target stimuli and therefore represented a further extension of information processing demand compared with the previous two tasks. The experimental stimuli were ten words, two drawn from each of the following five semantic categories: animal, furniture,

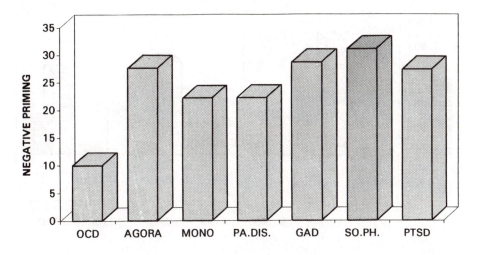

Fig. 10.3. Derived NP adapted Stroop task. (Key as for Fig. 10.2.)

tool, music, and body. The words were as follows: DOG, CAT, TABLE, CHAIR, HAMMER, SPANNER, GUITAR, TRUMPET, HAND, and FOOT. Stimuli were presented as two simultaneous, slightly overlapping words, one red and one green. Subjects were instructed to ignore the green word in each pair and to assign the red word to one of the five semantic categories. There were two priming conditions: repetition priming (NP) occurred when the ignored distractor prime was identical to the subsequent probe, for example red CHAIR/ green DOG, followed by red DOG; semantic priming (SNP) occurred when the ignored distractor prime was semantically related to the subsequent probe, for example red CHAIR/ green DOG, followed by red CAT. Beech *et al.* (1991) had reported reduced NP and SNP on this task in highly schizotypal compared with low schizotypal subjects.

We found (Enright and Beech 1993*b*) that OCD patients exhibited results very similar to highly schizotypal subjects (see Fig. 10.4) Compared with the OAD subgroups, OCD patients demonstrated the least NP and SNP. The amount of NP exhibited by OCD subjects differed significantly from four OAD subgroups: Agoraphobia, Generalized Anxiety Disorder, Social Anxiety, and Post-Traumatic Stress Disorder. The amount of SNP in OCD subjects differed significantly from all OAD subgroups.

The semantic facilitatory priming effect indicated that OCD subjects benefited from the ignored prime in naming the subsequent semantically related target. Beech *et al.* (1991) have suggested that this similar result in high schizotypes may reflect a difference in the relative strength of mechanisms of spreading facilitation (Collins and Loftus 1975) and spreading inhibition (Roediger and Neely 1982). The specific proposal is that highly schizotypal subjects exhibit weaker inhibition to semantically related concepts activated in memory by the target stimuli. This suggests that certain stimuli previously associated with specific symptoms in OCD

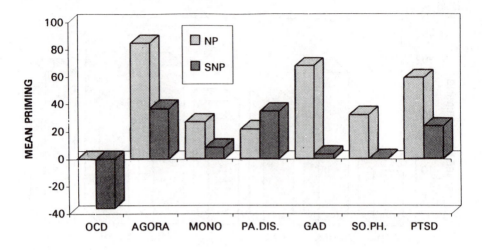

Fig. 10.4.   Derived NP and SNP semantic task.

patients might more readily serve as a reminder of these obsessional thoughts or actions, due to a failure to inhibit such associations pre-attentively.

Negative priming in the three experiments

Since the same group of subjects was used in all three NP experiments, derived priming measures were intercorrelated to examine whether each task was tapping a similar mechanism of cognitive inhibition. Results indicated that only the two measures from the semantic task were correlated significantly (at the 5 per cent level), both in the analysis of all subjects, and when analysing OCD subjects' results alone. Since the derived priming data from the semantic task were calculated by subtraction of the same control condition, care is warranted in the interpretation of these two significant findings. Statistical attempts to establish non-linear relationships amongst the derived priming measures also proved non-significant in all but the data from the semantic task.

The lack of an interrelationship between derived NP from the three experimental tasks suggests that each experimental task may reflect the employment of a different mechanism of cognitive inhibition. OCD subjects exhibited a greater failure of inhibition on all tasks, suggesting deficits across the complete range of inhibition mechanisms tapped by these tasks.

Conclusions regarding the NP findings

These four studies demonstrate the consistency of the differential NP effects between OCD and OAD subjects. Where comparative data are available, OCD subjects exhibit reduced NP similar to that found in highly schizotypal and schizophrenic subjects, whereas OAD subjects show NP effects similar to those of low schizotypy subjects. The differentiation of OCD and OAD groups becomes greater as the cognitive task complexity increases. The theoretical explanation for these effects suggests that reduced NP reflects less effective cognitive inhibition of the non-relevant stimulus and semantic associations provoked by the stimulus.

Several authors have pointed to the importance of a putative abnormality in the balance between facilitatory and inhibitory cognitive processes in other psychological disorders (see Power 1991 for review). These include post-traumatic stress disorder (Horowitz 1983), depression (Ingram 1990), and anxiety (Williams *et al.* 1988). Where empirical research has been conducted, these studies have tended to focus on cognitive processes involving emotionally charged experimental stimuli (either negative or threat-related words). It would seem likely from our failure to demonstrate a significant intercorrelation between different measures of priming that many different processes of inhibition may be in operation at different stages of pre-attentive and post-attentive processing. It would therefore be very premature to equate the suppression of disturbing thoughts cited in the anxiety literature with the putative processes of inhibition tapped by the current NP task. The importance of the present findings with OCD subjects (and of those previously reported for high schizotypy and schizophrenic subjects) is that evidence of reduced cognitive inhibition was demonstrated using emotionally neutral stimuli, suggesting a global deficit.

Finally, it should be noted that these data could be not explained as due to any experimental group being consistently less accurate or faster on the experimental tasks. There were no significant differences between OCD and OAD subjects in recorded error rates in any case. This fact need not be surprising since, although one might expect greater cognitive confusion from reduced cognitive inhibition, the task was very focal and the uninhibited distractors served to facilitate, not disrupt, performance in OCD subjects. The groups did not differ significantly in their overall reaction times to the stimuli when considered across all experimental conditions.

FINAL REMARKS

In summary, on psychometric measures, especially those related to positive symptoms and cognitive dysfunctional aspects of schizotypy, obsessional patients consistently exhibit results which imply a link with schizotypy and schizophrenia. The accumulated data from the NP studies suggest the tentative proposition (argued in greater detail in Enright 1996) that obsessionals may experience greater numbers of unwanted thoughts, due to a failure to inhibit intrusions from unconscious activation, this being associated with the spreading semantic activation from environmental stimuli, particularly those used as distractors, to unwanted thoughts.

The proposal that the clinical symptoms of OCD result from a failure to inhibit the semantic interpretations of external stimuli suggests a further link with the schizophrenias, where it has been suggested that first-rank symptoms arise as a result of ambiguous and unstructured sensory input and an abnormal assessment of causal relationships caused by a reduction in the influence of past regularities on current perception (Hemsley 1987, 1993). Morton (1979) suggests that hallucinations have their basis in real sounds that activate logogens preconsciously. The failure to inhibit incorrect activations leads to misinterpretation of the stimuli (Frith 1979). Likewise delusions have been hypothesized by Maher (1988) to arise as a result of abnormal percepts becoming available in consciousness, through a failure of inhibition, and then requiring some explanation. Frith notes that the more intelligent schizophrenic patient may be more likely to develop paranoid delusions, having the necessary cognitive framework to fit a number of irrelevant percepts into his or her cognitive schemata.

Clearly the hypothesis that high schizotypes, schizophrenics, and OCD subjects all share a common global deficit of cognitive inhibition cannot yet account for the different presentations of these categories. High schizotypes, though by definition at risk of developing psychopathology, are apparently able to compensate for a relative failure in the mechanism of inhibition with the expression of only mild symptoms. OCD subjects retain for the most part integrated and rational thought processes outside their obsessional focus, which usually remains very narrow. In these subjects, therefore, the failure of inhibition appears to become especially focused, such that a range of potential intrusions all converge to produce relatively stable, specific OCD symptoms, whilst also exhibiting schizotypy to varying degrees. Finally, in schizophrenic subjects, the breakdown of rational and integrated thought becomes complete, with an apparent, total failure to cope with unsuppressed stimuli.

The future for research in this area will be to develop more subtle techniques for identifying different types and degrees of cognitive inhibition and to identify which critical factors mediate and modify the integration of excessive and unwanted sensory input.

REFERENCES

Akhtar, S., Wig, N.N., Varma, V.K., Pershad, D., and Verma, S.K. (1975). A phenomenological analysis of symptoms in obsessive-compulsive neurosis. *British Journal of Psychiatry*, 127, 342–8.

Allport, D.A., Tipper, S.P. and Chmiel, N.J.R. (1985). Perceptual integration and post-categorical filtering. In *Attention and performance*, XI, (ed. M.I. Posner and O.S.M. Marin). Erlbaum, Hillsdale, New Jersey.

American Psychiatric Association (1994). *Diagnostic and statistical manual of mental disorders* (4th edn). American Psychiatric Association, Washington, DC.

Baer, L., Jenike, M.A., Riccardi, J.N., Holland, A.D., Seymour, R.J., Minichiello, W.E., and Buttolph, M.L. (1990). Standardized assessment of personality disorders in obsessive-compulsive disorder. *Archives of General Psychiatry*, 47, 826–30.

Beech, H.R. and Vaughan, C.M. (1978). *The behavioural treatment of obsessional states*. Wiley, London.

Beech, H.R., Ciesielski, K.T., and Gordon, P. (1983). Further observations of evoked potentials in obsessional patients. *British Journal of Psychiatry*, 142, 605–9.

Beech, A.R., Baylis, G.C., Smithson, P, and Claridge, G.S. (1989*a*). Individual differences in schizotypy as reflected in cognitive measures of inhibition. *British Journal of Clinical Psychology*, **28**, 117–29.

Beech, A.R., Powell, T.J., McWilliam, J., and Claridge, G.S. (1989*b*). Evidence of reduced cognitive inhibition in schizophrenia. *British Journal of Clinical Psychology*, **28**, 109–16.

Beech, A.R., McManus, D., Baylis, G.C., Tipper, S.P., and Agar, K. (1991). Individual differences in cognitive processes: Towards an explanation of schizophrenic symptomatology. *British Journal of Psychology*, **82**, 417–26.

Bentall, R. P., Claridge, G. S., and Slade, P. D. (1989). The multidimensional nature of schizotypal traits: A factor analytic study with normal subjects. *British Journal of Clinical Psychology*, **28**, 363–75.

Black, A. (1974). The natural history of obsessional neurosis. In *Obsessional states* (ed. H. R. Beech) Methuen, London.

Bland, R. C., Newman, S. C., and Orn, H. (1988). Epidemiology of psychiatric disorders in Edmonton. *Acta Psychiatrica Scandinavica*, **77**, Supplement 338.

Cameron, O. G., Thyer, B. A., Nesse, R. M., and Curtis, G.C. (1986). Symptom profiles of patients with DSM-III anxiety disorders. *American Journal of Psychiatry*, **143**, 1132–7.

Ciesielski, K. T., Beech, H. R., and Gordon, P. K. (1981). Some electrophysiological observations in obsessional states. *British Journal of Psychiatry*, **138**, 479–84.

Collins, A. M. and Loftus, E. (1975). A spreading activation theory of semantic processing. *Psychological Review*, **82**, 407–28.

Derogatis, L. R., Lipman, R. S., and Rickels, K. (1974). The Hopkins Symptom Checklist (HSCL): a self report symptom inventory. *Behavioural Science*, **19**, 1–15.

De Silva, P. and Rachman S. J. (1992). *Obsessive-compulsive disorder: The facts*. Oxford University Press.

Dowson, J. M. (1977). The phenomenology of severe obsessive-compulsive neurosis. *British Journal of Psychiatry*, **131**, 75–8.

Eisen, J. L. and Rasmussen, S. A. (1993). Obsessive-compulsive disorder with psychotic features. *Journal of Clinical Psychiatry*, **54**, 373–9.

Enright, S.J. (1996). Obsessive-compulsive disorder: Anxiety disorder or schizotype? In *Controversies in the anxiety disorders* (ed. R.M. Rapee). Guildford Press, New York.

Enright, S.J. and Beech, A.R. (1990). Obsessional states: anxiety disorder or schizotypy? An information processing and personality assessment. *Psychological Medicine*, **20**, 621–7.

Enright, S.J. and Beech, A.R. (1993*a*). Further evidence of reduced cognitive inhibition in obsessive compulsive disorder. *Personality and Individual Differences*, **14**, 387–95.

Enright, S.J. and Beech, A.R. (1993*b*). Reduced cognitive inhibition in obsessive-compulsive disorder. *British Journal of Clinical Psychology*, **32**, 67–74.

Enright, S.J., Claridge, G.S., Beech, A.R., and Kemp-Wheeler, S.M. (1994). A questionnaire assessment of schizotypy in OCD. *Personality and Individual Differences*, **16**, 191–4.

Fenton, W.S. and McGlashan, T.H. (1986). The prognostic significance of obsessive-compulsive symptoms in schizophrenia. *American Journal of Psychiatry*, **143**, 437–41.

Fey, E.T. (1951). The performance of young schizophrenics and young normals on the Wisconsin Card Sorting Test. *Journal of Consulting and Clinical Psychology*, **15**, 311–19.

Flor-Henry, P., Yeudall, L.T., Koles, Z.J., and Howarth, B.G. (1979). Neuropsychological and power spectral EEG investigations of the obsessive-compulsive syndrome. *Biological Psychiatry*, **14**, 119–30.

Foa, E.B. (1979). Failure in treating obsessive-compulsives. *Behaviour Research and Therapy,* 17, 169–76.

Foa, E.B. and Wilson, R. (1993). *Stop obsessing! How to overcome your obsessions and compulsions.* Bantam Books, New York.

Foulds, G.A. and Bedford, A. (1975). Hierarchy of classes of personal illness. *Psychological Medicine,* 5, 181–92.

Fransella, F. (1974) Thinking and the obsessional. In *Obsessional states* (ed H.R. Beech). Methuen, London.

Frith, C.D. (1979). Consciousness, information processing and schizophrenia. *British Journal of Psychiatry,* 134, 225–35.

Goodwin, D.W., Guze S.B., and Robbins E. (1969). Follow up studies in obsessional neurosis. *Archives of General Psychiatry,* 20, 182–7.

Gorman, J. M., Liebowitz, M.R., Fyer, A.S., Dillon, D., Davies, S., Stein, J., and Klein, D. (1985). Lactate infusions in obsessive-compulsive disorder. *American Journal of Psychiatry,* 142, 864–6.

Harvey, N.S. (1986). Impaired cognitive set-shifting in obsessive-compulsive neurosis. *IRCS Medical Science,* 14, 936–7.

Head, D., Bolton, D., and Hymas, N. (1989). Deficits in cognitive set shifting ability in patients with obsessive-compulsive disorder. *Biological Psychiatry,* 25, 929–37.

Heaton, R. K., Baade, L. E., and Johnsen, K. L. (1978). Neuropsychological test results associated with psychiatric disorders in adults. *Psychological Bulletin,* 85, 141–62.

Hemsley, D. R. (1987). An experimental psychological model for schizophrenia. In *Search for the causes of schizophrenia* (ed.) H. Hafner, W. F. Gattaz and W. Janzarik, Springer, Heidelberg.

Hemsley, D. R. (1993). A simple (or simplistic) cognitive model for schizophrenia. *Behaviour Research and Therapy,* 31, (7), 633–45.

Horowitz, M. J. (1983). *Image formation and psychotherapy.* Jason Aronson, New York.

Hwang, M. Y. and Hollander, E. (1993). Schizo-obsessive disorders. *Psychiatric Annals,* 23, (7), 396–401.

Ingram, I. M. (1961). The obsessional personality and obsessional illness. *American Journal of Psychiatry,* 117, 1016–19.

Ingram, R. E. (1990). Attentional nonspecificity in depressive and generalised anxious affective states. *Cognitive Therapy and Research,* 14, 25–35.

Insel, T. R. (1992). Towards a neuroanatomy of obsessive-compulsive disorder. *Archives of General Psychiatry,* 49, 739–44.

Insel, T. R. and Akiskal, H. S. (1986). Obsessive-compulsive disorder with psychotic features: A phenomenological analysis. *American Journal of Psychiatry,* 143, 530–2.

Jackson, M. and Claridge, G. S. (1991). Reliability and validity of a psychotic traits questionnaire (STQ). *British Journal of Clinical Psychology,* 30, 311–24.

Jenike, M. A., Baer, L., Minichello, W. E., Schwartz, C. E., and Carey, R. J. (1986). Concomitant obsessive-compulsive disorder and schizotypal personality disorder. *American Journal of Psychiatry,* 143, 530–2.

Joffe, R. T., Swinson, R. P., and Regan J. J. (1988). Personality features of obsessive compulsive disorder. *American Journal of Psychiatry,* 145, 1127–9.

Jorgensen, A. and Parnas, J. (1990). The Copenhagen high risk study: Premorbid and clinical dimensions of maternal schizophrenia. *Journal of Nervous and Mental Disease,* 178, 370–6.

Karno, M., Golding, J. M., Sorenson, S. B., and Burnam, M. A. (1988). The epidemiology of obsessive-compulsive disorder in five US communities. *Archives of General Psychiatry,* 45, 1094–9.

Kringlen, E. (1965). Obsessional neurotics: a long term follow up. *British Journal of Psychiatry*, 111, 709–22.

Launay, G. and Slade, P. D. (1981). The measurement of hallucinatory predisposition in male and female prisoners. *Personality and Individual Differences*, 2, 221–34.

Lenzenweger, M. F. and Korfine, L. (1994). Perceptual aberrations, schizotypy, and the Wisconsin Card Sorting Test. *Schizophrenia Bulletin*, 20, 345–57.

Lewis, S.W., Chitkara, B. and Reveley, A.M. (1991). Obsessive-compulsive disorder and schizophrenia in three identical twin pairs. *Psychological Medicine*, 21, 135–141.

Lindsay, D.A. and Norman, P.H. (1977). Human Information Processing. In *An introduction to Psychology*, (2nd edn). Academic Press, London.

Lo, W.H. (1967). A follow-up study of obsessional neurotics in Hong Kong Chinese. *British Journal of Psychiatry*, 113, 405–13.

Maher, B.A. (1988). Anomalous experience and delusional thinking: the logic of explanations. In *Delusional beliefs*. (ed. T.F. Oltmann and B.A. Maher). Wiley, New York.

Maina, G., Bellino, S., Bogetto, F., and Ravizza, L. (1993). Personality disorders in obsessive-compulsive patients: A study report. *European Journal of Psychiatry*, 7, 155–63.

Malmo, H.P. (1974). On frontal lobe functions: psychiatric patient controls. *Cortex*, 10, 231–7.

Markowitz, P.J., Calbrese, J.R., Schultz, S.C., and Meltzer, H.Y. (1991). Fluoxetine in the treatment of borderline schizotypal personality. *American Journal of Psychiatry*, 148, 1064–7.

Marks, I.M. (1987). *Fears, phobias and rituals*. Oxford University Press, New York.

Mavissakalian, M., Hamann, M.S., and Jones, B. (1990). Correlates of DSM-III personality disorder in obsessive-compulsive disorder. *Comprehensive Psychiatry*, 31, 481–9.

Mellman, T.A. and Uhde, T.W. (1987). Obsessive-compulsive symptoms in panic disorder. *American Journal of Psychiatry*, 144, 1573–6.

Minichiello, W.E., Baer, L., and Jenike, M.A. (1987). Schizotypal personality disorder: a poor prognostic indicator for behaviour therapy in the treatment of obsessive-compulsive disorder. *Journal of Anxiety Disorder*, 1, 273–6.

Montgomery, S. A. (1990). Is obsessive-compulsive disorder diagnostically independent of both anxiety and depression? In *Current approaches: Obsessive-compulsive disorder*. (eds. Montgomery S.A., Goodman, W.A. and Goeting N.). Duphar Medical Publications, London.

Morton, J. (1979). Word recognition. In *Psycholinguistics,* Vol. 2. (eds. J. Morton and J.C Marshall). Cambridge University Press, London.

Norshirvani, H. F., Kasvikis, Y., Marks, I. M., Tsakiris, F., and Monteiro, W. O. (1991). Gender-divergent aetiological factors in obsessive-compulsive disorder. *British Journal of Psychiatry*, 158, 260–3.

O'Kasha, A., Kamel, M., and Hassen, A. (1968). Preliminary psychiatric observations in Egypt. *British Journal of Psychiatry*, 114, 949–55.

Pitman, R. K., Green, R. C., and Jenike, M.A. (1987). Clinical comparison of Tourette's syndrome with obsessive-compulsive disorder. *American Journal of Psychiatry*, 144, 1167–71.

Pollitt, J. D. (1957). Natural history of obsessional states. *British Medical Journal*, 1, 194–8.

Power, M. J. (1991). Cognitive science and behavioral psychotherapy: Where behaviour was, there shall cognition be. *Behavioural Psychotherapy*, 19, 20–41.

Rachman, S. J. and Hodgson, R. J. (1980). *Obsessions and compulsions*. Prentice-Hall, New Jersey.

Raine, A., Sheard, C., Reynolds, G. P., and Lencz, T. (1992). Pre-frontal structural and functional deficits associated with individual differences in schizotypal personality. *Schizophrenia Research*, 7, 237–47.

Rapoport, J. L. (1990). *The boy who couldn't stop washing*. Collins, London.

Rasmussen, S. A. (1985). Obsessive-compulsive disorder in dermatologic practice. *Journal of the American Academy of Dermatology*, 13, 965–7.

Rasmussen, S. A. and Tsuang, M. T. (1984). The epidemiology of obsessive-compulsive disorder. *Journal of Clinical Psychiatry*, 45, 450–7.

Rasmussen, S. A. and Tsuang, M. T. (1986). Clinical characteristics and family history in DSM-III obsessive-compulsive disorder. *American Journal of Psychiatry*, 143, 317–22.

Rasmussen, S. A., Goodman, W. K., Woods, S. W., Heninger, G., and Charney, D. (1987). Effects of yohimbine in obsessive-compulsive disorder. *Psychopharmacology*, 93, 308–13.

Ratnasuriya, R. H., Marks, I. M., Forshaw, D. M., and Hymar, N. F. S. (1991). Obsessive slowness revisited. *British Journal of Psychiatry*, 159, 273–4.

Reed, G. F. (1985). *Obsessional experience and compulsive behaviour. A cognitive structural approach*. Academic Press, London.

Robins, L. N., Helzer, J. E., Weissman, M. M., Orvaschel, H., Gruenberg, E., Burke, J. D., and Regier, D. A. (1984). Lifetime prevalence of specific psychiatric disorders in three sites. *Archives of General Psychiatry*, 41, 949–58.

Robinson, S., Winnik, H. Z., and Weiss, A. A. (1976). Obsessive psychosis: justification for a separate clinical entity. *Israeli Annals of Psychiatry*, 14, 39–48.

Roediger, H. L. and Neely, J. H. (1982). Retrieval blocks in episodic and semantic memory. *Canadian Journal of Psychology*, 36, 213–42.

Rosen, J. (1957). The clinical significance of obsessions in schizophrenia. *Journal of Mental Science*, 103, 773–85.

Rosenberg. C. M. (1967). Familial aspects of neurosis. *British Journal of Psychiatry*, 113, 405–413.

Rudin, E. (1953). Ein Beitrag zur frage der Zwangskrankheit, insobesondere ihrere hereditaren Beziehungen. *Arch Psychiatr. Nervenkr.* 191, 14–54.

Salkovskis, P. M. (1989). Obsessive and intrusive thoughts: Clinical and non-clinical aspects. In *Advances in european behaviour research and therapy*, Vol. 4. (ed. P. Emmelkamp, W. Everaerd, F. Kraaymaat, and M. van Son). *Annual Series of European Research in Behaviour Therapy:* Vol. 4. Anxiety Disorders. Swets, Amsterdam.

Schneider, K. (1959). *Clinical psychopathology*. Grune and Stratton, New York.

Shakhlamov, A. V. (1988). One of the variants of schizophrenia with obsessional states. *Zhurnal Nevropatologii i Psikhiatrii*, 88, 87–92.

Solyom, L., DiNicola, V. F, and Phil, M. (1985). Is there an obsessive-compulsive psychosis? Aetiological and prognostic factor for an atypical form of obsessive-compulsive neurosis. *Canadian Journal of Psychiatry*, 30, 372–80.

Stanley, M. A., Turner, S. M., and Borden, J. W. (1990). Schizotypal features in obsessive-compulsive disorder. *Comprehensive Psychiatry*, 31, 551–8.

Steketee, G. S., Grayson, J. B., and Foa, E. B. (1985). Obsessive-compulsive disorder: differences between washers and checkers. *Behaviour Research and Therapy*, 23, 197–201.

Steketee, G. S., Grayson, J. B., and Foa, E. B. (1987). A comparison of obsessive-compulsive characteristics and other anxiety disorders. *Journal of Anxiety Disorders*, 1, 325–35.

Stroop, J. R. (1935). Studies of interference in serial verbal reactions. *Journal of Experimental Psychology*, 18, 643–62.

Toates, F. (1990). *Obsessional thoughts and behaviour*. Thorsens, Wellingborough.

Videbech, T. (1975). The psychopathology of anancastic endogenous depression. Acta *Psychiatrica Scandinavica*, 52, 336–73.

Walker, V. J. and Beech, H. R. (1969). Mood states and the ritualistic behaviour of obsessional patients. *British Journal of Psychiatry*, 115, 1261–8.

Weiss, A. A., Robinson, S., and Winnick, H. Z. (1975). Obsessive psychosis: a cross validation study. *Israeli Annals of Psychiatry*, 13, 137–41.

Westphal, K. (1878). Uber Zwangsvorstellungen. *Arch. Psychiatr. Nervenkr.*, 8, 734–50.

Williams, J. M. G., Watts, F. N., MacLeod, C., and Mathews, A. (1988). *Cognitive psychology and emotional disorders*. Wiley, Chichester.

Woodruff, R. and Pitts, F. N. (1964). Monozygotic twins with obsessional neurosis. *American Journal of Psychiatry*, 120, 1075–80.

World Health Organization. (1977). *Manual of the international statistical classification of diseases, injuries and causes of death, I and II* (9th revision). World Health Organization, Geneva.

Part IV Schizotypy in healthy subjects

11

Benign schizotypy? The case of spiritual experience

MICHAEL JACKSON

INTRODUCTION

This chapter focuses on the benign features of the schizotypal personality trait, and specifically the proposition that it may underlie what will be referred to as 'spiritual experience'. The latter is used here to include what previous researchers have variously termed religious, peak, self-actualizing, transcendental, cosmic, mystical, numinous, visionary, psychedelic, noetic, ecstatic, transpersonal, psychic, or oceanic experience. The most widely reported feature of such experiences appears to be the sense of an external presence: of a deceased person, a spiritual entity, or a sentient agency in nature. Feelings of profound insight, of being externally 'guided', anomalous perceptual experiences (voices, visions, synaesthesias), loss of ego boundaries, and ostensive ESP phenomena are also common features (Hardy 1979; Maxwell and Tschudin 1990). Spatial metaphors of height, depth, and being in 'another dimension' are widely used in descriptions of these states, conveying the sense of being in an altered state of consciousness. They are typically rare, emotionally positive, and deeply significant for the individual.

A number of large-scale surveys have revealed that, in Western cultures, experiences falling within this broad definition are reported by around 30–40% of the population (Back and Bourque 1970; Paffard 1973; Greeley and McCready 1974; Hay and Morisy 1978, 1985). This figure increases to 60–70% when more sensitive research methods such as interviews are used (Hay 1987). Such experiences are claimed to have profoundly positive outcomes for the experient, such as increased empathy, aesthetic sensitivity, ecological awareness, acceptance of bereavement, and altruistic feelings and behaviour. Surveys have found positive correlations with measures of well-being (Greeley and McCready 1974; Hay and Morisy 1978), self-assurance (Wuthnow 1976), and 'psychological adequacy' (Hood 1974). These observations have led some theorists to suggest that the capacity to have such experiences can be seen as an adaptive (but poorly understood) feature of human nature (Hardy 1966, 1979; Prince 1979; Hay 1987), perhaps serving the function of resolving existential crises such as bereavement (Batson and Ventis 1982; Persinger 1983; Valla and Prince 1989).

Alongside this positive view of spiritual experience, another theme that has attracted considerable interest is the relationship between these phenomena and the subjective experience of florid psychosis. As William James puts it:

In delusional insanity, paranoia as they sometimes call it, we may have a kind of diabolical mysticism, a sort of religious mysticism turned upside down. The same sense of ineffable importance in the smallest events, the same texts and words coming with new meanings, the same voices and visions and leadings and missions, the same controlling by extraneous powers; only this time the emotion is pessimistic: instead of consolations we have desolations; the meanings are dreadful; and the powers are enemies to life ... It is evident that from the point of view of their psychological mechanism, the classic mysticism and these lower mysticisms spring from the same mental level ... That region contains every kind of matter: 'seraph and snake' abide there side by side. (James 1902, p. 426).

Many subsequent commentators have reiterated and extended James' claim about the closeness of the phenomenological relationship between spiritual and psychotic experience. Others have disputed it, proposing a variety of distinctions between them concerning the form, content, and modality of hallucinations (Arieti 1976); the mode of onset, content, socio-cultural relevance, and incorrigibility of 'delusional' beliefs (Lenz 1983); the degree of control of the experient (Group for Advancement of Psychiatry 1976; Prince 1979); and the duration of experiences and their emotional tone (James 1902). Counter-examples to each have been collectively suggested by Prince (1979); Watson (1982); Lukoff (1988); Jackson and Fulford (1996).

Beyond the immediate form and content of psychotic and spiritual experience, parallels have been drawn between the broader dynamic processes within which each appears to be embedded, and between their hypothetical psychopharmacological and neuropsychological substrates. Both may involve precipitating stressors or life events, and a form of adaption to the stressor—whether 'constructive re-integration' (Batson and Ventis 1982) or psychotic resolution (Docherty *et al.* 1978; Wootton and Allen 1983). This theme of a common 'problem solving process' is taken up in more detail later in the chapter. Hallucinogenic drugs have been seen as providing an experimental model of both states (Dobkin de Rios 1990; Fischmann 1983; Pahnke and Richards 1966), and both have been proposed to involve temporal lobe abnormalities (Mandell 1980; Persinger 1983; Roberts 1991*a*).

In short, the nature of the relationship between benign spiritual experience and florid psychotic episodes presents us with an intriguing paradox. On the one hand, some commentators have argued that they are sufficiently phenomenologically similar to suggest the operation of a 'common psychological mechanism' or 'final common pathway'. On the other, they are associated with opposite pragmatic consequences: the 'fruits' which are the hallmark of spiritual experience (humility, wisdom, discernment, altruism, and creativity) versus the 'deficits' of psychosis (deterioration of self-care and social and occupational functioning). This paradox is heightened by the disturbing juxtaposition of the secular-scientific and religious world-views—potentially threatening to each—which this comparison raises. Not surprisingly, scholarly appraisals of the relationship have at times been polemic. At one extreme are those who reject the notion of any substantial overlap between the phenomena (Greeley 1974; Deikman 1977; Wilber 1980): 'It is a different kind of consciousness change, both in the nature of the experience ... and in its after effects. To compare mysticism with schizophrenia is like comparing bread with steak because they are both foods' (Greeley 1974). At the other extreme are those who attempt to explain one phenomena entirely in terms of the other. For example, on the basis of case studies, both of renowned mystics and contemporary spiritual seekers, the Group for the Advancement of Psychiatry (1976) concluded that 'As psychiatrists, reading the recorded descriptions of mystical states, we might well be inclined to make a diagnosis of some serious mental illness, most frequently hysteria or schizophrenia; occasionally manic-depressive illness'.

Between these extremes, others have suggested more integrative formulations which attempt to acknowledge and account for the diversity of the phenomena, and both the similarities and distinctions between them (James 1902; Campbell 1972; Wilber 1980; Buckley 1982; Watson 1982). These involve the general concept that, at some level, the same psychological processes may underlie both classes of phenomena, but that the contexts (whether psychological or environmental) in which such processes occur determine their pragmatic effects for the experient. The current hypothesis is that benign spiritual experiences may be phenomenological expressions of high levels of schizotypy, in the same way as are more pathological, psychotic experiences. In other words, it is suggested that the same constellation of schizotypal traits predispose to both benign spiritual experience and psychotic breakdown.

SCHIZOTYPY AND SPIRITUAL EXPERIENCE

The 'nervous type' model of psychosis (Claridge 1995; see also Chapter 1) proposes that a cluster of traits, collectively referred to as 'schizotypy', form a basic dimension of human inter-individual differences. Individuals who are relatively high in trait schizotypy have been shown to share various psychophysiological, neuropsychological, cognitive, and phenomenological characteristics with diagnosed psychotics. However, although high levels of schizotypy are conceived as involving increased risk of psychotic breakdown, they are not (on this model) thought of as being *essentially* pathological. Indeed, the proposed connection between schizotypy and creativity (see Chapter 13) suggests that there may be certain biological advantages in high schizotypy, 'schizophrenia being the penalty the human species pays for its unique adaptiveness and flexibility' (Claridge 1985). It will be suggested later in this chapter that spiritual experience can be seen as a special case of a more general creative 'problem-solving' process, and that it may have a specific psychological function. For our current purposes, it is sufficient to note that the schizotypy model suggests the existence of a population of psychologically healthy high schizotypes, prone to psychotic-like experiences, but not adversely affected by them. Precisely this population has been the focus of schizotypy research, although the latter has not concentrated in any depth on the nature of their subjective experiences.

The hypothesis of a connection between schizotypy and spiritual experience would predict that, in the normal population, high schizotypes should report relatively high levels of spiritual experience. On the same grounds, diagnosed psychotics, who are by definition highly schizotypal, should also report high levels of relatively benign spiritual experience. These were the basic predictions to be tested in the first study reported here. Neither had been directly tested previously, although some relevant research had been conducted. Lynn and Rhue (1988) found positive correlations between 'Fantasy Proneness' and the Schizophrenia and Hypomania subscales of the MMPI, and the Chapmans' schizotypy scales of Magical Ideation and Perceptual Aberration (Chapman and Chapman 1980). However, Fantasy Proneness is a considerably broader concept than spiritual experience, so these results, while supportive, cannot be regarded as adequately testing the hypothesis advanced here. By contrast, Caird (1987) found no association between Hood's Mysticism scale and Eysenck's personality factors, including Psychoticism. Again, while these results appear to contradict the hypothesis, as the results reported in Chapter 2 of this volume show, Psychoticism (in Eysenck's sense, Eysenck and Eysenck 1975) is not equivalent to Schizotypy, and the Mysticism scale (Hood 1975), in focusing on unitive mystical experience, as defined by Stace (1960), is much more restricted than the current concept of spiritual experience.

Although high rates of religious content have been found in psychotic symptoms (Beit-Hallahmi and Argyle 1977), relatively few studies have attempted to compare directly the frequencies of spiritual experience in psychotics and normals. Gallemore *et al.* (1969) estimated the incidence of 'conversion experience' in matched samples of manic-depressives and normals and found a substantially higher rate of report in the manic-depressives (52 versus 20 per cent). Against this, Bradford (1987) found that 'the experience of God' was reported by 30 per cent of a (small) sample of schizophrenics. He argued that, because surveys of spiritual experience have found a comparable level of positive response in the normal population, this result suggested that it was a 'sui generis phenomenon ... unaffected by the pathology of schizophrenia' (Bradford 1987, p. 31).

Case material has been widely used to illustrate how the phenomenology of positive-symptom psychotic disorders, particularly in the early stages, resembles that of spiritual experience, and has been variously defined (James 1902; Boisen 1947, 1952; Bowers and Freedman 1966; Laing 1967; Wapnick 1969; Buckley 1982; Watson 1982; Grof and Grof 1986; and Lukoff 1988). Grof and Grof 1986; Lukoff 1988). Although they do not directly address the question of the relative frequencies of spiritual experience in psychotic and normal populations, these studies strongly suggest the need for research in this area to consider the quality as well as the quantity of such experiences.

QUANTIFYING SPIRITUAL EXPERIENCE

Although relatively little empirical research has been conducted on spiritual experience, it is clear that the experiences described by the 30–40 per cent of the population responding affirmatively to survey questions are heterogeneous, both in quality and degree (Hardy 1979; Maxwell and Tschudin 1990). Valla and Prince (1989) suggest that this range of phenomena is most appropriately described in terms of continuously variable, rather than discrete, constructs. This has been reflected in previous attempts to map the 'varieties of religious experience' using quantitative methods (Margolis and Elifson 1979; Moehle 1983; Robinson and Jackson 1987; Ahern 1990) each of which have derived dimensional or prototypical systems of classification.

Previous measures of spiritual experience lack empirical validation, sensitivity, and comprehensiveness. In the first stage of the current study therefore, a new questionnaire was developed, yielding both qualitative information and quantitative scales derived from factor analysis (Jackson 1991). The guiding aim in developing the instrument was to maximize its representativeness of the relevant phenomena reported in the contemporary population. The working definition given in the Introduction—emotionally positive, exceptional experiences occurring in altered states of consciousness, with profound significance for the subject, and benign pragmatic effects—was used as a guideline in selecting a large pool of contemporary first-hand descriptions of experiences, from which more specific details could be abstracted. A principal source here was the unique archive of over 5000 first-hand descriptions of 'religious experiences', collected over the last 20 years by the Alister Hardy Research Centre in Oxford. This was supplemented by other collections of first-hand accounts, elicited using different strategies, by Laski (1961), Paffard (1973), and Robinson and Jackson (1987). The most salient, commonly repeated themes in this pool were used to guide the selection of a representative set of sample accounts of spiritual experience. These were then used in the questionnaire (a) to define the area of interest to subjects and (b) to generate a pool of detailed phenomenological items for rating subjects' own experiences. Operational measures of spiritual experience, in the form of continuous rating scales, were derived from factor analyses of the responses to this, and a second, revised questionnaire, using two different samples. A consistent structure emerged from both these factor analyses and a cluster analysis of content codings of free responses. This suggested two dimensional prototypes for benign spiritual experience: *mystical experience* (feelings of profound meaning, insight, well-being, and unity), and *numinous experience* (a sense of a guiding presence, extra-sensory perception, and feelings of being in an altered state). Scales indexing these forms of experience were constructed on the basis of the factor analyses. These had high internal reliabilities, and concurrent validity in relating predictably and coherently with freely written responses and other questionnaire items.

The study summarized below used this instrument to test the following predictions: (a) that report of benign spiritual experience is specifically associated with schizotypy in the normal population; and (b) that diagnosed psychotics will report a relatively high rate of spiritual experience. These hypotheses were tested quantitatively, by assessing the correlations between the spiritual experience and trait measures in the normal sample, and by comparing spiritual experience scores in a normal and a psychotic sample. They were also examined qualitatively, by comparing the content of reported experiences in normal and psychotic subjects. Full details of the study can be found in the original report (Jackson 1991).

A STUDY OF SCHIZOTYPY AND SPIRITUAL EXPERIENCE

Two instruments were used in the study, as follows:

The Spiritual Experience Questionnaire (SEQ)

Spiritual experience was measured using the revised SEQ. This includes a widely used survey question—'Have you ever been aware of a presence or a power, whether you call it God or not, which is different from your everyday self?'—and five brief accounts of different forms of spiritual experience, to define the concept to respondents. These are followed by 43 items describing core phenomenological features of spiritual experience ('Feeling that you were in the presence of a supernatural being, or source of power or energy'; 'Having the impression that everything around you was alive and aware'; 'Feeling that you could see things in a completely new way'; 'A feeling of sacredness or holiness', etc). Respondents are asked to rate how well these items apply to any experiences they have had, which they were reminded of by the initial accounts. Further questions elicit ratings of the frequency and duration of experiences, freely written descriptions, and more general biographical information. The phenomenological items were used to construct two scales measuring mystical and numinous forms of experience Finally, five open-ended questions solicited freely written descriptions of spiritual experiences.

The STQ

Schizotypy was measured using the STQ (Claridge and Broks 1984), which contains two scales—STA and STB—based on the DSM-III (American Psychiatric Association 1980). As discussed in Chapter 2, and elsewhere in this book, the STA scale of most interest here has well-established validity and reliability (see also Jackson and Claridge 1991). In the form used the questionnaire also contained the Eysenck Lie (L) scale.

In addition to the above, data on more general personality trait relationships were also already available for the control sample, in the form of EPQ scores from a previous study (Claridge and Hewitt 1987). This provided an opportunity to assess the relative strength and specificity of SEQ correlations with schizotypy.

Subjects

The complete control sample consisted of 242 mixed zygosity twins, obtained through the Birmingham twin register, who had 4 years previously completed the STQ and EPQ questionnaires. Of these, 102 (42.3 per cent) were males, and 140 (57.7 per cent) were females; the average age of the total sample was 29.1 years (range 16–40). Useable data were available for 227 subjects.

The clinical sample was a group of 56 diagnosed schizophrenics, obtained through the London based 'Voices' self-help group. While most of these completed the SEQ and STQ, there was a substantial amount of missing data on age and gender (possibly because some felt that this threatened their anonymity). Because of the relatively small size of this group, subjects who did not have valid scores on all variables were included in the analyses where appropriate, rather than being dropped, so the numbers in the following vary slightly in different statistics. Of 44 subjects specifying their gender 23 were male and 21 were female. There was no difference in the sex distribution of the two samples, but the clinical group was significantly older (mean age, 36.9 year; range, 20–60).

Results

Schizotypy and spiritual experience in the normal sample

Overall, 68 (28.1 per cent) of the normal sample responded affirmatively to the survey question, a similar proportion to that found in previous studies (Hay 1987). Mystical Experience scores were normally distributed, with no significant demographic effects. On the Numinous Experience scale, women scored significantly higher than men (t (226) = 2.34; $P < 0.01$).

The scale inter-correlations are given in Table 11.1. The STA scale, measured both concurrently and four years previously, was the only personality variable to correlate significantly with both spiritual experience scales. Extraversion, Neuroticism, and STB also had significant univariate correlations with individual spiritual experiences scales. (The time lapse reduced the magnitude of the correlations by up to 0.1 for the STQ scales, which indicates the probable underestimation of the EPQ correlations.) Numinous Experience correlated strongly with STA, and more moderately with Neuroticism and STB. Mystical Experience correlated moderately with both STA and Extraversion. Substantially the same pattern of correlations was found in males and females.

Spiritual experience in the clinical sample

Affirmative responses to the Survey Question were given by 87.3 per cent of the clinical sample, compared with 28.1 per cent of the normal sample ($\chi^2(1) = 65.1$; $P < 0.001$). This level of endorsement was dramatically higher than any reported in previous surveys. Differences between the groups on the SEQ are shown in Table 11.2. Both the STQ and the SEQ scales were significantly different across groups,

Table 11.1: Relationships between Spiritual Experience measures and the personality scales (Spearman's rho; $N = 227$)

Rho	STA2	STB2	L2	STA1	STB1	L1	E	P	N
Numinous Experience	.50	.28	−.15	.39	.17	−.09	.06	.0	.24
Mystical Experience	.24	.08	−.05	.23	.06	−.07	.25	−.01	.05

STA2, STB2, and L2 were measured concurrently with the SEQ, and STA1, STB1, L2, E, P, and N were measured four years previously.

Table 11.2. Comparison of normal and clinical groups on STQ and SEQ scales

Scale/group	N	Mean	SD	t	d.f.	P
Numinous Experience						
Normal	227	3.21	2.40			
Clinical	47	6.09	2.60	7.37	272	0.001
Mystical Experience						
Normal	227	3.93	2.44			
Clinical	47	5.82	2.59	4.78	272	0.001
STA						
Normal	227	14.50	7.40			
Clinical	47	21.23	7.53	5.66	272	0.001
STB						
Normal	227	6.15	3.81			
Clinical	47	9.40	4.09	5.26	272	0.001
Lie						
Normal	227	6.69	3.84			
Clinical	47	6.92	3.84	0.38	272	n.s.

while the Lie scale scores were closely similar. Interestingly, the effect size was larger for the Numinous Experience scale than for the Mystical Experience scale and both of the clinically based STQ scales (although the fact that the clinical group was older, and STA is negatively associated with age, may have reduced the STA contrast).

Item analyses

A more detailed comparison of the psychotic and normal samples was obtained by comparing endorsement rates for individual items on the SEQ. Table 11.3 shows the endorsement rates for the most and least discriminating items. All the highly discriminating items were endorsed more frequently in the psychotic group. Most were from the Numinous Experience scale. While this may indicate which aspects of spiritual experience are relatively more commonly found in psychotics, it is noteworthy that the same set of items received an average endorsement rate of 36 per cent in the normal sample. Low-discriminating items were mostly from the Mystical Experience scale, and these were all frequently endorsed in both groups.

A further item on the questionnaire asked about the *duration* of the respondent's experience. The modal response in both groups was 'minutes', but while only 6.2 per cent of the responding control subjects reported experiences that lasted for more than a few hours, over 40 per cent of the clinical group did. This indicates that although their experiences may have involved a number of similar features, these were considerably more extended than in the control group.

Table 11.3. High and low discriminating SEQ items. The percentage in each group responding positively and the correlation (rho) with the group (normal/clinical) are shown.

High discriminators	Normal	Clinical	Rho	Scale
(10) A feeling of being controlled by something outside of yourself	34.5	71.4	0.35	NUM
(19) Feeling that you had entered another level or dimension of reality	40.2	73.2	0.35	NUM
(26) Feeling that you were in the presence of a supernatural being	38.7	82.1	0.39	NUM
(34) Feeling that you were in communication with a spiritual being	24.4	65.5	0.35	NUM
(42) Feeling that you had lost your sense of time	45.3	76.8	0.32	MYS
Low discriminators				
(21) Being surprised by the intensity of your emotions	66.4	64.3	0.05	NUM
(29) Having the impression that everything around you was alive and aware	56.6	60.7	0.10	MYS
(32) Feeling that you were in some kind of harmony with your surroundings	59.8	60.7	0.07	MYS
(37) A feeling of love, or that you were loved	64.1	67.9	0.05	MYS
(41) Being in an unusually peaceful or serene state of mind	70.9	67.9	0.06	MYS

In summary, then, a substantial correlation between schizotypy (STA) and Numinous Experience scores was found in the control sample, higher than that between spiritual experience and other personality variables. The Mystical Experience scale had less striking personality correlates. The clinical group returned higher scores on each of the Spiritual Experience Questionnaire and STQ scales, and an extremely high affirmative response to the survey question; notably their scores on the Lie scale were not different from those in the non-clinical group. Numinous Experience was the most powerful predictor of clinical status, over and above both clinical scales. The duration ratings indicated that many of the psychotics were referring to relatively prolonged experiences.

Free responses

Five items on the Spiritual Experience Questionnaire invited respondents to describe aspects of their experiences in their own words. In the control sample, 58.7 per cent gave substantial free responses, as opposed to 85.4 per cent of the clinical sample ($X^2 (1) = 14.4$; $P < 0.001$). This contrast in itself was suggestive of the greater salience of the questionnaire for the clinical group. There is not space here to report the formal content analysis of these data. Instead some examples are provided below, in order to flesh out the preceding statistics.

The control group

The most frequently described form of experience was a transient impression of deep insight, or a fresh perspective on life, and an accompanying feeling of euphoria or well-being.

Feeling of mild elation not related to any particular event. Feeling that problems are absolutely minuscule and totally unimportant—different sense of perspective. Feel I have more understanding—more able to cope with life. Revitalises, rejuvenates and puts things into perspective.

Many described feelings of harmony or unity with natural surroundings:

A feeling of being so very small and that all I experience and think is really so trivial in comparison. A feeling of being just on the circumference of some profound harmony and not knowing how to go any further. A sense of peace and calm but barely restrained raw power. Extreme emotion.

A sense of a 'presence' which guided, comforted, or reassured was also widely described:

Sometimes when I'm sitting in my room in the quiet; it seems as if something is in the room with me giving me special thoughts about what I should do the next day, week or so. These feelings are hard to explain because you don't know if they're thoughts or something different because they feel strange and unexplainable.

I have on several occasions seen, and also have just been aware of my grandad since his death in 1977. He gives me a great feeling of comfort, security and confidence, especially as he only appears when I am unwell, anxious or worried.

A substantial minority of these involved explicitly religious content:

I have experienced a sense of God's presence on many occasions. When I first experienced it (in a church service at the age of 15) I actually felt physically drunk (I wasn't!) and could hardly walk. On other occasions, I have just felt an overwhelming sense of peace and love, and often forgot the time.

There were several classic conversion experiences, various forms of 'psychic' experiences, including apparitions, telepathy, precognition, and clairvoyance, two clear examples of out of body experiences (both in connection with childbirth), and some prototypical 'near death experiences'. A small number of negative experiences were described, mostly connected with fear of the dark and superstition.

The clinical group

In general, the descriptions offered by the clinical group were more disturbing, negative, and bizarre both in the way they were expressed, and in their content. However, there were strong parallels with the experiences described by the control sample, and some individuals described wholly positive, prototypical spiritual experiences:

I was looking for wild orchids in a local limestone wooded quarry near to where I live. I was greatly distressed in my heart by an obsessive sin I seemed unable to overcome. I was entirely alone in this quarry. It was very quiet. In my sadness I saw a figure in cool white clothes above the pine trees or in the trees above me and to the right. His face became clear. He had the kindest expression of tenderness as he looked directly at me that I have ever seen. I was feeling so full of guilt and failure and this face seemed to say I know all your temptations and failures but I love you so much unconditionally. His eyes were so beautiful, so kind, so strong. It lasted only a second or 2 or 3 at most. That was it . . .

I no longer believe in God. With all humility and trembling I have to say I KNOW Him and LOVE Him.

Usually when meditating I feel my consciousness spread outside me to encompass all things this happens usually when I am completely relaxed towards the end of meditation.

Time stopping but at the same time that moment encompassing all time. It relaxes me and makes me feel that life is worth living.

An intense, mystical awareness of nature was conveyed, if in slightly unusual terms, in many of the descriptions:

As a young naturalist approaching my fourteenth birthday, the taste of soil in me through digging up and eating earth-nuts/ pig-nuts, having walked across streets and estates and woodland, I followed a stream where damson and anemones flowered, a late spring, the ash and the oak only just breaking into leaf, I left the stream and walked across a muddy, hoof-pitted field, at the gate I turned and looked back, low yellow sun-rays illumined the ash and oak leafage: illumining Life as Earth against black cloud—the air crystal clear. A meteorological phenomena Constable captured in one of his paintings. Palpitations and shock seared me like electricity—awe, poignant awe—numinous at the beauty of living mother. I walked home like a shaken vision of St Paul on the road to Damascus. I wrote poetry obsessively as a result'.

A sense of presence was mentioned by most respondents, often with bizarre elaborations:

I woke up one night and my curtains were slightly open. I could see the moonlight streaming in and I was aware of a supernatural presence. I quickly closed the curtains but the awe-inspiring presence was still there. It was like a throbbing living being all around me. It pressurised me, I quickly got out my canvas and painted the experience, the following day I was urged to protect my room from these rays and influences by papering the inside with tinfoil.

In some cases, clearly psychotic experiences were described by some respondents as intensely positive from their point of view:

Ecstasy—in the way I imagine religious people use the term.

Crossing busy road junctions paying no heed to traffic—a feeling of invulnerability. A longing to regain it—comparable I'd guess to a junkie's desire for more crack. A desire to experience this high probably lies behind my attempts to give up anti-psychotic medication 3 times over the last 7 years—it doesn't work. I suppose my illness has gone beyond these peak experiences.

Finally, a number of the psychotic respondents made unsolicited comments about the relationship between the experiences the questionnaire had suggested to them, and those they considered to be a function of their illnesses, although there was no obvious consensus of opinion. Some simply explained all such experiences in terms of their illness:

I call the experiences which come into this category schizophrenic as they have not been a feature of my life outside these episodes . . . Being convinced that these experiences though usually pleasurable are not useful to day-to-day life and I cannot see their relevance—they're just misleading

Others felt that there was not a specific association between psychosis and this class of experience:

I would also like to add that you don't have to be mentally ill to have one of these experiences. They are common in people who have had no form of mental illness in their life. They are spiritual experiences which are common to all Christians or even the other religions.

Most who expressed an opinion suggested that there was a fundamental connection between their psychoses and their spiritual experiences.

Along with other 'psychotic' (possibly) experiences it has increased my faith in God (very much a personal God). I really needed a crisis to turn my life about and this seemed in part a spiritual crisis—it showed me where my priorities lay, made me realign my thoughts and helped relate to other people who had similar experiences. These are really indirect effects but for the overall effect of this horror and psychosis I would go through it again.

A formal content analysis of these data is described in detail elsewhere (Jackson 1991). The results supported the conclusions suggested by the quantitative study, particularly with respect to the interpretation of the SEQ scales, the distinction between numinous and mystical subtypes, and the differential contrast between them across the control and psychotic groups. The greatest between-group contrast of 20 blind ratings made for each free response was for 'awareness of a supernatural agency', and closer analysis found that this was largely explained by the much more common reference to the sense of a divine presence (as opposed to a 'mundane' presence such as a ghost) in the psychotic group. Where it was possible to rate the emotional tone and pragmatic effects of the experiences described, the majority were positive in both groups, although a higher proportion of the psychotic group's descriptions were rated as negatively toned than in the control group.

Discussion

The central hypothesis of the study described here was that benign spiritual experience is specifically associated with schizotypal personality trais. A crucial initial stage was the empirical derivation of two dimensions of spiritual experience: 'mystical experience' (feelings of unity, insight, tranquillity, and well-being) and 'numinous experience' (the sense of a supernatural presence, prominent sensory phenomena, volitional passivity, and intense emotions). The distinct profiles that emerged for these scales in the current study supported the utility and coherence of this distinction.

The central hypothesis was supported by the findings that the SEQ scale was correlated with schizotypy (STA) in the normal sample, over and above more general trait measures, and that Numinous Experience scores were markedly elevated in the clinical sample. At the same time, the nature of the hypothesized relationship was specified more closely by the finding that these associations were largely restricted to numinous experience. This pattern is consistent with the claims of previous theorists, most notably Hood (1974), and Deikman (1977), who argued that the 'higher' forms of mystical experience have little relevance for psychopathology, and with Caird's (1987) finding of a lack of association between mystical experience and Eysenck's personality variables.

The Numinous Experience scale predicted clinical group membership more strongly than the DSM-III based schizotypy scales. The sense of an external, spiritual presence thus appears to be a highly salient experience for many psychotics (particularly when the presence is interpreted as being divine rather than 'mundane'). This impression was supported by the high rate of free responses in the psychotic group and the content of these responses. It has also been reiterated in the feedback obtained from the Voices group from which the clinical sample was taken, and similar self-help groups, in response to workshop presentations of these results.

The hypothesis of a common schizotypal trait underlying both benign spiritual and psychotic experience offers the beginnings of an account of the phenomenological similarities between them. Insofar as schizotypy theory accounts for the phenomenology of psychotic experience, it may be equally applicable to spiritual experience. For example, central themes in schizotypy research have been anomalous patterns of attentional inhibition and instability of CNS homeostasis in high schizotypes and diagnosed psychotics (Claridge 1985; see also chapters 4, 5, and 12 in this volume). These have strong parallels in early theories of spiritual experience. James (1902), for example, suggested that 'persons deep in the spiritual life' are distinguished by relatively ready access to 'unconscious' contents: *'the door to this region seems unusually wide open'*. Underhill (1930) suggested that mystics have

thresholds of extraordinary mobility. That is to say, a very slight effort, a very slight departure from normal conditions, will permit their latent or subliminal powers to emerge and occupy the mental field. A 'mobile threshold' may make a man a genius, a lunatic, or a saint. All depends on the character of the emerging powers.

The relevance of such factors for spiritual experience could be assessed by investigating the distribution of these cognitive and neuropsychological variables across the spiritual experience scales.

However, while this line of research may take us further into the question of why spiritual and psychotic experience have phenomenological parallels, it would not address the question of why they are different, or in James poetic terms, why some find 'seraphs' and others, 'snakes'. If a 'common mechanism' underlies both forms of experience, progress on this question is perhaps more likely through an improved understanding of the personal, social, and cultural contexts in which specific 'schizotypal experiences' occur, rather than of the 'nuts and bolts' of the psychological processes underlying the production of the experiences. This was attempted in a second study which aimed to complement the quantitative emphasis of the questionnaire study, with a closely focused qualitative investigation of 'borderline' individuals.

A PROBLEM-SOLVING PERSPECTIVE

Case studies of 'benign schizotypy'

In much of the schizotypy literature, it is more or less assumed that schizotypal experiences involve some form of—perhaps muted—psychopathology. The key 'positive' features of schizotypy—magical ideation, perceptual abberation, and paranoid ideation—are defined in terms of how they depart from accurate, 'normal' reality testing. In this context, the claim that apparently schizotypal reality-testing of spiritual experience may be not only *not* pathological, but positively helpful and constructive for the individual, deserves serious examination. The fact that experients report that they have found such experiences beneficial, as some of the examples from the questionnaire study illustrate, does not provide sufficient grounds to establish that this is the case in any objective sense. The same claim is, after all, not unusual in psychotic illness (Roberts 1991*b*). Survey findings of a positive correlation between report of spiritual experience and measures of well-being are uninformative about the basis of the sense of well-being (and incidentally, the nature of the spiritual experiences in question). To assess this issue further, it is necessary to examine the evidence more closely in particular cases.

If it is the case that spiritual experience is benign, how do these anomalous experiences produce their benefits? How does it help an individual to experience an alternative reality, however 'spiritual'? Previous commentators have proposed that such experiences may be an integral component of a general *problem solving process* (Batson and Ventis 1982; Wootton and Allen 1983; Valla and Prince 1989), which has also been described in studies of 'inspirational' creativity in the arts and sciences (Wallas 1926; Harding 1942). The basic form of this process is a progressive sequence involving reaching an impasse, 'incubating' the problem, and experiencing a specific moment of insight, typically involving an altered state of consciousness and symbolic imagery. The textbook example is Kekule's discovery of the structure of the benzine ring, in the form of a dream of a snake biting its own tail (symbolizing the bonding of the aromatic ring). Batson and Ventis (1982), have suggested that in the case of spiritual experience the impasse is typically an existential crisis (rather than a purely intellectual problem), of which the prototypical example is bereavement. Stated baldly, the impasse here is that the deceased is a necessary feature of the bereaved person's life, but that they are dead. The spiritual experience is suggested to be a moment of insight which resolves the impasse, typically through effecting a 'paradigm shift' in the individual's goals or their perspective on the problem. A common spiritual experience in the context of bereavement is a period of awareness of the deceased person's presence, whether through a direct sensory perception or, less tangibly, simply the feeling that they are present. Through such experiences, people gain comfort in the face of bereavement in a more emotionally direct sense than would be available through relatively 'cold' cognitive processing, such as considering the arguments for the survival of the soul. Such experiences literally transcend logical consideration, and allow even sceptics the comfort of a direct experience of the *subjective* fact of survival.

This consideration may begin to account for the role of specifically schizotypal features in benign spiritual experience. Without the perceptual abberation and magical ideation necessary to generate a hallucinatory experience, and to attribute it to an external reality, it would not (at least from a materialist perspective) be possible to attain the benefits of this type of experience. The subjective authority (or what James termed the 'noetic quality') of spiritual experiences, which is a necessary feature for their benign effects, may depend on the capacity to have non-veridical experiences, and to believe in them.

In the following, the face validity of this account is assessed through an examination of two 'borderline' cases of benign spiritual experience. These were part of a larger series of case studies, described in Jackson (1991) and Jackson and Fulford (1996). The original study aimed to re-examine the phenomenological similarities and distinctions between spiritual and psychotic experiences, and to provide a broader perspective on the life situations of the experients and the contexts within which their experiences were embedded. The study involved detailed comparison of the case histories of two groups of strategically selected subjects. One group comprised healthy individuals who reported frequent, intense spiritual experiences with strong schizotypal features, but had no psychiatric history; the other comprised recovered diagnosed psychotics who viewed their psychotic experiences in spiritual terms. Case histories were elicited through a semi-structured interview developed for the purpose. Before going on to review two of these cases, the broad findings of the phenomenological comparison are summarized.

The general conclusions were that there were counter-examples for each of the phenomenological distinctions between psychotic and spiritual experiences proposed in the previous literature. *Undiagnosed* interviewees reported experiences involving both malignant and idiosyncratic spiritual entities; true and pseudo-hallucinations; mood congruent and incongruent hallucinations; and visual and auditory hallucinations. They lacked volitional control over their initial experiences (although they described acquiring increased control with the passage of time). They held grandiose beliefs about their status, spiritual role, and paranormal abilities, with full conviction. They described both emotionally positive and emotionally negative experiences, some of which continued for extended periods of time. Only a minority of experiences described in either group were obviously 'sub-culturally influenced'.

There were then, strong phenomenological parallels between the experiences described in the two groups, to the extent that the benign experiences met Present State Examination (PSE) (Wing *et al.* 1974) criteria for a range of psychotic symptoms. However, there were some marked differences of degree between the two groups. Most strikingly, the diagnosed participants had been relatively overwhelmed by their psychoses, and had effectively lost contact with consensual reality for extended periods of time, during which they acted out their delusions in bizarre behaviour. While the undiagnosed subjects experienced difficulties in integrating their experiences into their everyday lives, and their behaviour was affected, markedly in some cases, this did not create situations of serious social crisis for them, and they remained largely 'in touch' with those around them. In the short term, then, there was a clear sense in which the experiences described by diagnosed subjects were 'pathological', and most of those described by the undiagnosed subjects were relatively benign. The diagnosed group also differed in reporting a considerably higher rate of emotionally negative schizotypal experiences, while positive experiences were common in both groups.

Case vignettes

Case 1

'Sara' (43) was a married voluntary parish worker. She described her childhood in a Christian middle-class family as happy and conventional. She was educated at grammar school, trained as a secretary, and worked for a large industrial company. In her early thirties she was informed that she was unable to have children, and this precipitated a period of depression, which was neither diagnosed nor treated. This lifted when her career began to develop, and she achieved rapid promotion into middle management. As her career progressed, she became increasingly uncertain about her direction in life, and her first major experience occurred while she was thinking about this on her way to work:

I heard a voice say 'Sara, this is Jesus. When are you coming to work for me?' And my first reaction was, I honestly thought it was my brother hidden in the back of the car . . . I thought he was having me on. I turned round to look and there was nobody there. I turned back and thought 'He's put a tape in the car' because it was so real and there was nothing there. Then I heard it again.

This, together with subsequent experiences, met the PSE criteria for non-affective auditory hallucinations and visual hallucinations. Initially, these centred on the theme that she was being chosen by Jesus, then proceeded to explicate a detailed model of 'the workings of the kingdom of heaven'. She was initially deeply troubled by these experiences, and she confided in her vicar, who advised her that her experiences were authentic and that she should follow their promptings. She described this as a tremendous relief, and she duly gave up her career and became a lay parish worker. Her experiences have continued in the nine years since what she called her 'big bang', but they have changed in content (mainly involving clairvoyant insights concerning people she works with) and form, becoming less florid:

In the first five months it was ultra clear because I couldn't hear anything else, but God doesn't take your free will away . . . it was just that he'd turned his own volume up, if you like. When you equalise the volumes I can listen to Him or I can do my own thing. Most of the time I'm clear but not always.

She believed that she had exceptional paranormal powers and that God was directly helping her through synchronicity. These beliefs met the criteria for delusions of grandiose ability, and religious delusions, although they were clearly sub-culturally influenced.

She suggested that her experiences were similar to those of psychotics, but while the latter were mistaken in ascribing a divine source to theirs, she was not. She further commented

if I'm mad, so be it, but this is the most real thing I've ever known . . . it has always enhanced my life: it's brought a great deal to other people and it is benign; it is co-operative; it is loving; it helps me see the beauty of nature; hear the beauty of music; understand myself and understand others; reach out to others; begin to grasp something about ultimate reality and the way this universe is.

Case 2

'Sean' (53) was a married salesman with two grown-up children. He came from a stable, middle-class, non-religious family, and had left school at 16 without qualifications. He described himself as having been a 'militant atheist' before the onset of his main experiences. These began in his late forties, when he had recently lost his job, and had been told that he might have multiple sclerosis. He was 'worried sick' about these problems, as he walked through some local fields, when he 'heard words not of my choice, but like another voice within me saying my name—'Sean, none of this matters. You will always have what you need.' The 'voice' then 'instructed' him about the ephemeral nature of mundane reality and the value of an attitude of acceptance of events, rather than striving against them. After some time, when he reached the road, 'my own thoughts started to come back', and 'all the worry lifted'. This voice continued to speak to him for long periods 'almost daily', for about 9 months, and then less frequently, on the nature of the cosmic order and the pragmatic consequences of this for him. He reported that this 'instruction' was unrelated to any religious doctrine that he had encountered, although it involved recognizable perennial spiritual concepts, such as the insubstantiality of the material world, the interconnectedness of things, and the theme of non-attachment to material goals. His description of this experience met the PSE criteria for thought insertion and auditory pseudo-hallucinations.

He believed his communicants (who always referred to themselves as 'we') were from a 'higher' level of the cosmic hierarchy. He referred to 'them' as the CIA (Central Intelligence Agency), and had been told that he was 'sent the knowledge and it turns into a voice inside me'. He accepted the knowledge, and felt that it transformed him, enabling him to cope with his difficulties in an effective but relaxed way. He had never discussed his experiences with anyone except, once, his wife, who had laughed, assuming that he was joking.

At the time of interview, he no longer experienced the alien thoughts, although he still felt that he was 'guided'. He attributed his experiences to his extreme receptivity at the time when they started, because he had been so close to despair. Although he had acquired a new spiritually based philosophy, he had not joined any religious or spiritual groups. Despite the unworldiness of his philosophy, he seemed a very down-to-earth person, and was clearly functioning well, and at that time successfully self-employed. He was not worried about his sanity, although he had been when he started hearing the voice. He said in the interview:

I know me, I ain't no loony, I don't go and do crazy things. I lead a perfectly normal, respectable type of life, not because I have to but because it suits me . . . I am definitely sure . . . that I am open to hear things that most people aren't.

Finally, he doubted whether a doctor would be able to assess his experiences medically, but he would be worried about other people's reactions to a doctor's opinion: 'I just simply don't want anyone to know I'm a loony if I am!'

Clearly, both Sara and Sean strongly felt that their experiences had been beneficial to them. Both were financially secure, in steady, long term marital relationships, and led active, fulfilling lives in their occupations and local communities. Sara described her vicar's evaluation of her mental state as based on the following well-grounded considerations: 'I was behaving rationally, coping with my job, making decisions, talking to my husband about the fact that I needed to leave work . . . making sensible arrangements about changing my life and I wasn't showing any phobias, paranoias or whatever'. There were, then, some indications that both were functioning well and that their experiences had not had any obvious negative effects for them. It is not possible here to assess, through reference to any independent evidence, the stronger claim that these experiences were positively helpful.

In terms of the problem-solving process model, both of the individuals described above referred to going through a parallel sequence of events in which spiritual experience served a similar benign function. Their situations at the onset of their major experiences were very different forms of existential crisis. For Sara, while she was apparently achieving every success in her career, and was expecting to feel fulfilled by this, she found herself instead wondering why she was doing it, and yearning for a more meaningful direction. By contrast Sean was in a state of despair and helplessness about his future financial security and health. The initial experiences that they described appeared to directly address their specific problems. Sara found a new direction in the instruction that she should 'work for Jesus'. This required a relatively drastic change in her goals and lifestyle. It was arguably helpful for her that the impetus should come from 'beyond', rather than from her own inclinations. Indeed, she described how, quite apart from her own decision process, the 'revelation' was helpful in explaining her decision to her boss and her husband (her boss apparently commented 'they don't teach us to argue with God at business school'). Sean found a new perspective, involving stepping back from the problem and going with the flow, which he described as immensely helpful, allowing him to deal with matters in a calm, relaxed way—which before had rendered him virtually paralysed with despair. Again, the authority of this advice, in coming from 'the Central Intelligence Agency', may have helped him to use it more wholeheartedly than if he had received it in a more mundane form.

Both of these cases, then, provided anecdotal support for the general problem-solving process model. To recap, they each reached a point of existential impasse, which was resolved through their spiritual experience, and the non-veridical nature of their experiences was arguably important in facilitating this resolution. Similar conclusions were reached concerning the other cases of benign experience in the original study.

In benign spiritual experience, this general problem-solving process could be conceptualized as a negative feedback loop, in which the experience is triggered by high levels of dissonance or stress resulting from an existential crisis, and, once triggered, having the direct effect of reducing the triggering stressors. This would suggest that, in time, the experiences should cease as the factors which trigger them are resolved. There was some anecdotal support for this in the case studies. Both Sara and Sean described a 'quietening' of their voices over a period of about 6–12 months, as they made the life changes which their experiences had inspired. By contrast, the diagnosed subjects described an intensification of their psychotic experiences after the acute onset, involving a series of increasingly bizarre 'insights' which led to a state of full-blown psychosis. This downward spiral could perhaps be described as a positive-feedback loop, in which the initial 'insights' have the effect of increasing the individual's sense of crisis, precipitating further, increasingly desperate attempts to find resolution. To illustrate this process, one of these cases will be briefly described:

Case 3

'Phil' (24) was an undergraduate from a working-class, 'part-time Christian' family. His parents separated when he was 11. His initial psychotic experience occurred after he was attacked by an enraged policeman at an illegal Stonehenge festival. This experience brought home to him his own impotence in the face of the Establishment, and connected strongly with his experience of helplessness as an environmental activist. He developed the belief that he was 'the Rainbow warrior', with divine powers that could save the world. Again, there was a direct sense in which this 'revelation' answered his existential crisis. Unfortunately, it was not helpful in reducing his level of emotional turmoil. The announcement of his special status to his friends was (understandably) met with rejection, and he was sectioned after an incident in which he walked (shirtless) along a line of stationary traffic, demanding that the drivers switch their engines off to save the trees. The trauma of hospitalization, and the sense of isolation and lack of understanding he felt from psychiatric workers also increased his level of stress, although he was heavily medicated. He became more dogmatic in his assertion of his divine status and described a series of bizarre experiences involving exercising various magical powers, turning into a tree, and eventually transferring his divinity into a passing swan. His recovery followed a period of respite with his girlfriend's family who, as he described it, looked after him like a small child and provided a consistent atmosphere of emotional support and acceptance.

The anecdotal evidence supplied by Phil and other diagnosed participants was consistent with the proposal that a similar problem-solving process to that described for benign spiritual experience may be involved in some cases of full-blown psychosis. There were a number of examples of initial psychotic experiences occurring at times of intense crisis, and a clear sense in which these experiences involved content which appeared to address the individual's problems. By contrast with the benign cases, however, the net result of these experiences was to increase the level of crisis, usually through social conflict resulting from disclosure about the experience, or acting out central themes of the experience. In these cases, the initial psychotic insight led to an increasing cycle of bizarre experiences and a rapid trajectory into full blown psychosis.

To conclude this line of speculation, some suggestions will be briefly considered as to which factors might explain why the same problem-solving process may be self-resolving in some cases, and self-aggravating in others.

One contributory factor may be the level of predisposing schizotypy for a given individual. As we have seen, high schizotypes are more likely to report both benign and pathological schizotypal experiences. In terms of the problem-solving model, this might suggest that the threshold of emotional or cognitive stress at which such experiences are triggered is relatively low. This could result in an inherently unstable system, which is too prone to produce 'insight' experiences. (Conversely, it might be suggested, if the threshold is too high, individuals might be unable to achieve such experiences, even when they would be useful, and consequently may find it difficult to make major 'paradigm shifts' in their goals or belief systems.) This suggestion found some support in the case studies, in that the diagnosed participants described considerably more extensive schizotypal experiences throughout their lives than did the undiagnosed participants, and in this sense, could be described as being more schizotypal.

Secondly, it is possible that the social context in which experiences occur, or perhaps more importantly, the individual's appraisal of this context, may partially determine whether an insight resolves or aggravates an initial crisis. Sara described how her vicar's endorsement of her experiences 'was a tremendous relief' and helped her to accept them, whereas before she had been badly frightened, and afraid that she was going mad. It is interesting to speculate how her story would have developed had her vicar, like Phil's friends, rejected her insights. This proposal finds some support in the factors which diagnosed participants identified as helpful to them in the process of recovery. Each identified social contexts that provided some validation of their experience, in response to this line of questioning. For all except Phil, this included a supportive, spiritually oriented group (Bahais, practitioners of wicca, and Christadelphians) who offered a philosophy that had some common ground with the individual's psychotic insights. This provided the potential for dialogue, and a renegotiation of delusional beliefs allowing the individual to retain something of their psychotic beliefs, whilst letting go of the more bizarre components. As one participant put it 'I'm not the sun, but I can be a mirror which reflects it'. Similarly, the undiagnosed participants described either keeping their anomalous experiences quiet (like Sean), or carefully selecting whom to discuss them with (like Sara). They thus effectively avoided serious social confrontation about their beliefs and experiences, which may have increased their stress levels in the circumstances.

A further possibility is that the diagnosed participants simply came up with less useful insights, which necessarily resulted in increased conflict. Consistent with this suggestion, the belief in their own divinity was an initial insight for most of the diagnosed subjects, whereas the undiagnosed participants more modestly believed that they were specially chosen by a divine being, and in some cases had a special spiritual role or mission, but not that they themselves were divine beings. To complicate the picture, over a longer time period, and with some re-evaluation, the diagnosed interviewees felt that some of their psychotic experiences had involved profound, spiritually authentic insights, which became central foci in their spiritual lives after recovery. In this broader sense, even some of the more bizarre experiences—such as the belief that one is God—were seen as problem-solving by some interviewees.

CONCLUSIONS

To summarize, the general hypothesis that emerged from these studies was that both benign spiritual experience and acute psychotic experience involve the operation of the same underlying psychological process, which has also been described in studies of creativity. This involves a sequence in which a cognitive or emotional impasse triggers an altered state of consciousness which releases a potentially resolving insight or solution to the impasse, often in symbolic form. The subjective force of such experiences enables experients to make a paradigm shift in their goals or perspective on the problem; it is suggested that their non-veridical 'schizotypal' nature is essential in this respect. In benign cases, the insight successfully resolves the triggering crisis and the process is self-terminating. This becomes pathological when the insight increases the sense of crisis, triggering a further cycle of experiences and a spiral away from reality into full-blown psychosis. On this model, variations in schizotypy are conceived as individual differences in the threshold at which stressors trigger the process. Some suggested factors which may influence whether the process is benign or pathological in individual cases include the individual's level of schizotypy, their appraisal of the social feedback their insight produces, and the quality of the insight experience involved.

In so far as this model of the relationship between spiritual and psychotic experience is valid, it is likely to be restricted to a subset of examples of both categories. This would exclude psychotic illnesses with gradual onset and predominantly negative symptoms, such as Crow's (1980) concept of 'type II' schizophrenia, or conditions that have a relatively clear underlying biological aetiology, such as bipolar affective disorder. Similarly it would exclude non-sensate mystical experiences that are reached through disciplined and calm spiritual practice (Deikman 1977). Nevertheless, the evidence suggests that the most commonly reported context for contemporary spiritual experience is a crisis of some form (Hay 1987); similarly the role of stress and life events in triggering psychotic episodes is well-established and fundamental to the diathesis—stress model. The validity of the model for the relevant subgroups of spiritual and psychotic experience, then, could be assessed more formally and in considerably more depth. An interesting first step would be a study which used blind ratings to assess the degree to which the content of a larger sample of spiritual/psychotic experiences addressed the specific circumstances or concerns of the experients, and a more focused analysis of the variation between the different 'insights' involved, and how they are utilized.

More generally, the studies described here suggest a need for clinicians to recognize and to work with the more benign, spiritual experience component of psychosis, and for an attitude of openness towards its therapeutic potential. Many diagnosed psychotics feel that their intense and sometimes bizarre spirituality is pathologized by mental health and religious professionals alike, yet it may be that precisely this aspect of their psychology holds considerable promise for healing.

REFERENCES

Ahern, G. (1990). *Spiritual experience in modern society*. Alister Hardy Research Centre, Oxford.

American Psychiatric Association (1980). *Diagnostic and statistical manual of mental disorders* (3rd edn). APA, Washington, DC.

Arieti, S. (1976). *Creativity. The magic synthesis*. Basic Books, New York.

Back, K. W. and Bourque, L. B. (1970). Can feelings be enumerated? *Behavioral Science*, 15, 487–96.

Batson, C. P. and Ventis, L. W. (1982). *The religious experience*. Oxford University Press.

Beit-Hallahmi, B. and Argyle, M. (1977). Religious ideas and psychiatric disorders. *International Journal of Social Psychiatry*, 23, 26–30.

Boisen, A. T. (1947). Onset in acute psychoses. *Psychiatry*, 10, 159–67.

Boisen, A. T. (1952). Mystical identification in mental disorder. *Psychiatry*, 15, 287–97.

Bowers, M. B. and Freedman, D. X. (1966). Psychedelic experiences in acute psychoses. *Archives of General Psychiatry*, 15, 240–8.

Bradford, D. T. (1987). *The experience of God*. Peter Long, New York.

Buckley, P. (1982). Mystical experience and schizophrenia. *Schizophrenia Bulletin*, 7, 516–21.

Caird, D. (1987). Religiosity and personality; are mystics introverted, neurotic, or psychotic? *British Journal of Social Psychology*, 26, 345–6.

Campbell, J. (1972). *Myths to live by.* Viking, New York.

Chapman, L. J. and Chapman, J. P. (1980). Scales for rating psychotic and psychotic-like experiences as a continuum. *Schizophrenia Bulletin*, 6, 476–89.

Claridge, G. S. (1995). *The origins of mental illness* (new impression). Malor Books, Cambridge, Mass.

Claridge, G. S. and Broks, P. (1984). Schizophrenia and hemisphere function I. Theoretical considerations and the measurement of schizotypy. *Personality and Individual Differences*, 5, 633–48.

Claridge, G. S and Hewitt, J. K. (1987). A biometrical study of schizotypy in a normal population. *Personality and Individual Differences*, 8, 303–12.

Crow, T. J. (1980). Molecular pathology of schizophrenia: more than one disease process? *British Medical Journal*, 280, 66–8.

Deikman, A. J. (1977). Comments on the G. A. P. Report on Mysticism. *Journal of Nervous and Mental Disease*, 165, 213–17.

Dobkin de Rios, M. (1990). *Hallucinogens.* Prism Press, Bridport.

Docherty, J. P., Van Kammen, D. P., Siris, S. G., and Marder, S. R. (1978). Stages of onset of schizophrenic psychosis. *American Journal of Psychiatry*, 135, 420–6.

Eysenck, H. J. and Eysenck, S. B. G. (1975). *Manual of the Eysenck Personality Questionnaire.* Hodder & Stoughton, London.

Fischmann, L. G. (1983). Dreams, hallucinogenic drug states, and schizophrenia: A psychological and biological comparison. *Schizophrenia Bulletin*, 9, 73–94.

Gallemore, J. L. Jr, Wilson, W. P., and Rhoads, J. M. (1969). The religious lives of patients with affective disorders. *Diseases of the Nervous System*, 30, 483–7.

Group for the Advancement of Psychiatry (1976). Mysticism: spiritual quest or psychic disorder? *G A P Report*, 9, 705–825.

Greeley, A. M. (1974). *Ecstasy. A way of knowing.* Prentice-Hall, New Jersey.

Greeley, A. M. and McCready, W. C. (1974). *The mystical, the twice born and the happy: An investigation of the sociology of religious experience.* National Opinion Poll Research, Chicago.

Grof, S and Grof, C. (1986). Spiritual emergency: The understanding and treatment of transpersonal crises. *Re-Vision*, 8, 7–20.

Harding, R. E. M. (1942). *An anatomy of inspiration.* W. Heffer and sons, Cambridge.

Hardy, A. C. (1966). *The divine flame.* Collins, London.

Hardy, A. C. (1979). *The spiritual nature of man.* Clarendon, Oxford.

Hay, D. (1987). *Exploring inner space.* (2nd edn). Penguin, Harmondsworth.

Hay, D. and Morisy, A. (1978). Reports of ecstatic, paranormal or religious experience in Great Britain, and the United States—A comparison of trends. *Journal for the Scientific Study of Religion*, 17, 255–68.

Hay, D. and Morisy, A. (1985). Secular society/religious meanings: A contemporary paradox. *Review of Religious Research*, 26, 213–27.

Hood R. W. (1974) Psychological strength and religious experience. *Journal for the Scientific Study of Religion*, 13, 65–71.

Hood R. W. (1975). The construction and preliminary validation of a measure of reported mystical experience. *Journal for the Scientific Study of Religion*, 14, 29–41.

Jackson, M. C. (1991). A study of the relationship between spiritual and psychotic experience. Unpublished D. Phil. thesis. Oxford University.

Jackson, M. C. and Claridge, G. S. (1991). Reliability and validity of a psychotic traits questionnaire (STQ). *British Journal of Clinical Psychology*, 30, 311–23.

Jackson, M. C. and Fulford, K. W. M. (1997). Spiritual experience and psychopathology. *Philosophy, Psychiatry and Psychology.*

James, W. (1902). *The varieties of religious experience.* Longmans, New York.

Laing, R. D. (1967). *The politics of experience*. Penguin, Harmondsworth.

Laski, M. (1961). *Ecstasy. A study of some secular and religious experiences*. Cresset Press, London.

Lenz, H. (1983). Belief and delusion. Their common origin but different course of development. *Zygon*, 18, 117–37.

Lukoff, D. (1988). Transpersonal perspectives on manic psychosis. Creative, visionary and mystical states. *Journal of Altered States of Consciousness*, 20, 111–39.

Lynn, S. J. and Rhue, J. W. (1988). Fantasy proneness: Hypnosis, developmental antecedents and psychopathology. *American Psychologist*, 43, 35–44.

Mandell, A. (1980). Toward a psychobiology of transcendence: God in the brain. In *The psychobiology of consciousness* (ed. J. M. Davidson and R. J. Davidson). Plenum, New York.

Margolis, R. D. and Elifson, K. W. (1979). A typology of religious experience. *Journal for the Scientific Study of Religion*, 18, 61–7.

Maxwell, M. and Tschudin, V. (1990). *Seeing the invisible: Modern religious and other transcendent experiences*. Arkana.

Moehle, D. (1983). Cognitive dimensions of religious experience. *Journal of Experimental Social Psychology*, 19, 122–45.

Paffard, M. (1973). *Inglorious Wordsworths*. Hodder & Stoughton, London.

Pahnke, W. H. and Richards, W. A. (1966). Implications of LSD and experimental mysticism. *Journal of Religion and Health*, 5, 175–208.

Persinger, M. A. (1983). Religious and mystical experiences as artefacts of temporal lobe function: A general hypothesis. *Perception and Motor Skills*, 57, 1255–62.

Prince, R. (1979). Religious Experience and Psychosis. *Journal of Altered States of Consciousness*, 5, (2), 167–81.

Roberts, G. W. (1991 *a*). Schizophrenia: a neuropathological perspective. *British Journal of Psychiatry*, 158, 8–17.

Roberts, G. W. (1991 *b*). Delusional belief systems and meaning in life: A preferred reality? *British Journal of Psychiatry*, 159, (suppl. 14), 19–28.

Robinson, E. A. and Jackson, M. C. (1987). *Religion and values at sixteen plus*. Alister Hardy Research Centre, Oxford.

Stace, W. T. (1960). *Mysticism and Philosphy*. Lippincott, Philadelphia.

Underhill, E. (1930). *Mysticism. A Study in the Nature and Development of Man's Spiritual Consciousness (twelfth, revised edition)*, Methuen & Co, London.

Valla, J. P. and Prince, R. (1989). Religious experiences as self-healing mechanisms. In *Altered states of consciousness and mental health* (ed. C. A. Ward), Sage, London.

Wallas, G. (1926). *The art of thought*. Harcourt, New York.

Wapnick, K. (1969). Mysticism and schizophrenia. *Journal of Transpersonal Psychology*, 1, 49–68.

Watson, J. P. (1982). Aspects of Personal Meaning in Schizophrenia. In *Personal meanings* (ed. E. Sheperd and J. P. Watson), J. Wiley and Sons, London.

Wilber, K. (1980). The pre/trans fallacy. *Re-Vision*, 2, 51–72.

Wing, J. K., Cooper, J., and Sartorius, N. (1974). The measurement and classification of psychiatric symptoms. Cambridge University Press.

Wootton, R. J. and Allen, D. F. (1983). Dramatic Religious Conversion and Schizophrenic Decompensation. *Journal of Religion and Health*, 22, 212–320.

Wuthnow R. (1976). *The consciousness reformation*. Berkeley, California.

12

Hallucinations and arousability: pointers to a theory of psychosis

CHARLES MCCREERY

A MODEL FOR PSYCHOTIC PHENOMENA

Introduction: the study of hallucination in normal subjects

The idea of schizotypy as a dimension of personality along which the entire population may be ranged implies a degree of continuity between ostensibly well-adjusted and apparently psychotic persons. Such a model might well lead us to expect the occasional occurrence of such apparent abnormalities as hallucinatory experience even in normal subjects, if only at a sub-clinical level, i.e. less frequently perhaps in the normal than the psychotic individual, or accompanied by a less aversive affective tone. The anecdotal evidence for the occurrence of so-called 'out-of-the-body experiences' (OBEs) in a considerable percentage of normal subjects is consistent with this prediction, and has been supported by a number of surveys of random or near-random sections of the population using questionnaire techniques. These have characteristically yielded incidence figures of about 15 per cent in the general population and 25 per cent among students (see Irwin (1985) for a review).

An OBE may be defined as one in which the subject temporarily feels located in a different place from the physical body; it may take a fully 'perceptual' form, as when the subject seems to see his or her physical body from outside. From time to time in this chapter, I shall use the theory-neutral term 'ecsomatic experience', proposed by Green (1968*b*), as a synonym for 'OBE'.

In the context of schizotypy research, the study of hallucinatory processes in normal subjects presents a number of advantages over the comparable endeavour in diagnosed psychotics. There are not the same confounding effects of drugs, hospitalization, and the difficulties of communication and interpretation which Sarbin (1967), for example, discusses. The study of ecsomatic experiences offers the particular advantage that they are susceptible to experimental study, inasmuch as a minority of subjects report being able to induce them at will, by methods to which one may approximate in the laboratory. Some of the results of a laboratory study of this kind will be presented later in the chapter.

The comparative study of hallucinations of the sane and the insane also promises theoretical advantages to the student of schizotypy and schizophrenia. We may hope to shed light on such questions as why hallucinatory experiences seem to be predominantly maladaptive and aversive in diagnosed psychotics, but often emotionally neutral or even highly pleasurable in normals, for whom they may have on occasion an adaptive value. For example, some OBEs occurring at moments of physical or mental crisis for their subjects appear to leave them feeling better after the experience than before (Green 1968*b*). I shall be discussing the significance of this fact below.

In my own case the study of hallucinations in normal subjects, and of ecsomatic experiences in particular, has led me to a model of psychosis which takes as its starting-point the phenomenological similarity between psychosis and dreams. This has often been remarked upon before, but to my knowledge has never been satisfactorily explained. In the first half of this chapter I shall propose a model which I believe accounts for this coincidence of phenomenology, and in the second I shall support this theoretical framework by presenting empirical data on the personality and electrophysiological characteristics of subjects reporting OBEs.

Psychosis viewed as a waking dream

Aristotle is usually credited with the first observation on the phenomenological similarity between dreams and psychosis; in *de Somniis* he wrote: '[T]he faculty by which ... we are subject to illusion when affected by disease, is identical with that which produces illusory effects in sleep.' In more modern times Kant observed, 'the lunatic is a wakeful dreamer' (quoted in La Barre 1975, p. 12); and Jung (1909, p. 86) wrote: 'Let the dreamer walk about and act like one awakened and we have the clinical picture of dementia praecox.'

Among the resemblances between the two states we may note the following:

1. *Autism*, or the preoccupation with inner rather than outer events;
2. *Autonomy of mental content*: in the dream the subject is often the passive observer, or even the apparent victim, of events seemingly beyond his or her control, while the psychotic may experience various forms of loss of control over mental events, such as thought insertion or hallucination.
3. *Flattened or inappropriate affect*: one of Bleuler's (1911) defining conditions of schizophrenia; in dreams it may take such forms as the commission of 'crimes' with little emotional disturbance, or feelings of horror before anything occurs in the dream environment to justify it.
4. *Delusional beliefs.*
5. *Disorders of thought and language.* Mavromatis (1987) remarks that 'practically all of the schizophrenic thought disturbances are encountered in hypnagogia.'
6. *Lack of insight.* A defining condition of both dreams and psychotic states.

These many striking parallels between dreams and psychosis have so far never been satisfactorily explained. Attempts to look for EEG correlates of sleep in psychotics' waking EEGs have appeared unsuccessful. Perhaps as a result of these apparent failures, the hypothesis that there is a common mechanism underlying dreams and psychosis seems to have made little headway in recent times. Cutting

(1985), for example, in his comprehensive review of theories of schizophrenia, devotes a mere three parenthetical lines to the hypothesis.

In this paper I shall attempt to revive the hypothesis of a link between dreams and psychosis by proposing what I believe to be a new model in order to explain the similarities listed above. The basic premise is a simple one, namely that the psychotic appears like a person asleep because in fact he is asleep. That is to say he is subject to episodes of sleep, albeit possibly brief ones, which intrude into the waking state, and which go undetected by the subject. Thus far the model resembles some that have been put forward before, for example by Feinberg (1970), who suggested that the visual hallucinations of drug-withdrawal delirium represent the intrusion into waking consciousness of processes normally associated with sleep. However, there are two features which I believe are novel in my own model:

(1) the proposed mechanism whereby such sleep processes are generated in the middle of the waking state;
(2) the type of sleep that I suggest is associated with psychotic phenomena.

With regard to (1), I shall be proposing that the sleep processes in question are the result, not of de-arousal as in nocturnal sleep, but of hyperarousal, such as may occur in predisposed individuals in response to environmental stress. And with regard to (2), I shall be suggesting that what we should be looking for is evidence of Stage 1 sleep in the EEGs of schizophrenics, not rapid eye movement (REM) sleep of the type proposed by Feinberg (1970), for example.

The idea that sleep can occur as a response to extreme hyperarousal is at first sight a paradoxical one. However, there is both anecdotal and experimental evidence to support it. Oswald (1962) devotes a whole chapter to what he calls 'sleep as a provoked reaction'. On the anecdotal level he cites cases such as those of soldiers falling asleep while waiting to go into battle; and on the experimental level there is his own study (Oswald 1959) in which he was able to induce sleep in four out of six volunteers by administering powerful shocks at regular 10s intervals to the subject's wrist or ankle.

Fig. 12.1A represents the conventional view of arousal and its relationship to sleep, while Fig. 12.1B represents the view that underlies the present model. On the conventional view, arousal is a linear continuum with sleep at one end of it; according to the present view, arousal is still a continuum, but sleep supervenes at both ends.

The ideas in this chapter were stimulated by questionnaire and experimental studies of ecsomatic experiences in normal subjects (McCreery 1993). The findings of these studies may also be seen as providing considerable support for the model of psychosis to be proposed here. The second half of this chapter will therefore be devoted to presenting some of these findings in the context of the sleep/psychosis model. For the moment, however, let us consider the phenomenon of the ecsomatic experience itself, and how it illustrates the proposed mechanism for explaining the similarities between dreams and psychosis.

A. Conventional model

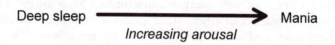

Deep sleep ⟶ Mania

Increasing arousal

B. Preferred model

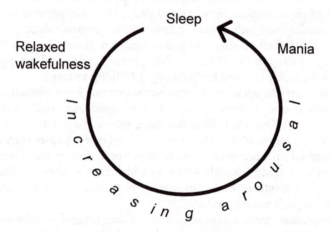

Fig. 12.1.   Two contrasting models of the relationship between arousal and sleep.

The out-of-the-body experience considered as a waking dream

As Irwin (1985) pointed out, the out-of-the-body experience seems to supervene on states of either extremely low or extremely high arousal. Green (1968 *b*), for example, found that three-quarters of a group of 176 subjects who reported a single OBE were lying down at the time, and 12 per cent of them considered they had been asleep when it started. By contrast, a substantial minority of cases occur under the opposite sort of condition, for example during rock-climbing falls, traffic accidents, childbirth, or musical performances in public.

Oswald (1962) refers to times when a sleep state 'results from overwhelming or terrifying stimulation', and this seems a good characterization of many of this second type of situation. The following is a case in point from one of my own subjects.

My ex-husband and I had a row in which he tried to strangle me . . . I seemed to float above my body and could see myself slowly slide down the wall. Everything seemed to be in slow motion, but also I have this very beautiful serene feeling . . . The next thing I knew, I was waking up lying on the floor . . .

My suggestion is that, whether the subject realizes it or not, the terms 'waking up' in this account have their normal, literal significance, and are not merely metaphorical. I suggest that the experience was a form of dream, occurring in a brief episode of sleep brought on by hyperarousal, this being the result of the extreme stress of the situation. I further suggest that the hallucinations of psychosis have a similar aetiology, as do all the other phenomenological features which psychosis shares with dreams, as enumerated above.

Incidentally, it is interesting to note that transient hallucinatory episodes of the ecsomatic type in non-clinical subjects may be accompanied by unusual affective responses, as indeed is the case in the example just quoted, where the subject refers to feeling 'serene' despite the extremity of her situation. However, one difference between such isolated episodes in normal subjects and protracted phases of psychosis in clinical subjects is that the former often seem to be of adaptive value to the subject, as mentioned above. Subjects who report ecsomatic experiences in connection with surgical operations, for example, may report feeling better after the experience than before. I have suggested the term 'happy schizotype' to denote members of the class who experience non-aversive, and even adaptive, hallucinations (McCreery 1993).

The 'happy schizotype' concept was suggested by the findings of a comparative questionnaire study of 450 people who had experienced at least one ecsomatic experience and 234 controls who had not. It was found that the significant differences between the two groups all concentrated on scales which loaded on Factor 1, 'Positive Schizotypy', in the Bentall *et al.* (1989) factor analysis of schizotypy scales. Thus, scales which consistently discriminated between out-of-the-body experiencers (OBErs) and controls were the Chapmans' Hypomania, Magical Ideation, and Perceptual Aberration Scales (Chapman *et al.* 1978; Eckblad and Chapman 1983, 1986), Claridge and Broks's (1984) STA Scale, and the Launay and Slade (1981) Hallucination Scale. In contrast there were no significant differences on Eysenck's Neuroticism scale (Eysenck and Eysenck 1975), which might be considered a general measure of adjustment to life, or Claridge and Broks's STB, which one can almost characterize as an unhappiness scale, containing as it does a number of items such as 'Do you often experience an overwhelming sense of emptiness?' (keyed Yes). Moreover, on the Chapmans' Physical Anhedonia scale (Chapman *et al.* 1976), OBErs scored consistently *lower* than controls, suggesting that in some ways they were actually enjoying life more than the average person (McCreery and Claridge 1995).

Arousability, hallucinations, and 'microsleeps'

The model of psychosis outlined so far clearly implies that arousability is a highly relevant variable in relation to schizotypy/psychosis-proneness. On the present view, we would expect people who are prone for whatever reason to extreme hyperarousal to be more liable to the various phenomena, including anomalous perceptual experiences, that characterize psychosis and which also occur in sub-clinical form in schizotypic normals.

One finding that is consistent with this prediction is the correlation that has been observed between the Chapmans' Hypomania (HoP) scale and scales tapping anomalous perceptual experiences such as their Perceptual Aberration scale (PAb). In my own data, derived from a total of 695 subjects, the correlation between HoP and PAb was 0.57, while that between HoP and the Launay-Slade Hallucination Scale (LSHS) was 0.63. PAb mainly taps disortions of the body image, whereas LSHS mainly taps anomalous auditory experiences.

It should be noted that there is no obvious overlap of content between the items of the Hypomania scale and scales such as PAb and LSHS. In the present context one may see the Hypomania scale as a measure of chronic lability of arousal. Some of the items are designed to tap episodes of hyperarousal, for example 'I often get into excited moods where it's almost impossible to stop talking' (keyed True). Others tap abnormal lability of arousal, for example 'I seem to be a person whose mood goes up and down easily' (keyed True).

A connection between arousal and hallucinations has been noted before, for example by Slade and Bentall (1988), who invoke enhanced arousal as one of a number of factors in the aetiology of auditory hallucinations. They suggest that high arousal interacts with the subject's current level of hallucinatory predisposition, and that 'minimal stress . . . may trigger hallucinations in highly predisposed individuals while severe stress would be necessary to trigger a comparable experience in a mildly predisposed person'.

What I believe has not hitherto been satisfactorily explained is *why* high internal-arousal levels should potentiate the individual's predisposition to hallucinate. The present model would explain this as follows: environmental stress raises the highly arousable individual's level of internal arousal to such a level that sleep supervenes—either partially, in the sense that certain sleep processes such as dreaming mentation intrude into waking consciousness, or completely for a brief period, so that he or she experiences an episode of sleep within the context of waking life.

Oswald's (1962) concept of 'microsleeps' may be relevant in this context. These are brief episodes, lasting just a few seconds, which occur during the waking state but which show all the normal electrophysiological signs of sleep, such as disappearance of the alpha rhythm of the EEG, slowing of the heart beat, and respiratory changes. What is particularly significant from the present point of view is that the subject may lack insight, even retrospectively, into the fact that he or she has slept. Indeed the person may strongly deny having slept for a moment and appear genuinely astonished when presented with unequivocal evidence for the fact of having done so, for example in the form of mechanically recorded failures at a vigilance task. Brief, but possibly frequent, lapses into sleep of this kind might well be sufficient to explain many of the phenomena of psychosis, such as hallucinations and other perceptual aberrations, which are often of short duration, even if their behavioural consequences are more long-lived. Certainly hallucinatory experiences of the sane are often of fairly short duration. For example, Green and McCreery (1975) found that about half of their 850 subjects reporting apparitional experiences estimated that these episodes had lasted less than a minute, and, among this half, 42 per cent considered that the experience had lasted less than 15 secs.

Psychosis as a Stage 1 sleep phenomenon

The chief objection to previous attempts to forge a theoretical link between dreams and psychosis seems to have been the apparent lack of electrophysiological evidence for continuity between them. Robbins (1988), for example, after reviewing studies of the EEG of psychosis, concludes 'The physiological correlates of dreaming and hallucinations appear to be different.' I believe that this failure to find electrophysiological evidence for a continuity between dreams and psychosis has been because investigators have been looking for it in the wrong place. That is to say, they have been looking for evidence of REM sleep processes in the waking state, whereas I suggest we should be looking for electrophysiological signs of Stage 1 sleep.

The search for signs of REM sleep appears to have been founded on the false assumption that dreams can only occur in connection with that phase of sleep. However, there seems no good reason to deny the term 'dream' to any mental event occurring during sleep, in which case we should include those mental events that occur during Stage 1, even if they consists merely of what subjects call 'thinking'. Moreover, the type of dramatic, narrative, and affectively charged sequences of mental events which people normally think of when the term 'dream' is used do not appear to be exclusively associated with REM sleep, as was assumed following the original studies of Aserinsky and Kleitman (1953). Later studies suggested that some narrative dreams may occur in other phases of sleep (see, for example, Foulkes and Vogel (1965)). It may also be relevant to note that normal subjects may even report the sort of dereistic mentation usually thought to be characteristic of sleep when they are ostensibly awake and resting, and showing a waking EEG (Foulkes and Fleisher 1975).

The idea that it is Stage 1 and not REM processes that are behind the phenomena of psychosis may be supported with three types of argument. First, there is the purely logical consideration that it is Stage 1 which is normally contiguous with the waking state, in which the main phenomena of psychosis occur, whereas REM sleep usually only supervenes after the subject has gone through a complete cycle of all the other stages of sleep (Stages 1 to 4). Secondly, there is the argument that REM sleep is characterized by lowered muscle tone, amounting to virtual paralysis, whereas there is little sign of a corresponding phenomenon in connection with psychotic states. Paralysis is occasionally reported in connection with various types of hallucinatory experience in the sane, including OBEs, apparitional experiences, and false awakenings, but such cases seem to be the exception rather than the rule (Green and McCreery 1994). Thirdly, the phenomenology of Stage 1 sleep shows many parallels with psychotic phenomenology, including the occurrence of dereistic thinking and autonomous imagery and hallucinations of various kinds (see Mavromatis (1987) for a review of this area; see also Oswald 1962; Schacter 1976; McKellar 1989).

Electrophysiological evidence relevant to the model

If we abandon the idea that it is REM sleep which underlies the phenomena of psychosis, and seek instead for evidence that Stage I processes are at work, then I think we can adduce various electrophysiological observations in support of the model.

First, there is the striking fact that the alpha rhythm responds in the same way to both an increase and a decrease in arousal, that is by disappearing or being masked by other sorts of activity. As Oswald puts it:

The alpha rhythm is a feature of a certain level of cerebral vigilance. It gets faster and disappears with increase of cerebral vigilance, and gets slower and disappears with fall of cerebral vigilance. The disappearance of alpha rhythm from the EEG of a person in whom it is normally present requires us always to ask the question, 'Is the individual now very alert or is he drowsy?' (Oswald 1962, p. 35)

One may also mention another curious symmetry, this one in relation to beta activity, namely the fact that it may occur with the approach of sleep, as well as in states of heightened arousal. I believe both these observations fit the model of the relationship between sleep and arousal represented in Fig. 12.1B rather than the 'common-sense' model of Fig. 12.1A.

Secondly, we may note the fact that a relative dearth of tonic alpha, and by contrast a relative abundance of beta, tends to be characteristic of the EEG of schizophrenics. As Flor-Henry (1979) puts it: 'Since Berger in 1937 noted the predominance of beta waves in "many mental disturbances" a very large number of studies have consistently found an excess of EEG power in the fast frequencies in the 20 to 50 Hz band.' This is what one would expect on the hypothesis that schizophrenics tend to be in a chronic state of heightened arousal, so that any unusual stress is likely to precipitate them into that state of hyperarousal in which sleep supervenes as a provoked reaction.

Thirdly, it is noteworthy that some studies have reported an elevated incidence of delta activity in the waking EEG of schizophrenics (see, for example, Sponheim et al. (1994)). Although delta waves are most characteristic of Stages 3 and 4 of sleep, short bursts of such slow waves may be observed even in Stage 1 sleep in certain subjects. Their observation in the waking EEG of some schizophrenics suggests that sleep processes are unusually 'near the surface' in such subjects, and waiting to break forth into consciousness under the influence of any abnormal stress.*

A final electrophysiological observation which may be adduced in support of the model concerns the relative weakness of schizophrenics' performance at tasks involving smooth-pursuit eye-tracking movements. Claridge (1994), after reviewing the many studies of this phenomenon, concludes that it is one of the most eligible candidates for being a marker for schizophrenia. I would suggest that in schizophrenics the normal mechanisms underlying the proper performance of smooth-pursuit tracking tasks may be disrupted, not by the rapid eye movements characteristic of REM sleep, but by the slow rolling eye movements which are characteristic of Stage 1. This might be either a direct effect of the intrusion of such slow eye movements into the waking state, or the indirect result of whatever disinhibitory mechanism gives rise to them.

Some possible objections considered

The question of motor function.

It might be thought a problem how people could continue to exercise any motor function at all successfully if they were subject to episodes of sleep during the waking state. The first point to note is that it is one of the advantages of positing Stage 1 as the type of sleep underlying the phenomena of psychosis, rather than the REM phase, that it is the latter and not the former which is accompanied by virtual paralysis. Moreover, there is anecdotal evidence that people can continue to perform quite complex perceptual motor skills while asleep, particularly if they are practised and habitual ones. Oswald (1962), for example, cites the case of soldiers sleeping while on the march. Finally, the episodes of sleep we are positing may be quite short. Indeed, they may amount in some cases to no more than the 'microsleeps' described above.

The psychotic's eyes are open.

Oswald (1962) makes it clear that a subject may enter brief periods of sleep lasting a few seconds while his or her eyes remain open. He found experimentally that subjects exposed to repeated electric shocks, timed to synchronize with loud jazz music and bright lights flashing on and off in front of the subject's face, showed the electrophysiological signs of sleep even though their eyes were 'glued and strapped so widely open that the pupil remained exposed wherever the eye was turned' (p.154). He also notes that more protracted episodes of sleep with the eyes open may be observed in children, and adults suffering from dehydration.

---

* This idea would fit well with the model proposed by Claridge, Clark, and Davis (in press) to explain their recent findings concerning the enhanced susceptibility of schizotypes to nightmares and emotionally charged dream experiences of any kind, including enjoyable ones. They propose that such subjects are characterized by enhanced 'permeability' of the normal boundary between conscious and preconscious processes.

Psychotics do not think they are asleep.

As we have already noted, lack of insight may be shown by normal subjects following microsleeps. In addition, it is relevant to note the phenomenon of the 'false awakening', in which the subject believes that he or she has woken up when in fact they are still asleep and dreaming (Green and McCreery 1994). In one form of this experience, which Green (1968a) labelled a 'Type 2' false awakening, the subject even seems to wake in his or her bedroom, which may appear highly realistic, and may not identify the experience as hallucinatory and occurring during sleep until he or she has experienced the state several times and has worked out methods for identifying it (see McCreery (1973), p. 118, for an example).

Of particular interest in the present context is the fact that the phenomenology of the Type 2 false awakening shows a remarkable resemblance to that of the so-called 'primary delusory experience', as described by Jaspers (1923), for example. In both cases there is a sense of something 'uncanny' which the perceptual content of the experience alone appears insufficient to justify. As Jaspers puts it of the psychotic experience, 'Something seems in the air which the patient cannot account for, a distrustful, uncomfortable, uncanny tension invades him . . .' (p. 98). In the case of the Type 2 false awakening Green (1968a) writes, 'the subject appears to wake up in a realistic manner, but to an atmosphere of suspense . . . his surroundings may appear normal, and he may gradually become aware of something uncanny in the atmosphere' (p.121). This phenomenological similarity becomes more understandable if both experiences are correctly to be interpreted as occurring during a form of sleep.

EXPERIMENTAL EVIDENCE FOR THE MODEL

Weakened inhibition and the schizotypal nervous system

The episodes of hyperarousal which we have postulated to underlie psychosis might result from a number of different factors. In some cases they might result from purely environmental conditions, such as the chance misfortune of living for prolonged periods in an extremely traumatic situation. In other cases the aetiology might be purely genetic. One possible constitutional factor which might give rise to episodes of hyperarousal is that of relative weakness in inhibitory mechanisms. This is the factor postulated to underlie psychosis-proneness in Claridge's (1967) theory. In this model the essential feature underlying individual differences in psychoticism/schizotypy is a loosening of homeostatic controls in the nervous system, due to relative weakness of normal inhibitory mechanisms. This relative failure of homeostatic control is seen as liable to manifest itself in two distinct forms: first, as a tendency to lability of arousal; and secondly, as a tendency to 'uncoupling' of different functional arousal systems within the CNS. This dissociation of arousal between different functional subsystems may give rise to unusual patterning when two or more electrophysiological variables are considered concomitantly; for example a cortical and an autonomic one (Claridge and Chappa 1973; Claridge and Clark 1982).

We shall have occasion to refer to Claridge's model throughout the remainder of this chapter, as it fits both with the experimental data to be reported and with the theory of psychosis as outlined above. Clearly, people with labile nervous systems due to weakness of homeostatic mechanisms could be the very people who are liable to reach those levels of hyperarousal that precipitate episodes of sleep in waking life.

Dissociation of arousal in the two cerebral hemispheres

The hypothesis of weakened inhibition as a basic characteristic of the schizotypal nervous system has received experimental support from a number of different strands of research in recent years. Among these are the latent inhibition paradigm (Baruch *et al.* 1998 *a*, 1998 *b*; Lubow *et al.* 1992), experiments on negative priming (Beech and Claridge 1987; LaPlante *et al.* 1992), and semantic activation without conscious identification or SAWCI (Evans 1992). All of these are discussed elsewhere in this volume.

My own experimental data bearing on the question of inhibition in schizotypes were derived from a study in which forty subjects attempted to induce ecsomatic experiences in the laboratory, while their EEG and skin conductance level (SCL) were monitored. Twenty of the subjects were people who had experienced at least one OBE before, and the rest were matched controls who had not. The experimental procedure in which they participated may be characterized as a period of relaxation, followed by mild sensory limitation and an imagery task. Subjects lay on a garden lounger and wore goggles made of halved ping-pong balls over their eyes, while an angle-poise lamp containing a 100 W bulb shone on the goggles from a distance of 18 inches to give an even, white 'ganzfeld'. Over headphones they listened to a 20 minute relaxation tape, consisting of a series of physical relaxation exercises based on the Jacobsen (1929) method, followed by a series of mental relaxation exercises, such as imagining lying on a beach. Following the 20 minutes of relaxation, they were exposed to 10 minutes of 'pink' noise, on which was superimposed a sine wave with a frequency of 350Hz. The frequency of the sine wave was slightly different in the two ears, producing the effect of a rhythmic beat at a frequency of 4 Hz. During the 10 minute sound phase, subjects attempted to imagine they were floating up to the ceiling of the laboratory and looking down on their body lying below.

Four of the OBE group and one control endorsed a question designed to tap the occurrence of OBEs in this situation. In addition, all but five of the OBErs reported an anomalous perceptual experience of some kind, whereas only eight of the controls did so. These anomalous experiences ranged from peripheral entoptic phenomena to fully externalized hallucinations, such as the perception of a girl in a red dress sitting on the garden lounger (McCreery and Claridge 1996*a*).

The main electrophysiological finding of the experiment was one that bears on the question of dissociation of arousal between different functional subsystems within the central nervous system, one of the two phenomena predicted by the Claridge (1967) model of the psychosis-prone nervous system. In my experiment this idea of dissociation of arousal was extended to an area that was not originally envisaged by the Claridge theory, but which seemed an apt one in which to look for it, namely the question of the relationship between the two hemispheres of the brain. As Claridge and Broks (1984) point out, 'The hemispheres are indisputably separate functional-anatomic units—unlike intrahemispheric regions, which are relatively poorly specified.' Moreover, there is considerable evidence, from a variety of disciplines and methodologies, for a degree of functional differentiation between the two cerebral hemispheres (see Springer and Deutsch (1981) for a review).

The specific hypothesis to be tested was that ecsomatic experiences might be associated with a relative activation of the right hemisphere (RH). To this end, two EEG electrodes were placed on the sites F3 and F4, which are symmetrically located over the left and right frontal lobes. The prediction concerning relative RH activation was based on the known phenomenology of the OBE, as analysed by Green (1968b) and others. In particular, such experiences appear not to be predominantly verbal or analytical, but to consist rather in a passive contemplation of predominantly visual imagery. As Green (1968b) puts it, OBE subjects 'do not appear to feel inclined to engage in analytical thought; their attitude appears, generally, to be that of an alert but usually passive observer'. Since the left hemisphere (LH) in right-handers tends to be preferentially involved in verbal processing and the right in visuo-spatial (see, for example, Robbins and McAdam (1974); Risberg et al. (1975)), this would suggest that an ecsomatic experience may involve relative activation of the right, in comparison with the left. In addition it is worth mentioning that Fenwick (1984, 1987) suggests that the right temporal lobe might be particularly involved in the mediation of 'mystical' or ecstatic experience, and extremes of positive affect are sometimes reported in association with OBEs.

The measure of arousal in the two hemispheres was the median frequency (M50) of the EEG amplitude spectrum. This is a measure which seems previously only to have been used in anaesthesia research (Stoeckel et al. 1981; Schwilden and Stoeckel 1987). It is that frequency which divides the area of an EEG 'spectrum' in half, so that as much of the curve lies above as below it. The spectrum itself is derived by applying Fourier analysis to the original complex EEG wave, thereby breaking it down into its constituent components at each frequency from (in this case) 1–30 Hz. A plot of the amplitude of the wave on the y-axis against frequency on the x-axis gives the spectrum at any given moment. M50 is a sensitive index of arousal since if the amplitudes of the component waves increase at the higher frequencies, i.e. in the beta and alpha bands, while the amplitudes at the lower frequencies, in the theta and delta bands, decrease or remain constant, then the median frequency will rise. Conversely, if delta and/or theta frequencies increase in amplitude while alpha and/or beta decrease or remain constant, then M50 will fall. (Delta and theta frequencies are, in general, characteristic of sleep or the hypnagogic state, whereas alpha and beta frequencies are more characteristic of wakefulness and arousal.)

In the experiment under discussion there was a significant group difference in M50's response to the experimental procedure: the controls' two hemispheres moved in parallel throughout the experiment, whereas the OBErs showed a relative activation of the RH towards the end of the sound phase (McCreery and Claridge 1996*b*). I would interpret this as a result at the level of individual differences, rather than an electrophysiological correlate specific to the ecsomatic experience itself. I suggest that the relative proneness of the OBE group to hallucinations and imagery of a spontaneous and autonomous kind may be correlated with a long-term dispositional tendency to relative activation of the RH.

Hemispheric results of this kind are often explicable in terms of more than one hypothesis about the precise hemispheric relationship involved. For example, the present data could be explained either by a model in which the RH of schizotypes is constitutionally in a relatively hyperactive state, or in terms of one in which the 'rational', linguistic LH normally exerts an inhibitory influence over the more 'spatial', holistic RH, but does so less effectively in schizotypes. Whatever the preferred model, the data seem compatible with the hypothesis that a relative weakness of inhibitory mechanisms is a fundamental characteristic of the schizotypal nervous system. This interpretation is also consistent with the fact that there was a nearly significant main effect for group, with the OBErs tending to have the higher level of tonic arousal, as measured by M50, regardless of hemisphere. In both hemispheres the mean M50 of the OBE group remained consistently above that of the controls throughout the experiment.

Inhibitory mechanisms and the coherence function of the EEG

In addition to the median frequency measure studied in the experiment described, an index of the coherence function of the EEG was also calculated. This, too, produced a result consistent with the hypothesis of weakened inhibition in schizotypes. The coherence function between two EEG electrodes may be thought of as a measure of the extent to which the signals coming from two EEG channels remain 'locked' with respect to phase and amplitude over time. A high value for the coherence function implies that the phase and amplitude relations between the two channels have remained relatively constant over the time period in question, while a low one implies the opposite. It should be noted that changes in the phase relationship contribute relatively more powerfully to changes in the coherence function than do changes in the amplitude relationship. There is some discussion as to whether high coherence values can be taken to imply a common source for the signals at the two electrode sites in question. Shaw *et al.* (1979) write: 'Sometimes the implication is that electrical dependence implies a structural connectivity, but other workers are more cautious, suggesting that only a functional coupling is implied.'

In my experiment, the forty subjects exposed to the experimental procedure described earlier showed a positive correlation of 0.4 between STA score and coherence in the alpha band at the end of the sound phase. Shaw *et al.* (1979), who in their study found higher coherence values in schizophrenics than controls, put forward a model of 'dysfunction of inhibitory mechanisms' to explain their results. They suggested that other studies of EEG coherence also 'suggest a model in which increased coherence is compatible with a more diffuse organisation of cortical function'. I suggest that my own data would fit with the idea that in schizotypes excitation may 'spill over' between spatially separated points, due to relative weakness of inhibitory mechanisms.

Cortical and muscular dissociation in the ecsomatic state

I was not able to find any unusual pattern of co-variation between cortical (M50) and autonomic (SCL) measures in my data, perhaps because of the relatively short time-scale of 30 minutes over which the measurements were made, or perhaps because I was looking for intra-individual divergences between the two measures, whereas the Claridge studies mentioned above were looking at *inter*-individual comparisons. However, there was an interesting indication in my experiment that OBErs are people with a tendency towards dissociation between cortical and *muscular* activation. Subjects were required, both before and after the experimental procedure, to rate their degree of physical relaxation on an analogue scale which ranged from 'As if in bed, just about to fall asleep' (scored 0) to 'Extremely tense, as before an exam' (scored 100). A statistically significant group-difference emerged on this measure. The two groups, OBErs and controls, started out with essentially the same mean physical relaxation score at the start of the experiment, but followed strikingly different courses over time. The OBErs ended the experiment more physically relaxed on average, while the controls rated themselves more tense. This finding presents an interesting contrast with the cortical measure, M50, where it was the OBErs who showed the tendency to greater arousal at the end of the experiment, at least in the right hemisphere, whereas the controls became less aroused in both hemispheres.

I suggest that this finding is compatible with the idea that schizotypes are people with a tendency to enter 'paradoxical' states of high cortical but low muscular activation. The finding fits with what is known of OBEs in their natural setting, from retrospective questionnaire studies. Green (1968b) found that nearly three quarters of a group of 176 subjects reporting a single OBE were lying down at the time of the experience, and 33 per cent rated themselves as having been more muscularly relaxed than usual whereas only 11 per cent rated themselves more tense. At the same time, more than half of the 176 subjects rated themselves as having been more awake and keenly observant than usual.

Meditation and dissociation of arousal

There was a further piece of evidence in my data for the proposition that schizotypes are people with a tendency to dissociation of arousal in different subsystems of the CNS. This concerns the prevalence of meditation practices among the OBErs. 44 per cent were regular or occasional meditators, as compared with only 31 per cent of the controls. Moreover, there was a significant positive association between incidence of meditation and number of reported OBEs. The number of regular meditators, in particular, increased with increasing number of OBEs reported.

It is worth noting here that McCreery and Green (1986) found that the practice of meditation was a significant predictor of hallucinatory experiences of another kind in a normal population. They carried out a follow-up study of subjects who had reported at least one experience of perceiving an 'apparition'. They found that 37 per cent of those who had gone on to have at least one further experience of this kind during a 10 year period were meditators, compared with only 18 per cent of those who reported no further hallucinatory experience of this kind during the period.

How do we explain this association between meditation and tendency to hallucinate? There is some electrophysiological evidence that meditation, in at least some of its forms, is a 'paradoxical' state of relatively high cortical arousal accompanied by extreme muscular relaxation (Das and Gastaut 1957; Wallace 1970). I suggest that if happy schizotypes are people with a constitutional tendency to dissociation of arousal, then this means that they are relatively liable to enter this paradoxical state, either spontaneously, as in an OBE, or more deliberately, as in meditation.

It is worth noting that there are a number of links between the ecsomatic and the meditative states. OBEs are often preceded by a state of sensory de-afferentation and muscular relaxation, two conditions which characterize many forms of meditation. Moreover, once established, the ecsomatic state seems to have some phenomenological similarity to meditative states. As we have already noted above, the OBE subject tends not to engage in much serial, analytical thought, but is occupied rather in the relatively passive contemplation of imagery. Similarly, the meditation subject is often preoccupied with the contemplation of a visual image, whether external or internal, this procedure being aimed at the suppression of the normal associative processes.

It is interesting to speculate as to whether meditation may involve relative dissociation, not only between cortical and muscular activation, but also between left and right hemispheres. Certainly the phenomenology of meditation, with the avoidance of serial analytical thought, might suggest this hypothesis. Moreover, Fenwick (1987) argues for the particular involvement of the right hemisphere in meditative states, on the grounds that the RH limbic system is particularly implicated in 'ecstatic' experiences, including those which occur in connection with certain cases of right temporal-lobe epilepsy.

Finally, it is interesting to note one further connection between OBEs and the meditative state, and this is the fact that they may actually occur together. Some habitual OBErs employ meditation as a tool in the deliberate induction of OBEs (Green 1968*b*), and ecsomatic experiences sometimes appear to be the accidental by-product of the practice of meditation, as in the following example:

'I was meditating. I used to sit with a group of friends once a week . . . I suddenly found myself standing at the side of my chair watching myself meditating. It was only for a minute or so and then I went back.'

Lability of arousal in schizotypes

So far we have concentrated on data suggestive of dissociation of arousal in presenting evidence for the hypothesis of weakened inhibition in the schizotypal nervous system. We shall now consider some evidence for the other prediction of the Claridge (1967) theory, namely lability. The idea that lability of arousal might be a feature of the nervous system of psychosis-prone individuals has previously received support from experimental observations that groups of schizophrenics show greater variance than controls on many electrophysiological measures. This enhanced variability may take the form of both between-subjects and within-subjects variation. In other words the same schizophrenic subject may show enhanced variability from test to retest, or a group of schizophrenics may show greater variability from one subject to another than a group of controls. As Claridge (personal communication) puts it, the only predictable thing about schizophrenics is their unpredictability.

In my own data there was evidence for both forms of increased variability. With regard to the first form—intra-subject variability—it was found that the cortical measure, M50, showed greater within-subject variability over time in OBErs than controls. This was demonstrated in the fact that there were lower correlations between successive measures in the OBE group than the controls. For example, in the correlation matrix for the six successive measures of M50 in the left hemisphere (each measure representing the averaging of data over a 5 minute period), only two of the fifteen possible correlations fell below 0.8 in the control group, whereas in the OBE group eleven of the fifteen correlations did so. A similar result emerged when comparison was made between the two matrices for the RH and also when correlations across hemispheres and over time were considered. These contrasting correlation matrices suggested a picture of greater instability or lability over time in the OBE group.

The other variable in my data that fitted the hypothesis of lability of arousal in schizotypes was the 'slope' of skin conductance level during the sound phase of the experiment. The SCL slope was computed by plotting the data points for this 10 minute period against time and calculating a regression line for each subject. Within-subject slope variables of this kind have the advantage of being independent of the absolute values of the physiological variables being measured. An example is the slope variable computed by Birchall and Claridge (1979) in relating visual evoked amplitude to stimulus intensity. In my data there was a significantly greater variance of slopes among the OBErs than among the controls. In other words there was a tendency for the the skin conductance level of the OBErs to vary more markedly over the course of the sound phase than that of the controls. This tendency was regardless of sign; the subjects might be showing either an increase or a decrease of SCL over time (McCreery and Claridge 1996*b*).

It is interesting to compare these results with the observation by Gruzelier and Venables (1972), and others, of a bimodal distribution when groups of schizophrenics are examined on measures of SCL responsiveness and habituation to non-informational stimuli such as tones. It is found that schizophrenics may be either hypo- or hyper-responsive to the tone, either not showing the normal orienting response at all, or, if they show it, not habituating to it on repeated exposure as normal subjects tend to do. Moreover, Claridge and Clark (1982) found that schizophrenics, if tested on more than one occasion, might be hypo-responsive on one occasion and hyper-responsive on another. I believe that these phenomena may be evidence for the present hypothesis concerning psychosis and sleep. Oswald (1962) writes as follows concerning the progress of the GSR (galvanic skin response) as an individual falls asleep:

The interesting thing about the human GSR was that, having disappeared as the individual fell asleep, we found it often returned as cortical vigilance fell even lower . . . not only did the GSRs return during medium or deep sleep in eight of our nineteen subjects but they disappeared again as cortical vigilance rose (p. 34).

I suggest that the variability of schizophrenics with respect to the GSR might be due to the fact that, unlike normal subjects, they are liable to marked qualitative changes of state, from waking to sleeping and vice versa, even during daylight hours. On any given day some members of a schizophrenic subject group might be liable to the intrusion of sleep processes during testing and some not, depending on whether they were in that state of hyperarousal which we have suggested may trigger the sleep state. This could account for the presence of both hypo- and hyper-responders in the same group. Moreover, on repeated testing, a particular subject might or might not be at the same phase of the sleep process, and thus might have changed from being a hypo- to being a hyper-responder, or vice versa.

Migraine and lability of arousal

A further indication of the relevance to schizotypy of arousability in general, and lability of arousal in particular, concerns the incidence of migraine among my happy schizotypes. Among the 450 OBErs 41 per cent claimed to be migraine sufferers, whereas among the 234 controls only 23 per cent did so—a highly significant difference. There was also a significant association between the number of OBEs a person reported and the incidence of migraine, with the proportion of migraine-sufferers increasing as the number of reported OBEs increased.

The case for migraine being essentially a disorder of arousal has been eloquently made by Sacks (1970). He characterizes a migraine attack as a 'centrencephalic seizure', originating in the mid-brain, and played out over a time-period of hours or days. Indeed Sacks goes so far as to draw an analogy between migraine and certain forms of psychosis, with regard to fluctuations of arousal:

The sequence of a full-fledged migraine . . . has essentially two stages: a stage of excitation or arousal, followed by a protracted stage of inhibition or 'dearousal'.

It is. in these terms that we may first perceive the proximity of the migraine cycle to that of epilepsy, on the one hand, and to the more leisurely cycles of waking and sleep, on the other; the prominent affective components of migraines demand comparison, more remotely, with the excitatory and inhibitory phases of some psychoses. (p.131)

I would add that dissociation of arousal between the two hemispheres may also be an underlying feature of migraine, since one-sided pain is almost a defining characteristic of the disorder. As Rose and Davies (1987) put it: 'A disturbance in one cerebral hemisphere could produce one-sided symptoms and a one-sided headache.' They point out that in addition to one-sided pain, there may also be loss of vision from just one half of the visual field and 'pins and needles' on just one side of the body.

Also significant for our present thesis is the association of migraine with hallucinations. The model I have proposed suggests a direct link between hyperarousal and hallucination, via the mechanism of sleep. If migraine is rightly to be regarded as a disorder of arousal, including episodes of heightened arousal as Sacks implies, then it is perhaps not surprising that hallucinations, and other anomalous perceptual experiences of various kinds, are sometimes to be found in association with migraine attacks. These anomalous perceptual experiences even include on occasion ecsomatic experiences, as Eastman (1962) pointed out. She drew attention to a paper by Lippman (1953) in which are discussed a number of examples of body-image distortions associated with migraine attacks; among them is the following:

While performing some accustomed mechanical action I will find myself in two places at once. I have the distinct impression that I am two people; one is going through the actions of eating, reading or sitting down, etc; the other 'me' is suspended up and above to one side, perceiving or contemplating myself in a detached sort of way. The impression comes and goes in a flash.

In the present model, schizotypy represents a tendency to episodes of hyperarousal. If migraine attacks also represent episodes of hyperarousal, as Sacks suggests, then it would make sense to expect schizotypes to be more prone to attacks of migraine than controls, and to expect such attacks to be occasionally accompanied by OBEs and other hallucinatory phenomena.

Age, arousability, and hallucinations

A final observation relevant to the model proposed here concern the age of subjects reporting different numbers of OBEs. One might expect that the older a person might be, the more out-of-the-body experiences he or she will tend to report, on the grounds that they have simply had longer in which to experience them. However, in my sample it was found that the more OBEs a subject reported the younger he or she was likely to be.

This somewhat paradoxical finding actually fits well with the model of psychosis in general, and the mechanism of ecsomatic experiences in particular, put forward above. On the present view schizotypy consists in a constitutional tendency to hyperarousal, leading to episodes of sleep intruding into waking life. In the case of isolated hallucinatory episodes such as OBEs, these may be supposed to occur, either to low schizotypes who happen to be exposed to an extreme of environmental stress, or to high schizotypes who are constitutionally predisposed to episodes of hyperarousal, even in the absence of environmental triggering factors. The high schizotype group may be expected to have already had a number of OBEs even at a relatively young age, whereas the low schizotypes may only ever have one, and its occurrence might be at any point in their life, depending on when the extreme environmental stress occurs. On this model we might expect to find, if we examine a population of OBE subjects who belong in a high age bracket, a relatively high proportion of people reporting a single OBE, simply because people in that age bracket have had longer to be exposed by chance to an extremely traumatic environmental situation. To test this hypothesis an analysis was made of the proportion of subjects in each age-band (16–29, 30–39, etc.) who reported a given number of OBEs, and it was found that there were indeed a significantly increasing number of people reporting a single experience as the age-band rose.

CONCLUSION

The model of the aetiology of psychosis developed in this chapter is summarized in Fig. 12.2. Arrows indicate the existence and direction of postulated causal influence. The genetic underpinning of the phenomenon is suggested to be a relative weakness of inhibitory mechanisms in the brain, following Claridge's (1967) theory. Its phenotypic expression is a lability of arousal. This interacts with environmental triggers to produce episodes of excessive arousal, which in turn lead to sleep. These intrusions of sleep into everyday consciousness may be individually short-lived, but give rise to the characteristic phenomenology of psychosis, shared with the dreaming state, such as hallucinations, delusions, and autism.

A specific advantage of the present model is that it explains an otherwise paradoxical finding concerning one manifestation of psychosis, catatonia. This is the fact that catatonia can be successfully treated with sedatives rather than stimulants. Stevens and Derbyshire (1958), for example, found that catatonic subjects initially became behaviourally more active with the administration of the sedative amobarbitol, before finally falling asleep in the normal way in response to an increase in dosage. They concluded that catatonia was a state of 'inner

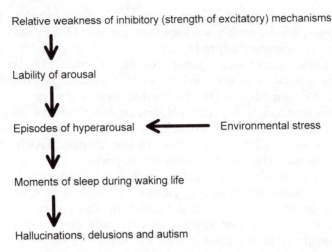

Relative weakness of inhibitory (strength of excitatory) mechanisms

Lability of arousal

Episodes of hyperarousal ⟵ Environmental stress

Moments of sleep during waking life

Hallucinations, delusions and autism

Fig. 12.2.   A model of the aetiology of psychosis.

seething excitement' despite the apparent inhibition of activity. I suggest that this apparent inhibition is a phenomenon of sleep, but triggered by a state of hyperarousal rather than relaxation.

The present model is compatible with the idea of some form of continuity between the various forms of psychosis. For example, it would fit with Eysenck's proposal that there is only one underlying form of madness, which takes different forms according to the individual's position on various long-term dimensions of personality (Eysenck 1992). This '*Einheitpsychose*' model, discussed elsewhere in this volume, is supported by a number of different sorts of empirical observation, such as the apparent genetic linkage between the two main forms of psychosis, with manic-depressive individuals being over-represented among the relatives of schizophrenics; the frequent interchangeability of the two main diagnoses when a single patient is considered over a sufficient time-span (Claridge *et al.* 1990); and the difficulty of allocating some individuals to one category or another, so that resort is made to the hybrid diagnosis of 'schizoaffective disorder'.

Finally, the present model is also compatible with the episodic and fluctuating nature of psychosis. If the basis of the disorder is a tendency to hyperarousal, one can imagine that the resulting symptomatology, such as hallucinations and delusions, might be present at some periods of an individual's life and absent at others, as the tonic level of arousal varied with changing life circumstances or other more 'internal' factors. In particular, the model would be compatible with the apparent reversibility of the psychotic process, even after decades of active psychosis, a phenomenon stressed by Manfred Bleuler (1968).

REFERENCES

Aserinsky, E. and Kleitman, N. (1953). Regularly occurring periods of eye motility, and concomitant phenomena, during sleep. *Science*, 118, 273–4.

Baruch, I., Hemsley, D. R., and Gray, J. A. (1988 *a*). Differential performance of acute and chronic schizophrenics in a latent inhibition task. *Journal of Nervous and Mental Disease*, 176, 598–606.

Baruch, I., Hemsley, D. R., and Gray, J. A. (1988 *b*). Latent inhibition and 'psychotic proneness' in normal subjects. *Personality and Individual Differences*, 9, 777–83.

Beech, A. R. and Claridge, G. S. (1987). Individual differences in negative priming: Relations with schizotypal personality traits. *British Journal of Clinical Psychology*, 78, 349–56.

Bentall, R. P., Claridge, G., and Slade, P. D. (1989). The multi-dimensional nature of schizotypal traits: a factor analytic study with normal subjects. *British Journal of Clinical Psychology*, 28, 363–75.

Birchall, P. M. A. and Claridge, G. S. (1979). Augmenting-reducing of the visual evoked potential as a function of changes in skin conductance level. *Psychophysiology*, 16, 482–90.

Bleuler, E. (1911). *Dementia Praecox or the group of schizophrenias* (trans. J. Zinkin). International Universities Press, New York (1950).

Bleuler, M. (1968). A 23-year longitudinal study of 208 schizophrenics and impressions in regard to the nature of sczhizophrenia. In *The transmission of schizophrenia* (ed. D. Rosenthal and S. S. Kety), pp. 3–12. Pergamon, London.

Chapman, L. J., Chapman, J. P., and Raulin, M. L. (1976). Scales for physical and social anhedonia. *Journal of Abnormal Psychology*, 85, 374–82.

Chapman, L. J., Chapman, J. P., and Raulin, M. L. (1978). Body-image aberration in schizophrenia. *Journal of Abnormal Psychology*, 87, 399–407.

Claridge, G. S. (1967). *Personality and arousal*. Pergamon, Oxford.

Claridge, G. S. (1994). Single indicator of risk for schizophrenia: probable fact or likely myth? *Schizophrenia Bulletin*, 20, 151–68.

Claridge, G. S. and Broks, P. (1984). Schizotypy and hemisphere function—I. Theoretical considerations and the measurement of schizotypy. *Personality & Individual Differences*, 5, 633–48.

Claridge, G. S. and Chappa, H. J. (1973). Psychoticism: A study of its biological basis in normal subjects. *British Journal of Social and Clinical Psychology*, 12, 175–87.

Claridge, G. S. and Clark, K. H. (1982). Covariation between two-flash threshold and skin conductance level in first-breakdown schizophrenics: Relationships in drug-free patients and effects of treatment. *Psychiatry Research*, 6, 371–80.

Claridge, G. S., Clark, K. H., and Davis, C. Nightmares, dreams and schizotypy. *British Journal of Clinical Psychology*. (In press.)

Claridge, G. S., Pryor, R., and Watkins, G. (1990). *Sounds from the bell jar: ten psychotic authors*. Macmillan, Basingstoke.

Cutting, J. (1985). *The psychology of schizophrenia*. Churchill Livingstone, Edinburgh.

Das, N. N. and Gastaut, H. (1957). Variations de l'activitié électrique du cerveau, du coeur et des muscles squelettiques au cours de la méditation et de l'extase yogique, in *Conditionnement et réactivité en Electroencéphalograhie*, Suppl. No. 6 of *Electroencephalography & Clinical Neurophysiology*, 211–19.

Eastman, M. (1962). Out-of-the-body experiences. *Proceedings of the Society for Psychical Research*, 53, 287–309.

Eckblad, M. and Chapman, L. J. (1983). Magical ideation as an indicator of schizotypy. *Journal of Consulting and Clinical Psychology*, 51, 215–25.

Eckblad, M. and Chapman, L. J. (1986). Development and validation of a scale for hypomanic personality. *Journal of Abnormal Personality*, 95, 217–33.

Evans, J. L. (1992). Schizotypy and preconscious processing. Unpublished D. Phil. thesis. University of Oxford.

Eysenck, H. J. (1992). The definition and meaning of psychoticism. *Personality and Individual Differences*, 13, 757–85.

Eysenck, H. J. and Eysenck, S. B. G. (1975). *Manual of the Eysenck Personality Questionnaire*. Hodder and Stoughton, London.

Feinberg, I. (1970). Hallucinations, dreaming and REM sleep. In *Origin and mechanisms of hallucinations* (ed. W. Keup), pp. 125–32. Plenum Press, New York.

Fenwick, P. (1984). Some aspects of the physiology of mystical experience. In J. Nicholson and B. Foss (eds.) *Psychological Survey*, 4.

Fenwick, P. (1987). Meditation and the EEG. In *The psychology of meditation* (ed. M.A. West). Clarendon Press, Oxford:

Flor-Henry, P. (1979). Laterality, shifts of cerebral dominance, sinistrality and psychosis. In *Hemisphere asymmetries of function in psychopathology* (ed. J. Gruzelier and P. Flor-Henry). Elsevier/North-Holland Biomedical Press, Amsterdam.

Foulkes, D. and Fleisher, S. (1975). Mental activity in relaxed wakefulness. *Journal of Abnormal Psychology*, 84, 66–75.

Foulkes, D. and Vogel, G. (1965). Mental activity at sleep onset. *Journal of Abnormal Psychology*, 70, 231–43.

Green, C. E. (1968a). *Lucid dreams*. Hamish Hamilton, London.

Green, C. E. (1968b). *Out-of-the-body experiences*. Hamish Hamilton, London.

Green, C. and McCreery, C. (1975). *Apparitions*. Hamish Hamilton, London.

Green, C. and McCreery, C. (1994). *Lucid dreaming: the paradox of consciousness during sleep*. Routledge, London.

Gruzelier, J. H. and Venables, P. H. (1972). Skin conductance orienting activity in a heterogeneous sample of schizophrenics. *Journal of Nervous and Mental Disease*, 155, 277–87.

Irwin H. J. (1985). *Flight of mind: A psychological study of the out-of-body experience*. Scarecrow Press, Metuchen, New Jersey.

Jacobsen, E. (1929). *Progressive relaxation: A physiological and clinical investigation of muscular states and their significance in psychology and medical practice*. University of Chicago Press, Chicago, Illinois.

Jaspers, K. (1923). *General psychopathology* (trans. J. Hoenig and M. W. Hamilton). Manchester University Press, Manchester. (First published in Germany, 1923, as *Allgemeine pathologie*.)

Jung, C. G. (1909). *The psychology of dementia praecox* (trans. F. Peterson and A. A. Brill. The Journal of Nervous and Mental Disease Publishing Company, New York.

La Barre, W. (1975). Anthropological perspectives on hallucination and hallucinogens. In *Hallucinations: Behavior, experience, and theory* (ed. R. K. Siegel and L.J. West). Wiley, New York.

Laplante, L., Everett, J., and Thomas, J. (1992). Inhibition through negative priming with Stroop stimuli in schizophrenia. *British Journal of Clinical Psychology*, 31, 307–26.

Launay, G. and Slade, P. (1981). The measurement of hallucinatory predisposition in male and female prisoners. *Personality and Individual Differences*, 2, 221–34.

Lippman, C. W. (1953). Hallucinations of physical duality in migraine. *Journal of Nervous and Mental Disease*, 117, 345–50.

Lubow, R. E., Ingberg-Sachs, Y., Zalstein-Orda, N., and Gewirtz, J. C. (1992). Latent inhibition in low and high 'psychotic-prone' normal subjects. *Personality and Individual Differences*, 13, 563–72.

McCreery, C. (1973). *Psychical phenomena and the physical world*. Hamish Hamilton, London.

McCreery, C. (1993). Schizotypy and out-of-the-body experiences. Unpublished D. Phil. thesis. University of Oxford.

McCreery, C. and Claridge, G. (1995). Out-of-the-body experiences a.. I personality. *Journal of the Society for Psychical Research*, 60, 129–48.

McCreery, C. and Claridge, G. (1996a). A study of hallucination in normal subjects—I: self-report data. *Personality and Individual Differences*, 21, 739–47

McCreery, C. and Claridge, G. (1996b). A study of hallucination in normal subjects—II: electrophysiological data. *Personality and Individual Differences*, 21, 749–58.

McCreery, C. and Green, C. (1986). A follow-up study of people reporting apparitional experiences. Unpublished MS.

McKellar, P. (1989). *Abnormal psychology: Its experience and behaviour*. Routledge, London.

Mavromatis, A. (1987). *Hypnagogia: The unique state of consciousness between wakefulness and sleep*. Routledge, London.

Oswald, I. (1959). Experimental studies of rhythm, anxiety and cerebral vigilance. *Journal of Mental Science*, 105, 269–94.

Oswald, I. (1962). *Sleeping and waking: Physiology and psychology*. Elsevier, Amsterdam.

Risberg, J., Halsey, J. H., Wills, E. L., and Wilson, E. M. (1975). Hemispheric specialization in normal man studied by bilateral measurements of the regional cerebral blood flow: A study with the 133-Xe inhalation technique. *Brain*, 98, 511–24.

Robbins, P. R. (1988). *The psychology of dreams*. McFarland, Jefferson, North Carolina.

Robbins, K. I and McAdam, D. W. (1974). Interhemispheric alpha asymmetry and imagery mode. *Brain and Language*, 1, 189–93.

Rose, C. and Davies, P. (1987). *Answers to migraine*. Macdonald, London.

Sacks, O. (1970). *Migraine*. Faber and Faber, London.

Sarbin T. R. (1967). The concept of hallucination. *Journal of personality*, 35, 359–80.

Schacter D. L. (1976). The hypnagogic state: a critical review of the literature. *Psychological Bulletin*, 83, 452–81.

Schwilden, H. and Stoeckel, H. (1987). Quantitative EEG analysis during anaesthesia with isoflurane in nitrous oxide at 1.3 and 1.5 mac. *British Journal of Anaesthesia*, 59, 738–45.

Shaw, J. C., Brooks, S., Colter, N., and O'Connor, K. P. (1979). A comparison of schizophrenic and neurotic patients using EEG power and coherence spectra. In *Hemisphere asymmetries of function in psychopathology* (ed. J. Gruzelier and P. Flor-Henry), pp. 257–83. Elsevier/North-Holland Biomedical Press.

Slade, P. D. and Bentall, R. P. (1988). *Sensory deception*. Croom Helm, London.

Sponheim, S. R., Clementz, B. A., Iacono, W. G., and Beiser, M. (1994). Resting EEG in first-episode and chronic schizophrenia. *Psychophysiology*, 31, 37–43.

Springer, S. P. and Deutsch, G. (1981). *Left brain, right brain* (revised edn). W. H. Freeman, New York.

Stevens, J. M. and Derbyshire, A. J. (1958). Shifts along the alert-repose continuum during remission of catatonic 'stupor' with amobarbitol. *Psychosomatic Medicine*, 20, 99–107.

Stoeckel, H., Schwilden, H., Lauven, P., and Schüttler, J. (1981). EEG parameters for evaluation of depth of anaesthesia. *Proceedings of the European Academy of Anaesthesiology*, In (ed M. Vickers 75–84. Springer-Verlag, Berlin.

Wallace, R. K. (1970). Physiological effects of transcendental meditation. *Science*, 167, 1751–4.

13
Creativity and schizotypy

J. H. BROD

DOES MADNESS UNDERLIE CREATIVITY?

Is there a causal relationship between states of 'madness' and concurrent acts of creativity? Do you *have* to be 'mad' to be creative? Could you be *more* creative if you were able, somehow, to hurl yourself into the depths of 'madness'? Of course not! The answer is 'no' to all three questions. States of 'madness', or, to use a less 'folksy' term, psychosis, involve a number of severely debilitating symptoms which tend to disable many of the cognitive, affective, and behavioural processes required for intelligently adaptive functioning in general. This includes creative functioning, unless your view of creativity is one which does not involve any discernible end product, or unless your criteria for judging an end product as creative do not include, in addition to novelty or originality, the notion of aptness, appropriateness, or whatever equivalent term within the aims and standards of a particular field of endeavour might be used to denote the 'fittingness' of that product (Glover *et al.* 1989).

Symptoms of states of full-blown psychosis can include wildly disordered and chaotic thinking, or, alternatively, tightly constricted, obsessive thinking such that any information unrelated to the focus of the obsession is either ignored or distorted to become incorporated into it: hallucinations, delusions, and paranoia; agitated hyperactivity, or lack of energy and volitional activity; and extreme anxiety, listlessness, or anhedonia. Although some of the symptoms listed can lead to frenetic cognitive activity, the diffuse and changeable attentional focus accompanying this energetic drive will result, either in an inability to pursue one direction of activity to its conclusion, or, alternatively, the end product will lack a number of qualities constituting organization, comprehensibility, and general appropriateness.

COULD THE PRODUCTS OF MADNESS BE CREATIVE?

There are, perhaps, some areas of creative endeavour where the lack of these qualities in an end product is either less noticeable, or less open to public argument or dismissal. For example, the processes and products in modern dance, or in some forms of art, tend to be fairly opaque to non-experts. From a non-expert and cynical point of view, it seems entirely possible that someone might offer an exhibit entitled 'Reflections on Non-reflection', consisting of a dead hedgehog upside down in a chamber pot, underneath a tilted mirror—and have it hailed as a creative product. In the view of the general public, this might well be seen as quite unintelligible, and quite possibly the product of some form of madness.

However, a product is creative or not by virtue, at the very least, of its comparative relation to other products, past and present, within a domain. Furthermore, it could be argued that domains themselves have meaning and relevance by virtue of how they stand in relation to the goals and products of other domains. Thus, the comparison and evaluation of a product leading to judgements about value, worth, and creativity must necessarily proceed on the basis of a hierarchy of criteria: some local, or particular to the domain— its history, structure, levels of complexity, goals, and internal dynamics (let us call it 'Domain Network Dynamic')—and others which are more global, or superordinate (although possibly more implicit), relating to the interaction between the domain and its products, and the messages and contents of other domains ('Interdomain Network Dynamic').

To return to the hedgehog and chamber pot example, it is arguable that whether or not this exhibit is judged creative would depend upon at least three factors: first, whether the judge is generally capable of understanding and appreciating symbolic ideas; secondly, the nature of the relationship, or of the fit, between the symbolic messages conveyed by the example and its Domain Network Dynamic; and thirdly, the nature of the relationship, or of the fit, between the symbolic messages conveyed by the example and its Interdomain Network Dynamic.

Presumably, some areas of creative endeavour appear more opaque than others to non-experts, either because they involve symbolic representations, thus bringing individual differences into play in terms of a general ability to process symbolic material; or because one cannot perceive their Interdomain Network Dynamic. However, the preceding arguments do militate against a domain-expert judgement of creativity for the products of psychotic functioning where, to repeat, if there is a finished product, it will in all probability lack a number of qualities constituting organization, comprehensibility, and general appropriateness. That is, if a product is disorganized, incomprehensible, and inappropriate in terms of its Domain Network Dynamic, it is unlikely to be a creative product, even though it might be original or unique.

HOW THEN IS PSYCHOSIS LINKED TO CREATIVITY?

If full-blown psychotic states preclude concurrent creativity, what is one to make of the wealth of literature presented further on in this chapter, suggesting a relationship between the two? A number of researchers (for example Prentky 1980, 1989; Claridge *et al.* 1990; Eysenck 1993, 1994) have already pointed out, in different ways, that the relationship is not between actual psychosis and creativity, but, rather, between 'schizotypy' or 'psychoticism' and creativity. In other words, the putative link is with non-clinical expressions

of schizotypal temperament and information processing style, along a personality dimension that leads from 'normality' at one end, through differently weighted combinations of schizotypal traits, towards full-blown psychosis at the other end. The point is made again here, because it seems,
as yet, not to have permeated the comprehension of many researchers, both
within the field of creativity research and outside it. One possible reason
for this confusion is that the terms 'schizotypy' and 'psychoticism' are too
similar to the terms used to denote actual states of mental illness, and therefore their use automatically activates concepts and images which cloud the
understanding.

The notions of originality and creative insight are as highly prized in the
scientific community as they are in the arts. Nevertheless, the conservative
attitudes and values of the former community, together with its intellectual
and emotional detachment from the human being (or equivalent nervous system)
that is the subject of theory and experimentation in academic psychology, appear
inevitably to demand that creativity be linked with the folk-psychological concepts
of 'stability' and 'control'. Against such a background, it may be difficult for
many researchers, in considering the nature of creativity, to distinguish between
psychopathology and its non-clinical manifestations, since both may be viewed
in the same prejudicial light.

The construct of schizotypy employed here refers to a set of behavioural,
affective, and cognitive 'eccentricities' which, in addition to forming some of
the underpinnings for episodes of psychotic illness, also exist in the normal
population at a non-clinical level. It is also assumed that there is a necessary
(backward) connection between actual psychotic illness and schizotypy, but
no necessary (forward) connection between schizotypy and actual psychotic
illness. In other words, a person can have above average to high scores
on one or several of the schizotypy scales and never develop a psychotic
illness. This will not depend just upon an interaction between schizotypy
and psychological stressors, but also upon a number of other interacting
influences.

Indeed, the notion of schizotypy as a single normally distributed dimension
of personality shading into psychosis at one end of the continuum would,
perhaps, be better represented and understood as a set of genetically-weighted
information processing and temperamental vectors, interacting with one another,
and with other vectors for temperament, information processing, and physical
and psychological environmental factors, to provide many different matrices
of potential outcomes in schizotypal personality, cognitive style, and mental health.

These different matrices might also be expected to result in different levels
of probability for creative talent and expression, and perhaps different types
of creative potential within schizotypal subtypes. Unfortunately, despite the
bulk of evidence for a general relationship between creativity and schizotypal
traits, very little work has been carried out that might elucidate which *particular* sets of interacting influences (or vectors), from within and outside

the range of schizotypal traits, might give rise to which *particular* creative outcomes.

EVIDENCE FOR THE LINK

The 'wealth of literature', mentioned earlier, that reveals some link between creativity and psychopathology, though not its actual nature, includes a few familial-genetic and experimental studies, and a great deal of anecdotal, biographical, and psychobiographical evidence. Both Plato and Aristotle suggested a relationship between artistic creation and madness, and this view has persisted down the ages, partly fostered by a notion of creativity as involving divine intervention or dictate, i.e. some kind of mystical, mysterious, and inchoate eruption from the 'sea of unconsciousness', the supposed communicative interface between man and the gods, from which madness was also, popularly, thought to emerge. By the nineteenth century, however, this view was superseded in the literature by a conception of creativity as allied to degeneracy and inferior genes. Such genes could also give rise to early death, criminality, or lunacy (Babcock 1895), the latter now regarded in a totally negative and contemptuous light.

From the anecdotal, biographical, and psychobiographical evidence it is possible to derive a very long list of so-called geniuses and eminent achievers in the fields of art, literature, poetry, musical composition, philosophy, science, and politics, all of whom are recorded as having displayed aberrant, borderline, or psychotic behaviours, including actual episodes of psychotic illness, and some suicides or suicide attempts (Alston 1972; Becker 1978; Bell 1972; Broad 1981; Bychowski 1973; Claridge *et al.* 1990; Dale 1952; Edel 1975; Ellrich 1974; Gibson 1889; Goertzel *et al.* 1978: Grant 1968; Holton 1978; Jamison 1993; Juda 1949; Karlsson 1978; Krebs & Shelley 1975; Lange-Eichbaum 1932; Larkin 1970; Lélut 1836; Lombroso 1891, 1910; Ludwig 1992; Martindale 1972, 1990; Murphy 1979; Nisbet 1912; Nordau 1900; Pickering 1974; Post 1994; Reichsman 1981; Robinson 1977; Solomon 1975; Storr 1976; Trethowan 1977; Trilling 1950; Tsanoff 1949; Winslow 1971). The names of these eminent achievers are too numerous to mention, but a few examples from each category are as follows. Artists: Goya, Michelangelo, Monet, Picasso, Van Gogh; writers and poets: Balzac, Blake, Byron, Coleridge, Conrad, Kafka, Plath, Proust, Shelley, Woolf; composers: Chopin, Handel, Schumann, Beethoven, Wagner; philosophers: Buber, Heidegger, Nietzsche, Schopenhauer, Wittgenstein; scientists: Darwin, Einstein, Faraday, Helmholz, Mayer; and politicians: Churchill, Disraeli, Hitler, Mussolini, Stalin.

Retrospective diagnoses and descriptions of gifted individuals in the lists include schizophrenia, paranoia, depression, hypomania, manic-depression, cyclothymia, schizoaffective illness, borderline personality disorder, psychopathy, neurosis, hysteria, megalomania, narcissism, compulsions, and hypochondria. Many of these individuals were said to suffer from (one or several of) hallucinations, delusions, violent rages, extreme anxiety, poor socialization, and (what might today be termed) 'existential problems'. A raging sexual appetite and promiscuity, or sexual obsessions and fetishes, or, alternatively, sexual inadequacies, are often mentioned, as are unreasonable and unrealistic squandering of money; alcohol and substance abuse; cruel or unfeeling behaviour towards others, including close friends, lovers, and family members, sometimes alternating with behaviour of great charm and charisma; and reclusive behaviour. The family histories of many of the individuals examined in this literature, also show evidence of psychopathology or psychosocial problems. In Post's (1994) psychobiographical analysis of 291 subjects, 55.5 per cent had relatives with histories of schizophrenia, depression, suicide, alcoholism, and other instabilities.

It is important to emphasize, at this point, that the creative products attributed to these individuals were not the products of rabid psychosis. Lange-Eichbaum's (1932) biographical investigations of the temporal relationship with psychosis found that many of them became psychotic only after they had made their major contributions. The descriptions provided in these biographical accounts in general do not support any notion of organized and coherent creative output contiguous with mental illness. Instead, the creative periods and products occurred before the illness, during periods of remission from periodic illness, during the lead up to or away from the full-blown state, or, simply, from a background of sub-clinical but 'deviate' symptoms or behaviours, that by conventional standards might appear 'abnormal' or outrageous, but which appeared to constitute the usual self of the individual.

Before leaving the biographical evidence, it is worth examining the details of Post's (1994) psychobiographical analysis, which was carefully based on factual and available medical material, from the complete and sufficiently detailed biographies of 291 eminent achievers living in the nineteenth and first half of the twentieth century, and subjected to diagnoses in accordance with DSM-III-R (American Psychiatric Association 1987). His subjects comprised visual artists, novelists and dramatists, composers, scholars and thinkers (philosophers), statesmen and national leaders, and scientists. The data were distinguished into two overall categories: lifelong psychopathology (deviations of personality), and episodic disorders (psychiatric illnesses, including persistent ones). Post found that episodic psychiatric conditions had occurred in 69.4 per cent of subjects, of which in just over half (35.4 per cent) they had not caused any serious disabilities, but in 34 per cent, psychiatric illnesses had interrupted or terminated creative work. From the persistent psychopathology analysis, he found only 6.5 per cent of subjects with 'no remarkable personality characteristics'. Some 'unusual' features, not found among the criteria of any DSM personality disorder, were observed in 25.4 per cent of subjects. DSM traits occurred in 54 per cent of subjects.

Looking at the different types of creative individual, scientists had the least amount of abnormalities, but these were trivial or completely absent in only one-third of cases, and the amounts of DSM trait-cluster psychopathology increased from scientists (42.2 per cent), through composers (61.6 per cent), politicians (63 per cent), thinkers (74 per cent) artists (75 per cent), to writers (90 per cent). Severe psychopathology (interrupting work and sometimes requiring treatment) exceeded less disruptive psychopathology in the case of artists, composers, and writers. Overall, the creative writers appeared to have suffered most, with unhappy childhoods, psychiatric family histories, alcohol abuse, psychosexual and marital difficulties, and depression (72 per cent). Four per cent of the writers exhibited mainly traits from DSM Cluster A paranoid, schizoid, and schizotypal disorders; 40 per cent exhibited mainly Cluster B traits of antisocial, borderline, histrionic, and narcissistic personality; and 46 per cent showed mainly Cluster C traits of avoidant, obsessive-compulsive, and dependent personality, to which affective traits were added.

Moving from the past and the internationally famous, to less eminent but nevertheless gifted individuals in more recent times, several family studies have confirmed a genetic link between creative talent or achievement and psychosis. Andreasen (1987) studied prominent American writers from the University of Iowa Writers' Workshop, and their families. She found that the rate of mood disorders in first-degree relatives was much higher for the writers than for the controls. Heston (1966) looked at the offspring of schizophrenic mothers, who were raised by foster mothers. About half of them were successful adults, showing artistic talent at higher levels than that of a control group; the other half showed psychosocial disability. Karlsson (1970, 1981, 1984) found a high incidence of creative achievement among the relatives of psychotic patients, as well as in the patients themselves, and an increased risk of mental illness in successful scholars and their relatives. McNeil (1971) also found significant and positive correlations between the mental illness rates of biological parents and creative abilities of their adopted offspring.

Experimental studies comparing the rate of mental disorder in creatives with controls matched on other variables and/or with rates in the general population have been carried out by Akiskal and colleagues (cited in Jamison 1993), Andreasen and Canter (1974), Andreasen (1987), Jamison (1989), and Richards *et al.* (1988). Except for the Richards study, which assigned creativity ratings on the basis of subjects' scores on the Lifetime Creativity Scales (measuring putative creativity in everyday life), the subjects in these studies were all artistic creatives: writers (novelists, playwrights, and poets) and artists (painters and sculptors), plus one group of Blues musicians. Results revealed significantly enhanced levels of affective disorder in the artistic creatives.

Andreasen's (1987) study, in which she applied formal psychiatric diagnostic criteria and a structured interview technique, found that 80 per cent of her writers could be diagnosed as meeting criteria for major mood disorder, compared to 30 per cent for the comparison group. Symptoms of full-blown manic-depressive illness, bipolar I, or the less full-blown variant, bipolar II (major depressive illness with a history of hypomania) were shown by 43 per cent of the writers, compared to 10 per cent of controls. At least one episode of major depressive illness had been experienced by 37 per cent of the American writers, compared to 17 per cent of controls (but this difference was not significant), and 30 per cent of writers, as opposed to 7 per cent of controls, were diagnosed as alcholic. These findings were based on a rather small sample of writers (*N* = 30), and the percentage of mood disorders in the control group was much higher than is normally estimated in the general population (around 1 per cent for manic-depressive illness, 1–2 per cent for cyclothymia, and 5 per cent for major depressive disorder), so some reservations about the results may be in order. However, with regard to the latter point, estimations of levels of mental disorder in the general population might well increase dramatically if psychiatrists had the opportunity of interviewing people in similar 'non-patient' contexts to that of Andreasen's study. A raised incidence of mental disorder in the general population, from mild to borderline, would, in any case, be predicted from a dimensional view.

The two studies by Akiskal and colleagues (Jamison 1993) were carried out on 20 award-winning European writers, poets, painters, and sculptors; and on Blues musicians (subject numbers unrevealed). The results of 'extensive psychiatric interviews' showed, in the first study, that around half of the subjects had suffered from a major depressive episode, and nearly two-thirds displayed recurrent cyclothymic or hypomanic tendencies. Similar results were obtained for the Blues musicians.

Jamison's (1989) study of 47 British writers and artists aimed at determining the actual rates of treatment for disorder in this group, found that 38 per cent had been treated for a mood disorder, mostly depression, but approximately one-third reported histories of severe mood swings, and one-quarter reported having experienced extended elated mood states.

Results of the experimental studies mentioned so far appear, on the whole, to emphasize states of mood disorder which are less than the full-blown, manic-depressive bipolar I disorder. Depression, hypomania, and cyclothymia appear to predominate. The results of Richards *et al.* (1988) explicitly reinforce this conclusion. They compared the scores of 17 manic-depressive and 16 cyclothymic patients, plus 11 of their 'normal' first-degree relatives (group 1), with 15 'normal' control subjects, and another group of psychiatric controls, on the Lifetime Creativity Scales. The interesting finding was that the cyclothymics and normal first-degree relatives of group 1 displayed higher creativity (with similar scores to each other) than the manic-depressives and normal control subjects (who also had similar scores to each other). Richards *et al.* conclude:

Overall peak creativity may be enhanced, on the average, in subjects showing milder and, perhaps, subclinical expressions of potential bipolar liability (i.e., the cyclothymes and normal first-degree relatives) compared either with individuals who carry no bipolar liability (control subjects) or individuals with more severe manifestations of bipolar liability (manic depressives). (p. 287)

This is in line with the assertion, made earlier on, that the link is not between creativity and full-blown psychosis, but, rather, between creativity and schizotypy. To reinforce the point once more, consider Jamison's (1989) study of British writers and artists. This included an analysis of mood and productivity ratings over a 36 month period, and the concordance between these ratings was contrasted between the group whose members had been treated for depression or manic-depression illness, and those without a history of treatment for mood disorders (but many of whom had reported mood swings and prolonged elevations). The mood and productivity curves of the latter group corresponded quite closely with each other, whereas in those for the group with a history of treatment, the peaks for productivity precede and follow the peaks for mood by three to four months. Jamison (1993) suggests that:

[the] elevated mood of the treatment group . . . probably reflects more true hypomania (that is, greater distractibility, irritability, increases in seeking out of other people, and alcohol abuse) than does just an expansive, elevated, and creative mood; this might well lead to less productivity in the acute phase. In the group with no history of treatment, the periods of increased mood and productivity may represent a milder form of hypomania (or simply an intensification of normal mood), with cognitive and mood changes only. (pp. 139–40)

A further source of evidence which is sometimes cited as confirmation of a link between creativity and mild(er) psychopathology comes from investigations of the personality profiles of creatives (for example MacKinnon 1960, 1962; Barron 1969). MacKinnon looked at groups of architects classified as highly creative by their professional peers. He found that these individuals scored around one standard deviation higher than the average on the MMPI (Minnesota Multiphasic Personality Inventory) scales for Psychopathic Deviate, Schizophrenia, and Femininity. Barron's comparison of creative groups (architects, mathematicians, and writers) with average and non-creative groups, also found raised scores on *all* the MMPI measures, compared with the mean for the general population. Their average scores for Hypochondriasis, Depression, Hysteria, Psychopathic Deviate, Paranoia, Psychasthenia, Schizophrenia, and Hypomania ranged from 11 to 18 points above the general mean of 50. MacKinnon and Barron both pointed out that, in addition to this evidence of psychopathology, there was also clear evidence of adequate control mechanisms or 'ego strength'.

Before leaving this section, it is important to note that the bulk of the evidence (anecdotal, biographical, and experimental) for a link between creativity and psychopathology, whether mild or severe, comes from male subjects.

CREATIVITY, SCHIZOTYPY, AND INTELLIGENCE

The set of vectors which give rise to a person's level of intelligence are important, both for adjusting the probability of psychotic illness and for the testing and predicting of creative achievement.

Claridge and colleagues (1990, 1995) suggest that higher levels of IQ give some protection for schizotypal personalities who might otherwise be prone to psychopathology, by providing them with more flexible psychological resources to help cope with stress, and by promoting achievements that are socially valued, thus strengthening self-esteem. Of course, this does not mean that all individuals who *do* suffer periods of psychotic illness are not intelligent—as already suggested there are multiple vectors involved.

IQ and creativity are also thought to be correlated up to around IQ 120 (Guilford 1981; Eysenck 1983; Simonton 1984; Vernon 1987; Findlay and Lumsden 1988), which is approximately the average IQ of a university under-graduate (Jackson 1984; Rushton 1990), after which creativity and IQ become independent of each other. Some researchers suggest that the relationship con-tinues even higher up the IQ scale. Rushton (1990), for example, suggests that individuals with IQs of 120 would have great difficulty competing successfully in some of today's most creative scientific professions, such as astrophysics, computer engineering, and mathematics, and cites several studies which have shown a rather higher level of IQ in professional scientists.

Haensly and Reynolds (1989) point out that the relationship between measures of creativity and IQ can vary, depending on a number of factors, including the nature of the creative talent which is supposedly tapped. For example, Guilford and Hoepfner (Guilford 1968) looked at the correlations between the California Test of Mental Maturity (a measure of IQ) and a range of divergent thinking (trait creativity) tests. The figural divergent thinking measures were found to have much lower correlations with the IQ test than the measures of symbolic and semantic divergent thinking. It is possible, then, that creative talents which find expression in some forms of visual art do not require the same levels of intelligence—at least, of the kinds normally tapped in IQ tests.

The exact relationship, then, between intelligence and actual creative achieve-ment in particular fields, remains somewhat problematical as yet, but this is only to be expected, considering the number of unresolved issues and the complexity surrounding both constructs. However, it is clear from the literature that a higher than average intelligence is necessary for most types of creative achievement; it is the level of sufficiency of the former which appears open to argument. If one also accepts the argument that higher levels of intelligence supply a protective cloak for psychosis-prone individuals, then any analysis of the relationship between schizotypy and creativity will require intelligence to feature in the equation. There is unlikely to be a link between creativity and schizotypy in individuals with average to low levels of IQ, except, possibly, in the visual arts.

SCHIZOTYPAL PROFILES AND THEIR IMPLICATIONS FOR PROFILES OF CREATIVITY

Schizotypal profiles

The results of at least eight factor analyses of various schizotypal trait question-naire scales or items (Gruzelier 1995; Claridge *et al.*; 1996; and six analyses discussed in Venables 1995), provide strong evidence for the existence of a minimum of two, but probably at least four, separate profiles or syndromes of schizotypy (see Chapter 2).

The first is essentially a profile of cognitive and perceptual eccentricity (labelled 'Unusual Experiences', or Unex, by Mason *et al.* (1995), and 'Unreality' by Gruzelier), which is very similar, at a symptom-muted level, to the positive symptom dimension of schizophrenia (Venables 1995). It consists of traits of magical thinking, perceptual aberration, a tendency to experience hallucinations, a tendency to cyclothymia (hypomanic personality, or HoP), and some paranoid ideation and suspiciousness.

The second syndrome, of negative symptom traits, reflects the withdrawn schizoid factor in schizophrenic symptomatology. The scales which load on this factor are social anhedonia, physical anhedonia, and (if included in the analysis) introversion. This syndrome essentially describes 'Introvertive Anhedonia' (Intan), with flat affect and few or no close friends.

The third factor is a profile which, as well as describing some social impairment or anxiety, particularly yields 'Cognitive Disorganization' (Cogdis) effects, centring upon attentional difficulties and distractibility. Venables (1995) suggests that this is a second positive symptom factor. It includes traits of borderline personality (STB), schizophrenism, STA (magical thinking, unusual perceptual experiences), introversion, and neuroticism.

The fourth, more marginal, factor in Claridge *et al.*'s (1996) analysis ('Impulsive Nonconformity', or Impnon), consists of traits of borderline personality, hypomanic personality, Eysenck's psychoticism (P) scale, and extraversion. Claridge *et al.*'s description of the profile of this factor is of 'asocial behaviour with associated impulsiveness and mood-related disinhibition'.

These four profiles of schizotypy should be used to aid future research on the creativity-schizotypal trait link, principally because the experimental literature relating (or potentially relevant) to this link appears to contain non-unitary themes and results, as does the literature on creativity in general. Before going on to discuss the possible enhancement of creativity via a link with schizotypy, it is necessary to point out that each of the four profiles can also be associated with traits of paranoia (see Chapter 3), which could, instead, undermine creativity. Non-clinical manifestations of paranoia could result in the making of illegitimate associative connections, and in such a narrowing of the focus of attention that relevant and legitimate connections are excluded from consideration. Creativity expression could either be prevented, or the quality, originality, or aptness of the end product could be reduced.

Profiles of creativity

Impulsive nonconformity

Claridge *et al.*'s (1996) factor analyses of schizotypal traits, both with and without the inclusion of Eysenck's neuroticism (N) and extraversion (E) personality scales (Eysenck and Eysenck 1975), show the same schizotypal profiles, standing in their own right without N and E. This is hardly surprising, since the personality scales on their own yield little useful information about the nature and contents of cognition that essentially define psychosis-proneness. However, since the inclusion of Eysenck's P scale in the analysis resulted in a fourth profile of schizotypy, it is necessary to consider his claim (1993, 1994) that the degree of P is the underlying cause of both creativity and psychopathology.

Higher levels of P, in Eysenck's theory, result in greater creativity, partly as a result of behavioural traits associated with the construct. Roger and Morris (1991) found two subfactors in their analysis of the P-scale: callousness, paranoia, and intolerance; and impulsiveness and non-planning. The dimension is associated generally with deceitful, asocial, amoral, and unnecessarily aggressive behaviours. With this in mind, it is possible to see a link between P and public attributions of creativity and eminence. High P individuals would use their P qualities to obtain judgements of creative merit, by influencing (through the use of persuasion, intimidation, deceit, or other means of effecting control) those individuals or situations which bring their products to public notice. In other words, one can question how creative are the products of many 'eminent' individuals. Eysenck (1993) himself suggested something along these lines.

However, when it comes to actual creative *ability*, is P the causal factor? Eysenck's claim is that P increases creative potential at the cognitive level, via an association with:

(1) scores on divergent thinking tests (for example Woody and Claridge 1977), which supposedly tap fluency, flexibility, and originality in the production of associative links from long-term memory;

(2) patterns of unusual word association and concept formation (word-sorting) performance ('overinclusive' or 'allusive' thinking) shown by normals (schizo-typal traits unmeasured), psychosis-prone subjects, psychotics, and biological relatives of these groups (see Eysenck 1993 for relevant studies).

'Divergent thinking' (Guilford 1950), 'overinclusive thinking' (Cameron 1938, 1947; Cameron and Magaret 1951; Payne and Hewlett 1960; Payne 1969, 1973), and 'allusive thinking' (McConaghy and Clancy 1968) essentially refer to the same construct, although overinclusive and allusive thinking are terms which were originally coined in the context of psychotics' performance on cognitive tasks. The construct describes a loosening of boundaries between concepts, with a consequent widening of the associative horizon, greater amounts of available associations, and more unique associations to stimuli presented.

Links with P in the word-association and sorting performances are made either as a result of scores on the P-scale itself, or, more generally, via Eysenck's (1992) general claim that the P dimension (from low to high scores) actually defines the full range of personality types, from 'altruistic' and 'socialized' at the very low P-score end, through 'aggressive' and 'psychopathic', to schizophrenia at the highest scoring end.

The results of the Claridge et al. factor analysis, however, showed P loading *only* on the fourth, more marginal, factor—Impnon—with HoP and STB (and E, when included in the analysis). HoP loads far more strongly on the Unex factor, and STB loads at a slightly stronger weighting on the Cogdis factor. The first conclusion must therefore be that P is not the dimension which defines schizotypy. Rather, P is just one vector among others; it enters the picture more marginally by virtue of some similarity of attributes or relations with two other scales, which themselves load more strongly with *other* profiles of schizotypal traits. (Presumably, HoP and STB load additionally with P here, because they also include some elements of paranoia, aggression, and/or nonconformity.)

The second conclusion is that P, as just one trait in a marginal factor, cannot, therefore, underly the predisposition towards creativity in intelligent schizotypes *in general*. With regard to the particular processes of divergent thinking shown in the word-association and concept word-sorting performances, evidence for this as a feature of schizotypal thinking stands in its own right, from experimental studies with schizophrenics, schizoaffectives, manic-depressives, and non-psychotic relatives. If this kind of divergent thinking has any predictive value for actual creative performance at the product level, it should be equally well (or better) explained in terms of the other three main profiles of schizotypal traits.

The other positive symptom factors on which HoP and STB load more strongly essentially describe the *cognitive* features of schizotypy: cognitive and perceptual eccentricities, attentional difficulties, and distractibility. The fourth factor, on the other hand, simply defines deviance or nonconformity at the affective, aggressive, and behavioural levels. The fact that E loads significantly on this profile together with P, implies a low resting-level of cortical arousal (Eysenck 1967), and a consequent need for arousal-boosters via P-type interactions with (or manipulations of) external sources. The third conclusion, then, is that the correlations obtained between P and divergent thinking test results or word-association responses, are simply due to nonconformist, sensation-seeking behaviour, such that high P subjects are more willing to 'perform' and say anything that comes into their minds, irrespective of its quality, value, appropriateness, truth, or shockingness. The point would be that P is not related to creativity *per se*, but to the nature and performance of its expression.

Positive versus negative trait creativity?

According to Eysenck's (1967) theory, the greater the degree of extraversion, the lower the levels of cortical arousal; extraverts look 'outwards' to external stimuli, to increase their level of arousal to some optimal level. Introverts, on the other hand, have high resting levels of cortical arousal; their focus of awareness is more internally engaged, and extra stimulation from external sources is avoided. These differences in levels and directions of cortical arousal would affect both the spread and the strength of activation across neuronal networks in response to external and internal input, and in combination with schizotypal differences in hemispheric asymmetry, degrees of anxiety, and other interacting biochemical and psychological variables may effect changes in the weightings on synaptic connections, to yield different profiles of cognitive outcome.

It should be noted that it is introversion which is regularly associated with personality profiles of creatives, and, when included in Claridge *et al.*'s (1996) analysis, loaded significantly on the Intan and Cogdis factors at 0.53 and 0.33, respectively. Extraversion, on the other hand, loaded on Impnon at 0.30 and on Unex, at 0.25.

However, Prentky (1980) proposed a model of psychosis and creativity which allows for different kinds of creative processing from schizotypes of *both* the introverted *and* the extraverted kind. The neurocognitive dimension of information processing proposed in his model shows a 'normal range' of 'ambicognitive thought processes' in the middle, psychotic thought disorders of the active and withdrawn types at opposite ends of the continuum, and two different expressions of creativity sandwiched towards the ends, between normality and each type of psychosis. His model was based, in part, on a two-dimensional model of arousal proposed by Claridge (1967), which has implications for sensory input regulation, information processing below the level of working memory, and strength of attentional focus.

In Claridge's model, differing personality outcomes from interactions between traits of extraversion–introversion, neuroticism, and psychoticism can be explained in terms of the strength of association between tonic arousal on the one hand, and a homeostatic system of arousal modulation on the other. Tonic arousal is described as a dimension running from high to low anxiety drive, whereas the high to low endpoints of the dimension of arousal modulation refer to the opposite homeostatic arousal goals of introverts versus extraverts. Psychosis is the result of a dissociation between the two arousal dimensions. Active (positive symptom) psychosis results from poor modulation of sensory input and poor inhibitory control over tonic arousal, whereas retarded (negative symptom) psychosis results from excessive inhibition of sensory input and a reduction in tonic arousal.

In Prentky's model, the creative profiles of both the A-type (abstract) individual towards the positive symptom end of the continuum and the C-type (concrete) individual towards the negative symptom end of the continuum are described in terms of the kinds of information processes inferred from the interactions and dissociations between arousal dimensions proposed in the Claridge model.

Thus, the A-type person, with high tonic arousal and low arousal modulation, is characterized by hyper-alertness of the whole system, low-resolution parallel-processing of large amounts of sensory input, rapid habituation to stimuli, high distractibility, a weak attentional focus, and easy attentional shift. The cognitive style involves a loosening of ideational boundaries (i.e. 'overinclusiveness'), and, in the pure type, is more likely to be synthetic. Clinically, affective symptoms would predominate: lability, depression, and agitation. Impulsivity and aggression also feature in the Claridge model.

The C-type person, with low tonic arousal and high arousal modulation, is characterized by a constriction of the attentional field with high sensory-input registration, slow habituation to stimuli, low distractibility, a strong attentional focus, and difficult attentional shift. The cognitive style involves a tightening of ideational boundaries (i.e. 'underinclusiveness'), and, in the pure type, is more likely to be analytic. In problem solving, these individuals will 'zero in on the absolutely critical relations or the unexpected but meaningful anomalies' (Prentky 1980, p.73) Clinically, schizoid-like symptoms would predominate, including flat affect, withdrawal, and apathy.

It should be emphasized that the Claridge model which Prentky draws upon does not attribute introversion and extraversion in the normal Eysenckian sense, to these profiles of psychosis. Such attributions could not be made, because the psychotic dissociations between Claridge's two arousal dimensions drive the individual beyond the normal descriptive boundaries of introversion and extraversion, as well as distorting their normal psychobiological parameters. However, at non-clinical schizotypal levels of personality, introversion and extraversion would map on to Prentky's C and A-type profiles, though without capturing the full range and essence of these traits.

Prentky's model is a good starting point for reflecting on the nature of the schizotypy–creativity link. However, we have four profiles of schizotypy now, rather than two, to reflect upon. Two of these four have an introverted tendency (Intan and Cogdis), and two are more extraverted (Unex and Impnon). In each pair, one could be viewed as having traits associated with high anxiety-drive (Cogdis and Unex), and one with low anxiety-drive (Intan and Impnon).

In addition, any dissociation between arousal mechanisms will only be partial, temporary, cyclic, or 'threatened' (rather than actual) in schizotypal, as opposed to clinically psychotic, states. One possibility is that there are additional neuropsychological or psychobiological mechanisms that act in some compensatory fashion to reverse the direction of one or other of the two arousal dimensions whenever a partial or threatened dissociation occurs. If there are such mechanisms, they may, perhaps, provide the underpinnings for the 'ego strength' associated with schizotypal creativity.

The point is that we need to find some way of relaxing the divergence between A and C-type cognition in order to accommodate the four schizotypal profiles. We also need to be able to accommodate evidence such as that provided by Katz and Pestell (1989), which shows the use of both highly focused *and* unfocused attentional strategies in the same (putatively) creative subjects, depending on task demands. These researchers found that a group of subjects high on remote associative ability (RAT) (as shown by RAT performance scores) picked up more stimulus information than low RAT scorers on divided attention tasks, but picked up less background item information than low RAT scorers when the task demanded focused attention.

Of the four schizotypal profiles, one, Intan, is unambiguously composed of negative symptom traits—social and physical anhedonia, in addition to introversion. This profile maps on to Prentky's description of C-types. Such individuals, who avoid social contact and find little pleasure in sensual and cooperative activities, and are protected by a lack of anxiety and reactivity to external stimuli (neuroticism loads –0.06 on this factor), are, in effect, 'walled off' from the 'reality' of the external world. Thus, for intelligent individuals of this (non-clinical) type, with little activity or disturbance at the sensory, social, and emotional levels, there is a high probability of accelerated intellectual activity, with strong attentional focus. One could argue that these individuals could be equally well classified as divergent thinkers, as those showing positive symptom profiles, owing to the likelihood of large and proliferating amounts of 'incestuous' connectivity in the contents of information processing. However, since the cognitive contents would be, to a great extent, the products of cognitive 'incest', they would exhibit qualities of internal relatedness or cohesiveness, and would build up to greater levels of sophistication (or divergence) via processes of 'lawful' or logical regularity. Creativity of the goal-directed or goal-constrained type seems a more likely outcome of this profile of traits, and the direction of creativity would tend to be more towards science and philosophy, and away from the emotionally expansive elements underlying much artistic creativity. In view of Gruzelier's (1995) findings of a right hemisphere advantage for this schizotypal profile, it is possible that the creative processes may involve the employment of controlled imagery and visuospatial manipulation.

Of the remaining three schizotypal profiles, one, Unex, is unambiguously composed of positive symptom traits—including hypomania, which maps on to Prentky's description of A-type traits. Although its important traits of perceptual aberration, magical ideation, and the tendency to experience hallucinations are not really captured by Prentky's profile description, Jamison (1993) has gone to some lengths to associate these elements of cognition with manic-depression and cyclothymia. On the other hand, agitated hypomanic states can equally be associated with delusional and hallucinatory states in schizophrenia. In any case, the loading of hypomania and cognitive and perceptual eccentricities, all on the one factor, indicate a non-specificity of the dimension of positive symptoms at the non-clinical level—the level at which creativity is possible. This is also the set of traits which anecdotal, observational, and experimental studies have associated with overinclusive and divergent thinking.

It looks as if these two schizotypal profiles, of the four, provide the best fit for Prentky's A and C types. However, for several reasons, Unex, with Intan, does not provide a satisfactory polarization of creative attributes and processes, even though Unex and Intan together provide an appropriate polarity of direction of psychosis-proneness. Two of these reasons are: first, that creativity goes hand in hand with introversion, which does not load on Unex; and secondly, that creative acts demand some union of opposite processes— functional, conceptual, and attentional—via some connecting link, which Unex does not provide directly. It will be argued later that there *is* a connection between Unex and Intan, but that this serves to increase the amount or quality of creativity, and the direction of its expression, rather than providing a polarizing influence.

It is Cogdis which provides the most satisfactory polar opposite and linking attributes for Intan. This is an introverted profile, with high tonic arousal and traits of tension, anxiety, stimulus-reactivity, and emotionality. The elements of self-reflection, the hyperacuity and sensitivity towards environmental cues, the richness of associative connections born of high levels of arousal coupled with high pick-up from broad-scan pre-attentional mechanisms, and the overriding theme of emotionality altogether suggest a boiling cauldron of complexity and contradiction.

The type of creativity expressed by this profile of schizotypal traits would be of the open-ended type, since the individual would have difficulty in controlling and constraining the flood of ideas and any associated emotions. The content of creativity would have an emotional reference, and may also include a good deal of symbolism. The lability of affect associated with this profile implies either some hemispheric 'freedom of entry' or more 'seepage' of right to left hemisphere communication. Thus, in addition to creative activities such as poetry and literature, other spheres of emotionally and symbolically tinged open-ended creativity, such as dance and musical composition, would also belong here.

Intan and Cogdis are, in many ways, opposite sides of the *same* coin. Both profiles look inwards, both 'brood' over the contents of their cognitions to bring new insights into being, and both experience aversive effects from environmental interactions. The difference is in their emotionality and responsivity to external events, which colour the contents of cognition, the means of ideational proliferation, and the manner of its expression.

As suggested previously, it seems possible that in schizotypy, as opposed to psychosis, there may be some compensatory mechanisms which (sometimes, or always) reverse the direction of either the tonic arousal or the arousal modulating system, whenever the individual is on the brink of dissociation. If this suggestion is a sensible one, it would indicate a (possibly fluctuating) relationship, in the same individual, between some of the traits in both profiles—and/or between Intan traits and some of the Unex traits, since the latter tend to correlate highly with those of Cogdis (see Chapter 2).

Transliminality

So far, we have two potentially creative profiles, the descriptions for which could simply be boiled down to a combination of intelligence and different temperamental traits, which together determine the direction of interest, the degree of interest, and the strength of concentration. However, there is nothing in these profiles to suggest any real motivation to express their effects, or to present them in terms of a finished product, to the world at large. The urge for expression must be the outcome of interacting effects with the more extravertive traits of Unex and Impnon. However, there is little, so far, to deny a charge that so-called creativity is merely the outcome of a great deal of application, using perfectly 'normal' information processes, in line with the hard-work/normal-processing theory of Weisberg (1986, 1988), and the high intrinsic motivation theory of Amabile (1983); see also Hennessey and Amabile (1988). The only real link with psychopathology would be that, at their extremes, the temperamental traits involved could lead to some 'weird' and 'pathetic' isolate behaviour, or to some 'over the top' behaviour, with deviant social interaction or complete social inadequacy. However, this mild psychopathology by itself could not bear any causal relationship to creativity, since the latter will then have lost its 'deviate' information processing status.

While the main thrusts of Amabile's and Weisberg's theories cannot be rejected, it can be argued that there *is* often something more than this behind creativity, and that there is some common underlying cause which can give rise to both psychopathology and creativity. The key appears to lie with the first positive factor, Unex, containing those features of cognition and cycles of affect (energy, drive, and arousal) which particularly define schizotypal (as opposed to non-schizotypal or schizotypy-neutral) traits.

Thalbourne and Delin (1994), using similar components to those here defining the unusual experiences factor, but also including a scale which measures creative personality, found a single factor which they called 'transliminality', from the Latin 'trans', meaning 'across', and 'limen', meaning 'threshold'. They suggested that transliminality operates as an individual difference in 'the selectiveness with which the barrier or gating mechanism between subliminal and supraliminal [contents of cognition] is operating . . .' (p. 22) (see also Chapters 4 and 5). Individuals high in transliminality would have a 'largely involuntary susceptibility to large volumes of inwardly generated psychological phenomena of an ideational and affective kind', and 'because of the inescapable fecundity of their conscious life' would pay more attention to inner processes and attach more meaning to the products of inner processes (p.25). The operation of transliminality in creatives, they suggest, allows novel ideas or solutions to problems, and connections between elements, to occur in ways that appear not to be the result of direct reasoning. Similarly, manic flights of ideas, delusions of grandeur, hallucinations (and, presumably, aberrations of perception), and paranormal beliefs are all essentially forms of 'associative creativity'—the connecting-up of diverse phenomena arising contiguously as a result of enhanced access to subliminal realms.

While the language of Thalbourne and Delin's arguments may not appeal to many researchers, their arguments are supported by evidence that can be couched in appropriately 'drier' information processing terms. On the one hand, results of Shaw and Conway (1990), using an anagram problem-solving test, detection and identification threshold-assessment procedures, and word-clue primes, presented both sub- and suprathreshold, found that high creatives had significantly faster detection and identification threshold times, and used more non-conscious clues and non-consciously primed solutions than did low creatives. On the other hand, the results of Evans (1992; see also Chapter 5), using lexical decision tasks, threshold assessment procedures, and semantically associated or non-associated word primes, found that subjects high on positive-symptom schizotypal traits were more responsive to subliminal primes than low schizotypes.

It is suggested that it is this factor of transliminality-underlying, pervading, and operating in conjunction with the cognitive, affective, and behavioural traits defining the two creative profiles outlined above—that is responsible for both the schizotypy–creativity link, and the *quantitatively* extraordinary processes of creative insight and elaboration. Basically, the same 'normal' cognitive processes of associative thought, employment of heuristics, mental representation of material in working memory, retrieval of knowledge from long-term memory, and so on, would operate during the course of creative enterprise. However, there would be a greater amount and diversity of associative connections made, thus more divergence of thought. In addition, heuristics are more often likely to be applied without the individual's conscious knowledge or intention. The quantitative differences in schizotypal-creative as opposed to non-schizotypal-creative processing, may result in qualitative differences at the product end.

It is further suggested that the underlying cause of transliminality itself involves, perhaps, schizotypal differences in hemispheric asymmetry or inter-hemispheric communication.

HEMISPHERIC DIFFERENCES UNDERLYING SCHIZOTYPY AND CREATIVITY

A number of researchers have found 'abnormal' cerebral hemispheric asymmetries in schizotypes (for review, see Lencz *et al.* 1995; see also Chapter 8). It could be speculated that these abnormalities may indicate a 'freeing-up' of right-hemisphere processes, and their involvement in tasks for which the left hemisphere is normally specialized. Such indications map on to similar notions about creativity, which have been part of folk psychology for many years. However, the hemisphere picture in relation to both schizotypy and creativity is actually far more complicated than that presented in 'popular psychology' books espousing the theme. The experimental findings also include different patterns of creative performance *within* the groups of high scorers on schizotypal traits.

Poreh *et al.* (1994) used two groups of male subjects—high and low scorers on some of the Unex scales (perceptual aberration, magical ideation, and STA)—and administered a dichotic listening test, in addition to trait creativity tests of divergent thinking. The schizotypal subjects performed significantly better than controls on the Figural Fluency and Originality divergent thinking tests—a finding which is consistent with the notion of enhanced right-hemisphere processing, in schizotypes, of the perceptual stimuli for which it is normally specialized. Of particular interest, though, was the finding that, within the schizotypal group, those with a left-ear (right-hemisphere) preference for the identification of syllables, scored significantly higher on the STA scale, than those with a right ear (left hemisphere) preference. In addition, these left ear schizotypes also performed significantly better on the Verbal Fluency and Originality scales of the divergent thinking tests. Although Thalbourne and Delin (1994) did not include the STA scale in their factor analysis, its content maps on to other scales which they did include. Thus, it seems feasible to assume that the STA scale taps into his transliminality factor.

Unsurprisingly, studies of schizotypes have also found an increased incidence of left-and mixed-handedness (Chapman and Chapman 1987; Kelley and Coursey 1992; Kim *et al.* 1992; see also Chapter 8). Left-handers similarly show an enhancement of right hemisphere processing activity (over normal right-handers) in spatial tasks for which it would normally be specialized (Hermann and Van Dyke 1978; Porac and Coren 1981), and these abilities have been used to explain greater mathematical talent in left-handers (Peterson, 1979; Annett and Kilshaw 1982), greater chess ability in left-handers (Cranberg and Albert 1988), and an increased proportion of left-handed artists and architects (Peterson and Lansky 1977; Mebert and Michel 1980) and science students (Coren and Porac 1982; Kimura and D'Amico 1989). Some research has also reported more divergent thinking by left-handers on the figural subscales of the Torrance (1970) divergent thinking tests (Newland 1981; Burke and Chrisler 1989).

Again, however, superior performance on verbal divergent-thinking tasks (for which the left hemisphere would normally be specialized) have also been found in left- and mixed-handers, but only for males. Coren (1995), using a large student population, found no differences in left-, mixed-, and right-handed females, in three divergent thinking experiments tapping verbal and semantic ability. However, in two of these experiments, the results for males showed a significant increase in divergent thinking for left- and mixed-handers over right-handers, and a linear increase in divergent thinking with greater degrees of sinistrality. These results were not due to any confounding with convergent thinking ability (related to IQ and involving 'convergence' on the correct answer by use of contextual knowledge and application of contextually relevant rules) because Coren's fourth experiment with an inductive-reasoning convergent-thinking test found no advantages for left-handed males or females. In fact, the results showed a linear trend, in males and females combined, in the opposite direction: higher convergent thinking scores for right-handers.

Owing to the raised incidence of left- and mixed-handedness in schizotypes, it seems feasible to postulate that the creativity of both schizotypes and sinistrals is due to similar causes—even in schizotypes who are right-handed, but who show similar patterns of deviant cerebral processing. However, as shown by Poreh et al.'s results (in addition to other dichotic-listening and negative-priming results), there are some differences within this overall deviant pattern for schizotypes, both between and within sexes. The differences may depend partly on measures of additional schizotypal traits which are not usually taken (those that measure Intan and Cogdis). In other words, they may depend partly on which schizotypal profile, in addition to (or instead of) transliminality, is most descriptive of the individual. Males generally score more highly on the Intan profile, whereas females tend to obtain higher scores on Cogdis; however, there are individual differences. Each profile may reflect a different relationship with hemisphere activity.

Gruzelier's (1995) results imply relationships between right-hemisphere over-activation and 'withdrawn' traits and left-hemisphere over-activation and 'active' traits (which appear to reflect some combination of Cogdis and Impnon), and inconsistent relationships between 'unreality' traits and cerebral asymmetry—indicating a lability in lateralized activation for this profile. It is also possible that the differences in cerebral processing within schizotypes are partly a function of sex differences in the arousal dimensions, interacting with each profile of traits.

Gruzelier (1995) found no sex differences in arousal for the 'withdrawn' factor, but there were differences for high-scorers in 'active' and 'unreality' traits. His two dimensions of activation were 'stress', ranging from tense and anxious to calm and placid, and 'arousal', ranging from sleepy and tired to activated and vigorous. High 'unreality' scorers, if female, tended to be anxious and tired, as opposed to males, who were calm and active. High-scorers on the 'active' profile showed high arousal, overall, but in females there were significant effects with stress.

Thus, the overall picture of deviant hemisphere functioning in schizotypes contains inconsistencies and non-unitary themes. However, in view of the claims for non-lateralization of the Unusual Experiences profile, in particular, it seems plausible that it is this—with its transliminal qualities, and deviating effects on 'normal' associative and perceptual processes—which, in interaction with other positive or negative schizotypal traits of information processing and with particular outcomes of arousal, yields difference in creative abilities. Depending on the nature of these interactions, they may simply enhance the normal cognitive processes underlying creativity, or they may bring about unusual cognitive abilities as a result of some undermining of normal processing activity.

CONCLUDING REMARKS

The arguments presented merely indicate pointers to areas for future investigation—they obviously do not provide any real explanations of the processes underlying creativity. Such explanations should no longer be pursued through the use of trait creativity tests, isolated measures of hemisphere functioning, random use of individual schizotypal scales, and grossly selected groups of subjects. Rather, they should be sought through the use of performance measures of actual creative achievement, thoughtfully selected tasks and schizotypal scales related to different profiles of creativity, and the sorting of subjects into groups according to more fine-grain individual characteristics.

In addition, it seems important to find some appropriate term to replace 'schizotypy' and 'psychoticism' for future research. These labels are contaminated by the theoretical contexts in which they were originally conceived (see Chapter 1). More importantly, they confuse the understanding of other researchers, as well as students of psychology. What is required is a new term that reflects the explanations given for schizotypy in relation to temperament, behaviour, and information processing, but which does not automatically activate concepts associated with mental illness. 'Bioeccentricity', perhaps? Without some appropriate new term to clear away the prejudices, there is unlikely to be much progress and synthesizing of research on creativity from different perspectives. Rather, as has happened so far, repetitive attempts at recapitulation and clarification will simply continue to occur periodically in the future.

REFERENCES

Alston, E. F. (1972). James Barrie's 'M'Connachie'—His 'writing half'. *American Imago*, **29**, 257–77.

Amabile, T. M. (1983). *The social psychology of creativity*. Springer-Verlag, New York.

American Psychiatric Association. (1987). *Diagnostic and statistical manual* (3rd edn, revised). APA, Washington, DC.

Andreasen, N. C. (1987). Creativity and mental illness: prevalence rates in writers and their first-degree relatives. *American Journal of Psychiatry*, **144**, 1288–92.

Andreasen, N. C. and Canter, A. (1974). The creative writer: psychiatric symptoms and family history. *Comprehensive Psychiatry*, **15**, 123–31.

Annett, M. and Kilshaw, D. (1982). Mathematical ability and lateral asymmetry. *Cortex*, **18**, 547–68.

Babcock, W. L. (1895). On the morbid heredity and predisposition to insanity of the man of genius. *Journal of Nervous and Mental Disease*, **20**, 749–69.

Barron, F. (1969). *Creative person and creative process*. Holt, Rinehart & Winston, New York.

Becker, G. (1978). *The mad genius controversy*. Sage, Beverley Hills, CA.

Bell, Q. (1972). *Virginia Woolf: A biography*, Vol. 2. Harcourt Brace Jovanovich, New York.

Broad, W. J. (1981). Priority war: Discord in pursuit of glory. *Science*, **211**, 465–7.

Burke, B. F. and Chrisler, J. C. (1989). The creative thinking, environmental frustration and self-concept of left- and right-handers. *Creativity Research Journal*, **2**, 279–85.

Bychowski, G. (1973). Marcel Proust and his mother. *American Imago*, **30**, 8–25.

Cameron, N. (1938). Reasoning, repression and communication in schizophrenics. *Psychological Monograph*, **50**, 1–33.

Cameron, N. (1947). *The psychology of behaviour disorders*. Houghton Mifflin, Boston.

Cameron, N. and Magaret, A. (1951). *Behavior pathology*. Houghton Mifflin, Boston.

Chapman, J. P. and Chapman, L. J. (1987). Handedness of hypothetically psychosis-prone subjects. *Journal of Abnormal Psychology*, **96**, 89–93.

Claridge, G. (1967). *Personality and arousal*. Pergamon Press, Oxford.

Claridge, G., Pryor, R., and Watkins, G. (1990). *Sounds from the bell jar. Ten psychotic authors*. Macmillan, London.

Claridge, G. and Beech, T. (1995). Fully and quasi-dimensional constructions of schizotypy. In *Schizotypal Personality* (ed. A. Raine, T. Lencz, and S. A. Mednick), pp. 192–216. Cambridge University Press.

Claridge, G., McCreery, C., Mason, O., Bentall. R., Boyle, G., Slade, P., and Popplewell, D. (1996). The factor structure of 'schizotypal' traits: a large replication study. *British Journal of Clinical Psychology*, **35**, 103–15.

Coren, S. (1995). Differences in divergent thinking as a function of handedness and sex. *American Journal of Psychology*, **108**, 311–25.

Coren, S. and Porac, C. (1982). Lateral preference and cognitive skills; an indirect test. *Perceptual and Motor Skills*, **54**, 787–92.

Cranberg, L. and Albert, M. (1988). The chess mind. In *The exceptional brain* (ed. L. Obler and D. Fein), pp. 204–22. Guilford Press, New York.

Dale, P. M. (1952). *Medical biographies. The ailments of thirty-three famous persons*. University of Oklahoma Press, Norman.

Edel, L. (1975). The madness of art. *American Journal of Psychiatry*, **132**, 1005–12.

Ellrich, R. J. (1974). Rousseau's account of a psychological crisis. *American Imago*, **31**, 80–94.

Evans, J. L. (1992). Schizotypy and preconscious processing. D.Phil thesis. University of Oxford.

Eysenck, H. J. (1967). *The biological basis of personality*. Thomas, Springfield, IL.

Eysenck, H. J. (1983). The roots of creativity: cognitive ability or personality trait? *Roeper Review*, 5, 10–12.

Eysenck, H. J. (1992). The definition and measurement of psychoticism. *Personality and Individual Differences*, 13, 757–85.

Eysenck, H. J. (1993). Creativity and personality: suggestions for a theory. *Psychological Inquiry*, 4, 147–78.

Eysenck, H. J. (1994). The Measurement of Creativity. In *Dimensions of creativity* (ed. M. A. Boden), pp. 199–242. MIT, Cambridge, Mass.

Eysenck, H. J. and Eysenck, S. B. G. (1975). *Manual of the Eysenck Personality Questionnaire*. Hodder and Stoughton, London.

Findlay, C. S. and Lumsden, C. J. (1988). The creative mind: toward an evolutionary theory of discovery and innovation. *Journal of Social and Biological Structures*, 11, 1–189.

Gibson, C. (1889). *The characteristics of genius. A popular essay*. Walter Scott, London.

Glover, J. A., Ronning, R. R., and Reynolds, C. R. (ed.) (1989). *Handbook of Creativity*. Plenum Press, New York.

Goertzel, M. G., Goertzel, V., and Goertzel, T. G. (1978). *Three hundred eminent personalities*. Jossey-Bass, San Francisco.

Grant, V. W. (1968). *Great abnormals*. Hawthorn Books, New York.

Gruzelier, J. (1995). Syndromes of schizotypy: patterns of cognitive asymmetry, arousal, and gender. In *Schizotypal personality*, (ed. A. Raine, T. Lencz, and S. A. Mednick), pp. 329–52. Cambridge University Press.

Guilford, J. P. (1950). Creativity. *American Psychologist*, 5, 444–54.

Guilford, J. P. (1968). *Intelligence, creativity and their educational implications*. Robert Knapp, San Diego, CA.

Guilford, J. P. (1981). Potential for creativity. In *Creativity: Its educational implications* (2nd edn) (ed. J. C. Gowan, J. Khatena, and E. P. Torrance), pp. 1–5. Kendall/Hunt, Dubuque, IA.

Haensly, P. A. and Reynolds, C. R. (1989). Creativity and intelligence. In *Handbook of creativity*, (ed. J. A. Glover, R. R. Ronning, and C. R. Reynolds), pp. 111–31. Plenum Press, New York.

Hennessey, B. A. and Amabile, T. M. (1988). The conditions of creativity. In *The nature of creativity* (ed. R. J. Sternberg), pp. 11–38. Cambridge University Press.

Herrmann, D. J. and Van Dyke, K. (1978). Handedness and the mental rotation of perceived patterns. *Cortex*, 14, 521–9.

Heston, L. L. (1966). Psychiatric disorders in foster home reared children of schizophrenic mothers. *British Journal of Psychiatry*, 112, 819–25.

Holton, G. (1978). *The scientific imagination: Case studies*. Cambridge University Press.

Jackson, D. N. (1984). *Multidimensional aptitude battery manual*. Research Psychologists Press, Port Huron, Michigan.

Jamison, K. R. (1989). Mood disorders and patterns of creativity in British writers and artists. *Psychiatry*, 52, 125–34.

Jamison, K. R. (1993). *Touched with fire. Manic-depressive illness and the artistic temperament*. The Free Press, New York.

Juda, A. (1949). The relationship between highest mental capacity and psychic abnormalities. *American Journal of Psychiatry*, 106, 296–304.

Karlsson, J. L. (1970). Genetic association of giftedness and creativity with schizophrenia. *Hereditas*, 66, 177–82.

Karlsson, J. L. (1978). *Inheritance of creative intelligence*. Nelson-Hall, Chicago.

Karlsson, J. L. (1981). Genetic basis of intellectual variation in Iceland. *Hereditas*, 95, 283–8.

Karlsson, J. L. (1984). Creative intelligence in relatives of mental patients. *Hereditas*, 100, 83–6.

Katz, A. N. and Pestell, D. (1989). Attentional processes and the finding of remote associates. *Personality & Individual Differences*, 10, 1017–25.

Kelley, M. P. and Coursey, R. D. (1992). Lateral preference and neuropsychological correlates of schizotypy. *Psychiatry Research*, 41, 115–35.

Kim, D., Raine, A., Triphon, N., and Green, M. (1992). Mixed handedness and schizotypal personality. *Journal of Nervous and Mental Disease*, 180, 131–3.

Kimura, D. and D'Amico, C. (1989). Evidence for subgroups of adextrals based on speech lateralization and cognitive patterns. *Neuropsychologia*, 27, 977–86.

Krebs, H. A., and Shelley, J. H. (ed.) (1975). *The creative process in science and medicine*. Proceedings of the C. H. Boehringer Sohn Symposium. Kronberg, Taunus, 16–17 May, 1974. American Elsevier, New York.

Lange-Eichbaum, W. (1932). *The problem of genius* (trans. E. Paul and C. Paul). Macmillan, New York.

Larkin, E. (1970). Beethoven's medical history. In *Beethoven: The last decade*, (ed. M. Cooper), pp. 439–66. Oxford University Press, London.

Lélut, L. F. (1836). *Du demon de Socrate, specimen d'une application de la science psychologique a celle de l'histoire*. Trinquart, Paris.

Lencz, T., Raine, A., Benishay, D. S., Mills, S., and Bird, L. (1995). In *Schizotypal Personality*, (ed. A. Raine, T. Lencz, and S. A. Mednick). Cambridge University Press.

Lombroso, C. (1891). *The man of genius*. Walter Scott, London.

Lombroso, C. (1910). *The man of genius*. Charles Scribner's Sons, New York.

Ludwig, A. M. (1992). Creative achievement and psychopathology: comparisons among professions. *American Journal of Psychotherapy*, 46, 330–56.

McConaghy, N. and Clancy, M. (1968). Familial relationships of allusive thinking in university students and their parents. *British Journal of Psychiatry*, 114, 1079–87.

MacKinnon, D. W. (1960). What do we mean by talent and how do we test for it? In *The search for talent*, pp. 20–9. College Entrance Examination Board, New York.

MacKinnon, D. W. (1962). The personality correlates of creativity: a study of American architects. In *Proceedings of the XIV International Congress of Applied Psychology, Copenhagen, 1961* (ed. G. S. Nielsen), Vol. 2, pp. 11–39. Munksgaard, Copenhagen.

McNeil, T. F. (1971). Prebirth and postbirth influences on the relationship between creative ability and recorded mental illness. *Journal of Personality*, 39, 391–406.

Martindale, C. (1972). Father's absence, psychopathology, and poetic eminence. *Psychological Reports*, 31, 843–7.

Martindale, C. (1990). *The clockwork muse: the predictability of artistic change*. Basic Books, New York.

Mason, O., Claridge, G., and Jackson, M. (1995). New scales for the assessment of schizotypy. *Personality and Individual Differences*, 18, 7–13.

Mebert, C. J. and Michel, G. F. (1980). Handedness in artists. In *Neuropsychology of left-handedness*, (ed. J. Herron), pp. 273–8. Academic Press, New York.

Murphy, G. (1979). Shumann: a short, troubled life. *Rochester Democrat and Chronicle*, 2 December, p. 5C.

Newland, G. A. (1981). Differences between left- and right-handers on a measure of creativity. *Perceptual and Motor Skills*, 53, 787–92.

Nisbet, J. F. (1912). *The insanity of genius: and the general inequality of human faculty physiologically considered*. Stanley Paul, London.

Nordau, M. (1900). *Degeneration*. D. Appleton, New York.

Payne, R. W. (1960). Cognitive abnormalities. In *Handbook of abnormal psychology*, (1st edn) (ed. H. J. Eysenck). Pitman, London.

Payne, R. W. (1973). Cognitive abnormalities. In *Handbook of abnormal psychology*, (2nd edn) (ed. H. J. Eysenck). Pitman, London.

Payne, R. W. and Hewlett, J. H. G. (1960). Thought disorder in psychotic patients. In *Experiments in personality*, Vol. 2 (ed. H. J. Eysenck), pp. 3–104. Routledge & Kegan Paul, London.

Peterson, J. M. (1979). Left-handedness: differences between student artists and student scientists. *Perceptual and Motor Skills*, 48, 961–2.

Peterson, J. M. and Lansky, L. M. (1977). Left-handedness among architects: partial replication and some new data. *Perceptual and Motor Skills*, 45, 1216–18.

Pickering, G. (1974). *Creative malady*. Oxford University Press, New York.

Porac, C. and Coren, S. (1981). *Lateral preferences and human behaviour*. Springer-Verlag, New York.

Poreh, A. M., Whitman, D. R., and Ross, T. P. (1994). Creative thinking abilities and hemispheric asymmetry in schizotypal college students. *Current Psychology*, 12, 344–52.

Post, F. (1994). Creativity and psychopathology. A study of 291 world-famous men. *British Journal of Psychiatry*, 165, 22–34.

Prentky, R. A. (1980). *Creativity and psychopathology: a neurocognitive perspective*. Praeger, New York.

Prentky, R. A. (1989). Creativity and psychopathology. Gamboling at the seat of madness. In *Handbook of creativity* (ed. Glover, J. A., Ronning, R. R., and Reynolds, C. R.), pp. 243–69. Plenum Press, New York.

Reichsman, F. (1981). Life experiences and creativity of great composers: a psychosomaticist's view. *Psychosomatic Medicine*, 43, 291–300.

Richards, R. L., Kinney, D. K., Lunde, I., and Benet, M. (1988). Creativity in manic-depressives, cyclothymes, and their normal first-degree relatives: a preliminary report. *Journal of Abnormal Psychology*, 97, 281–8.

Robinson, L. (1977). Visionaries and madmen: are creativity and schizophrenia linked? *Lawrence Berkeley Laboratory News-Magazine*, 2, 7–10.

Roger, D. and Morris, J. (1991). The internal structure of the EPQ scales. *Personality and Individual Differences*, 12, 759–64.

Rushton, J. P. (1990). Creativity, intelligence, and psychoticism. *Personality and Individual Differences*, 11, 1291–8.

Shaw, G. A. and Conway, M. (1990). Individual differences in nonconscious processing: the role of creativity. *Personality and Individual Differences*, 11, 407–18.

Simonton, D. K. (1984). *Genius, creativity and leadership: Historiometric inquiries*. Harvard University Press, Cambridge, Mass.

Solomon, M. (1975). The dreams of Beethoven. *American Imago*, 32, 113–44.

Storr, A. (1976). *The dynamics of creation*. Penguin Books, Harmondsworth.

Thalbourne, M. A. and Delin, P. S. (1994). A common thread underlying belief in the paranormal, creative personality, mystical experience and psychopathology. *Journal of Parapsychology*, 58, 3–38.

Torrance, E. P. (1970). *Creative learning and teaching*. Dodd, Mead, New York.

Trethowan, W. H. (1977). Music and mental disorder. In *Music and the brain: Studies in the neurology of music* (ed. M. Critchley and R. E. Henson), pp. 398–442. Heinemann, London.

Trilling, L. (1950). *The liberal imagination: Essays on literature and society*. Viking Press, New York.

Tsanoff, R. A. (1949). *The ways of genius*. Harper & Brothers, New York.

Venables, P. H. (1995). Schizotypal status as a developmental stage in studies of risk for schizophrenia. In *Schizotypal personality* (ed. A. Raine, T. Lencz, and S. A. Mednick), pp. 107–31. Cambridge University Press.

Vernon, P. E. (1987). Historical overview of research on scientific abilities. In *Scientific excellence: Origins and assessment* (ed. D. N. Jackson and J. P. Rushton). Sage, Beverly Hills, Calif.

Weisberg, R. W. (1986). *Creativity, genius and other myths*. Freeman, New York.

Weisberg, R. W. (1988). Problem solving and creativity. In *The nature of creativity* (ed. R. J. Sternberg), pp. 148–76. Cambridge University Press.

Winslow, J. H. (1971). *Darwin's Victorian malady*. American Philosophical Society, Philadelphia.

Woody, E. and Claridge, G. (1977). Psychoticism and thinking. *British Journal of Social and Clinical Psychology*, **16**, 241–8.

Part V Conclusions

14

Final remarks and future directions

GORDON CLARIDGE

An advantage of being the Editor of a book like this is that one can have the last word, hence imposing a personal interpretation on the material that has gone before and, implicitly or not, passing a judgment on the relative significance of its different parts. I know my co-authors well enough to realize that none of them will agree with everything in this final chapter and some will agree with very little of it! But there is, I feel sure, a unanimity about two *general* themes that run through the book and which brought us together in the first place. One is the idea that madness is, to a degree, present in everyone, or, put more formally, that so-called 'psychotic' traits form part of normal individuality. The other is that, although the expression of such traits can vary enormously, the label 'schizotypy'—with all its faults as a misnomer—does seem to serve quite well to articulate the commonality of what we have been writing about. At least there appears to be no other construct or set of constructs around in psychology at the moment that can suitably embrace all of the information we have presented, given the need to cover historical, theoretical, and empirical aspects.

Nevertheless—to pursue the nomenclature question one last time—it would undoubtedly be preferable if an alternative to 'schizotypy' could be found. For the problem with the term is not merely scientific: it is not just about a literal failure to denote the breadth of the subject matter to which it is supposed to refer. There is also an emotive element. Any word with 'schizo—' as its root has sinister overtones, even more so than 'psychosis' and its various derivatives. The implied association to what can be devastating mental illness gets in the way of other, more healthy, interpretations. This of course is especially so with respect to the connection to creativity, a conjunction which many people find hard to stomach, even when it is explained to them, as Brod does several times in the previous chapter. (Interestingly—and, for reasons brought out in this book, without any good scientific reason—associations of creativity with *manic-depression* appear to be altogether more palatable.)

Unfortunately, finding a usable alternative to 'schizotypy' is not easy. Brod suggests 'bioeccentricity'; she also refers to the descriptor 'transliminality', introduced by Thalbourne (Thalbourne and Delin 1994), which covers many of the ideas discussed in the present volume. But such neologisms rarely catch on because they emerge from no historical or linguistic tradition. The best hope, perhaps, is that shifts in intellectual and empathic understanding of psychosis, especially schizophrenia, will eventually make the matter much less of an issue.

Turning to the actual content of the previous chapters, it could of course be argued that the very breadth of the material presented there is its weakness, our attempt to bring it under a single heading misguided, and its integration, even eventually, impossible. I shall take this objection, in its several aspects, as the subject of my concluding remarks here.

On the clinical side, the most obvious example of the above criticism comes from the section of the book demonstrating that a high level of 'schizotypy' is not just confined to individuals who are diagnosably psychotic, or even located on the schizophrenia spectrum: it can be found in other abnormal conditions too. The instances given here were obsessive-compulsive disorder (OCD) and some forms of adult dyslexia. The authors of the relevant chapters (Chapters 9 and 10) give their own cogent explanations of their respective data and here I shall confine myself to some comments about the finding, as a general phenomenon.

One opinion about such 'overinclusiveness' in schizotypy is that this does indeed undermine the latter's validity as a useful construct. Schizotypy should, after all, relate only to schizophrenia—or at most, in an enlarged form, to recognizably psychotic disorder. However, that is to ascribe a pre-eminence to psychiatric classification and description that it probably does not deserve. It could equally well be argued that the findings here simply reflect badly (and yet again, for we are by no means the first to say these things) on attempts by psychiatrists to find uniquely definable, aetiologically distinct, clinical disorders. A discrete-category, non-overlapping nosology in psychiatry might simply be wrong, even when judged, that is, over and above the *Einheitpsychose* model and the psychosis spectrum—themselves providing well-established evidence for weak boundaries between alleged clinical entities. It is, after all, merely psychiatry's medical tradition that has dictated the form of classification it has evolved, and its influence as a profession that has made others believe that it offers the only possible starting-point for studying mental illness.

There is now an awareness, even within psychiatry itself, that criticisms of its classificatory system might be valid; as witness the growing concern over the problem of 'co-morbidity', viz. the tendency for individuals simultaneously to meet the diagnostic criteria for more than one disorder, whether—in DSM terms—Axis I (mental illness) or Axis II (personality disorder), or both. In a recent discussion of this phenomenon, van Praag (1996) notes that there is an urgent need to reconceptualize psychiatric nosology in a more flexible form, and suggests several, not necessarily mutually exclusive, ways in which one might interpret co-morbidity. One, already familiar here, is through the greater recognition of continuities between personality, personality disorder, and major mental illnesses. Another is by exploring the possibility that psychiatric syndromes and the behaviour patterns associated with them actually form hierarchies, rather than existing as separable entities. Although van Praag does not mention it, the latter interpretation coincides very much with that put forward many years ago by Foulds, whose ideas I discussed in a different context in Chapter 1. Foulds also proposed a psychiatric classification that was essentially hierarchical (Foulds and Bedford 1975). According to such a scheme, the major psychiatric syndromes, as currently recognized, were thought to be better arranged in a descending order of severity—downwards, from the most disintegrative forms of psychosis to mild neurosis and personality disorder. The hierarchy was envisaged as of such a form that it did not preclude individuals simultaneously meeting—as they frequently do—the psychiatric glossary criteria for disorders at different levels, i.e. being both 'neurotic' and 'psychotic' at the same time. Foulds' system—largely ignored at the time and since—nevertheless proved to be very accurate in practice, and able to accommodate such facts as the tendency, say, for neurotic symptomatology often to herald schizophrenic breakdown or to be unveiled after recovery from a psychotic episode.

Looked at from the perspective of such a model of classification, the observations made in Chapter 10 about OCD, for example, cease to be particularly odd. Relieved of the unnecessary obligation to explain why data do not fit into current psychiatric thinking about classification (and hence aetiology), it is possible to direct attention towards the more important question—in this case the common processes possibly responsible for obsessional and schizophrenic thinking. This is what Enright and Beech have done in their application to the problem of the notion of cognitive inhibition. Here it is worth noting that, although more laboratory-based than most, the general style of their analysis is becoming increasingly common in clinical psychological research, viz. to set aside the diagnostic issues and concentrate more on trying to unravel the underlying mechanisms of individual symptoms. This approach has become especially popular, and is proving very fruitful, in schizophrenia research, where the scramble for a single global cause of the illness has turned out to be a hopeless, probably illusory endeavour (Bentall 1990).

Of course, even if we accept a more Fouldsian view of psychological disorders, we still need to explain why individuals who have descriptive features in common—and hence share the same functional mechanisms for symptoms—nevertheless develop different conditions. Applied to the particular examples of interest here, this means: given their apparently high level of 'psychosis-proneness', who *do* dyslexics and most OCD patients not develop a full-blown psychosis? Alternatively, what causes other, in important respects similarly endowed, individuals to do so? The general answer presumably lies in the multifactorial nature of aetiology. Cognitive inhibition, latent inhibition—even the mechanisms of hemispheric processing—are relatively narrow (and low-level) formulations and could only possibly describe one small part of the chain of events that contribute to the outcome of disordered psychological functioning. For example, even though it might be a significant component, there is no earthly reason why mixed cerebral laterality should, *per se*, be a cause of abnormality, any more than being tall is a compelling reason to join the Coldstream Guards! This principle of sufficient and necessary cause is therefore crucial and must operate in all spheres in which the question of aetiology is addressed.

Disentangling the multiple influences at work here can be undertaken from various angles. One is by looking at interacting effects among the many personality and cognitive traits that contribute to the predispositions for illness. Variations even within schizotypy itself will be important. As shown in Chapter 2 and illustrated in various ways throughout the book, 'schizotypy' is not a unitary set of traits. It consists, instead, of several reliably identifiable components, not all of which need be present—or present to the same degree—even in individuals who are high on the overall characteristic. This could be significant in helping to explain why, among equally schizotypal individuals who develop disorder, only some become diagnosably schizophrenic. In the two non-psychotic outcomes discussed here it is notable that the high schizotypy was mostly expressed as raised scores on the so-called 'positive symptoms' aspect, or tendency to unusual experiences. The latter seems to lie at the core of 'psychoticism' and is perhaps a necessary prerequisite for clinical psychosis. Yet it is clearly not a sufficient condition, given its high rate in other groups. Perhaps the emergence of specifically *psychotic* symptoms requires, among other things, the presence of additional components of schizotypy, a particular profile of traits. This would certainly fit with the observations made by the Chapmans in their test of the predictive validity of their own scales (L. J. Chapman *et al.* 1994). The especially deviant individuals at follow-up were those who were high, not just in magical ideation (part of the 'positive symptoms' complex), but also in social anhedonia.

The Chapmans' results point to the usefulness of trying to define 'schizotypy' according to profiles that might map on to different disorders. This is illustrated in the application of cluster analysis to the problem, exemplified in the work of Leanne Williams, reported here (Chapters 2 and 4). As she has shown, measures of the components of schizotypy group together into several profiles, 'deviant' in different ways; these could represent risks for a variety of disorders, not all necessarily psychotic. However, it does appear that social anhedonia— probably best interpreted as 'schizoid asociality' (J. P. Chapman *et al.* 1995)— has a particularly 'schizophrenic' weighting when occurring alongside the more cognitive elements of psychosis-proneness. It would be instructive to extend such analyses to include measures of the paranoia/suspiciousness component to which Rawlings and Freeman draw our attention in Chapter 3. As they point out, this has been rather neglected in past research, but might be expected to reveal profiles describing individuals whose primary tendencies to schizotypy have a specifically paranoid flavour.

Broad as it has now become, schizotypy of course covers only a small part of the individual differences domain; other temperamental and cognitive characteristics—for example intelligence—will also interact with it to shape the outcome in any given individual. Even so, the constellation of traits that describe the person's make-up still only provides the dispositional background against which other formative factors act. In schizophrenia and schizotypy research, this aspect has been recently pursued mostly from a biological standpoint: for example, along the lines that insults to the brain, especially at birth, will exacerbate genetically determined (schizotypal) tendencies and so enhance risk for later psychotic breakdown (Kendell *et al.* 1996). The approach certainly finds support in considerable evidence that diagnosed psychotics, especially schizophrenics, do show evidence of deviant brain structure and function. However, it is important to note that such abnormalities are very variable across individuals and quite heterogeneous: a recent meta-analysis by Chua and McKenna (1995) of published research demonstrated that, despite what individual investigators might claim for their own findings, there is no real evidence of a *consistent* brain pathology in schizophrenia. It seems that we need to conclude that such cerebral abnormality as does occur acts only as a very non-specific trigger, though it could certainly help to explain why among equally schizotypal individuals some go on to develop frank psychosis and others do not.

Throughout psychiatry's new organic phase of the 1980s and 90s, less interest has been shown in social environmental factors as formative influences in the aetiology of psychosis. Correspondingly, there has been little concern with psychosocial explanations of psychotic behaviour (except as residual deficits from an underlying neuropathology). Yet there are some notable exceptions and some signs of change. One is to be found in the work of Tienari (1991) showing that, to be translated into psychotic illness, the genetic predisposition to schizophrenia also requires exposure to horrible parenting. Another is the suggestion that purely biological accounts of schizophrenia have gone too far and that researchers need to pay more attention to the psychology of the disorder, including the content of the subjective experience (*Schizophrenia Bulletin* 1989). Then, on a broader front still, there is the remarkable recent book by Sass (1992), *Madness and modernism*. In it the author shows how it is possible to embed our knowledge and construction of insanity in a proper cultural context, in which art, philosophy, and madness are all one, stemming from an acute self-consciousness. Importantly, Sass manages to sustain his argument without falling into the fallacies of earlier 'psychodynamic' or anti-biological accounts of psychosis; instead he cleverly reconciles his thesis with much of the conventional scientific literature on schizophrenia.

Against this broadening backcloth of idea about schizophrenia, it is appropriate to turn to that majority of cases where the outcome in high schizotypy is not pathological at all; or where, if it *is* unusual, it is something that would not immediately be labelled 'illness'. It is the existence of these phenomena—such as the out-of-the-body experience (OBE) and the profound spiritual experience—that gave rise to the notions of the 'happy schizotype', quoted by McCreery in Chapter 12, and 'benign schizotypy', introduced by Jackson in Chapter 11. As I commented in Chapter 1, for our transatlantic colleagues working on schizotypy, these are impossible concepts: schizotypy is, by definition, neuropathological in origin. Yet Jackson and McCreery seem to make a good case for the idea that some outcomes for 'psychosis-proneness', however strange, need not be psychiatrically deviant, in which case we have no right to attempt to pathologize them. On the contrary, spiritual experiences can actually serve a healthy, problem-solving, reconstructive purpose for the individual.

What determines the life path for the high schizotype—healthy or maladjusted—is perhaps one of the most interesting (and, not least for the mentally ill, important) questions raised by the present volume. As a passing observation on that, it is instructive to recall 'Sara', one of Jackson's subjects who chanced—with happy results—to seek advice on her 'psychotic' experiences, not from the medical profession, but from her vicar. What, one wonders, would the outcome have been had her choice been different?

Apart from such luck in life—which I personally believe is more influential than is generally supposed—other factors that might shape schizotypy into a happy or benign form look similar to those discussed earlier, with respect to less severe, but ill, outcomes. According to McCreery and Jackson, in both OBE subjects and the spiritually moved the signs of high schizotypy are again largely confined to the 'positive symptom' component; once more the schizoid, anhedonic features are absent. This confirms that hallucinatory or similar perceptually aberrant experiences (often thought to be the sign, *par excellence*, of madness) are actually neutral with respect to psychopathology: it is only how they are reacted to or worked upon, or how they interact with other factors, that causes them to become distressing or judged deviant in a medical sense.

Before moving on to develop that point further, it is worth noting a purely psychometric implication for the validity of 'schizotypy'—so helping to counter a particular criticism of the latter's status as a specifically *psychosis-relevant* construct As the factor analyses of psychosis-proneness scales have shown, the positive symptom/unusual experiences part of schizotypy is its strongest, most face-valid, component. At first glance, it is this aspect, more than any other, that one would expect to be unambiguously confined to *psychotic* expressions of the overall trait. Yet this is not the case. It is precisely this—the most bizarre, 'positive symptom', feature—that frequently occurs outside a narrowly defined psychotic (or even clinical) domain; being associated, as we have seen, with a range of outcomes, both benign and morbid. It cannot therefore be argued that schizotypy is merely a general personality dimension with some rather non-specific psychopathological overtones, which might be the case had the dominant components been those weighted on affective and social responsiveness, impulsive nonconformity, or even cognitive disorganization. The most 'mad' part of schizotypy is very much *not* the sole preserve of the clinically insane.

A further extension of the ideas discussed above—concerning schizotypy having potentially quite healthy outcomes—is the supposed connection with creativity, discussed in the previous chapter. Before considering this, we might just note that, compared with out-of-the-body and spiritual experiences, creativity is a much more drastic instance of the supposed 'normality' of schizotypy. Indeed, it could be claimed that OBEs and spiritual experience are rather flawed instances. For both refer to 'weird' psychological events which, as in Sara's case referred to earlier, might well in another context have had the person labelled 'ill'. True, the subjects themselves judged the experiences to be positive, even enjoyable or beneficial. But, to the average person, the feeling of leaving one's body, or hearing the voice of the Almighty might, understandably, be considered a sign of mental illness—one which, for reasons not yet clear, did not in these particular cases result in the individual entering psychiatric treatment. Admittedly, in the spiritual examples this stance does force us to confront the awkward dilemma that Jackson presents us with at one point: either religious experience is a sign of madness or the mad have an insight beyond the majority of ordinary mortals. But so be it.

If one chose to pursue a certain line of argument, the observations on spiritual experience could be readily squared, if one wished, with a straightforward disease theory of schizotypy and schizophrenia: in other words, they could perfectly well fit the quasi-dimensional model outlined in Chapter 1.

The connection with creativity, however, is more difficult to reconcile with that essentially deficit-based model. For the proposal about creativity is that schizotypy mediates, or has underlying processes in common with, *superior* intellectual qualities which it would be eccentric in the extreme to label a sign of disease. This raises its own dilemma: how to resolve the apparent contradiction of psychotic illness as a disabling condition and schizotypy as a trait of psychological strength. The question was partly addressed in Chapter 13, but deserves a further brief comment.

In giving her own account of schizophrenic cognition (Chapter 5), Evans draws our attention to the notion of a 'leaky' barrier between preconscious and conscious, as an explanation of why psychotics are often overwhelmed by unwanted thoughts and images. But she also stresses how, in normal but highly schizotypal individuals, the same mechanism can be a vehicle for enhanced performance; in appropriate contexts this might issue as creative activity. In order to explain the flip from normal to abnormal, all we might need to do therefore is to propose a more leaky, or more dysfunctional, barrier in the clinically psychotic—whether occurring as a relatively fixed trait, or as an intermittent state characteristic. The creative person might simply, for some reason, have greater control over, or be able to do more with, the material that spills over into consciousness. As Brod discusses in the previous chapter, from a purely biological standpoint, these effects could represent styles of cerebral organization (related to laterality), variations in arousability, or differences in homeostatic modulation of neural functioning. Speculations on the biology of schizotypy offered by other contributors to the book could lead to a similar conclusion. All refer, in one form or another, to a single, simple idea: that the schizotypal nervous system is characterized by weak regulatory, or inhibitory, control. At a 'low' level, this can be observed as fluctuations in arousal and responsivity; at higher levels it is reflected, among other things, in loosened or more flexible styles of cognitive processing. Viewed in this way, it is easy to see how, depending on the setting of critical parameters in different cases, both pathological and healthy, adaptive, even creative, functional states could ensue.

Nevertheless, such accounts are relatively static and reductionist in nature—and become more so the more microscopic the level at which they are formulated. Indeed, this is one particularly deceiving facet of the reductionist fallacy: that temptingly precise though the biological analysis might be, it can only hope to specify the 'machinery' that subserves, or whose functioning is correlated with, mental events. It does not address the latter directly, and—crucially— not on an individual basis. This is true even of cognitive formulations which, although usually cast in a more psychological language, are also largely concerned with generalizations, rather than with the individual person, and with process rather than content. An illustration is the fact that most laboratory experiments testing cognitive paradigms—including those referred to here, such as negative priming and SAWCI—make use of standardized stimuli, rather than information drawn from the subject's own experience. I would argue that this is a point of considerable importance if we are to get down to the detail of how schizotypy can lead to such a wide range of outcomes—from insanity to creativity. The 'leaky barrier' idea, referred to above, provides an appropriate way-in to how we might examine this question.

Consider the following, as a concrete example. If the hallucinatory voices or other intrusive cognitions—reflecting the enhanced spillage into consciousness to which the high schizotype is supposedly more prone—convey negative messages, then is it not more likely that, compared with the case where the contents of consciousness are benevolent, the outcome will be clinically psychotic? In other words, knowing *what* leaks into the individual's current awareness is as important as knowing *how* and *how much* it leaks. As noted earlier, it is the very neglect of these subjective personal experience data that has been the most obvious flaw in recent mainstream schizophrenia (and schizotypy) research. A revived interest in this topic would, in my view, give the whole field a much more mature appearance and take it on to a new stage, of understanding how psychological and biological events conspire to produce a gradation of functioning that encloses both the adaptive and the maladjusted.

Pursuing such a line of enquiry would begin to draw upon information and research strategies that, with a little thought, easily connect to the subject matter of this book. Here I am thinking particularly of the study of life experience data— both mild and severe trauma—which have repeatedly been shown to be important in the aetiology of psychiatric illness, including schizophrenia (Greenfield *et al.* 1994; Norden *et al.* 1995; Viinamäki *et al.* 1995). Laid down in long-term memory, it is these impressions that constitute the mental products that are potentially available for 'leakage' as malign psychotic symptoms, fleeting but disturbing images and emotions, benign schizotypal experiences, or inspirations for creative activity. Studies at this interface between mechanism and content could give us some of our best insights into the dynamics of healthy schizotypy, 'borderline' disorder, and frank psychosis.

Evidence already available on this score suggests that there are several meth-odologies waiting to be explored. One, already hinted at, is the use of personally tailored stimulus material in experimental procedures such as SAWCI. Another, very different, method is to examine in more detail than hitherto the direction of causation between life events and psychosis-proneness. Most current researchers take it for granted that schizotypal characteristics are genetically determined and scarcely bother to go beyond that assumption in formulating a view about vulnerability to psychosis. Yet a recent study (Lawrence *et al.* 1995)—interest-ingly, undertaken entirely outside schizophrenia research—showed that one effect of even mild early trauma was to enhance the later tendency to superstitious and magical ideation; both of which are, of course, signs of schizotypy. Further study of how life experience interacts with the genetic disposition and shapes the phenotypic expression of schizotypy would, therefore, be well worthwhile.

An extension to that interest—and already in place as an undeservedly marginalized part of the existing high-risk literature on schizophrenia—is the continued investigation of how life experience, schizotypy, and learned coping strategies influence one another. Someone who has written extensively on this is Anthony (1987), under the heading of the so-called 'invulnerable child.' It is an interesting notion in itself that some individuals who, judging from their genetic and environmental background should be at increased risk for schizophrenia, actually turn out to be least vulnerable. As Anthony notes, in intellectually talented individuals a flight into creativity is often adopted as a way of dealing with life stress, even though this may turn out to be an incomplete coping strategy. To describe such individuals Anthony makes use of the notion of 'skinlessness', a term that we have also employed elsewhere in discussing the creatively psychotic person (Claridge *et al.* 1990). It is a label which, like other evocative descriptors mentioned here—'leaky barrier' and 'acute self-consciousness' (Sass 1992)—tries to capture the exquisite sensitivity and enhanced imaginativeness which, contrary to much popular belief about psychosis, characterizes schizotypy. Surely here, more than in any other dispositional trait for disorder, the biography of the individual is something we must know about if we are to understand why persons of similar make-up are, alternatively, devastated or protected by their life experiences.

As a related theme, and one which connects well to McCreery's theorizing in Chapter 12, colleagues and I have recently undertaken the study of the dream/nightmare experience, as an expression of schizotypy (Claridge *et al.*, in press). We have found that, among normal volunteers, high schizotypes have stronger emotional experiences of pleasant dreams, as well as of nightmares—a sign that they are more impressionable, both positively and negatively. The nightmare connection to schizotypy supports other findings (Levin and Raulin 1991) and has led us to a new interest, which is to see how these observations can be exploited as a way investigating life experience in psychosis and borderline disorders. A representative methodology for doing this has already been developed by Belicki and her colleagues for use in the study of sexual and physical abuse victims (Cuddy and Belicki 1992). Belicki's argument is that quantitative analysis of the sleep disturbance—evaluation, for example, of recurrent nightmares—can provide a way of tapping into individual life experiences of a traumatic nature that may have preceded disorder. The method should be ideally suited to the study of such phenomena in psychotic and related conditions, as well as in the exploration of the psychic contents of healthy schizotypes.

This view of a future direction for schizotypy research is of course based on a personal interest and does not minimize the importance of other likely developments. Indeed, each part of this book implicitly or explicitly signals lines for future research. Notwithstanding the dangers of reductionism, cautioned against earlier, a strong continuing trend will certainly be to explore the biological correlates of schizotypy. Two adjacent chapters here are illustrative of contrasting interpretations of this perspective. Paul Broks, in his analysis of social cognition (Chapter 6), adopts a classic neuropsychological approach: he sees the way forward as lying in the discovery of relatively macroscopically defined brain modules that map onto complex psychological processes. In contrast, Helen Cassaday's authoritative review of latent inhibition in Chapter 7 places more emphasis on the animal modelling and psychopharmacology of schizophrenia; it therefore concentrates on an appropriately simple, narrowly defined phenomenon which, it is nevertheless claimed, can mimic a core feature of the disorder.

One other aspect of the biology of schizotypy that will certainly continue to receive attention is its genetics. This has not been been represented directly in the present volume, though a sense of its importance has lain in the background throughout the book (and explicitly discussed in speculative vein by Richardson, in Chapter 9, as a supposed connecting link between schizotypy and dyslexia). Several of the experimental paradigms discussed here have a possible application in genetics research. This arises from their dual status as research tools: on the one hand, as procedures for exploring mechanisms or processes of, say, schizotypal cognition; on the other hand, simply as objective indicators of psychosis-proneness, one stage on from questionnaire scales. In the latter capacity they have the potential to serve as what Gottesman and Shields (1972) introduced into schizophrenia research as the notion of 'endophenotypic markers', defined by Gottesman (1991) as 'data not available to the naked eye that are intermediate to the phenotype and the genotype for schizophrenia'. The idea and the research strategy to which this gives rise are important because it begins to seem unlikely that the genetics of schizophrenia (or psychosis in general) will be unravelled solely through studies in which the phenotype is defined in terms of gross, often arbitrary, diagnostic features. Although also not without its own problems (Claridge 1994), a more promising approach is to investigate the heritability of relevant endophenotypic markers, established elsewhere in schizotypy and other high-risk research.

The ideas discussed here also have implications for the management of serious mental illness. For decades, treatment has been dominated by physical, mostly pharmacological, methods. Given the evident biological nature of many of the signs of psychotic behaviour, there is some rationale for this and if criticism is to be levelled at such treatments it needs to be done sensibly, with due regard to the complexity of the therapeutic problem. That was not always the case in the past, especially during the heady 1960s when schizophrenia took on an almost romantic aspect, becoming an icon of protest against the traditional family structure and the wider society. The exclusively social and sociological explanations of psychotic behaviour that then took root left little room for the organic and, correspondingly in treatment, for pharmacology. Unfortunately, the backlash, when it came, was, and remains, equally unbalanced. Contemporary observations that careless therapeutic practices in the use of neuroleptic drugs for the treatment of serious mental illness continue to perpetuate a 'toxic psychiatry' (Breggin 1993) are regarded by the defenders of such methods as time-warped, rather than still valid. (Although proprietary brands for antipsychotic drugs have proliferated, the generic substances themselves have scarcely changed in 40 years!) Even where deficiencies in pharmacotherapy are acknowledged, these are seen as signs of the immaturity of the scientific endeavour, rather than as a warning that a paradigm shift is perhaps required in the way we view disorders like schizophrenia.

Nevertheless, some signs of change are apparent and, although the debate still has the flavour of confrontation rather than cooperation, a more broadly based psychobiological view of the treatment needs of clinically diagnosable psychotic individuals does seem to be very slowly emerging. A central tenet of this new approach is the idea that the schizophrenic's psychological experience needs to be recognized, not just as a symptom of illness, but as having a content that is important in its own right, one which it is necessary to understand and manipulate as a way of bringing about therapeutic change. In other words, contrary to a longstanding belief in (organic) psychiatry, talking to the psychotic patient about his or her delusions and hallucinations *is* a good thing. With some notable exceptions (Romme and Escher 1993; see also Jenner *et al.* 1993), this challenge to the received wisdom has been spearheaded mostly by clinical psychologists intent upon developing psychological methods for helping schizophrenics cope with their experiences (Birchwood and Tarrier 1994). These techniques are not of the psychotherapeutic, 'depth analysis' type to which organic psychiatrists have traditionally objected (perhaps rightly, though even that might turn out to be misguided): instead, they are of a more pragmatic, cognitive-behavioural variety, designed to coax the client away from self-destructive delusional belief or towards a better understanding and management of an hallucinatory experience. Nor are the procedures in question intended to substitute for drug treatments, but rather to be used in conjunction with them and to complement their effects, for example by employing medication as an initial strategy for bringing the person more within psychological reach. There is nothing here, therefore, to which an empathic observer of the mentally ill could object. Yet it has taken a century for this more holistic perspective on the treatment of schizophrenia to even begin to affect clinical practice, and even now only minimally and against some resistance—to the extent that, as one commentator remarked, 'until quite recently, proponents of such views might even have been seen as themselves just a bit crazy!' (Hughes 1994).

In conclusion, as the varied material and opinions found in this book attest, the indications are that, in spite of a currently dominant (and often arrogant) organic psychiatry, research in the area we have covered will somehow continue on a healthily broad front, spanning both biological and psychological perspectives. It will certainly need to. For, as we have emphasized several times, 'schizotypy'—or whatever generic term is eventually settled upon to cover this domain of individual differences—is a particularly good example of a *psychobiological* construct. Having some of its roots in a blatantly neuropathological conception of disease, others in a more mentalistic tradition, and yet others in a personality-based experimental psychopathology, it presents a puzzle that no faction has yet solved, or is likely to without reference to the others' contributions. The particular need here to find a meeting-point between the biological and the psychological, the dimensional and the discontinuous, the healthy and the ill is not a new idea, of course. It is embedded in the history of the topic, expressed in the struggle by Eugen Bleuler to understand schizophrenia, and in the emergence of the notion of 'schizoid'. The modern equivalents, derivatives, and elaborations of that concept still carry the same message as that which Manfred Bleuler (1978), from whom I quoted in Chapter 1, considered to be the 'magic touch' of 'schizoid', as an insight. It invites us, non-judgmentally, to set aside our prejudices about the mentally ill and consider that what constitutes madness is, as he says, 'not quite so crazy psychologically'.

REFERENCES

Anthony, E. J. (1987). Children at high risk for psychosis growing up successfully. In *The invulnerable child* (ed. E. J. Anthony and B. J. Cohler), pp. 147–84. The Guildford Press, New York.

Bentall, R. P. (1990). *Reconstructing schizophrenia*. Routledge, London.

Birchwood, M. and Tarrier, N. (ed.) (1994). *Psychological management of schizophrenia*. Wiley, Chichester.

Bleuler, M. (1978). *The schizophrenic disorders* (trans. S. M. Clemens). Yale University Press, New Haven.

Breggin, P. (1993). *Toxic psychiatry*. Fontana, London.

Chapman, J. P., Chapman, L. J., and Kwapil, T. R. (1995). Scales for the measurement of schizotypy. In *Schizotypal personality* (ed. A. Raine, T. Lencz, and S. A. Mednick), pp. 79–106. Cambridge University Press.

Chapman, L. J., Chapman, J. P., Kwapil, T. R., Eckblad, M., and Zinser, M. C. (1994). Putatively psychosis-prone subjects 10 years later. *Journal of Abnormal Psychology*, **103**, 171–83.

Chua, S. E. and McKenna, P. J. (1995). Schizophrenia—a brain disease? A critical review of structural and functional cerebral abnormality in the disorder. *British Journal of Psychiatry*, **166**, 563–82.

Claridge, G. (1994). Single indicator of risk for schizophrenia: probable fact or likely myth? *Schizophrenia Bulletin*, **20**, 151–67.

Claridge, G., Pryor, R., and Watkins, G. (1990). *Sounds from the bell jar. Ten psychotic authors*. Macmillan, London.

Claridge, G., Clark, K., and Davis, C. (in press). Nightmares, dreams, and schizotypy. *British Journal of Clinical Psychology*,

Cuddy, M. A. and Belicki, K. (1992). Nightmare frequency and related sleep disturbance as indicators of a history of sexual abuse. *Dreaming*, **2**, 15–21.

Foulds, G. A. and Bedford, A. (1975). Hierarchy of classes of personal illness. *Psychological Medicine*, **5**, 181–92.

Gottesman, I. I. (1991). *Schizophrenia genesis: the origins of madness*. W. H. Freeman, New York.

Gottesman, I. I. and Shields, J. (1972). *Schizophrenia and genetics: a twin study vantage point*. Academic Press, New York.

Greenfield, S. F., Strakowski, S. M., Tohen, M., Batson, S. C., and Kolbrener, M. L. (1994). Childhood abuse in first-episode psychosis. *British Journal of Psychiatry*, **164**, 831–4.

Hughes, I. (1994). Psychological approaches to the management of psychosis, Withington Hospital, Manchester, June 3rd, 1994 (Conference report). *Journal of Mental Health*, **3**, 551–4.

Jenner, F. A., Monteiro, A. C. D., Zagalo-Cardoso, J. A., and Cunha-Oliveira, J. A. (1993). *Schizophrenia. A disease or some ways of being human?* Sheffield Academic Press, Sheffield.

Kendell, R. E., Juszczak, E., and Cole, S. K. (1996). Obstetric complications and schizophrenia: a case control study based on standardised obstetric records. *British Journal of Psychiatry*, 168, 562–70.

Lawrence, T., Edwards, C., Barraclough, N., Church, S., and Hetherington, F. (1995). Modelling childhood causes of paranormal belief and experience: childhood trauma and childhood fantasy. *Personality and Individual Differences*, 19, 209–15.

Levin, R. and Raulin, M. L. (1991). Preliminary evidence for the proposed relationship between frequent nightmares and schizotypal symptomatology. *Journal of Personality Disorders*, 5, 8–14.

Norden, K. A., Klein, D. N., Donaldson, S. K., Pepper, C. M., and Klein, L. A. (1995). Reports of the early home environment in DSM-III-R personality disorders. *Journal of Personality Disorders*, 9, 213–23.

Romme, M. and Escher, A. (1993). *Accepting voices*. MIND Publications, London.

Sass, L. A. (1992). *Madness and modernism*. Basic Books, New York.

Schizophrenia Bulletin. (1989). Issue theme: Subjective experiences of schizophrenia and related disorders. 15, No. 2, 177–324.

Thalbourne, M. A. and Delin, P. S. (1994). A common thread underlying belief in the paranormal, creative personality, mystical experience and psychopathology. *Journal of Parapsychology*, 58, 3–38.

Tienari, P. (1991). Gene-environment interaction in adoptive families. In *Search for the causes of schizophrenia* (ed. H. Häfner and W. F. Gattaz). Springer-Verlag, Berlin.

van Praag, H. M. (1996). Comorbidity (psycho) analysed. *British Journal of Psychiatry*, 168, (suppl. 30), 129–34.

Viinamäki, H., Niskanen, L., Haatainen, J., Purhonen, M., Väänänen, K., and Lehtonen, J. (1995). Do mental traumas in childhood predict worse psychosocial functioning in adulthood? *Nordic Journal of Psychiatry*, 49, 11–15.

Appendices

Appendix I
STQ items and normative data

A. QUESTIONNAIRE ITEMS

Note: All items are scored for 'Yes' response.

STA scale: Schizotypal personality

Do you believe in telepathy?

Do you often feel that other people have it in for you?

When in the dark do you often see shapes and forms even though there's nothing there?

Does your own voice ever seem distant, far away?

Does it often happen that almost every thought immediately and automatically suggests an enormous number of ideas?

Do you ever become oversensitive to light or noise?

Do you often have vivid dreams that disturb your sleep?

When you are worried or anxious do you have trouble with your bowels?

Have you ever felt when you looked in a mirror that your face seemed different?

Do you feel it is safer to trust nobody?

Do things sometimes feel as if they were not real?

Do you feel lonely most of the time even when you're with people?

Do everyday things sometimes seem unusually large or small?

Are you often bothered by the feeling that people are watching you?

Do you feel that you cannot get 'close' to other people?

Do you dread going into a room by yourself where other people are already gathered and are talking?

Does your sense of smell sometimes become unusually strong?

Are you sometimes sure that other people can tell what you are thinking?

Have you ever had the sensation of your body or part of it changing shape?

Do you ever feel sure that something is about to happen even though there doesn't seem to be any reason for you thinking that?

Do you ever suddenly feel distracted by distant sounds that you are not normally aware of?

Do you ever have a sense of vague danger or sudden dread for reasons that you do not understand?

Have you ever thought you heard people talking only to discover that it was in fact some nondescript noise?

Do your thoughts ever stop suddenly causing you to interrupt what you're saying?

Do you feel that you have to be on your guard even with your friends?

Do you ever feel that your thoughts don't belong to you?

When in a crowded room do you often have difficulty in following a conversation?

Do you sometimes feel that your accidents are caused by mysterious forces?

Do you feel at times that people are talking about you?

Do you believe that dreams can come true?

Do you ever feel that your speech is difficult to understand because the words are all mixed up and don't make sense?

Are your thoughts sometimes so strong that you can almost hear them?

When coming into a new situation have you ever felt strongly that it was a repeat of something that has happened before?

Have you ever felt that you were communicating with another person telepathically?

Are you easily distracted from work by daydreams?

Are you very hurt by criticism?

Do you ever get nervous when someone is walking behind you?

STB scale: Borderline personality

Do you often feel the impulse to spend money which you know you can't afford?

Do you often change between intense liking and disliking of the same person?

Do you frequently have difficulty in starting to do things?

Do you hate being alone?

Do you often experience an overwhelming sense of emptiness?

Do you at times have an urge to do something harmful or shocking?

Do you at times have fits of laughing or crying that you can't control?

Do you often have periods of such great restlessness that you aren't able to sit still for more than a very short time?

Do you frequently gamble money?

Does life seem entirely hopeless?

Do you often have the urge to hit someone?

Have you ever felt the urge to injure yourself?

Do you often overindulge in alcohol or food?

Do you often feel like doing the opposite of what other people suggest, even though you know they are right?

Do you often feel that there is no purpose to life?

Do you ever have the urge to break or smash things?

Do you ever have suicidal thoughts?

Are your thoughts about sex often odd or bizarre?

B. TOTAL GROUP AND AGE/SEX NORMS FOR STQ
Table A1.1   STA scale

	Mean	SD	N	Range
TOTAL GROUP				
Overall	15.95	7.44	1997	0–35
By age range				
1–20	18.38	6.90	255	3–33
20–29	16.31	7.40	717	0–35
30–39	16.26	7.56	357	1–35
40–49	14.96	7.94	288	1–35
50–59	15.05	6.81	190	0–33
60–69	13.61	6.75	116	1–31
70+	12.53	7.21	74	1–35
MALES				
Overall	15.20	7.48	925	0–35
By age range				
1–20	18.23	6.88	155	3–33
20–29	15.58	7.26	368	0–35
30–39	14.97	7.88	148	1–35
40–49	13.18	7.59	125	1–35
50–59	13.41	6.77	56	2–31
60–69	12.43	6.74	42	1–28
70+	11.67	7.14	31	2–28
FEMALES				
Overall	16.61	7.35	1072	0–35
By age range				
1–20	18.63	6.94	100	3–33
20–29	17.08	7.46	349	1–35
30–39	17.17	7.21	209	2–33
40–49	16.32	7.70	163	3–33
50–59	15.74	6.73	134	0–33
60–69	14.28	6.72	74	2–31
70+	13.14	7.28	43	1–35

Table A1.2 STB scale

	Mean	SD	N	Range
TOTAL GROUP				
Overall	6.35	3.90	1433	0–18
By age range				
1–20	9.29	3.48	153	2–16
20–29	7.32	3.83	444	0–18
30–39	6.45	3.76	273	0–17
40–49	5.48	3.63	224	0–16
50–59	4.93	3.16	168	0–15
60–69	3.99	2.97	102	0–15
70+	2.93	2.64	69	0–12
MALES				
Overall	6.41	4.02	562	0–18
By age range				
1–20	9.61	3.39	75	2–16
20–29	7.18	3.86	194	0–18
30–39	6.18	3.87	98	0–17
40–49	5.29	3.66	83	0–15
50–59	4.83	3.03	48	0–11
60–69	3.83	3.30	36	0–15
70+	2.64	2.82	28	0–12
FEMALES				
Overall	6.31	3.83	871	0–18
By age range				
1–20	8.97	3.55	78	2–16
20–29	7.43	3.81	250	0–18
30–39	6.60	3.71	175	0–16
40–49	5.59	3.62	141	0–16
50–59	4.97	3.23	120	0–15
60–69	4.08	2.79	66	0–14
70+	3.12	2.52	41	0–8

Appendix II
The Oxford-Liverpool Inventory of Feelings and Experiences (O-LIFE)

The O-LIFE contains four psychosis-proneness scales in addition to the STA scale given in Appendix I. These are the Unusual Experiences, Cognitive Disorganization, Introvertive Anhedonia, and Impulsive Nonconformity scales; a list of the items for each appears below.

All are answered YES or NO: 'Y' indicates that the item is positively scored when confirmed and 'N' that the item is positively scored when disconfirmed.

UNUSUAL EXPERIENCES

Are the sounds you hear in your daydreams usually clear and distinct? Y

Are your thoughts sometimes as real as actual events in your life? Y

Does it often happen that nearly every thought immediately and automatically suggests an enormous number of ideas? Y

Are your thoughts sometimes so strong that you can almost hear them? Y

Do you think you could learn to read others' minds if you wanted to? Y

Have you felt that you have special, almost magical powers? Y

Do ideas and insights sometimes come to you so fast that you cannot express them all? Y

Can some people make you aware of them just by thinking about you? Y

Does a passing thought sometimes seem so real that it frightens you? Y

Does your voice ever seem distant, faraway? Y

Do you sometimes feel that your accidents are caused by mysterious forces? Y

Do people in your daydreams seem so true to life that you sometimes think they are? Y

Is your hearing sometimes so sensitive that ordinary sounds become uncomfortable? Y

Have you felt that you might cause something to happen just by thinking too much about it? Y

Are you so good at controlling others that it sometimes scares you? Y

Do you ever have a sense of vague danger or sudden dread for reasons that you do not understand? Y

Have you sometimes had the feeling of gaining or losing energy when certain people look at you or touch you? Y

Have you ever thought you heard people talking only to discover that it was in fact some nondescript noise? Y

Have you occasionally felt as though your body did not exist? Y

On occasions, have you seen a person's face in front of you when no one was in fact there? Y

Do you often have a day when indoor lights seem so bright that they bother your eyes? Y

Have you wondered whether the spirits of the dead can influence the living? Y

Have you felt as though your head or limbs were somehow not your own? Y

Now and then when you look in the mirror, does your face seem quite different than usual? Y

Do you ever feel that your thoughts don't belong to you? Y

Do you ever suddenly feel distracted by distant sounds that you are not normally aware of? Y

When in the dark, do you often see shapes and forms even though there's nothing there? Y

Have you sometimes sensed an evil presence around you, although you could not see it? Y

Does your sense of smell sometimes become unusually strong? Y

Do you ever feel sure that something is about to happen, even though there does not seem to be any reason for you thinking that? Y

COGNITIVE DISORGANIZATION

Do you often hesitate when you are going to say something in a group of people that you know more or less? Y

Do you frequently have difficulty in starting to do things? Y

Do you often worry about things you should not have done or said? Y

When in a crowded room, do you often have difficulty in following a conversation? Y

No matter how hard you try to concentrate, do unrelated thoughts always creep into your mind? Y

Are you easily hurt when people find fault with you or the work you do? Y

Do you easily lose courage when criticized or failing in something? Y

Do you seem to be a person whose mood goes up and down easily? Y

Are you sometimes so nervous that you are 'blocked'? Y

Do you find it difficult to keep interested in the same thing for a long time? Y

Do you dread going into a room by yourself where other people have already gathered and are talking? Y

Do you often have difficulties in controlling your thoughts when you are thinking? Y

Do you often feel that there is no purpose to life? Y

Do you worry about awful things that might happen? Y

Are you easily distracted from work by daydreams? Y

Are you easily confused if too much happens at the same time? Y

Do you worry too long after an embarrassing experience? Y

Do you often feel lonely? Y

Do you often experience an overwhelming sense of emptiness? Y
Do you often feel 'fed up'? Y
Would you call yourself a nervous person? Y
Is it hard for you to make decisions? Y
Do you ever feel that your speech is difficult to understand because the words are all mixed up and don't make sense? Y
Are you easily distracted when you read or talk to someone? Y

INTROVERTIVE ANHEDONIA

Have you had very little fun from physical activities like walking, swimming or sports? Y
Do you enjoy many different kinds of play and recreation? N
Has dancing, or the idea of it, always seemed dull to you? Y
Is trying new foods something you have always enjoyed? N
Are there very few things you have ever really enjoyed doing? Y
Are you much too independent to really get involved with other people? Y
Do you think having close friends is not as important as some people say? Y
Are you rather lively? N
Does it often feel good to massage your muscles when they are tired or sore? N
Do you like mixing with people? N
On seeing a soft, thick carpet have you sometimes had the impulse to take off your shoes and walk barefoot on it? N
Are people usually better off if they stay aloof from emotional involvements with most others? Y
Can just being with friends make you feel really good? N
Have you often felt uncomfortable when your friends touch you? Y?
When things are bothering you do you like to talk to other people about it? N
Do you have many friends? N
Do you prefer watching television to going out with other people? Y
Is it true that your relationships with other people never get very intense? Y
Do you love having your back massaged? N
Is it fun to sing with other people? N
Do people who try to get to know you better usually give up after a while? Y
Can you usually let yourself go and enjoy yourself at a lively party? N
Are the bright lights of a city exciting to look at? N
Do you usually have very little desire to buy new kinds of foods? Y
Do you like going out a lot? N
Do you feel very close to your friends? N
Do you feel that making new friends isn't worth the energy it takes? Y

IMPULSIVE NONCONFORMITY

Do you often overindulge in alcohol or food? Y

When with groups of people, do you usually prefer to let someone else be the centre of attention? N

When you catch a train, do you often arrive at the last minute? Y

Do you often change between intense liking and disliking of the same person? Y

Have you ever cheated at a game? Y

Do you at times have an urge to do something harmful or shocking? Y

Are you usually in an average sort of mood, not too high and not too low? N

Would you take drugs which may have strange or dangerous effects? Y

Do you stop to think things over before doing anything? N

Have you ever blamed someone for doing something you know was really your fault? Y

Would being in debt worry you? N

Do you think people spend too much time safeguarding their future with savings and insurance? Y

Do you ever have the urge to break or smash things? Y

Have you ever felt the urge to injure yourself? Y

Would it make you nervous to play the clown in front of other people? N

Do you consider yourself to be pretty much an average kind of person? N

Have you ever taken advantage of someone? Y

Would you like other people to be afraid of you? Y

Do you often have an urge to hit someone? Y

Do people who drive carefully annoy you? Y

Do you sometimes talk about things you know nothing about? Y

Do you often feel like doing the opposite of what other people suggest, even though you know they are right? Y

Do you often feel the impulse to spend money which you know you can't afford? Y

Appendix III
The Paranoia/Suspiciousness Scale (PSQ)

Items are grouped according to subscale. With the exception of items 23, 26, and 38, all are scored for being endorsed 'Yes'.

Number   Item

INTERPERSONAL SUSPICIOUSNESS/HOSTILITY (IS)

2.   Do you sometimes feel that no one understands you?
3.   Are you sometimes eaten up with jealousy?
8.   Are you sure you are being talked about?
11.   Do you wonder why sometimes you feel so bitter about things?
14.   Do people you are with have a strong influence on your moods?
15.   Do you tend to be envious of other people's good fortune?
20.   Do people sometimes say insulting things about you?
27.   Do you often get involved in things you later wish you could get out of?
33.   Do you sometimes feel that people are laughing at you behind your back?
42.   Do you often feel that people have it in for you?
43.   Do you feel at times that people are talking about you?
47.   Are you often bothered by the feeling that people are watching you?

NEGATIVE MOOD/WITHDRAWAL (NM)

13.   Do you think that you feel more intensely than most people?
18.   Are you more sensitive than most people?
26.   Are you happy most of the time?
38.   Do you agree that there are really more nice people than objectionable people in the world?
44.   Do you feel that you have to be on your guard even with your friends?
45.   Do you feel it is safer to trust nobody?
46.   Do you feel lonely most of the time, even when you're with people?

ANGER/IMPULSIVENESS (AI)

9.   Do you often get into a jam because you do things without thinking?
17.   Do you sometimes feel 'like a powder keg ready to explode'?
23.   Are you an 'even tempered' person?

29.	Do you get so 'carried away' by new and exciting ideas that you never think of possible snags?
31.	When put in charge of something, do you insist that your instructions are followed, or else you resign?
35.	Do some of your friends think you are a hothead?
36.	Do you find that you can't help getting into arguments when people disagree with you?
37.	Do you sometimes fly off the handle for no good reason?
40.	Do you have trouble controlling your temper?

MISTRUST/WARINESS (MW)

7.	Do you tend to assume that all people have a vicious streak and it will come out when they are given the chance?
19.	Do you believe in never trusting anyone who has a grudge against you?
22.	Do you suspect that people who act friendly to you can be disloyal to you behind your back?
25.	Do you get suspicious of over-friendly strangers?
32.	When people are especially nice, do you wonder what they want?
34.	Do you doubt the honesty of people who are more friendly than you would expect them to be?

PERCEIVED HARDSHIP/RESENTMENT (PH)

4.	Do you feel that it is other people who always seem to get the breaks?
5.	Do you feel that you have often been punished without cause?
6.	Would you have been more successful if others around you had not put difficulties in your way?
10.	Have you had an awful lot of bad luck?
16.	Do you feel that you have had more than your share of things to worry about?
24.	Do you feel at times that you've got a raw deal out of life?
28.	Have you had more trouble than most?

(NO SUBSCALE)

1.	Do people generally seem to take offence easily?
12.	Do you believe you will never be satisfied?
21.	Do people mean to do and say things to annoy you?
30.	Do you often notice your ears ringing or buzzing?
39.	Do you get upset when people don't notice how you look when you go out in public?
41.	Would you like to be in a position where people were frightened to defy you?

Author index

Subject index

affective psychosis 6–7, 10; *see also* manic-depression *and* bipolar disorder
Aggression Questionnaire 45
agoraphobia 213, 214, 215
allusive thinking 284; *see also* divergent thinking
alpha rhythm 256
Alzheimer's disease 5
amobarbital 269
amphetamine 125, 126, 130, 131, 132, 138
amygdala 111, 112–13, 117, 119
anhedonia 26, 31; *see also* Introvertive Anhedonia
  absence of as healthy sign 179–80, 189–90, 211, 255, 304
  and cognitive performance 68–9, 287–8
  and handedness 152
  Physical Anhedonia scale 20, 21, 210, 255
  Social Anhedonia scale 20, 21, 210
antidepressants 134
Antisocial personality disorder 279
anxiety disorders 213–16
arousal 253–4
  and creativity 286, 291–3
  dissociation of 260–3, 264–6, 287
  lability of 266–8
  and sleep 253–4
attention-deficit-hyperactivity-disorder (ADHD) 172, 182–3
autism 102–4, 106–7, 115–18, 252, 270
automatization deficit 174, 183, 191
Avoidant personality disorder 279

benzodiazapines 205
beta-blockers 205
'Big-5' personality theory, *see* five-factor personality theory
'bioeccentricity' 293, 301
bipolar disorder 6–7, 280; *see also* manic-depression
Borderline Personality Disorder (BPD) 10, 39, 209, 279
Borderline Personality scale, *see* STB scale
brain imaging 149, 150, 155, 161, 182, 209

caffeine 134
callosal inhibition 146
cannabis 130
catatonia 269
cerebral lateralization
  arousal effects in 261–3
  and creativity 291–3
  drug effects on 136, 154
  in dyslexia 173, 174–5, 176, 182–3
  in psychosis 148–51, 153–5
  and schizotypy 151–3, 154–6, 157–60
ceronapril 135
chlordiazepoxide 137
chlorpromazine 72
cluster analysis 30–2, 68, 231
Cognitive Disorganisation, *see* O-LIFE
Cognitive Slippage scale 20
Combined Schizotypal Traits Questionnaire (CSTQ) 27, 91, 179
confirmatory factor analysis 28–9
Combined Schizotypal Traits Quesionnaire (CSTQ) 27, 91, 179
confirmatory factor analysis 28–9
corpus callosum 150
creativity 93, 229, 240, 307–9
  and arousal 286–7
  and cerebral lateralization 153, 291–3
  and intelligence 281–2
  and psychopathology 277–81
  and schizotypy 180, 190, 282–9
cyclothymia 280
cyclothymic mood disorder 10

delusions 252, 270, 288
  cognitive theories of 42–3, 64, 82, 84–5
  as primary delusional experience 260
  psychological therapy for 311
  scales of 210, 211
dementia praecox 5, 39
dependent personality disorder 279
developmental dyslexia, *see* dyslexia
Diagnostic and Statistical Manual (DSM-III, IIIR, and IV)
  criteria for Axis II personality disorders 8, 9–10
  highly creative assessed with 278–9
dichotic listening 156–8, 292